D0936550

Ed Barrow

Ed Barrow

*The Bulldog Who
Built the Yankees'
First Dynasty*

Barrow

DANIEL R. LEVITT

UNIVERSITY OF NEBRASKA PRESS • LINCOLN

LONGWOOD PUBLIC LIBRARY

© 2008 by Daniel R. Levitt ¶ All rights
reserved ¶ Manufactured in the United
States of America ¶ ∞ ¶ Library of Congress
Cataloging-in-Publication Data ¶ Levitt,
Daniel R. ¶ Ed Barrow : the bulldog who
built the Yankees' first dynasty / Daniel R.
Levitt. ¶ p. cm. ¶ Includes bibliographical
references and index. ¶ ISBN 978-0-8032-
2974-7 (cloth : alk. paper) ¶ 1. Barrow,
Edward Grant, 1868–1953. ¶ 2. Baseball
managers—United States—Biography. ¶
3. New York Yankees (Baseball team)—
History. ¶ I. Title. ¶ GV865.B3L48 2008 ¶
796.357092—dc22 ¶ [B] ¶ 2007040521 ¶
Set in Adobe Garamond by Kim Essman
¶ Designed by R. W. Boeche ¶

To Charlie and Joey, the best boys in the whole world

Contents

Part 1: Every Job in Baseball, 1868–1920

Part 2: The Yankees Years, 1920–1953

Illustrations

Following page 222

Tables

Preface

I lived for nights like these, moving across the city's great broken body, making connections among its millions of cells. I had a crazy wish or fantasy that some day before I died, if I made all the right neural connections, the city would come all the way alive.

Ross MacDonald, *The Instant Enemy*

Reconstructing a life is a fascinating exercise. Edward Grant Barrow spent fifty years in baseball as a central character in many of its most interesting and entangled situations. During the first half of the twentieth century, the baseball establishment was run by a tight circle of executives. These men argued, schemed, collaborated, and traded. The ever-evolving relationships between them shaped the baseball environment of the era. Because Barrow was an actor in the middle of so many key events, following him allows us to decipher their origin and effect. Barrow's life strings together two critical metaquestions of the half-century: how did baseball's competitive environment evolve? and how did the Yankees come to dominate it?

He held practically every job, except player. As president of the International League during the second decade of the twentieth century, Barrow led the battle against the upstart Federal League, a self-declared Major League backed by some of the biggest industrialists of the era. He managed Babe Ruth and the Boston Red Sox to their last World Series championship before the "curse."

During the first eighteen years of their existence, the New York Yankees had never won a pennant. In October 1920 bickering Yankees owners Jacob Ruppert and Tillinghast L'Hommedieu Huston hired Barrow from the Boston Red Sox as de facto general manager. Under Barrow's leadership, the Yankees captured their first pennant in 1921 and went on to become the most successful sports franchise in American history. The story of Barrow's assembling and maintaining the great Yankees dynasty affirms his genius for organizing, for recognizing baseball talent, and for taking advantage of the economic environment in which he operated.

Note on money: Throughout this book I often refer to dollar amounts. Because of economic differences between Barrow's era and today, these amounts can have meaning only if put in context. In his book *How Much Is That in Real Money*, John J. McCusker has spliced together several price series to create a price index back to colonial times. Based on McCusker's index, the following table indicates the factor by which to multiply a dollar in the shown year to adjust to a 2006 dollar.

1900	1910	1915	1920	1925	1930	1935	1940	1944
24	21	20	10	11	12	15	12	11

For example, one dollar in 1930 is equivalent to twelve dollars in 2006 in terms of the goods one could purchase.

To some degree, however, converting prices to 2006 dollars, even with a price index, can be misleading. The price index accounts for the effects of inflation over the past century. The overall economy, however, now has much more money in the system, not just because of inflation but also because the economy itself has expanded tremendously. The growth of the economy can be broadly attributed to two factors: an increase in population and an increase in productivity. Because of the increase in productivity, incomes have increased much faster than inflation. That is, an average income today can purchase many more goods than an equivalent (i.e., inflation-adjusted) income could have in the past. For example, adjusting Babe Ruth's then-astronomical salary of $80,000 in 1930 to $960,000 today implies an equivalent purchasing power; it does not mean $960,000 would be his current salary. As professional sports revenue has exploded due to many factors (larger attendance, television, luxury boxes, etc.), team revenues and salaries have jumped by much more than inflation alone would suggest.

Barrow spent several years in Canada. During his time there, both the United States and Canada were on the gold standard, which pegged the two countries' dollars at parity. Thus, a Canadian dollar was equivalent to a U.S. dollar.

Acknowledgments

I would like to thank a number of people for their assistance in the production of this book. Lyle Spatz, Stew Thornley, Bill Nowlin, Bill Ayrovainen, Tom Swift, Rich Arpi, Robert Tholkes, David Poremba, and my brother Matt Levitt each read one or more chapters or otherwise helped them along. Matt also combed the archives of the Harry Frazee papers at the University of Texas and uncovered previously unresearched documents.

Mark Armour generously reviewed the entire manuscript and offered several improvements, both large and small. Jim Wyman helped me interpret the financial information available in the Yankees' business and financial records at the National Baseball Hall of Fame Library. Steve Steinberg directed me to a number of valuable source materials.

Jane Dorward (Toronto), Ralph Christian (Des Moines), John Thorn, Steve Gietschier, Jim Meier, and Steve Steinberg provided help with the necessary research. Donald Honig, Bob Creamer, Chris Lamb, and Paul Ferrante graciously responded to my inquiries, and Ray Robinson generously shared some thoughts from his own research. Bill Deane provided a professional fact-checking review, and Barb Wojhoski helped clean up the text. Skip McAfee prepared the index and suggested a number of clarifications along the way. Any remaining errors are mine.

Dave Eskenazi, Mike Mumby, Mark Rucker, Pat Kelly, and Marcia Schiff eased the process of finding interesting photographs.

The State Historical Society of Iowa, the University of Minnesota Wilson Library, and the Hennepin County Southdale Library tracked down a range of articles and documents. Gabriel Schechter and Helen Stiles helped me navigate the terrific resources at the National Baseball Hall of Fame Library.

Rob Taylor at the University of Nebraska Press endorsed the project and helped guide it from its initial proposal to final product.

Ed Barrow

Every Job in Baseball, 1868–1920

1. "The Best Deal the Yankees Ever Made"

Boston Braves rookie manager Dave Bancroft believed he had pilfered a budding pitcher from his old manager, John McGraw, when, in 1924, he claimed Dinty Gearin on waivers from the New York Giants for the four-thousand-dollar waiver price. Unfortunately, Bancroft was not familiar with the waiver rule. A team claiming a first-year player like Gearin also had to reimburse his original purchase price. The Giants had paid twenty-five thousand dollars to the Minor League Milwaukee Brewers to acquire Gearin's contract. Thus the Braves were technically on the hook for the full amount the Giants had spent on him.

The impoverished Braves of the mid 1920s had no interest in shelling out twenty-five thousand dollars for Gearin's services. To recoup as much as possible, the Braves sent Gearin back to Milwaukee, salvaging ten thousand dollars in return. They quickly sent these funds to the furious Giants, who naturally demanded the remaining fifteen thousand dollars as well. In the end, the Braves weaseled out of their obligation by arguing that Bancroft was not authorized to make a waiver claim, and that the claim should never have been accepted by the league in the first place. They successfully contended that unless otherwise delegated, only the team president was authorized to make waiver claims (although as this story makes clear, this rule was not always adhered to).

At the time, most baseball teams were still run like small businesses. As American business historian Alfred Chandler has pointed out, prior to the explosive growth of American corporations in the half century after the Civil War, even the largest firms were directed by a president or a treasurer, and a general superintendent, who "personally supervised the labor force." Baseball teams were similarly directed well into the twentieth century. Nearly all were administered by the president, typically the controlling member of the ownership group, and the manager, who guided the players (the labor force) on and off the field. The distribution of authority between manager and president depended mainly on the level of control the president wished to retain for himself. Many owners (I often use "owner" and "president" interchangeably in this book), such as Barney Dreyfuss in Pittsburgh or Charles Comiskey in Chicago, prided themselves on their baseball smarts and maintained control over player personnel moves and decisions. Others, like Charles Stoneham of the New York Giants, employed a manager such as the willful genius John McGraw. Outside of a veto on significant cash outlays, Stoneham allowed McGraw essentially free rein on all personnel matters.

Teams also employed a business manager in their front office. Historically the business manager's job had been to administer the team's back-office functions such as accounting, ticket sales, and stadium operations. He also arranged travel, booked hotels, and oversaw the bats, balls, and uniforms. The business manager had no responsibility for the acquisition or disposition of players; his was a purely back-office position. The president and the manager were responsible for the product on the field.

Baseball ownership syndicates prior to the First World War were generally made up of upper-middle-class professionals and businessmen. Most included local politicians or those well connected to them. The syndicate typically named its largest investor or most baseball-knowledgeable man as team president. By the second decade of the century, as Organized Baseball became more accepted within upper-class society, several wealthy industrial magnates began to covet the prestige of owning a baseball team. Furthermore, with competition from the self-declared major Federal League, the established leagues actively sought wealthy owners to bolster undercapitalized franchises. When Organized Baseball accepted a few well-heeled owners as part of the Federal League dissolution settlement, these new men began to rethink the composition of their front office, that branch of a baseball team's operation responsible for the product on the field.

In the wake of the Federal League's demise, ice-plant builder Philip De-Catesby Ball acquired the St. Louis Browns. Ball recognized his lack of baseball knowledge and the potential drawbacks of saddling his manager with both personnel acquisition and on-field duties. Accordingly, he hired Bob Quinn to run the club and granted Quinn the powers of a modern-day general manager—a role he had fulfilled successfully for Columbus in the high Minors. Chewing-gum magnate William Wrigley also joined the baseball ownership fraternity when he purchased a controlling interest in the Chicago Cubs. Wrigley brought in sportswriter Bill Veeck Sr., initially as vice president and treasurer. Wrigley soon promoted Veeck to the position of president, but like Quinn, he functioned as a modern-day general manager.

One of the central dilemmas—if not the central dilemma—for any organization is the level of centralization of decision-making authority. Overcentralize and one loses the flexibility and spontaneity of smart employees on the front lines; decentralize too much and the organization can lose its focus and necessary administrative constraints. Wealthy industrialists such as Wrigley and Ball, who faced this conundrum in their own businesses, recognized the value of adding a front-office executive with responsibility for player procurement.

By late 1920 New York Yankees co-owners Jacob Ruppert and Tillinghast Huston realized they needed a seasoned baseball man to run their franchise. Over the first six years of their ownership, the duo spent considerably to improve the team, culminating in the purchase of Babe Ruth prior to the 1920 season. And although the team improved significantly that season, the pennant again eluded them. When business manager Harry Sparrow died in May 1920, Huston himself hoped to assume a leading role in the front office. Trained as an engineer and with numerous outside interests, he lacked the skill and dedication for the position. With Ruppert's prodding, Huston grudgingly accepted his unsuitability for the task. Moreover, the relationship between the partners was becoming difficult. Ruppert and Huston had contracted a marriage of convenience to purchase the team, but they were not particularly close. A recent managerial disagreement and its carryover further stalemated the decision-making process of the team.

Ruppert, a brewery owner, in particular recognized the opportunity for better administration. He had observed firsthand the struggles of American corporations to develop an efficient management structure. Organizational administration must address two distinct areas: oversight of day-to-day operations and attention to the long-term. As baseball evolved into a more mature business after World War I, Ruppert realized that a more sophisticated front-office structure was required. No longer could a manager and an amateur owner maintain sustainable excellence from a baseball team.

In late October 1920, with the blessing of the financially strapped Harry Frazee, the owner of the Boston Red Sox, the Yankees' owners offered Boston field manager Ed Barrow a job as the Yankees' business manager. Although he may not have recognized it, Barrow had trained his entire life for the position. He was almost the antithesis of what we think of today as a professional manager, and he would have bristled at the characterization. Nevertheless, he proved the perfect fit. Then fifty-two, Barrow had begun organizing baseball teams and leagues in Des Moines as a teenager and had successfully held just about every conceivable baseball job (except that of player) since then. At the time sportswriter Dan Daniel may have best characterized Barrow as "forceful, alert, crafty, and when required, vitriolic." Barrow was a large man who, in his youth, boxed and relished physical confrontation. His demeanor and occasional vitriol could intimidate even robust professional athletes.

The quality that most impressed Ruppert and Huston, however, was his workaholic dedication to excellence. Barrow had proven his administrative capabilities as a Minor League owner, Minor League president, and big league manager with significant autonomy in team operations and player procurement. Barrow also had a surprising eye for detail; for example, since his youth he had prided himself on his penmanship. In Barrow the Yankees' owners landed a competent administrator who was also a knowledgeable baseball man with a competitive spirit.

Like Quinn and Veeck, Barrow was thrust into a baseball position that remained largely undefined. The Yankees' owners recognized they needed more than just a business manager; they also needed a baseball man to help make player personnel decisions and mediate between the owners and the manager. They willingly delegated much of their authority over the players to Barrow and over time allowed him to reorganize and assume control over nearly all of the front office. Immediately after his hiring, Barrow and the two owners restructured the Minor League and amateur scouting system to be more geographically regionalized. During his years in New York, Barrow aggressively oversaw the scouting department. Perhaps more than any other single factor, Barrow's energetic administration of the player acquisition function sustained the longevity of the Yankees dynasty. The Ruth purchase placed America's best baseball player and biggest sports celebrity in its largest city. The Barrow acquisition a year later ensured that the short-term boost from Ruth would be solidified and prolonged into one of the great sports dynasties of the twentieth century.

Many years later sportswriter Joe Williams called the Barrow hiring "the best deal the Yankees ever made." Before Barrow the Yankees had never won a pennant; after his addition they became one of the legendary dynasties in all of sports: "The Ruths had done the hitting, the Pennocks the pitching, the Dickeys the catching, and the Lazzeris the fielding, but it was Barrow who knitted the organization together, gave it pattern and a far-seeing program, directed its overall energies. That's why we say he represents the best deal the Yankees ever made."

2. Hustling and Scrapping

The post–Civil War America into which Ed Barrow was born was a complex, changing world that beheld both incredible possibilities and fearsome consequences. Economic historian Melvyn Dubofsky described the era as a "time of chaos." Millions of young men developed an American consciousness through military service; many headed west to escape the mundane life they returned to after the terror and excitement of army life. The nature of work was evolving as well, from one based on the personal relationships and community norms of the farm or early industrial firm, to the routine and detachment of the large corporation. (Obviously, these generalizations are applicable almost exclusively to white males.)

Barrow's father, John Williams Barrow, from English-Irish stock, grew up on a farm in Chillicothe, Ohio. Of only medium height, John became physically strong as a result of farm life. Ed Barrow remembered his father as quick-tempered but quick to forget as well. In 1863, at the height of the Civil War, he joined the Third Regiment of the Ohio Volunteers. The army discharged John after the war in 1866, and he returned home. Although he was not wounded in the war, military service was not kind to John Barrow. He suffered from dysentery, had lost his hearing—one can imagine the constant noise of the cannon and rifles—and was in generally poor health.

On a trip to Hillsborough, Ohio, soon after his return from the war, John met Effie Ann Vinson-Heller. The two fell in love and were married by the middle of the following year. Effie was of Dutch-French heritage, and Ed Barrow remembered her as a "handsome spirited woman with a determined chin." After his stint in the army and with a new wife, John Barrow had little interest in small-town life in Ohio. Under the Homestead Act of 1862, the federal government made the lands of the Great Plains available to settlers. For a total filing fee of eighteen dollars, any head of household at least twenty-one years old could claim a 160-acre parcel of land. The Barrow clan resolved to leave Ohio and take advantage of the opportunity to stake out land on the plains. John and his bride joined his two brothers, two sisters, and their mother for a journey to a new life in Nebraska. The family traveled west in four covered wagons in search of new lands to farm.

The Barrows were at the forefront of a massive migration. After the Civil War, the plains states saw a huge influx of settlers as many young Americans looked for fresh land to farm. Between 1870 and 1890 the population of the plains states increased fivefold. For many reasons, however, the new life for these farmers required a massive adjustment. Fundamentally, American farming in the eastern and Old Northwest states resembled that of northwest Europe because of a similar climate, vegetation, and geography. The plains of the Midwest, however, presented unique challenges to farmers accustomed to the Ohio Valley. Rainfall occurred less often and droughts were more common; less timber existed for construction of housing, fencing, and other farm needs; and rivers were fewer and farther between. The difficulties in farming this new land were further exacerbated by the general unpleasantness of life. The extreme temperatures in both winter and summer could be brutal when compared to those seasons back east. Furthermore, the psychological toll of living in relative isolation from other people because of large farm sizes and distances from the few towns should not be underestimated. Eventually, of course, the pioneer farmers developed the technology to harness the plains into some of the world's most productive farms, but during the early years life could be quite bleak.

It was in this bleak environment that John Barrow and his family hoped for a new life of self-sufficiency. The trip to Nebraska was quite an extended odyssey. For the winter of 1867–68, the Barrows camped at the hemp farm of a relative in Springfield, Illinois. There, on May 10, 1868, Edward Grant Barrow was born. His middle name was bestowed by his father after his hero, the Union general (and soon to be U.S. president) Ulysses S. Grant. During young Barrow's first year, the family became sidetracked from their Nebraska destination and ended up spending the next winter in Johnson County, Missouri. While in Missouri, Barrow's first brother, William Franklin, who would be known as Frank, was born.

Eventually the family made it to Nebraska and settled near Nebraska City, not far from the Iowa border. John Barrow and his brother each assumed a homestead and began the arduous struggle of earning a living. Barrow remembers his father telling him of the plagues that afflicted farmers on the prairie: tornadoes, floods, droughts, grasshoppers, and fires. His father also complained about the Native Americans, who resented the homesteaders as they witnessed their communities disintegrate from the settlers' far-reaching impact.

After six hard years on the farm, John Barrow sold out to his brother and moved his wife and three sons (the third son, Charles Oscar, was born while the family was in Nebraska) off the prairie. They spent the first winter in Council Bluffs, Iowa, on the Nebraska border. From there the family moved east to a farm ten miles outside Des Moines, Iowa, where John hoped the farming might be a little less taxing. Their sojourn on the farm lasted only a couple of years. John's health continued to deteriorate, making the rigors of farming beyond his capabilities. He pulled up his family and with another of his brothers, James, moved into the city of Des Moines. To earn a living, John Barrow became an expressman (generally a laborer engaged in the delivery of goods, which often involved driving a wagon) in the transfer, grain, and feed business. While in Des Moines, John and Effie had their fourth and final son, George Harvey.

When he reached school age, Ed attended the Third Ward School in Des Moines as did all his brothers. Barrow, who as a youth went by "Eddie," began his love affair with baseball while attending school; he played and pitched on the high school team. The health of his father continued to decline, and Barrow quit to help support the family.

Barrow once recalled his first job was as a roller-skating instructor at the Exposition Rink. He quickly advanced to floor boss and became manager at the rival Arena Rink. Shortly thereafter Barrow's roller-rink career ended unceremoniously when he used excess force to quell a disturbance and evict some regular customers. It's hard to know what to make of Barrow's roller-skating recollection. He mentioned it in only one biographical reminiscence, but circumstantial evidence suggests a strong likelihood of his involvement with the activity. Buoyed by the introduction of a new skate, roller-skating became extremely popular in the decades after the Civil War. For a big, tough, active youth from a family struggling financially, an after-school roller-rink job would seem a natural.

In any case, the fifteen-year-old Barrow next landed a job at the *Des Moines Daily News* as a mailing clerk. Barrow remembered stiff competition for this job, which mainly required neat handwriting to address the labels for mailing to subscribers. Barrow won the job and throughout his life prided himself on his attractive handwriting, a surprising vanity for someone who enjoyed boxing and fighting. Barrow was later reassigned to the position of city circulator—making him boss of a pack of unruly newspaper boys. This job fit the physically powerful and aggressive Barrow perfectly: at six feet tall and nearly two hundred pounds, he liked to box and relished confrontation. One time a newsboy threw a brick at Barrow when his back was turned. Fortunately it missed. When reminiscing on this incident many years later, Barrow remarked: "They were tough kids in those days." And Barrow believed he was the toughest of the bunch.

Sometime in late 1886, after a couple of years at the *Daily News*, Barrow switched papers, taking a job at the *Des Moines Leader*. He again started as a mailing clerk; his hustle and intelligence were soon rewarded, however, and Barrow was promoted, first to city circulator and later to advertising manager. As his responsibilities grew, he also occasionally filled in as city manager. After Barrow's promotion to selling ads as an advertising manager, the *Leader* also allowed him to do a little reporting on ball games and the theater.

While not working, Barrow played baseball for a YMCA team and then for several local teams. A big, strong lad, Barrow could pitch quite well and dreamed of advancing to the big leagues. This was the heyday of some of the great nineteenth-century pitchers such as Mickey Welch, John Clarkson, Old Hoss Radbourn, and Tim Keefe, and Barrow hoped to emulate them. In 1886 while pitching in a game—one he sometimes recalled as a city championship game—Barrow developed a sore arm around the fifth inning. Despite the onset of a cold rain, Barrow remained on the mound. Later that evening his arm and shoulder swelled and stayed tender and sore. Barrow maintained that this episode led to neuritis in his shoulder, and that he could never again throw with any velocity. He tried unsuccessfully to prolong his playing career by transitioning to first base. Although Barrow's playing career ended while he was still in his teens, he had been bitten by the baseball bug. He quickly shifted gears to become a baseball promoter and business manager to stay near the game.

Barrow's interest in organizing amateur baseball coincided with a huge upsurge in baseball's popularity throughout the Midwest. Geographically large, regionally organized sports leagues became possible in the decades after the Civil War with the maturation of two new technologies. Most obviously, efficient rail service became available between many midwestern cities. Just as important, news organizations expanded their recognition of the opportunities available through the telegraph. Game accounts and box scores could now be transmitted electronically, allowing newspapers to offer their readers current information. The ability to follow a team on a daily basis greatly expanded the interest in doing so. Finally, but not so critically, camera technology also matured during and after the Civil War. Newspaper photographs further enhanced interest in organized athletics. Des Moines was no exception to this mushrooming interest in Organized Baseball. The city acquired its first professional team in 1887 and won a Minor League pennant the following year.

Barrow experienced his first taste of Major League Baseball in late April 1887 when Cap Anson brought his Major League Chicago National League club to Des Moines for two exhibition games. The first game drew between five thousand and six thousand fans, a huge number for the time, despite bad weather, which led to a rain-out in the fourth inning. With storms again threatening the second game, a still respectable crowd of three thousand showed up to witness what turned out to be another rain-shortened exhibition.

As baseball fever swept Des Moines, in June 1887 a group of young men, including Barrow, organized the Des Moines League, a mostly amateur baseball circuit for older boys in their late teens. Barrow always had a little bit of the hustler in him, perfect for organizing and recruiting players to an amateur team. As an organizer, Barrow demonstrated executive abilities and salesmanship as well as hustle. He engaged local sports enthusiast and cigar-store owner Ed L. Moore to sponsor a team (Moore's store also sold sporting goods and other items). In his newsboys Barrow had a ready supply of talent, and he enlisted the better players for his team, named "E.L.M.'s Stars" in honor of the team's patron. Barrow and Moore later added a second team of younger lads, at one point nicknamed "Ed's Mascots" (for Moore, not Barrow) and soon shortened to simply the "Mascots."

Barrow was developing into a solid administrator, and both of the teams that he assembled became the best in the area. In 1889 the Mascots won the Des Moines Boys City League for younger boys; by Barrow's last seasons in 1889 and 1890, both the Stars and the Mascots excelled at their respective levels. After the 1889 season Barrow and Moore staged an exhibition between the two teams, charging fifteen cents admission to the usually free games. The Stars needed to double the score on the Mascots to win 75 percent of the purse; otherwise they would receive only 25 percent. In the event, the Stars barely covered, 7–3, to gain the 75 percent share.

Barrow publicized and financially subsidized his teams in several creative ways. Prior to a two-week barnstorming tour of northern and eastern Iowa in August 1889, he helped organize a benefit for the ball club, selling tickets for the send-off party at Moore's store for fifty cents each. Barrow also contrived to use the *Leader* to help promote the team and the games. The paper devoted a disproportionate amount of space to amateur baseball, and the Stars and the Mascots received an overindulgent share of the coverage. Barrow almost surely convinced his editors to allow him to write the short blurbs and game stories for inclusion in the paper. To generate additional buzz for a game in June 1890, the Stars—with Barrow as the likely initiator—hired a parachutist to jump out of a hot-air balloon into the ballpark. In July 1890, in response to the disbanding of Des Moines's Minor League franchise, Moore proposed (in an open letter in the *Leader*), probably at Barrow's instigation, organizing a local professional league from the talent available in the amateur leagues. He hopefully suggested that area businessmen could profitably own local teams in a "commercial league." In the event, Barrow did not remain in Des Moines long enough to immerse himself in such an enterprise.

One of Barrow's players was future Hall of Fame left fielder Fred Clarke. Clarke's family, like Barrow's, had moved to Des Moines after conceding that life farming the plains was too inhospitable. As a youngster Clarke found a job at the newspaper as one of Barrow's charges. Clarke recalled a fight with another newsboy in which he pushed the kid through a window. Barrow made him pay for the glass. "It cost me thirty-five cents, and that was a lot of money back then," remembered Clarke. Barrow recruited him to the team after recognizing that Clarke was by far the fastest of his seventeen newsboys. Clarke quickly established himself as the team's first baseman and part-time pitcher. Later Clarke, along with Barrow's younger brother, George, tried out with Hastings in the nearby Nebraska State League; only Clarke made the grade and stuck with team. Barrow remembered recommending Clarke, but the timing does not quite fit, as Clarke and George Barrow did not try out until the spring of 1892, by which time Barrow had left Des Moines (although Barrow could have mentioned Clarke in a previous season). A complementary story had the Hastings club first hearing of Clarke through an advertisement the youngster placed in the *Sporting News*.

Barrow's two youngest brothers, Charles and George, found routine employment, the former as an expressman like his father, the latter as a clerk. But Frank, like Ed, had a willingness to take risks and a strong desire to escape the limits of small-town life. In 1888 the African American inventor R. N. Hyde received a patent for a carpet-cleaner formula. Hyde took on a white partner, and the two introduced America to the product known as H&H Soap. Barrow's brother Frank became convinced that this new soap product offered an opportunity for great wealth, and he persuaded Barrow of its potential. The two brothers acquired the rights to H&H Soap for Pennsylvania and decided to relocate to Pittsburgh to make their fortune as soap magnates. They possessed only about five hundred dollars between them and needed to borrow the family savings of three thousand dollars to embark on the venture. In 1891 Barrow and his younger brother used the family's capital to load up on an inventory of this supposedly revolutionary cleaning solution. After a tearful good-bye, the two brothers headed off for Pittsburgh by train, accompanied by box lunches prepared by their mother.

In Pittsburgh they took up residence at the Taylor Hotel, later renamed the Staley, and began the process of introducing H&H Soap to Pennsylvania. Unfortunately, despite the brothers' best efforts demonstrating the cleaner on soiled rugs and cloth, the business flopped, and they soon ran out of money. Frank landed a job as a hotel clerk and worked until he could save up enough money to return home. The cocky Barrow, however, was too embarrassed to return home a failure and would not head back for seven years. Even then he returned only in response to the deaths of his two youngest brothers, a month apart in late 1897 from typhoid fever.

With the failure of the cleaning-product business, Barrow tried his hand at several jobs to earn a living. He first fell back on advertising, a skill he had acquired with the Des Moines papers. Instead of newspaper space, he sold advertising space on hotel registers and in theater lobbies. He also tried his hand at selling oil pumps. Finally, after his brother returned to Des Moines, Barrow assumed his job at the hotel, eventually becoming an assistant manager.

For a young sports enthusiast and hustler, Barrow worked and lived in the perfect place. His boss, hotel owner John Staley, was a big gambler and knew most of the sportsmen in town. Known as a theater and sporting hotel, the back dining room at the Staley was the epicenter for much of Pittsburgh's gambling crowd. Barrow also hobnobbed with the more upscale sporting clientele that lived at the better hotel next door. While working at the Staley, Barrow spent much of his time mingling with Pittsburgh's sporting community. By his own admission, Barrow patterned himself after this crowd, grew a handlebar moustache, and began dressing like a dandy.

Barrow recalled once that he almost boxed Jim Corbett, who became heavyweight champion in 1892 after knocking out John L. Sullivan. Corbett's manager, the smooth, publicity-seeking William Brady—who operated along the lines of a modern sports agent—cashed in on Corbett's popularity by having him tour the country for boxing exhibitions and stage appearances. In Pittsburgh Brady had apparently heard about a clerk at the Staley who was reputed to be a pretty good fighter. He sent Corbett's trainer to find Barrow.

"Your name Barrow?" he asked.

"Yes," said Barrow.

"How would you like to make $150?" the trainer asked.

"Doing what?" Barrow inquired.

"Boxing Jim Corbett," the trainer said, then quickly added, "Corbett won't hurt you, he's a gentleman."

Barrow demurred—one of the few times he ever shied away from a fight—suggesting instead a top police heavyweight. After the police commissioner rejected this match-up, Barrow offered a few more suggestions, and Brady eventually found a taker. Although he refrained from really hurting his exhibition partner, Corbett, nonetheless, bloodied his opponent badly.

Barrow later became friendly with Corbett and joked about how close they had come to fighting that day back in Pittsburgh.

Corbett asked, "What would you have done if you had been in there?"

"I'd have kicked you in the groin," Barrow told him.

When relating this story, Barrow added, "And I would have."

While hanging around the Pittsburgh sport scene, Barrow became friends with "Score Card" Harry Stevens. Stevens emerged as one of the great characters in baseball around the turn of the last century. He had come to America from England in his early twenties and like most immigrants hoped to find opportunities in the New World. After a short time at a steel mill in Ohio, Stevens, a naturally hard-working huckster, tried his hand at sales.

Around 1886 in Columbus he began peddling Civil War general John Logan's book, *The Great Conspiracy*. Through his sales efforts, he became acquainted with the state's politicians, including Governor J. B. Foracker. He also landed the score-card concession at the Columbus ballpark, where he entertained the fans in his red coat and battered hat while hawking his wares. Columbus rejoined the then–Major League American Association in 1889, and Stevens remained in Columbus until the league folded in 1891.

By then Stevens had assumed the score-card concession in Pittsburgh and moved there with his family. While in Pittsburgh he secured the right to sell programs in a number of local theaters. Barrow was looking to move beyond an assistant managership in the hotel business and met Stevens through his sporting connections. It was through Stevens that Barrow landed his gig selling advertising space in theater lobbies. Stevens recognized a fellow hard-driving salesman, and in the winter of 1893–94 allowed himself to be persuaded to offer Barrow a partnership in the business. During the 1894 baseball season, the twenty-six-year-old Barrow spent most of his days at the Pittsburgh ballpark selling score cards and concessions while overseeing the business for Stevens. While at the park he naturally became friendly with several ballplayers, including Connie Mack, and realized how much he missed being an active part of baseball.

3. Forcing His Way into Baseball

Pittsburgh sportswriter George Moreland envisioned a new Minor League that would serve a number of the smaller Ohio cities. Because his new league, as eventually constituted for the 1895 season, included Wheeling, West Virginia, Moreland named it the Inter-State League. He retained the Steubenville, Ohio, franchise for himself. At the time, the idea of a sportswriter forming a baseball Minor League was not particularly noteworthy. The capital requirements for a Minor League were relatively modest, and like most small businesses, they often failed. Moreland turned to some of his Pittsburgh sporting cohorts, including Barrow, to back the Wheeling franchise in his new league. Barrow saw an opportunity to enter professional baseball and eagerly accepted Moreland's offer. He joined up with Harry Stevens and ex-Pirates manager Al Buckenberger; each invested one hundred dollars to acquire the franchise rights. Buckenberger became team president and Barrow the business manager. The duo hired former Cincinnati pitcher Will White to manage.

Barrow had become friendly with Buckenberger during the latter's three years as the Pirates' skipper. Pittsburgh's principal owner, Captain William Kerr, hired Buckenberger prior to the 1892 season. In 1893 he brought the Pirates home second in a twelve-team league, raising expectations for 1894. Unfortunately, 1894 proved a disappointment, and with the club just below .500 after 110 games, Kerr canned Buckenberger and promoted his thirty-one-year-old catcher, Connie Mack, to manager.

During the off-season Buckenberger flirted with joining a new American Association that hoped to challenge the National League's Major League monopoly. Three years earlier, after the 1891 season, the Major League American Association folded, and four of its franchises joined the National League. With this collapse and merger, the new twelve-team National League gained a monopoly over Major League Baseball, which its magnates strove to preserve. They reacted quickly and forcefully by threatening to blacklist any ballplayers or managers involved with the new league. Buckenberger, who was also looking at several other baseball opportunities, quickly backed away. Cleared by the National League, St. Louis hired Buckenberger as manager for the upcoming 1895 season. With Buckenberger's departure for St. Louis, Barrow assumed full control over Wheeling's day-to-day operations. To staff his ball club, Barrow recruited several of the top available players in the Pittsburgh area, along with any decent ballplayers he could find in Wheeling. Barrow also signed Zane Grey, a capable ballplayer who later became famous as an author of western novels.

Now that he had his first professional franchise to run, Barrow needed a ballpark to play in. Barrow approached Harry Schmulbach, a local brewer with a farm on Wheeling Island, an island in the Ohio River, about the possibility of constructing a sports ground. Schmulbach agreed on the condition that Barrow persuade the city council to allow beer sales at the park. Barrow again demonstrated his salesmanship and negotiated permission to sell liquor on the island. The delighted Schmulbach honored his end of the bargain and built the ballpark.

By midseason the Inter-State League had collapsed and Moreland returned to sportswriting. Prior to the league's dissolution, Wheeling manager Will White had grown frustrated with the uncertainty and confusion surrounding the league and quit. His resignation forced Barrow to assume the managerial reins. To perform his new duties, Barrow commuted between Wheeling and his home in Pittsburgh. Because he was in first place when the league effectively disbanded, Barrow liked to believe that he had won the pennant in his first attempt at professional baseball stewardship.

For the second half of the 1895 season, Barrow's Wheeling franchise along with the Twin Cities (Dennison and Uhrichsville) club joined the Iron and Oil League, another new league inaugurated by a Pittsburgh sportswriter. Unfortunately, this new league suffered from many of the same financial weaknesses as the Inter-State League, and several teams struggled to finish out the season. In the anarchy of a failing league, Barrow found himself defending his behavior against some tenuous allegations from two folding franchises, Oil City and Celeron. The two charged that Barrow had shortchanged them on their share of Wheeling's gate receipts. Barrow denied he had promised to pay any part of the receipts from his ladies' day admissions to the visiting clubs. He further ridiculed the accusation that the teams did not receive their guarantee fee of sixty dollars. He noted that most teams received much more than the minimum from a trip to Wheeling. Barrow indignantly concluded: "The complaint comes with poor grace from the Oil City and Celeron teams when it is considered that both received more than the guarantee money here and Wheeling was lucky to get the thirty-five-dollar guarantee when on its trips, the managements finding it necessary to go down into their pockets to make up that amount."

By late in the 1895 season it was clear that the Iron and Oil League had little hope of surviving. With preliminary discussions under way regarding the formation of a new, stronger Central League for 1896 (a plan that did not come together), Barrow hoped to strengthen his team to enhance his prospects of joining the new league. He smartly signed ex-Major League shortstop Jack Glasscock, a thirty-five-year-old Wheeling native. Glasscock had been released by Washington because of arm trouble and had retired home to Wheeling.

Barrow managed his team to a solid half-season. In late August he and the first-place Warren, Pennsylvania, team agreed to play a best-of-seven series during the West Virginia state fair. Warren boasted Al and Honus Wagner, the latter a future star Barrow would soon recruit for his own club. Wheeling won the series, and both clubs made out surprisingly well financially. The season was not yet officially over, however, and a controversy erupted over the league's rightful champion. The league president awarded the pennant to Barrow, who later liked to boast that he had won two pennants in his first year of Organized Baseball.

With the demise of the Iron and Oil League, Barrow was twenty-seven years old and at a crossroads. He still technically managed the Pittsburgh concessions for Stevens but was determined to make a career in baseball. When another sportswriter, Sam Crane from New York, conceived the Atlantic League that off-season, Barrow angled for a franchise. For a short time Barrow thought he had secured a club for Hartford, Connecticut. His friend Al Buckenberger had originally been awarded a team for Trenton, New Jersey, but subsequently accepted the presidency of Toronto in the more prestigious Eastern League. Buckenberger planned to transfer the franchise rights to Barrow in exchange for three players he could take with him to Toronto. Barrow then intended to move the franchise to Hartford. In the meantime, however, Crane sold the Hartford franchise to Billy Barnie, another well-known baseball operator. Buckenberger and Barrow were livid at this turn of events; Buckenberger claimed Crane had agreed to his transfer scheme and that the deal had been witnessed by Stevens. Barrow had already signed three players for Hartford and advanced money to cover expenses. Despite Buckenberger's subsequent threats, Crane held firm, leaving Barrow out in the cold.

Barrow, however, remained committed to securing an Atlantic League franchise. Rasty Wright, owner of the Paterson, New Jersey, team in the new league had assembled a decent nucleus of eleven players. Barrow and partner Charles McKee approached Wright about buying him out, eventually settling on a price of eight hundred dollars for the team and players. At the time, Paterson was one of the nation's midtier cities; with a population of just over 105,000, it ranked as the thirty-second largest city in America.

With the challenge and time commitment of owning and administering a baseball franchise in New Jersey, Barrow could no longer operate the concession business for Stevens in Pittsburgh. Stevens had recently landed the account for the Polo Grounds (the National League New York Giants ballpark) and proposed that Barrow accompany him to New York to help run the operation. Barrow, committed to a life in baseball, declined, although the two remained lifelong friends. Stevens eventually became extremely wealthy through his concession business. He later added ice cream and soda pop to the score cards and soon thereafter introduced the hot dog. He eventually landed the concessions at a number of sporting venues and bragged he had grown the business "from the Hudson to the Rio Grande." Years later Barrow would reminiscence that selling out his interest in Stevens's business was the first of his three great missed opportunities for accumulating vast wealth.

Barrow needed a venue for his new club. The franchise would be Paterson's first professional team, and the city had no stadium suitable for a competitive Minor League franchise. Barrow called on politician Garret A. Hobart, one of the area's most prominent citizens, to finance a ballpark. Hobart owned the local streetcar line and was active in New Jersey politics. In fact, in November Hobart, on the Republican ticket as William McKinley's running mate, was elected vice president. His death in 1899 cut short further political advancement that in retrospect seems certain, given President McKinley's assassination two years later. As a civic enterprise, and to generate ridership for his business, Hobart consented to build Olympic Park between Paterson and Passaic at a cost of around four thousand dollars.

Still living in Pittsburgh, Barrow needed to stock his franchise—whichever one he ended up with. He remembered being "accosted" in Johnny Newell's café by the "now famous baseball plunger," Shad Gwillam, who later became better known in gambling circles. At this time nearly all cities in the Northeast were populated by baseball enthusiasts who promoted local baseball talent, typically in exchange for a modest fee or some sort of favor in kind. They often managed or organized local teams as well to keep abreast of the top local players. Gwillam asked Barrow if his team was fully assembled, because if not, he knew of a Dutchman named John (Honus) Wagner in Carnegie, near Pittsburgh, who would "someday be the best player in the world." The promoter added that while Wagner was "no college graduate, as far as education went, he was great at anything requiring mechanical skill such as pool, billiards, etc."

Barrow knew something of Wagner's ability from competing against him during the 1895 season in both the Inter-State League and the Iron and Oil League. Also, Wagner had a ball-playing older brother, Al, who had received some local recognition while a teammate of Honus's. Gwillam's forceful encouragement provided Barrow enough motivation to head to Carnegie the following day. Upon inquiring as to Wagner's whereabouts, Barrow was directed to a local poolroom. There, Barrow was dispatched to the railroad yards, where Wagner and friends were engaged in a contest to see who could throw a rock the farthest. Barrow remembers arriving just as Wagner completely outclassed the competition by throwing a stone weighing around a pound about three hundred feet. Barrow immediately attempted to sign Wagner to a contract for his Paterson club, but Wagner remained hesitant. To procure him, Barrow offered the undecided Wagner $125 a month, $25 above the league limit of only $100.

Barrow's timing proved fortunate. Earlier that off-season the Pittsburgh Pirates had attempted to sign Wagner for one hundred dollars per month but planned to option him to Kansas City for some further seasoning. Wagner had rarely ventured far from home—he had become homesick the previous season while playing in Michigan—and was reluctant to travel so far away. The day after Barrow signed him, George Moreland, now back to sportswriting, again approached Wagner on behalf of the Pirates—possibly to sweeten the offer—only to learn that Barrow had already landed Wagner. Moreland followed up with Barrow, who had little interest in relinquishing his prize ballplayer, but Barrow did promise the Pirates the first shot at Wagner when (and if) he decided to sell him.

Barrow believed Wagner possessed the best baseball hands he had ever seen. They were almost always in the right place at the right time. However, one day while Wagner was playing first base, a ground ball was hit that the shortstop bobbled. Before the pitch Wagner had dug down into his hip pocket to grab a hunk of chewing tobacco. As the shortstop was rushing his throw to Wagner at first, Wagner was jumping up and down and yelling at him to hold on to the ball, while at the same time making frantic jerks with his hand at something in his pocket. But the shortstop had already let go with a hard throw to beat the runner. Just in time Wagner put up his glove hand—at the time baseball gloves were little more than leather hand gloves—and caught the ball for the third out. After the catch, the team all converged on Wagner to see what was wrong. It turned out that his hand was stuck in his pocket. As Barrow described it: "In his hurry to get his hand out of his pocket, he had failed to open it, and the pocket not having been built for a ham, balked, and the more he pulled the tighter he became fastened, the pocket lining holding his hand in a viselike grip." To finally release his hand, they had to cut the pocket off.

Barrow always considered Wagner the best baseball player ever. This evaluation no doubt stemmed in part from his pride of discovery, but Wagner truly was a tremendous player. Barrow recognized his leadership abilities even at a young age. "Like all Germans," Barrow remarked, "Honus liked his glass of beer, but had no use for 'lushers' and 'called' more than one of the boys in his quiet way, when he thought a defeat had been caused by the bad effects of too much celebrating the night before." Surprisingly, most of his teammates accepted a rebuke from young Wagner because they appreciated his skill and desire to win.

In his appreciation of Wagner, Barrow subtly touted his own player evaluation skills as well. "He was so big and raw-boned that he sometimes appeared awkward," Barrow observed, "and anyone seeing him for the first time would imagine he couldn't get out of his own way. That was one of the reasons why good judges like Frank Selee and Pat Donovan and others passed him up after only a look at him." Only by evaluating Wagner day after day could one recognize his great skills.

In addition to Wagner, Barrow's Paterson team was stocked with a number of players who would advance to creditable Major League careers, most notably outfielders Bill Armour (who also became a big league manager) and Emmet Heidrick. The team started the season quickly, and on June 15 had a considerable lead in the pennant race: Paterson at 30-17 was well ahead of second-place Hartford at 25-22. Despite an injury to Wagner in June, the team remained solidly in first. Just prior to the Fourth of July, there was some discussion of closing out the first half of the season and creating a split season with the first-half winner, Paterson, playing the second-half victor. But this scheme quickly died.

For the typical July Fourth doubleheader in Wilmington, Delaware, Barrow and Wilmington manager Denny Long cooked up a unique scheme for some additional revenue. The two decided to add a third game to start at 8:00 p.m. under lights. For this novel game, played with an extra large ball to help visibility, only two hundred fans showed up. The lighting technology was not up to the task, however, and visibility was inadequate. Barrow remembered the bizarre sudden ending many years later. In the sixth inning Wilmington pitcher Doc Amole threw a giant "torpedo" (a small explosive) disguised as a baseball to the unsuspecting Wagner. When Wagner hit the "ball," it naturally exploded. The players ran for the clubhouse, and the fans onto the field, many unsuccessfully demanding their money back. Possibly because of this fiasco, Barrow never reconciled himself to night baseball when running the Yankees many years later.

The second half of the season started amid turmoil. Andrew Freedman, owner of the National League's New York Giants, owned the New York Metropolitans in the Atlantic League. The Metropolitans played in the Polo Grounds when the Giants were either out of town or otherwise idle. Freedman was one of the most disagreeable owners in baseball and best described as "overbearing and highhanded." As of early July he had not paid his league dues—the only team in arrears—and offered only a partial payment under threats from the league. Freedman was bitter because before the season he had forced through an arrangement that allocated all revenues to the home team in games played by the Metropolitans. Freedman obviously believed that a team in New York offering twenty-five-cent Minor League ball when the Giants were away would outdraw the league's smaller cities. In fact, New Yorkers had little appetite to watch Freedman's farm club, while several of the other cities, including Paterson, drew quite well. Furthermore, in a game on June 18 against Wilmington, Freedman held up the proceedings to berate the umpire. A Wilmington player told Freedman to "don a uniform if he desired to take part in the game." Freedman then banned the Wilmington player from again entering the Polo Grounds. In early July when Freedman carried out his threat and barred the player from a game, the umpire forfeited the game to Wilmington.

Freedman's shenanigans came to a head in the second week of July. League organizer Sam Crane and the owners (with the strong support of Barrow) kicked Freedman and his team out of the league. In its place they brought in the Athletics of Philadelphia (referred to as a "kindergarten" for the Major League Philadelphia team, just as the Metropolitans were for the New York Giants). The league also replaced the struggling New Haven franchise with one in Lancaster, Pennsylvania. Not surprisingly, Freedman threatened a lawsuit against the league, claiming several thousand dollars in damages.

As the second half started, Barrow also found himself shy a pitcher for a short time. One of his best hurlers, Sam McMackin (who later made it to the Majors for a few innings), was hit hard early in a game because he was drunk—euphemistically described as "in bad condition." An angry Barrow fined and suspended McMackin for several games. Over the second half of the season, the standings tightened considerably. By August 12 the race had devolved into essentially a three-way tie: by one count Hartford led by percentage points at 54-45, Paterson was second at 56-47, and Newark followed closely at 53-45. These three teams played neck and neck over the remainder of the season as additional controversies erupted. In a game at Hartford, Barrow, who had become unhappy with the league's poor umpiring in general, pulled his team off the field after some egregious calls. The umpire had missed a clear tag by Wagner at third, which led to three Hartford runs, and later refused to call a strike on a Hartford batter. With the Paterson team off the field, the umpire had little choice but to award a forfeit to Hartford.

As the season wound down, Barrow petitioned Crane to issue official league standings. The *Paterson Guardian* acknowledged that the Newark and Philadelphia papers showed different standings. Furthermore, Barrow brought up the matter of eight Newark exhibition game victories for which they were credited in the various standings. Hartford also was awarded a couple of disputed games that could further tilt the standings. The Newark and Hartford teams convinced Crane to defer any ruling until a league meeting well after the season. Crane went even further. He told a Newark paper that the Atlantic League had decided not to allow any protests of suspect games. Thus, when Newark won their last two games, they clinched a disputed pennant. At the season's finale on Sunday, four thousand spectators, a huge Minor League crowd for the era, turned out to watch a final Paterson victory.

After the season, wealthy baseball enthusiast Charles Soby agreed to sponsor the Soby Cup, a best-of-seven series between the first-and second-place ball clubs. The series was modeled on the Temple Cup of the National League, which also pitted the pennant winner against the second-place team. Despite Newark's nominal first-place finish, the Soby Cup pitted Paterson against Hartford. Hartford won the first game of the Soby Cup, but Paterson fought back and won the series four games to two. Prior to the start of the Soby Cup, Barrow scheduled a game with the Boston National League team, a pretty good first-division ball club. In a close fought battle in front of one thousand fans, the Boston regulars defeated Paterson 2–0.

Several years later when managing the Detroit Tigers, Barrow told a story about managing a team in Atlantic City and his catcher then in the Major Leagues. Given that Barrow did not manage in Atlantic City and his regular catchers were not active in the Majors six years later, the following reminiscence may be slightly embellished. In Barrow's account he was managing during a big series with Newark when a club employee ran out to the bench and told him that a deputy sheriff was there from Ohio to arrest his catcher "on a charge of breach of promise." Barrow fretted, mainly because it was the fifth inning and he had no reserve backstop available.

Barrow hustled out to the gate and found the deputy there with an angry young woman. She had come all the way from Cleveland to have Barrow's catcher arrested. The deputy and the young woman intended to carry out their mission in the middle of the game and haul him off to jail. Barrow hurried back inside to confer with his backstop.

"There's a girl out there from Cleveland who says you promised to marry her. Is that right?"

Seeing the young catcher turn pale, Barrow asked, "What sort of a girl is she, anyway?"

"Oh, she's the finest. I'd have married her last winter if I had had the money," replied his catcher.

Concerned over the loss of his catcher in midgame, Barrow asked, "Why don't you marry her now?"

The young catcher agreed. Barrow quickly made arrangements with a justice of the peace who officiated right across the street from the ballpark. While his team batted in the seventh, Barrow and the deputy acted as witnesses as his catcher and the young woman from Cleveland were married. And Barrow remembers everything worked out fine: the catcher made it back in time for the eighth inning, and the team won. He even concluded, "And I might add that the couple got along beautifully."

Not until the league meetings in late November was Newark officially awarded the pennant. No games were thrown out, and Crane's standings were accepted as correct. Over the course of the 1896 season, Crane had antagonized several owners and announced he would not run again for league president. After Crane removed himself from consideration, Barrow actively sought the position. In the election he defeated future Philadelphia Phillies president Horace Fogel five to three for the Atlantic League presidency. Barrow was much more ambitious and aggressive than he appears in his autobiographical writings; he often presents himself as being drafted into positions he actually had to pursue.

Despite some rough edges, the respect Barrow had earned from his fellow owners is evidenced by an incident in August during the just-completed season. Hartford and Newark were disputing the rights to a pitcher; instead of having Crane adjudicate the disagreement, the two teams named Barrow "referee" to decide the issue. For 1897 Barrow turned over the day-to-day operations of the Paterson franchise to his partner, McKee.

As the president of a young Minor League, Barrow adjudicated interowner squabbles, wrangled with the Majors over player and territorial rights, dealt with numerous player grievances, and managed the umpires. A Minor League president at the time also faced a unique set of business and financial challenges. The cultural and financial elites of American society generally disdained any interest in baseball. Team ownership prior to World War I fell mainly to politically connected, sports-minded, middling and small-time businessmen. Trolley and streetcar owners in particular were enthusiastic owners and investors, regarding franchises as a way to generate ridership. By the very nature of establishing their operations, which required negotiating rights-of-way, these owners were highly connected politically. Because the capital requirements to buy into a team, particularly in the Minor Leagues, were relatively modest, team employees were also a rich source for new owners. Often a manager or business manager would line up the capital necessary to acquire his own franchise.

Many of these poorly capitalized, politically connected baseball aficionados had little accumulated net worth and minimal ability to weather negative cash flow for long. It was not uncommon for teams and leagues to fold at midseason. Many owners had little experience in running a business, and like small business startups in all industries at the time, the failure rate was quite high. Furthermore, unlike the situation today, Minor League teams were not typically owned or controlled by Major League teams. Each team worked to find and sign the best players, while at the same time remaining solvent.

A stable and successful Minor League requires an organizational structure incorporating two essential features. First, the various franchises and leagues need to recognize one another's territorial integrity. A large portion of a franchise's value is derived from a team's monopoly over a defined geographic location. Clearly, financial planning becomes much more problematic if a franchise is at risk from a competitor invading its geographic area.

Second, teams need to have recognized control over their players. Prior to the advent of free agency in the 1970s, Major League teams had players in perpetuity through the "reserve clause." (The reserve clause was technically a section in each Major League contract "reserving" the player at the end of his contract; essentially the clause arrogated to the team the right to unilaterally renew the contract.) While the Major League clubs enjoyed the benefit of the clause themselves, they had no inherent reason for honoring it with independent Minor League teams. To survive within the structure that the Major Leagues had created, the Minors needed the Major Leagues to recognize their reservation rights as well.

The merger of four teams of the old American Association (a Major League from 1882 to 1891, after which it dissolved) into the National League in 1892 reduced baseball to a single Major League. As part of the documentation of the new arrangement, a National Agreement was negotiated granting recognition of the Minor Leagues' reservation rights. In return the Minor Leagues conceded drafting rights that permitted the Major Leagues to draft players from the Minors for a set price. The Minors also agreed to pay a protection fee to the Majors. The draft also led to the classification of Minor Leagues, with the better capitalized leagues in the bigger cites receiving a higher classification. The draft system further provided for higher classification Minor Leagues to draft from those of a lower class.

"Farming" was another practice that chafed the Minor Leagues of this era. Major League teams often signed amateur players who required some additional seasoning before being ready for Major League–caliber competition. The Majors would then "loan" these players to Minor League teams, while retaining the players' rights. This practice circumvented some of the usefulness of the draft by denying the Minor League team the profit of either the draft price for the player or the sale price in the event of an outright sale to a Major League club. Of course, the Minor League team always had the option of simply not accepting players controlled by Major League clubs. This was easier said than done, however. Typically men under Major League control were good ballplayers. Thus, if a team didn't accept them, they might find themselves at a competitive disadvantage.

The National League monopoly also worked to hold down Major League salaries. The lack of meaningful pennant races and boorish player and fan behavior discouraged attendance during the 1890s, though several Major League teams fared quite well. The New York Giants, for example, earned around $60,000 against stockholders equity of $250,000 in 1897. That season the *Sporting News* estimated salaries for the various professional baseball leagues including the Atlantic League (see table 1).

To further control salaries the lower Minor Leagues also instituted a team salary cap, then called a salary limit. Specified in terms of overall payroll allowed per month, the cap was designed to prevent any single or small group of owners in a small regional league from buying up all the best regional talent and dominating the league. Not surprisingly, unless strictly monitored, teams often violated the salary limits in the quest for the best players.

In sum, throughout the 1890s a poorly coordinated and managed baseball hierarchy attempted to prosper under the National Agreement of 1892. Despite significant friction between the Major and the Minor Leagues (and within each assemblage as well), the system functioned adequately for the magnates until the new challenge of a second Major League in 1901. It was within this framework that Barrow worked to keep the Atlantic League solvent and his owners satisfied.

During the winter before the 1897 season, Barrow traveled out west for a three-week hunting trip. His partner, Charles McKee, returned to Pittsburgh and spent the winter recruiting players. At a preseason meeting, the Atlantic League formally banned "farming," except in the case of the Athletics in Philadelphia. Manager Billy Sharsig argued that, because the team fell within the five-mile limit of a Major League club, certain concessions had to be made. Therefore, but for Philadelphia, the league ruled that "no drawing from other clubs would be allowed."

In March 1897 Jim Corbett lost his boxing title to Bob Fitzsimmons despite being a heavy favorite. He was leading in points when Fitzsimmons felled him in the fourteenth round with a famous punch to the solar plexus. The popular Corbett was also a decent baseball player—he had appeared in two Eastern League games in 1895—and he decided to play baseball over the summer to take advantage of his popularity. Barrow, who knew Corbett and his manager, William Brady, from his Pittsburgh days, helped recruit Corbett for a number of games in the Atlantic League. In July and August 1897 Corbett played in several regulation games in the Atlantic League, mostly at first base. Corbett was not a great player, but adequate enough not to embarrass himself, and he drew big crowds. Corbett would often receive as much as 50 percent of the gate receipts. One estimate had Corbett earning seventeen thousand dollars that summer, including both regulation and exhibition games.

As league president, Barrow capably oversaw league business. At a time when leagues often lost teams during the season, all Barrow's teams finished. With the exception of the Athletics, the teams fared well financially. For 1898 the league replaced the Athletics with a team in Allentown, Pennsylvania; the others all returned. Given the tenor of the times, Barrow struggled, with only limited success, to defend his umpires from abusive players and managers. But at least he took the challenge seriously.

That summer of 1897 Barrow and McKee cashed in on their star, Honus Wagner. Harry Pulliam, then a minor flunky with the National League's Louisville club (and a future National League president), was in New York with his team. As Pulliam remembered the episode, upon returning to his hotel after spending a night on the town, he found an old acquaintance from his hometown waiting for him. The visitor, for whom Pulliam had once done a favor, gushed about the greatest player in America playing in Paterson. Pulliam heeded this advice and took off for New Jersey. After watching Wagner for five days, Pulliam became a believer. Pulliam offered McKee and Barrow $2,000 for Wagner, a large amount for a Minor Leaguer at that time. Barrow, remembering his promise to Captain Kerr and the Pirates—and hoping to create some competition for his star—wired Kerr about the offer. Kerr replied he would match it. Pulliam pleaded for a little more time and contacted Louisville owner Barney Dreyfuss for permission to increase his bid. Dreyfuss agreed, and they upped their offer to $2,100. Barrow hoped to keep the auction alive and wired Kerr the new bid. When he received no response, Barrow sold his star to Louisville for $2,100.

Undeterred by his failed cleaning-product venture or his short-lived partnership with Stevens, until late middle-age Barrow nurtured a desire to succeed in a business sideline. With the league office and his residence now in Philadelphia, during the off-season Barrow took advantage of his experience with Stevens and acquired the concession business at Franklin Field, used mainly for college football. He also took on a local partner and became a fight promoter. With his boxing experience and familiarity with the fighters and promoters, Barrow had little difficulty presenting some pretty good bouts.

Despite, or possibly because of, their monopoly, during the 1890s the National League's owners failed to generate their anticipated attendance. The poor turnout is generally attributed to the league structure and a weak economy. The National League's twelve teams were not organized into divisions; the team with the best record at the end of the season was awarded the pennant. Given the wide disparity of playing strength among the teams, several teams were hopelessly out of the race early in the season. Economically, the depression that began in 1893 was the worst dislocation between the Civil War and World War I. The unemployment rate jumped above 18 percent in 1894 and stayed above 12 percent for five years.

Atrocious player and manager behavior during the decade further inhibited interest in baseball. Players and managers were both verbally and physically abusive toward umpires and one another. Furthermore, with only one umpire on the field, players took advantage of the arbiter's inability to see the entire field at one time. These shenanigans included runners skipping bases and fielders hiding balls in the outfield and impeding base runners by either grabbing or tripping them as they rounded the bases. When Ban Johnson challenged the status quo by declaring the American League a Major League in 1901, he highlighted a crackdown on unruly behavior as a major difference between his new league and the National.

At the Atlantic League meeting on March 24, 1898, Barrow and the owners made final preparations for the season. To support his umpires Barrow asked for the authority to suspend players for up to five days without pay for foul language or "ungentlemanly behavior." After some discussion, the owners granted the umpires, who reported to Barrow, the authority to suspend players up to two days. In general, the team owners of the Atlantic League did not feel rowdyism was a significant problem in their league and granted Barrow less authority in levying fines and suspensions than he had requested. In fact, while the league may not have been as riotous as the National, the players and managers often mistreated the umpires. On another front, in order to discourage farming from Major League clubs, the owners required that all players be signed for a full season. By thus binding a player to his Minor League club, a Major League team could not stash a player in the Atlantic League for less than its full season. Many of the league's owners correctly sensed the weak Minor League outlook for 1898. In a potentially short-sighted but money-saving amendment, the league reduced a team's fine for a forfeited game from eight hundred to one hundred dollars.

The Spanish-American War and the attendant patriotic fervor negatively affected baseball attendance and interest in 1898. The rapid succession of American victories during the summer absorbed much of the public's attention. Baseball attendance in the National League fell to only 2.3 million, compared to 2.9 million in 1897. As in many situations, those operating with the least cushion suffered the worst in the downturn, and the Minor Leagues struggled terribly during 1898. To maintain interest in his Minor League, Barrow experimented with a number of entertainment expedients.

He brought Corbett back for several exhibitions. He also used former heavyweight champ John L. Sullivan to umpire several games. Some of the most memorable exhibitions sponsored by Barrow, though, involved female pitcher Lizzie Arlington. Born Elizabeth Stroud, she assumed the name Arlington to enhance her baseball marketability. Stroud was a stocky twenty-two-year-old from coal-mining country and stood about five feet tall. She had learned to pitch under the tutelage of Jack Stivetts, an aging Major League hurler. That summer Arlington acquired an agent who paid her one hundred dollars per week and booked her at various baseball exhibitions.

Barrow recognized her potential appeal and engaged Arlington for a number of Atlantic League exhibitions to renew interest in the league. She appeared in only one regulation game, on July 5 for Reading, Pennsylvania, against Allentown and played mainly second base. The game drew one thousand fans, a large turnout for the time. With Reading ahead 5–0, Arlington went in to pitch the ninth inning. She loaded the bases before finally retiring the side without allowing a run. A local reporter described her pitching: "The sluggers of the Atlantic would soon put her out of business. She, of course, hasn't the strength to get much speed on and had poor control. But for a woman she is a success."

Despite these efforts, by midseason two of Barrow's franchises were in dire straits. On July 5 the Newark players went on strike because they had not been paid. Barrow reacted vigorously, suspending the players for two weeks and fining them as well. During their suspension, many of the players participated in Minor Leagues unaffiliated with the National Agreement. Barrow effectively used the suspension period to reorganize the bankrupt franchise on a "cooperative basis." Under this structure, the players were essentially given an interest in the profits in lieu of their salaries. Barrow created fourteen shares, thirteen for the players and one for the owner, who relinquished control for the remainder of the year but not his franchise rights.

The Hartford franchise also failed to meet its obligations at midseason. Barrow assumed ownership on behalf of the league and convinced the players to accept the cooperative plan. To help the club finish out the season, the guaranteed minimum paid to visiting clubs was reduced to only a token amount. After the league and players assumed control, the franchise sold two players to raise funds. At the end of the season, the team was sold and the profits divided among the players who remained.

Barrow was widely credited for his efforts in keeping the Atlantic League afloat during the financially disastrous season. For his services, the league's magnates awarded him a three-year contract. Unfortunately, any satisfaction Barrow felt from his extended contract would be short-lived. Most of the off-season was spent shoring up the ownership of the weakest franchises or relocating them to new cities with fresh ownership and fan enthusiasm. When Norfolk dropped out of the league, Barrow organized a franchise in Scranton. The Newark franchise wanted to jump to the more stable Eastern League, and despite the threat of a lawsuit, Barrow and the Atlantic League magnates refused to sanction the transfer. Barrow abandoned Hartford, which entered a team in the Eastern League, and replaced it with Wilkes-Barre.

Ever the optimistic entrepreneur, during the winter Barrow again put up his life savings for a risky moneymaking venture. At the instigation of Richmond manager Jake Wells, Barrow and Wells teamed up to enter the theater business in Richmond. The two leased the old Ford's Theater building, then occupied by the Spence Shoe Company, at a well-regarded location at Eighth and Broad. They signed a three-year lease, intending to open a "high-class variety house" in January. To finance the venture, Barrow put up his savings of $1,400 and borrowed $3,000 from the Atlantic League treasury. One can only imagine how this went over with his cash-strapped owners. For his part, Wells pawned his wife's jewelry. Bad weather delayed the opening, and the new business started slowly.

Barrow, now thirty years old, did not limit his new ventures to financial matters. On December 8 he married Alice Calhoun in New York City. Also thirty, Alice performed on stage in New York, presumably as a dancer. Interestingly, in his many autobiographical articles, I have never come across any reference by Barrow to this marriage. It was not a particularly blessed or lengthy one, and Barrow apparently had little interest in reliving it later.

The 1899 Atlantic League season was a financial disaster. Without a team in Norfolk, the cost of travel to Richmond became onerous for the league's other clubs. At midseason the new Paterson ownership forfeited its franchise back to the league. Barrow worked with colorful owner Abner Powell of the New Orleans team in the recently defunct Southern League to move his team up to Paterson. To renew interest, Barrow contacted Brady to help line up boxing champion James J. Jeffries to umpire a game. The promotion drew 4,500, a very large crowd for the time, but was little more than a stopgap measure amid a faltering season.

Despite difficulties in his new theater business, Barrow devoted his energies to the league presidency. Remarking on his struggle to preserve the Paterson team, the *Sporting News* declared: "Without Barrow the Atlantic League would have been a thing of the past long ago." The pressure of a failing league and a money-losing theater venture was taking its toll. Usually a strong backer of the umpires, Barrow became less supportive as the season dragged on. He fined umpire Sandy McDermott ten dollars for missing a game in Allentown. McDermott had been unable to make the trip because he had been hurt while umpiring a game in Lancaster. Soon thereafter McDermott missed a game owing to some confusion that was mostly Barrow's fault; nevertheless, Barrow docked him again. McDermott quit soon afterward.

Barrow soon realized he could not devote the necessary time to both baseball and the theater business, and he decided to get out of the latter. He persuaded his old Paterson partner, Charles McKee, to purchase his interest in the theater business. Barrow actually made some money when he sold out: McKee paid him $2,500 in cash and assumed his $3,000 debt to the Atlantic League. One can only wonder what became of this obligation when the league later collapsed.

By July 1899, with Paterson and Scranton no longer functioning, the league declared the first half-season over and discussed plans for a six-team second-half season. But the remaining teams had too many different agendas. Lancaster wished to continue the season, but the Eastern League was again courting Newark, and James Manning from the Western League's Kansas City team came east looking to buy players from the failing Wilkes-Barre and Richmond franchises. On August 6, Wells and Allentown manager Billy Sharsig called on Barrow in his Philadelphia office to discuss the league's situation. No official announcement was made, but statements by the meeting's participants made it clear that the league had closed down. Soon after the league collapsed, Barrow publicly offered three reasons for its demise: a failure by the teams to abide by the salary limits, a lack of business acumen by some owners, and a "do-others-or-they'll-do-you" spirit among many of them.

4. A Pennant in Toronto

With the collapse of the Atlantic League, Barrow once again needed to find a job in baseball. When the National League announced it was contracting from twelve to eight teams for the 1900 season, baseball positions suddenly became scarcer. Pursuing a lead, Barrow traveled to Washington to meet with Arthur Irwin. Irwin was the brother of John Irwin, an acquaintance of Barrow from his days managing in the Atlantic League. A Toronto native, Arthur Irwin owned a minority interest (Barrow remembered it as one-quarter share) of the Toronto franchise in the Eastern League, one of the top Minor Leagues. Ten years Barrow's senior, Irwin had spent many years in baseball as a player, manager, and minority owner. In 1898 Irwin began the season as Toronto's manager before taking the helm of the National League's Washington team at the tail end of the season. He remained as manager in Washington for the 1899 season and then returned to Toronto. Irwin's partners in the ownership syndicate included the team's majority owner, the Toronto Ferry Company, and Larry Solman. With their concurrence, Irwin hired Barrow as Toronto manager for 1900.

At the time, Toronto's baseball park was located on an island. Like the streetcar companies that owned baseball teams, the ferry company envisioned the ball club as a way to increase passengers. The company expected a ridership boost to and from the island on game days. Nominally named the Maple Leafs, the team was often referred to as the "Islanders."

With Washington one of the four teams being contracted, Irwin remained unsure of his next move. Initially it appeared as if Irwin would return to Toronto as team president—in fact rumors suggested Irwin was trying to gain control of the franchise and transfer it to the Western League—but he chose instead to take the managerial position in Syracuse, another Eastern League team. To facilitate the move, he sold his Toronto interest to Barrow, now flush with a little cash after the sale of his interest in the theater to Charles McKee. One needed to be careful when dealing with Irwin, one of the slimier men in baseball. Waite Hoyt, who later became a star pitcher under Barrow, once described Irwin as "probably the most disgusting man

[he] ever knew." After Irwin's death it was revealed that he had led a double life for many years. He had children and grandchildren with a wife in Boston and a common-law wife in New York. Until his death, neither wife knew of the other's existence.

Prior to the 1900 season, baseball was reentering the tumult of the early 1890s amid rumblings of challenges to the monopolistic National League. Western League president Ban Johnson renamed his league the American League and put a team in Cleveland, one of the contracted National League cites, and St. Paul owner Charles Comiskey transferred his team to Chicago, in direct competition with the National League club. Although Johnson's league was still technically a Minor League for 1900, Johnson clearly had designs on higher status. At the same time a number of baseball men, including John McGraw, Cap Anson, and *Sporting Life* editor Francis Richter, were working to organize a new American Association. Barrow, who knew Johnson from their days as Minor League presidents, scoffed at the suggestion that Johnson's league was in "revolt." He believed—wrongly—that the interim moves by Johnson were part of a big bluff worked out between Johnson and John Brush (the Cincinnati Reds' owner, a minority stockholder in the New York Giants, and one of the National League's most powerful magnates) to scare off the American Association.

The Eastern League was made up of many of the largest cities in eastern North America not already in the National League, and the quality of play was significantly above that of the Atlantic League. The team Barrow inherited had finished .500 in 1899. He immediately began hunting for new players to improve his team. One of his first signings was Mohawk Indian Louis Bruce from a semiprofessional team. The diminutive Bruce could pitch as well as play just about any position on the field. With his size and versatility, Bruce became something of a local celebrity in Toronto. Given baseball's organizational structure and small roster sizes, it was not uncommon for marginal players to bounce between the Major and the Minor Leagues. Of Barrow's recruits and trade targets, several had Major League experience in either their past or future. For example, at catcher he had ex-Atlantic Leaguer Harry Bemis, who would go on to a lengthy Major League career.

Minor League operations during the time Barrow managed in the Minors required a very small staff. The team president owned an interest in the team and was authorized by the ownership entity to represent the team at league meetings and for other major decisions affecting the franchise. Frequently the manager owned a percentage of the club and would also fulfill the team president function. The manager's functions also included matters that today a general manager would handle. That is, the manager was responsible for all the personnel moves and trades as well as overseeing the team on the field. To stock his roster, a Minor League manager used his relationships and contacts throughout baseball to generate leads on potential players. The manager's responsibilities did not quite equal two full-time jobs, however, because the roster sizes were generally fifteen players or fewer, reducing the complexity of the position. Also, to help with the on-field managing, a player would often be designated team captain; his duties sometimes included organizing workouts and getting the team onto the field. A Minor League club also typically employed an underpaid team secretary to help administer travel and other sundry items (uniforms, balls, etc.).

Barrow's Toronto Maple Leafs started slowly in 1900 and never really recovered. On May 27 the team was in last place with a record of 7-16. Further magnifying the poor start, a noticeable minority of Toronto's fans were Americans who ferried across Lake Ontario and cheered for the visiting club if it was from the States. Second-division Minor League teams rarely made money, and some began to question the relatively high-profile hiring of Barrow. Barrow was certainly making an effort and becoming increasingly frustrated—by early July he had tried around thirty-one players. One reporter asserted, with some overstatement: "I believe manager Ed Barrow has broken all previous records in signing players." Another report a month later noted that he had run through forty players but could not improve the club. With reports of Arthur Irwin leaving Syracuse, rumors naturally circulated insinuating his imminent return to Toronto.

For the annual July 4 doubleheader, Toronto was scheduled to play at Rochester, managed by Barrow's old friend and partner Al Buckenberger. For several hours prior to game time, a heavy rain fell, finally stopping around 9:00 a.m. But "dense banks of dark clouds remained in the sky," and it appeared as if no game could be played. Due to the weather, Barrow did not bother to bring his club out to the ballpark. He maintained that one of the Rochester owners told him that there would be no game. The Toronto club's secretary-treasurer further confirmed that he had been notified that the game was called off. Nevertheless, the Rochester team showed up, and after the customary couple of minutes, the umpire forfeited the morning game to Rochester, 9–0. Back at the hotel Buckenberger told Barrow what had happened, infuriating him.

Exactly what happened next remains lost to history, but piecing together various reports suggests that as the argument heated up, at some point Buckenberger called Barrow a liar, which brought things to a boil. Buckenberger may or may not have tried to push Barrow, but in any case, Barrow punched Buckenberger in the face. Toronto player Henry Lynch then grabbed Buckenberger from behind, and Barrow landed several more blows. After the altercation, Barrow was arrested for third-degree assault and then released. When he did not return to Rochester for his court date on July 9, he was fined twenty-five dollars. An angry Buckenberger also filed a civil suit asking five thousand dollars in damages for assault and battery. It is not surprising that later in July Buckenberger had little interest in negotiating player moves with Barrow, refusing to part with infielder Frank Bonner despite Barrow's offer of eight hundred dollars.

Buckenberger was well acquainted with Barrow's love of fighting as is clear from his account of an incident with Barrow several years earlier. One night after a game, Barrow and Buckenberger went for a stroll around town. When the two reached a remote spot, Barrow removed his coat.

"What are you doing?" Buckenberger asked.

"I understand you are something of a scrapper, and I am going to try you out. Come on, take your coat off," Barrow responded.

Buckenberger sensed Barrow was serious and thought he was crazy. He needed five minutes to persuade Barrow that he had never posed as a fighter. Finally Barrow reluctantly put his coat back on, and the two walked back to the hotel. Buckenberger concluded his reminiscence: "Now take a tip from me; don't ever go walking with Barrow and tell him you are a bit of a boxer."

Now that he was no longer a league president, Barrow criticized umpires with a vengeance whenever he felt wronged, which was often. Late in the season back in Rochester, Barrow again felt cheated out of a victory. After the game he wired the Toronto offices: "Deliberately robbed in the ninth innings today by umpire Egan." Despite his best efforts, Barrow experienced little success in 1900 with the ball club. In his five years in Organized Baseball, Barrow had developed a wide network of contacts and player relation-ships. He used this network to aggressively replace players he felt were not performing but could not improve on the .500 record of the previous sea-son. The Maple Leafs finished 63-67 and in sixth place.

By the close of the 1900 season, the Toronto Ferry Company wanted out of ownership; the team was not particularly profitable, and the island ballpark likely inhibited patronage due to slow boats and cold weather in the spring and fall. Barrow aggressively assumed the lead position in restructuring the ownership. In late September he secured an option to purchase the fran-chise for six thousand dollars. He envisioned a stock company ownership with a large contingent of local businessmen and professionals purchasing a significant number of shares each. Given the issues with the stadium's lo-cation, Barrow also pursued a new stadium on the mainland.

Ban Johnson and his American League owners resolved to become a Ma-jor League for the 1901 season. Johnson publicly professed his hope to ac-complish this peacefully, but no executive as sharp as he could have rea-sonably expected the National League to relinquish its monopoly without a fight. Johnson also recognized that to challenge the Nationals as a Major League he needed some teams in the more populous eastern North Amer-ican cities. The American League had started as the Western League in some of the larger cities of the Midwest, but even after adding Chicago and Cleveland for 1900, the league lacked enough major cities to truly pro-claim itself major.

One reason Barrow assumed a leading role in the new ownership drive was his hope of landing the team in the newly major American League. The sentiment in Toronto clearly favored maneuvering into Johnson's cir-cuit. In October Barrow traveled to Buffalo—whose team was a member of the 1900 American League and would itself be dropped in the reorganiza-tion—to meet with that team's ownership regarding an American League franchise. After the meeting Barrow released to the newspaper his projected cities of the restructured American League: Toronto, Buffalo, Louisville, Indianapolis, Milwaukee, Chicago, Detroit, and Cleveland. Johnson had clearly not taken Barrow into his confidence regarding the ultimate plan: only the last four teams would be included in the new American League. To give his league a more national appeal, Johnson abandoned several medium-sized Midwest markets and moved teams into Baltimore, Washington, Philadelphia, and Boston.

As a self-declared Major League, the American League refused to accept Minor League status under the Major League–Minor League draft as defined in the National Agreement. By opting out of the National Agreement, the American League captured an additional competitive advantage over the National: it was no longer constrained by the agreement's other provisions regarding contract status and territorial rights. Thus the American League could raid the existing Major and Minor Leagues for players, and while it had to respect contractual rights, the reserve clause was another matter. Naturally, as the new Major League looked to boost its talent level, its teams looked to two main sources: the National League, and the top Minor League, the Eastern. Barrow would spend the better part of the next two seasons battling to prevent many of his top players from jumping to the American League. In this he was more aggressive and successful than some of his competitors.

Although unsuccessful in securing a franchise in the new American League, Barrow successfully quarterbacked the Toronto franchise's reorganization. Barrow hoped to raise $10,000: $6,000 to acquire the franchise and $4,000 for operating capital and to cover part of the cost of a new ballpark. A new publicly owned company was established, and by March the shares of stock were almost fully subscribed; of the $10,000 target, only $1,100 remained unsold. The new company had a board of five directors led by President Ed Mack, an old-time Canadian baseball star. For the upcoming season the team set the cost of general admission at twenty-five cents, the grandstand at forty cents, and reserved seats at fifty cents. This compared to a typical National League charge of fifty cents; the American League offered a twenty-five-cent general admission ticket during its inaugural season.

During the off-season Barrow reportedly signed a couple of players who went on to longtime Major League careers. These players never ended up on Toronto's roster, however. Barrow thought he had purchased catcher Red Dooin from a semiprofessional independent league, but Dooin played the 1901 season in the Western League. Barrow also believed he had landed Christy Mathewson, a pitcher who went on to become one of the all-time greats. Barrow may have known Mathewson from a college football game in Franklin Field a couple of years earlier when he held the concession rights.

Several other teams were also angling to sign Mathewson that off-season. Connie Mack offered him $1,500 to join his American League Philadelphia Athletics. Also, Cincinnati owner John Brush and New York Giants owner Andrew Freedman conspired to manipulate the Minor League draft rules so that Freedman could acquire Mathewson cheaply. Unfortunately for Barrow's pennant chances, the reports of Mathewson heading to Toronto were short-lived and he ended up in New York.

Throughout the off-season Barrow worked to improve his club. Now that the team had a more aggressive recapitalized ownership, Barrow was allocated a larger allowance to purchase ballplayers. He secured future Major League star pitcher Nick Altrock from Syracuse for a salary of $175 per month. He also finally landed second baseman Frank Bonner from Rochester. The franchise was now financially secure enough that Barrow felt he could afford to turn down an offer of around $2,000 from St. Louis for third baseman Bob Schaub. Furthermore, Barrow acted proactively by sending advance money to his players in March to keep them from signing with the American League.

Barrow's busy off-season also included finding a site and building a new stadium. His initial efforts to lease a municipally controlled site met with resistance. Barrow's attempts to negotiate a stadium site with the city highlighted an element of his personality that would serve him poorly as he advanced into positions of prominence: he demonstrated little skill or tolerance in lobbying decision-making bodies. When Barrow needed to influence an association or group comprised of anyone other than close associates, he almost always failed to achieve his goal. Surprisingly, for someone who seemed politically adept in smaller settings, he never developed the skills necessary to exert his will over larger bodies.

Barrow and the Toronto club eventually found a site on which to build a ballpark, agreed on a five-year lease, and immediately began construction of Diamond Park. Because of the late start, the stadium was not ready for the home opener. At a league meeting, the other owners objected to Barrow's appeal to delay the Toronto home opener, causing Barrow and team president Ed Mack to petition league president Pat Powers. Powers was unwilling to rule unilaterally but provided Mack a letter of approval and sent him to meet with the other owners. Mack then successfully lobbied his fellow owners to revamp the early schedule.

In early April, Barrow brought his team to familiar territory—Paterson, New Jersey—for spring training. He arranged several spring training games, mostly with other Minor League clubs, but also with Philadelphia and New York. Barrow planned to carry fourteen players during the season: four pitchers, two catchers, and eight others. Players like Bruce who could both pitch and play the field offered important versatility when competing for minimal roster spots. When one player asked Barrow, "In case you release me, where do I go?" the unsympathetic Barrow responded, "Well, I guess you're a dead one. And you know your life's history better than I do." In addition to getting his team ready to play, Barrow also voiced his opposition to a misguided proposed rule that would eliminate awarding the batter first base when hit by the pitch. At the end of spring training, Barrow may have wished for an even broader rule when he suffered a split lip after getting hit by a thrown ball.

Because of the stadium construction difficulties, Toronto played its first thirteen games on the road. Barrow was enthusiastic over his team's 8-5 start and, ever the optimist, forecasted a pennant. Back home, opening day festivities included a big celebration with a parade scheduled for 2:15 p.m. followed by a 3:30 p.m. ball game. Early season attendance was strong, allowing Barrow the freedom to purchase and trade players as he continuously fine-tuned the team. As of midsummer Barrow had his team playing well and battling Rochester for first place. He even successfully protested a game that an umpire had called due to rain with Toronto down by one run.

In early May Barrow and his wife suffered a tragedy when their first child died of respiratory complications shortly after birth, possibly indicating a premature birth. It is unlikely Alice ever fully recovered; she and Barrow seemed to drift apart after this unfortunate incident. As near as can be determined, Barrow never mentioned this incident publicly, and he would never father any additional biological children.

In late July, Barrow's club began to lose ground to Buckenberger's Rochester team, mainly due to injuries to right fielder George Brown—described in a *Sporting News* article as the best batter in the league—and Schaub. Already irritable following the death of his infant son, Barrow grew increasingly bellicose as his club fell behind: when he lost both games of a doubleheader in late July at home to Rochester, both by one run, he loudly and publicly accused umpire Al Warner of incompetence. A couple of days later in a game against Buffalo, Barrow refused to allow Warner, the scheduled umpire, onto the field and found two locals (one a former big league official) to umpire. For the next day's game, Powers ordered Warner to umpire. When Barrow ignored Powers's instruction, Buffalo refused to play without a league umpire. Barrow's two local umpires then forfeited the game to Toronto.

Barrow's aggressive, self-indulgent performance created one of the biggest brouhahas of the league's season. Powers briefly suspended Warner and called a league meeting in Buffalo to rule on the validity of the forfeited game. At the contentious meeting Powers upbraided Barrow "for making the statement that [President Powers was] not competent to hold his position and everybody in the Eastern League Circuit thought it time for a change."

Instead of denying the statement, Barrow retorted, "I am not the only one who has made the remark."

Buffalo president James Franklin feared Barrow was implicating him and shouted: "Don't you dare make any insinuations in my direction; don't you dare do it! I am loyal to our president and you know it."

"I didn't say anything about you, and didn't mean you," Barrow shot back.

Rochester executive John Nash then jumped in and also upbraided Barrow for his actions.

Powers ended the scene by drawing a line in the sand: "Mr. Barrow may speak the truth when he says I am not competent to hold my position as president of the Eastern League. If I am not, then it is your privilege to retire me, but until you do retire me I propose to be president, and shall insist on my orders being carried out."

Despite the hullabaloo, the league failed to reach a resolution on the issues because the meeting fell short of a quorum of owners not directly involved in the outcome. Barrow's lack of diplomacy again did him a disservice. Powers had been elected president in 1893 and had stabilized the league. During his nine-year reign he had naturally consolidated his position while occasionally alienating some. Even assuming Barrow correctly gauged the sentiments of his fellow league executives, it was highly unlikely they would be willing to back Barrow in this controversy against their own teams' interests. Barrow's naiveté in understanding group dynamics is evidenced by his surprise at the unwillingness of the other magnates to confront Powers—on terms other than their own—in midseason over a controversy of Barrow's own making. This blind spot seems particularly startling given his three years as a league president.

On the field the remainder of the 1901 season was anticlimactic for Barrow and his squad. The team played capably but could never close the gap on Rochester, which won the pennant by nine games over second-place Toronto. Off the field chaos reigned throughout baseball. The American League was proving surprisingly successful, and its teams continued to target top Minor League players. In August the National League, reeling from the success of the American, also withdrew from the National Agreement, creating a player free-for-all. The Majors now recognized neither one another's nor the Minors' player reservation rights. In these frenzied circumstances Barrow continuously signed and released players as he tried to improve his club and prevent his own stars from defecting. In August he landed Patsy Flaherty, a pitcher who would go on to a respectable Major League career.

Barrow received generally high marks for bringing his team in second. Nevertheless, Mack intended to jettison Barrow and hire a player-manager. Mack's stated reason for the move was financial. The American League's struggle for Major League status significantly affected the health of the Minor Leagues. One Eastern League franchise, Hartford, suspended operations in early September; the team's players had not been paid since August 22 and the team had lost $7,400. The stockholders refused to infuse any more money, and the team canceled its remaining games. Mack claimed that only two franchises made money, Toronto, which earned a measly $952 (see table 2 for a summary financial statement), and Rochester. He further reported that the league had to subsidize the Buffalo, Syracuse, and Hartford clubs.

On its face the cost savings gained from a player-manager does not seem sufficient to fire a competent manager. (By using a player-manager a team gets two jobs for the price of a little more than one—Mack argued the saving would be $1,200, but a board supporter of Barrow maintained it would be closer to $600–$700.) Mack admitted that he and Barrow "had a few words after the close of last season" but insisted the argument had nothing to do with his wanting a player-manager. Other sources reported that the "words" were over baseballs for a player benefit game. Mack objected to the players receiving new baseballs for the game; Barrow sided with the players. One stockholder alleged that Mack decided then and there to fire Barrow. A rumor also surfaced that Barrow had explored purchasing the Buffalo franchise; it appears that this inquiry, however, came after he learned that Mack was angling for his ouster.

On November 15 Toronto's board of directors, in a contentious three to two vote, voted to hire a player-manager for 1902, effectively firing Barrow. The two directors who supported Barrow and a number of shareholders vehemently opposed the dismissal. They organized a shareholder meeting to conduct a vote by the full ownership on Barrow's status. Prior to the meeting Barrow was frustrated but philosophical: "When one satisfies both press and public, as well as those whose finances are at stake and then learns that, in spite of his success, he is to be turned down, he is apt to become just a little bit disgusted with things in general and baseball in particular. However, the matter will be definitely settled Monday night, and I will be glad of it, no matter which way it goes."

The stockholders emphatically supported Barrow, voting down Mack's proposal for a player-manager, fifty-eight to twenty-nine. His supporters pointed out that a winning club would bring in more money than a mediocre player-manager would save. They also highlighted the importance of Barrow's hustle and personality when he helped raise the funds to refinance the club. Mack, not one to lose gracefully, extracted a petty, price-saving dig by cutting Barrow's salary. In 1901 Barrow earned $1,500 plus a $300 bonus for finishing second. For the 1902 season the team reduced his salary to $1,200 with a bonus of $400 for winning the pennant and $300 for a second-place finish. Shortly after agreeing to stay at the reduced salary, Barrow received an offer of the presidency of the Southern League. Barrow chose to honor his agreement and remain with Toronto.

To combat the Major League's player raids, in the fall of 1901 the Minor Leagues organized themselves into the National Association of Professional Baseball Leagues. During its fall meetings, the National Association recodified the reserve rule, established league classifications, set salary limits, and elected Barrow's nemesis, Pat Powers, as president. In any case, without an agreement with the Majors, a purely Minor League organization remained mostly impotent to control the existing baseball conflicts. Further player and territorial competition came from a newly formed American Association, a high Minor League occupying some of the large midwestern cities abandoned by the American League. The American Association refused to join the National Association and viewed the other Minor League clubs as a source of talent.

Now rehired after the bitter battle, Barrow needed to retool his team for the 1902 season. After Mack's cry of poverty, however, Barrow lacked the financial resources of the previous season. Also, player rights remained tenuous among all the broken alliances, and a number of players deserted Toronto for greener pastures. Pitcher Nick Altrock and catcher Harry Bemis both signed with American League clubs. Barrow lost the rest of his 1901 pitching staff as well, including Flaherty. Schaub signed with Louisville in the American Association. The team sold outfielder George Brown to the Phillies.

Barrow also sold Frank Bonner, who was planning to jump to the Majors anyway, to the Cubs. The Bonner sale instigated a series of contacts between Barrow and Bonner that left Barrow feeling betrayed. When Cleveland offered Bonner a $2,400 salary for 1902, Barrow conceded that he could not compete with a salary roughly $1,000 higher than Toronto could pay. Barrow asked Bonner to go to Chicago instead of Cleveland because the Cubs were willing to pay Toronto $600 for him. Bonner agreed, but asked for $100 of the $600 purchase price. Barrow, recognizing the player's negotiating leverage and that $500 was better than nothing, granted Bonner's request. He even forwarded the $100 immediately when Bonner claimed he needed the money up-front because of an illness in his family. Bonner reneged, however, and signed with Cleveland, leaving Barrow stuck for the $100 advance.

Throughout the spring Barrow aggressively sought new talent for his team, signing numerous players he hoped could help. Many of these players came from the New York State League. In his pursuit of players Barrow was willfully ignorant of current contract status. He often shifted his view of baseball controversies depending on his own particular circumstances. When his need for new players was acute, he only loosely adhered to the constraints of other teams' player contracts. In fact, in 1902 Barrow reportedly had more cases before the National Board than any other manager and lost them all. Regardless of his methods, many lauded the talent he landed in his off-season maneuvering; Toronto was now considered the pennant favorite in some quarters.

The league itself replaced two of its weakest franchises, Hartford and Syracuse, with two larger cities in the New York metropolitan area, Jersey City and Newark. For spring training, Mack thought the club could save one thousand dollars by staying home, so the team trained in cold, wintry Toronto during April. Most of the spring training games would thus be against local college and semiprofessional teams as opposed to Major and Minor League clubs. Despite this lack of early-season competition, the team started off acceptably, and Barrow remained optimistic.

Early in the season, the pressure of the pennant race and poor umpiring again got the best of Barrow. In a May game at Worcester, the umpiring was apparently horrible for both teams, with poor decisions followed by "make-up" calls. In the ninth when his runner was called out sliding into home, Barrow charged out and began haranguing umpire Thomas Kelly. When he lightly touched the umpire's cap, Kelly gave Barrow a "left-hand jab that rocked the manager's top piece." Barrow quickly retaliated with "a thump on the jaw and a solar plexus blow." The fans surged onto the field during the exchange of punches, but the police quickly emerged and escorted the umpire out of the stadium. The lack of any significant repercussions from the league office for this incident highlights the looseness of the administration in the Minor Leagues at the time.

In late June, Barrow had the Maple Leafs at 32-17 and in first place, but by mid-July he had fallen to second behind Buffalo, managed by his friend and rival George Stallings. Over the rest of the summer, Toronto and Buffalo battled back and forth for first place. Approximately fifteen thousand spectators showed up for the season-ending doubleheader against Providence. Toronto won both games as pitcher Jimmy Gardner hurled a one-hitter in the first game and a six-hitter in the second. When the final standings were tabulated, Toronto captured the pennant by the slimmest margin, one-half game over Buffalo. (At the time seasons could end with teams having played different numbers of games regardless of the effect on the pennant race.) To wrap up the season, Barrow organized an exhibition game the next day against the National League champion Pittsburgh Pirates. The Pirates started their regulars and defeated the Maple Leafs 7–3. To celebrate the pennant, the stockholders threw a big end-of-season party for Barrow and the players. As an added bonus, a special performance was held at Shea's Theater with the players receiving the evening's proceeds.

The *Sporting News* reprinted an anonymous letter critical of Barrow's distribution of the receipts from the Pittsburgh exhibition game, which were split evenly with the Pirates. Of Toronto's half, Barrow divided the proceeds fifty-fifty with the players. Therefore, each player received $22.83, while Barrow received $357.43, in addition to a $300 bonus for arranging the game. Not surprisingly, his players were unhappy when they learned of the split percentages. That the organizer should retain the bulk of the proceeds squares with Barrow's personality and his history as a fight promoter and entrepreneur.

The Toronto organization was anxious to tie Barrow up for another season after what was also a tremendously successful year financially. The team turned a profit of $3,692—on stockholder's equity of $10,000—despite an increase in the team payroll to $14,837. The team drew around 130,000 fans with only fifty-seven home dates, an average of nearly 2,300 per game. This was an astonishing total for a Minor League team; Toronto actually outdrew two National League teams in fewer games. Flush from the successful season, the team decided to buy out the ground lease under its ballpark. When the ball club originally gained control of the site, the team had executed only a five-year ground lease with a three-year purchase option. With funds now available, the stockholders seized the opportunity to secure a permanent home.

Barrow received a number of attractive offers from other clubs, including one to manage San Francisco in the Pacific Coast League. He also turned down a managerial inquiry from the muddled Philadelphia Phillies ownership. To hold on to Barrow, the directors upped his salary to two thousand dollars with a five-hundred-dollar bonus for winning the pennant. Barrow reportedly accepted this offer and began the process of retooling for 1903. He also helped bring the American Association back into the fold of Organized Baseball. (Despite his inability to advocate adeptly for his own interests with political equals, Barrow often proved surprisingly effective in a "referee" role.) Along with Francis Richter, editor of *Sporting Life*, Barrow persuaded the leaders of the American Association to come to the National Association meeting for a negotiating session. Eventually, the two sides hammered out a compromise, removing the "outlaw" designation from the American Association. To wrap up his fall athletic activities, Barrow arranged a rugby match pitting several of the Toronto ballplayers, including himself, against a team made up of newspaper men and a couple of the Toronto directors, including Ed Mack. Barrow, still only thirty-four years old, must have enjoyed this match immensely.

5. Major League

Organized Baseball's two-year chaos persisted into the 1902–3 off-season. The ownership of more than a few players remained in dispute between the two Major Leagues. Also, the Minor Leagues, no longer protected by an agreement with the Majors, were contesting a number of Major League player signings. In the battle between the leagues, the better organized, less fractious, and more competently led American League maintained the initiative. To formalize his league's Major League status, American League president Ban Johnson transferred the Baltimore franchise to New York for 1903 over the objections of the New York Giants ownership. Also, Johnson considered shifting the Detroit Tigers to Pittsburgh to challenge the Pirates for supremacy there. Pirate owner Barney Dreyfuss believed a deal was fully negotiated, and that Johnson had found Pittsburgh-area investors to purchase the Tigers for thirty-six thousand dollars and transfer the franchise.

Johnson first considered moving the Detroit franchise to Pittsburgh after the 1901 season because of both the city's significantly larger population base and his irritation with the existing Detroit ownership. Irrespective of the possible shift, once Johnson became disgusted with the Detroit ownership, which included manager George Stallings, he actively maneuvered its replacement. He encouraged and offered financial support to local Detroit entrepreneur Sam Angus to purchase the club. Angus ran an insurance agency and was also a railroad contractor. Like many owners of the era, he was not particularly wealthy, but with Johnson's help he acquired and recapitalized the franchise. In his insurance agency Angus employed a thirty-one-year-old analyst, Frank Navin, destined to become one of the key figures in Detroit baseball. Navin had attended law school, but after an unsuccessful run for political office and the imprisonment of his brother for embezzlement, he retreated to the anonymity of the insurance office. When Angus gained control of the Detroit franchise, Navin eagerly sought the opportunity to manage the team's books.

In January 1903 the National League blinked and reluctantly agreed to recognize the American League as an equal. As part of the peace agreement, the American League maintained its recently acquired New York presence but agreed not to invade Pittsburgh. The settlement process also adjudicated claims to the various contested players, who were then assigned to teams. The Tigers retained the rights to three excellent ballplayers: Sam Crawford, Bill Donovan, and Kid Elberfeld. Crawford and Donovan had jumped to Detroit and, therefore, were satisfied with the settlement. Elberfeld, however, had played in Detroit in 1902. Nicknamed the Tabasco Kid because of his explosive personality, Elberfeld had grown disgruntled in Detroit and signed with the Giants after the 1902 season. The agreement thus left Detroit with a mercurial star unhappy with his situation.

At the conclusion of a dismal 1902 season in which the team finished 52-83, the Detroit Tigers fired manager Frank Dwyer. Owner Sam Angus targeted twenty-eight-year-old pitcher Win Mercer to take over the team, offering a salary of $3,800 for a player-manager role. Over the winter Mercer toured the West Coast with an all-star team of American Leaguers for a series of games against a National League team. Mercer, as treasurer of the American League team, maintained its finances and cash. While on this trip, in mid-January, Mercer committed suicide by asphyxiating himself in his hotel room in San Francisco. He attributed his despondency to gambling and women who got the better of him (which he did not expand upon). On the journey west he had also visited his brother, who was suffering from tuberculosis. The meeting clearly shook Mercer, who feared he might catch the disease as well. Initial reports suggested that some of the money Mercer held for the players might have gone missing, but after a final accounting, the finances appeared in order.

With the death of Mercer, Angus needed to quickly find a new manager for 1903. On the recommendation of Ban Johnson, Angus approached Barrow. Despite a pennant-winning team in Toronto, Barrow eagerly accepted a chance to manage for an apparently stable ownership in the Major Leagues. Just shy of thirty-five years old, Barrow had recently shaved his handlebar mustache; his more mature appearance befitted his new job. Recognizing his own limitations as an evaluator of baseball players, Angus also delegated the team-building function to his new manager. So, as in Toronto, Barrow had practically free rein to assemble the ball club as he saw fit (subject, of course, to Angus's oversight of the financial impact). To restock the Tigers, Barrow targeted Eastern Leaguers (as opposed to National Leaguers), now that the fragile peace agreement was in effect. He contemplated bringing in Lou Bruce, his favorite utility player in Toronto, and pursued Jimmy Gardner, his star hurler of 1902. The Maple Leafs, though, held on to Gardner by offering him Barrow's manager position for 1903, and Bruce never appeared for the Tigers. To shore up his infield, Barrow signed Charles Carr, his first baseman in Toronto in 1901. He also swapped second basemen with the New York Giants, trading Kid Gleason (one of Elberfeld's pals) for Heinie Smith, whom Barrow had managed in Paterson and now named team captain. To address the weakness at third base, Barrow converted pitcher (and occasional fielder) Joe Yeager to be his regular third baseman.

Once again Barrow's aggressive tactics in pursing players generated some animosity. Carr was on the Jersey City reserve list, and the club publicly and vigorously objected to his signing with Detroit. Although the National Agreement was not yet technically reinstated, with the new peace agreement accepted in principle, a gentlemen's agreement to recognize reserve rights of teams in Organized Baseball was generally in effect. Eastern League president Pat Powers, Barrow's old nemesis, protested the Carr signing and threatened to invade American League cities if not fairly compensated. Johnson paid lip service to Powers's complaint, but Carr remained in Detroit. A couple of weeks later, Barrow further thumbed his nose at the Jersey City ownership (and Powers) by signing outfielder Wallace Clement. Barrow lost this round, however; later that spring he sent Clement back to Jersey City and signed Boston Brave discard Billy Lush.

Unfortunately for his construction of the team, Barrow lost much of the month of February to pneumonia. Despite this setback, he remained optimistic he could build a solid Major League ball club. For spring training Barrow brought his squad to Shreveport, Louisiana, for two weeks of training and three weeks of exhibition games throughout the South. He also hoped to instill toughness and stamina by hiring middleweight fighter Willie Campbell to be his trainer for the spring. Back in Detroit the team increased the seating capacity of Bennett Park by adding new bleachers to left field.

Detroit opened at home against Cleveland on April 22. Because Cleveland's best pitchers were tall, Barrow ordered the mound lowered in the hope that this would increase their wildness. While this strategy may or may not have been the cause, Detroit swept all three games from the Indians. After this nice start, the team played around .500 ball and appeared materially improved over the dismal 1902 version.

From the end of May through early June, Detroit played seven consecutive games against the St. Louis Browns. After winning the first, the Tigers lost the last six. Kid Elberfeld had been sulking for some time leading up to this series, and as reported in the *Sporting News*, "it so happened that in three of the six games lost to St. Louis, Elberfeld made a muff, fumble, or wild throw at the moment of a critical stage, the error in each instance taking the game away from Detroit." Elberfeld desperately wanted out of Detroit, which made Barrow suspicious of his errors. Other managers, including John McGraw of the Giants and Jimmy McAleer of the Browns, were clearly tampering with Elberfeld and encouraging him to force his release from the Tigers. While in St. Louis, McAleer and Elberfeld went so far as to have Elberfeld actually practice with the Browns while the Browns regular shortstop, future Hall of Famer Bobby Wallace, shifted to third.

When Elberfeld fielded particularly egregiously on June 1 after a return to Detroit—a game the Tigers lost after Elberfeld booted a routine double play with one out and the team up by two in the ninth—Barrow could stand it no longer. He confronted Elberfeld after the game and blistered him with his disgust. Despite his small stature, the hard and violent Elberfeld refused to be cowed by Barrow's indignation. Elberfeld offered to buy his release from the Tigers for one thousand dollars, claiming he had been offered a salary in excess of three thousand dollars. Elberfeld clearly hoped to force his way to either the St. Louis Browns or back to the Giants. Barrow angrily declared that after his actions he would never trade Elberfeld to one of those two teams.

Barrow, with Angus's acquiescence, fined Elberfeld two hundred dollars, suspended him indefinitely, and released a damning statement to the press: "He utterly disregarded the rules and regulations, refused to obey the orders of his captain and manager to such an extent that we feel called upon to put a stop to it. I thought he tried to lose some of the games while we were in the South [i.e., at St. Louis], but said nothing about it." Barrow's public accusation of deliberately throwing the game ended any possibility of a reconciliation in Detroit (assuming that either side wanted one in the first place). As an above-average shortstop, Elberfeld was a valuable player, although his reputation likely exceeded his ability. When it became clear that Elberfeld was available, a number of teams approached Barrow and Angus for their asking price. Elberfeld, however, continued to insist he would only go to the Browns or the Giants; otherwise he would jump to an outlaw league on the Pacific Coast or retire home to Tennessee.

To relieve the stalemate Ban Johnson and White Sox owner Charles Comiskey, another key league executive, traveled to Detroit to meet with Barrow and Angus. Comiskey had some limited hopes of landing Elberfeld for himself. Johnson, however, had broader objectives: he feared the negative publicity of a prolonged stalemate with one of the league's star players, including a potential jump back to the National League. Furthermore, he recognized an opportunity to strengthen the New York American League club (today known as the Yankees). Disregarding the suspension, Johnson was determined to reach a resolution compatible with his objectives. To this end, although Barrow argued for a greater return, Johnson helped engineer a trade with New York manager Clark Griffith for shortstop Herman Long, a one-time great shortstop now well past his prime, and Ernie Courtney, a journeyman third baseman. Cincinnati purportedly offered four thousand dollars for Elberfeld; it is unlikely the cash-strapped Angus would have turned this down but for Johnson's influence.

Given the charged atmosphere of the time, one should not be surprised that Johnson's machinations did not end the controversy. Elberfeld agreed to join the Yankees, but New York Giants owner John Brush, a reluctant supporter at best of peace with the American League, loudly protested the move. He had lost Elberfeld in the peace settlement and was now witnessing him come to New York to star for his direct competitor. In retaliation Brush attempted to legally enjoin Elberfeld from appearing with the Yankees. He also convinced National League president Harry Pulliam that the trade violated the peace agreement. Brush should, therefore, be permitted to play his own disputed shortstop, George Davis. The peace agreement had awarded Davis to the Chicago White Sox, but Davis had held out rather than report. Brush's playing of Davis clearly violated the settlement and threatened to reignite the baseball war between the leagues. Only pressure from the other National League owners, most importantly Cincinnati's Garry Herrmann, induced Brush to back down. He reluctantly agreed to withdraw his injunction request and stop playing Davis.

Barrow received considerable criticism in the press for his inability to control Elberfeld and the resulting far-reaching complications. There can be little doubt that Barrow's dictatorial and overbearing style chafed the independent-minded Elberfeld, but Elberfeld was predisposed to resent any manager after his forced return to Detroit. Elberfeld's outlook further deteriorated when Barrow named Heinie Smith, the player his friend Kid Gleason had been traded for, team captain instead of him.

Barrow remained enamored with the fight game. While in Boston shortly after his confrontation with Elberfeld, he attended a boxing match along with several Detroit and Boston players. Seated close by was Sandy Ferguson, a local Boston heavyweight of some renown. Ferguson quickly became drunk and obnoxious with the patrons seated near him. Eventually he challenged Barrow. Wound up after watching a boxing match and in a general state of anger over the Elberfeld incident, Barrow readily accepted. He landed the first punch to Ferguson's stomach, stunning the big fighter. Fortunately, before Ferguson could retaliate, Boston first baseman Candy LaChance jumped in and separated the two men.

At the end of July the Tigers stood 41-40, and Barrow hoped to fine-tune his club, both for the pennant race and the upcoming 1904 season. He maintained his aggressive posture on signing ballplayers regardless of their status. When he learned that Jimmy Gardner was in danger of losing his Toronto managerial position to Arthur Irwin, Barrow contacted his ex-hurler with an offer of $2,500. Gardner declined the offer, most likely because he was under contract with the Maple Leafs and not free to jump. Barrow also conceded that the trade for Smith was a mistake; in August he released his captain, who assumed the manager's job at Rochester in the Eastern League. To rebuild his depleted middle infield, Barrow once again tried to sidestep Minor League rights and signed John Burns, most recently in an outlaw league in California. The National Commission, however, ruled that Burns was still technically the property of Toledo, and Detroit had to return him. Eventually, because Burns coincidently happened to be on Detroit's draft list, Barrow worked out an agreement whereby Detroit could acquire him by paying Toledo $750. Barrow remained unrepentant about skirting the lines of Minor League player rights. When he read that the National Association had failed once again to ratify the latest draft of the National Agreement, Barrow "chuckled" and remarked: "If they will only stick to that a few days until I can close a few deals with Eastern League players, I'll have my 1904 team complete."

Barrow dickered with his old friend George Stallings, now manager at Buffalo, to acquire a couple of players for the 1904 season. Stallings agreed to sell outfielder Matty McIntyre and pitcher Al Ferry if Barrow would also include a couple of players in return. When Ernie Courtney (a player Barrow never really wanted in the first place) refused to be one of them, Barrow suspended him, claiming he was out of shape and playing poorly. Barrow and Stallings then agreed on several players to be named later in the fall. For such a trade, Barrow needed the consent of the other seven American League owners (so that they would not put in a waiver claim on the players being shipped to the Minors). Because the other owners also often traded or sold players to the Minor League teams, a gentlemen's agreement of a "round robin truce" was generally in effect, to the detriment of the players.

Prior to the end of the season, Barrow lined up shortstop Charlie O'Leary from Des Moines for the 1904 season to strengthen his depleted infield. Barrow also spent considerable effort trying to line up young pitchers for 1904. He remained dissatisfied with Yeager at third. During much of the season he unsuccessfully targeted Columbus third baseman Terry Turner, who went on to a long career with the Indians. When he learned of the strained relationship between St. Louis Cardinals third baseman Jimmy Burke and manager Patsy Donovan, Barrow offered cash but was turned down.

When Detroit pitcher John Skopec was released late in the season, he alleged dissension existed on the team between Barrow and a number of players. Both Barrow and the players denied this charge, and Barrow further denigrated Skopec:

> *Skopec was all in, so far as we were concerned when he refused to come east with the team because he could not have a lower berth in the sleeper. I had promised to pay the St. Paul team $200 for his release if he made good, and found that he did not, and had made up my mind to release him Monday anyway. But with Donovan and Carr suspended, and Burns taken away from us, I concluded to bring him east for a short time and give him notice here. When, however, he refused to take an upper berth in the sleeper, I thought*

that was about the limit, and directed him to turn over his uni-
form and go to the office in Detroit and get what money was due
him and consider himself released forthwith.

Although the players denied any discord, reading between the lines of
Angus's response to Skopec's accusations suggests he may have expressed a
fairly pervasive dissatisfaction with Barrow's methods: "I have noticed a disposition on some sides to take up the cudgel of undesirable players against
the manager of the team; but I wish to say that as long as I am connected
with baseball in Detroit, Mr. Barrow will manage the team. I quite agree
with his policy, his discipline and consider him the best-equipped manager
in this league today, else he could never have done what he has with this
team." What he did was improve the club by twelve and one-half games to
65-71. Crawford and Jimmy Barrett starred in the outfield, Carr held his
own at first base, and the pitching staff's top three of George Mullin, Bill
Donovan, and Frank Kitson gave Barrow a strong nucleus. Late in the year,
however, his infield became so thin that on a trip to Washington Barrow
was forced to sign and use local amateur Simon Nicholls at shortstop.

When the 1903 season ended, Barrow found himself at the center of two
baseball stories. In mid-October several newspapers ran articles linking Barrow to Powers's job as the Eastern League president. One story reported that
Barrow could count on the support of four of the eight teams. Barrow, under
contract with Detroit for 1904, unsure of his level of support in the Eastern
League, and generally optimistic regarding the team he was assembling for
the upcoming season, did not actively pursue the opportunity. Pittsburgh
owner Barney Dreyfuss instigated the second controversy when he claimed
he owned the draft rights to McIntyre and Ferry, and that the sale to Detroit violated his rights to those players. Dreyfuss elevated his case to the
National Commission, which ruled in favor of Barrow and Detroit.

As the sniping at his managerial methods followed him into the off-season, Barrow felt the need to respond publicly. He sent an open letter to the
press defending himself against the charge of being "a hard man to work
for, of being too strict, and of not being on good terms with my players,
etc." The managerial philosophy he outlined seems remarkably enlightened, even from the vantage of over a century later. In dealing with play-

ers, Barrow occasionally threatened "dire punishment" but rarely found it necessary to follow through. Usually a "heart to heart" talk proved at least as effective. He also moved quickly to resolve any conflicts between teammates. Barrow believed in being firm and enforcing discipline. He recognized, though, that some players need "flattery and praise" while others require reprimands.

Barrow outlined three basic behavioral rules the players were required to follow: in by midnight (although an exception could be made in extenuating circumstances); no drinking in the morning before games; and no poker or craps games for large stakes. Barrow was convinced that many of his problems resulted from players who did not take the game seriously enough. These players wanted to have a "good time," and when they encountered a manager who pushed them, they complained he was a "mean chap." Barrow's description of his managerial style strikes one as eminently reasonable. Of course, Barrow was short-tempered, physically imposing, and sarcastic. He often did not deliver the message articulated in his press release quite as reasonably as he purported. Furthermore, with no field staff of assistant coaches and lots of free time after day games and on long train rides, close, regular supervision was problematic, and the more structured in-season regimen players have today simply did not exist. Thus many players may have found Barrow's more active off-field supervision—which is commonplace today—highly confining. As Barrow reminisced many years later:

> In those days the players generally were not smart and there was nothing but haphazard play and rugged manners. Of course, the aces of those vivid days were geniuses just as they are now, but organization has put finish and polish to the game. Comparably with the theater of today—the casting, staging and lighting effects—baseball's casting, staging and general conduct are on a much higher plane than they once were. All the haphazardness has been taken out of the game and it is conducted from beginning to end just as any other well-organized business. Call it inside baseball, if you wish, but I call it balance.

After two years of ownership, Angus had tired of the financial uncertainty and stress of overseeing a Major League baseball operation. In the fall Barrow traveled with Angus on two separate hunting trips, one for ducks and the second for deer. As they relaxed and discussed the future of the franchise, Angus told Barrow that he had decided to sell the team, either in total or just a percentage depending on the demand. Angus had passed the same message along to Frank Navin and encouraged both men to help him locate a buyer.

Navin either showed more initiative or was simply luckier in the hunt for a new owner, but in any case, he identified William Clayton Yawkey, a lumber and mining baron and one of the richest men in Michigan. Before negotiations could advance, however, Yawkey suddenly died. Navin pursued the idea with Yawkey's son, the twenty-five-year-old William H. (Bill) Yawkey, to whom Yawkey had reportedly left $10 million. As an aside, Bill Yawkey was the uncle and foster father of Tom Yawkey, who bought the Boston Red Sox just under three decades later. Bill Yawkey paid $50,000 for the franchise and allocated $5,000 worth of stock to Navin and $2,500 to Barrow.

In the opening chapter I noted that the concept of a general manager did not materialize until late in the second decade of the last century. To Barrow's consternation, however, business manager Navin soon became involved with some of the player procurement functions typically associated with a general manager. In 1908 Navin assumed the presidency of the team as Yawkey retreated to the background. But for the several years prior to his promotion, Navin had more influence over personnel moves than most managers would find comfortable, especially the single-minded Barrow.

For a man known as "baseball's poker face," Navin was a surprisingly warm and emotional man. He often helped old ballplayers in need of financial support. Navin was also remarkably tolerant of the human foibles of his friends and trusted associates. Notwithstanding some of these softer qualities, he was extremely driven and shrewd. He was able to maneuver his limited stake in the Tigers into a personal fortune and standing as one of the key front-office executives of the first half of the twentieth century. Upon Yawkey's acquisition of the franchise, Navin immediately began ingratiating himself into his confidence. Barrow and Navin would cross paths many times over the next thirty years until the latter's death in 1935.

With the exceptions of third base, where Barrow was dissatisfied with Yeager, and with the catcher, where thirty-nine-year-old Deacon McGuire was showing his age, Barrow remained upbeat over the outlook for 1904. He liked his outfield of McIntyre, Barrett, and Crawford. At first base, Carr was a longtime Barrow favorite, and he expected satisfactory seasons from the young O'Leary and Burns (whom Barrow overrated considerably). The pitching staff was anchored by Mullin and Donovan and included a number of hurlers Barrow thought capable, such as Kitson, Ed Killian (acquired from Cleveland), and Ferry.

Barrow remained obsessed with finding an adequate third baseman. He and Ban Johnson, the latter ever vigilant in improving the competitiveness of his league—particularly the new New York club—worked out a deal that would send Mullin to New York. In return Barrow would receive third baseman Bill Coughlin from Washington and pitcher Jesse Tannehill from New York. Barrow became so sure of this impending transaction that he announced to the press: "Practically, one may say that the exchange of players has already been made, but the deal cannot be closed up until the machinery for reimbursing Washington for Coughlin is set in motion by President Johnson." Unfortunately, the compensation for Washington could not be "closed up," and Barrow remained shy a third baseman. As a temporary fix, Barrow purchased Ed Gremminger from the Boston Braves.

For spring training Barrow led his troops back to Shreveport. Catcher Fred Buelow related a spring training story that illustrates both Barrow's personality and the laxity of training regimens compared with today. Buelow and fellow catcher Frank McManus went out on the town one evening with Wild Bill Donovan. Donovan was a popular evening companion because of his fun-loving personality. More importantly, though, Donovan did not drink alcohol, and if a player came in late with him, he would generally avoid punishment. Buelow remarked that he had "worked the dodge several times and got away with it."

One evening Buelow, McManus, and Donovan were out late dancing. In the course of the night, Donovan ditched his two intoxicated companions, who, with daybreak approaching, needed to sneak back into the hotel. As they approached their lodging, they spotted Barrow out front waiting for his curfew-breaking ballplayers. McManus suggested, "We'll go round the block and duck into the barroom, and have one drink if it's our last on earth." Buelow noticed Barrow spot them sneaking into the bar and ordered lemonade, but McManus, fortified by an evening on the town, ordered another beer. Barrow followed them inside and exploded: "Well, I have a great pair of catchers here." Buelow tentatively showed Barrow he was drinking lemonade and slunk off to bed, while Barrow concentrated his wrath on McManus. The next morning McManus moped around. Buelow tried to show some pepper and was humming the George M. Cohan song "Always Leave Them Laughing When You Say Goodbye." Barrow felt Buelow was trying to show him up and called him away from the field. He lit into Buelow, who remembers promising "never to sing again or take a drink, or stay out late or speak to McManus or do anything that a player should not do." In fact, chastising a player behind the bench like this was a trademark approach of Barrow's when he felt it necessary to admonish one of his charges.

After spring training, the team traveled through the South playing several exhibitions. In a game at Nashville, Carr's nose was broken by a pitch that hit him in the face. An outraged Barrow berated the umpire and the Nashville club. In response several Nashville fans surrounded the Detroit bench and "jeered and hooted" at the Tigers. Barrow ordered them away, and when they would not retreat, he threw a bucket of water at them. Unfortunately, most of the water missed the hoodlums and hit a "curious spectator" instead. Only with great difficulty was a riot prevented; the police tried to arrest Barrow for his water throwing, but the riled Barrow forcibly resisted. Eventually he calmed down, and two policemen escorted him to the police station, where he posted a ten-dollar bond. The next morning when the court considered the provocation, it discharged him.

Jimmy Barrett, one of the league's best on-base men, chafed under Barrow's autocratic control. Barrow, who remained obsessed with the weakness at third base, believed he had lined up a trade with the Giants, sending Barrett in exchange for third baseman Art Devlin and outfielder Moose McCormick. The trade fell through, and Barrow later maintained that it broke down because Navin influenced Yawkey to veto it. Navin had as much baseball authority as any business manager in baseball, but Barrow's assertion is unconvincing. It is almost inconceivable that just a couple of months after Yawkey had purchased and reorganized the franchise Navin would have secured the type of influence needed to overrule an experienced manager on the cusp of what many expected to be a solid season.

As the season opened, Barrow continued to try to strengthen his team. Burns was not the answer at second, and he needed another catcher as well. To man second, Barrow signed Bobby Lowe, a one-time star now past his prime. Lowe had broken his kneecap while with the Cubs in 1903. He had initially tried to come back in 1904 with Pittsburgh, but the Pirates released him at the end of spring training. Barrow again found himself in hot water with a Minor League when he tried to sign Shreveport's second baseman. To bolster his catching, Barrow outbid two Minor League teams to sign thirty-eight-year-old Bob Wood. Although Barrow liked signing youngsters, he often relied too heavily on journeymen that other Major League teams no longer believed in. Sometimes, of course, this practice allows one to economically capitalize on the misjudgment of others, but it needs to be used as a targeted approach for specifically identified players; a scattershot method simply leaves a team with too many discarded veterans.

Early in the season the team played adequately, including one game in Chicago at a temperature of only twenty-three degrees. Unfortunately, Barrow's club quickly fell apart. In early June the Tigers bottomed at 13-26, well out of the pennant race. Barrow remained obsessed with finding a quality third baseman; he reportedly offered fifteen thousand dollars, a huge amount at the time, to Washington for Coughlin and pitcher Case Patten, a solid rotation regular. Washington rejected the offer, possibly influenced by Johnson, who was closely entangled with that franchise and wanted to see it improve. Barrow did, however, strengthen the team for the future by purchasing shortstop Germany Schaefer from Milwaukee in the American Association for 1905 delivery.

In his desperation to improve the team, Barrow agreed to an atypical player acquisition that hastened his exit. After a protracted negotiation, Barrow acquired mediocre outfielder Frank Huelsman from Charles Comiskey and the White Sox for $1,250. It seems, however, that Barrow had most likely also agreed to return the player at season's end for the original purchase price if so requested by the White Sox. Comiskey claimed this option agreement had been agreed upon as a condition of the trade, at which point Navin inserted himself into the transaction. He asserted that there had been a misunderstanding, annulled the deal, and returned Huelsman to Chicago. Barrow came off as amateurish in this player purchase. Either he had agreed to acquire a player on option for the remainder of the year, a short-term strategy at best—if Huelsman had panned out, Comiskey would certainly have repurchased him—or he had purchased and played a player without resolving the contract terms.

The team's decline and Barrow's acquisition gaffe led in early June to rumors of his firing, accompanied by stories of dissatisfied Detroit players wanting to get away from Barrow's nagging. An unhappy Mullin wanted to go to New York, where manager Clark Griffith was offering a higher salary. Trade rumors surrounding Jimmy Barrett had supposedly "broken him up." According to a story in the *Sporting News*, certain players never spoke to Barrow as they passed by. In early July, as Barrow became increasingly frustrated and recognized his imminent departure, he publicly blamed poor seasons by Carr and Crawford for much of his team's failure.

Finally, on July 24 with the club at 32-46, Barrow officially tendered his resignation, a move clearly forced by Navin (with Yawkey's backing). Many of the players disliked Barrow's heavy-handed approach to managing, but after his exit they could also more fully appreciate his effort and determination. Several days later when Barrow returned to pick up some of his belongings, Donovan and the players presented him with a diamond locket and thanked him for his service. The Tigers also finally consummated the Coughlin acquisition, paying eight thousand dollars to Washington for the third baseman. Coughlin started the next few years but did little to justify his high purchase price and Barrow's obsession. From 1907 through 1909 Detroit would capture three consecutive pennants. A number of key performers on those teams, including McIntyre, Killian, Schaefer, and O'Leary, were Barrow acquisitions.

In retrospect it is hardly surprising that Barrow and Navin could not co-exist. Both were young and ambitious: at the time of his departure, Barrow was still only thirty-six and Navin three years younger. Furthermore, Navin carved out a front-office position that previously had not existed: a de facto general manager, that is, a nonowner with responsibility for personnel. No manager at the time would have been comfortable sharing player decisions with anyone other than the team president, and Barrow surely had less tolerance for this arrangement than most. The Tigers' front office would operate under this system for only a few more years, until Navin assumed the team's presidency in 1908. Ironically, it would be Barrow himself who would, many years later, epitomize the ideal for this position.

6. Back to the Minors

After his departure from Detroit, Barrow wasted little time in returning to the maelstrom of Minor League managing. On the recommendation of his friend (and Buffalo manager) George Stallings, Montreal snapped him up for the remainder of the season. Barrow headed to Buffalo to take over the team while it was on a road trip. While most players looked forward to playing for a former Major League manager, several remained loyal to his predecessor, Charles Atherton. In fact, two players Barrow had managed in Detroit—Joe Yeager and Frank McManus—were now in Montreal and protested that they had no desire to again play under the aggressive, dictatorial Barrow.

After arriving in Buffalo, Barrow was on the bench by August 9. In his first game, he showed that his tour with the Tigers had matured him briefly. When the umpire called a Buffalo runner safe at home, the Montreal fielders surrounded and berated him for blowing the call. During the confrontation, the Buffalo batter ran all the way around from first and scored. Barrow's players became apoplectic at this additional setback and verged on triggering a forfeit. Barrow cooled his charges down and led them back to the field. When Montreal won the game, Barrow's composure deserved much of the credit.

Several days later Barrow controlled a game by managing to the elements. Conditions were muddy and the sky was dark during much of a game against Toronto. In the sixth inning Toronto started hitting Montreal's tiring pitcher. Montreal continued to lead into the seventh, so Barrow began slowing the game by having his players kick mud onto the plate. The umpire tired of cleaning it off and called the game due to darkness, even though, according to a Toronto sportswriter, the sky "was lighter than at any time during the contest." Montreal finished the season just over .500, and many anticipated a competitive season under Barrow in 1905. The club's finances remained tenuous, however—the team reportedly lost around ten thousand dollars for the season—and rumors of a franchise shift to Richmond, Virginia, persisted.

At the American League meetings in early December, Barrow met with the Yankees' owners, but despite speculation in the press, an offer of the New York manager's position was not forthcoming. Thus, when Charles Ruschaupt, owner of the Indianapolis Indians in the American Association, offered a two-year managerial contract, Barrow eagerly accepted this new challenge.

As he had everywhere else, Barrow immediately began reconstructing his team. Ruschaupt provided the funds for Barrow to purchase players, including several from Major League teams. Barrow executed a number of trades as well. Typical of the era, a couple of acquired players would then be resold or retraded prior the start of the season. He purchased pitcher Ed Siever and catcher Mike Kohoe from the St. Louis Browns, but the latter balked at returning to the Minors, and the former ended up in Minneapolis. Barrow also remained unafraid to acquire reputedly hard-to-manage players. New pitcher Wee Willie McGill was supposedly fine if, as the *Sporting News* put it, he let "the booze alone." Recently acquired second baseman Bill Hallman, who had been a manager in the Western League, did not want to play under a manager with a reputation as a strict disciplinarian. Barrow also brought in his jack-of-all-trades from Toronto, Lou Bruce.

The short-tempered Barrow became increasingly frustrated as Indianapolis started slowly. With the team in seventh place, Barrow again lost his patience with the umpires. In a game against Kansas City, Indianapolis trailed 2–1 with one out and two on, including a runner on third. At that point the umpire called the game due to darkness, although according to one report it was no darker than it had been fifteen minutes earlier. The upset Barrow berated the umpire, who fired back with his own insults. The two men then squared off and exchanged several blows before the players and police separated them.

Several weeks later Barrow again found himself in the middle of a row, this time between players. During a game against Toledo, Barrow had positioned John Farrell, his team captain and second baseman, as third base coach. Throughout the game Farrell insulted and harassed Toledo third baseman George Moriarty. Eventually Moriarty, a tough, intolerant player, lost his cool and attacked Farrell. Barrow rushed into the fray and with great difficulty pulled Moriarty off Farrell. Moriarty promptly attacked another Indianapolis player and took another swing at Farrell. Barrow had to practically choke Moriarty to end his rampage. That Barrow, and not one of the players, the policemen, or the umpire, took on Moriarty testifies to both Barrow's physical strength and his enjoyment in putting it to use.

Barrow, of course, did not save his wrath for only the opposition and the umpires. In a game in early July in Louisville, he lambasted outfielder Tom McCreery when the veteran returned to the bench after letting a catchable fly ball drop. The argument became especially heated, and several spectators claimed they witnessed Barrow hit McCreery. Barrow denied striking the player, and the location of the bench effectively blocked any definitive views other than those of the players themselves. McCreery left Louisville immediately following the game, but Barrow explained that his departure was due to his wife's illness. He further stated that any issues between him and McCreery had been worked out. In any case, McCreery soon returned to the club.

Barrow later recounted how he had missed out on a chance to buy Ty Cobb that season because Ruschaupt began tightening the purse strings. Cobb's Minor League manager at Augusta, Andy Roth, approached Barrow regarding the possibility of Indianapolis purchasing both Cobb and infielder Clyde Engle, another future Major Leaguer. Roth was asking eight hundred dollars for both or five hundred dollars for one. Ruschaupt authorized Barrow to spend up to three hundred dollars, and he negotiated with Roth for a couple of days to land the future legend. But Barrow could not convince Roth to part with his young outfielder for less than five hundred dollars. His failure to land Cobb became a particularly bitter pill later in the season when his nemesis of the previous season, Frank Navin, purchased him for nine hundred dollars.

As the season entered the homestretch, Barrow's frustrations in Indianapolis showed little sign of abating. His relationship with Ruschaupt deteriorated as the owner became increasingly meddlesome while his team languished. Barrow did not like interference, especially from someone whose knowledge he did not respect. In late August, Toronto fired manager Dick Harley and installed team captain Jack White as interim manager. When Toronto approached Barrow around the same time regarding the manager's job for 1906, Barrow actively negotiated for his release from the second year of his two-year contract. As Barrow remembered it, he was owed eight hundred dollars for the balance of the season's salary. To buy his release, Barrow agreed to forgo this income. He hoped to return to Toronto in time to manage the final games of the season but could not wrap up his duties in Indianapolis in time. The team finished the year in sixth place, which was particularly disappointing after the early season hype surrounding Barrow and his reshaping of the team.

Unhappy in his marriage, Barrow began an affair with Frances Taylor around 1902, when he lived in Toronto. I have been unable to uncover any record of a divorce from Alice. After his departure from Detroit, the *Toronto Star* reported that "Mr. and Mrs. Barrow [would] probably spend a couple of weeks on the island," evidencing that he remained married to Alice at that time. Nevertheless, in his autobiography Barrow relates that one of the reasons he desired Toronto's managerial position was to be near Frances. Frances herself was married to Harry Briggs, and in the middle of 1906 gave birth to a daughter, Audrey.

Once again Barrow dove into the challenge of rapidly rebuilding a team. The 1905 Maple Leafs had finished last, but the fans remembered that Barrow's most recent season in Toronto had ended with a pennant. Team president James J. McCaffrey gave Barrow essentially free rein to retool the team. Barrow enthusiastically accepted his mandate and nearly completely turned the team over—by the start of the 1906 season only three players remained from the previous year. The return of the pennant-winning manager and his celebrated moves brought a sense of optimism back to the club. Barrow brought in several former Major Leaguers: outfielder Jack Thoney, whom he imported from Indianapolis, would lead the league in batting; pitcher Fred Mitchell, whom Barrow would face years later as a manager under much different circumstances; and Herman Long, a mainstay of the championship Boston teams during the 1890s.

In December 1905, a joint Major League–Minor League committee was convened for the purpose of proposing rule changes that would increase scoring. Barrow expected three new rules to be adopted: three balls for a walk; fair territory to be extended ten feet outside the first and third base lines; and repeal of the foul-strike rule that had just been adopted in 1901, but only with respect to not counting line drive and long fly fouls as strikes. Barrow once again showed a surprising naiveté on how large committees work. None of these rules passed. Only the third, championed by Clark

Griffith, had any chance, but the National League had no interest in re-scinding the foul-strike rule.

Barrow brought his squad of prospective players to Preston Springs, On-tario, for spring training in March 1906. He intended to evaluate a large contingent of hopefuls with the expectation of uncovering a few quality ballplayers. After filtering though the candidates, Barrow set his roster and brought the team back to Toronto. Once again the home opener was a civic occasion, with a parade and the usual marching across the field by the play-ers. Unfortunately, the optimism and excitement of the off-season faded quickly. The team stumbled from the gate at 3-10, and by mid June, with the team at 14-28, the cocky, aggressive Barrow began to panic. During June and July he made wholesale changes to the club, bringing in a host of new players. Barrow also began to feel the sting of negative publicity from the press. Many were particularly unhappy with the trade of outfielder John White, a six-year veteran in Toronto, for Bob Wood, an aging catcher Bar-row had managed in Detroit. The *Toronto Star* published a little rhyme ti-tled "The Busy Barrow," poking fun at his search for players.

> *He ranges o'er the continent*
> *Where'er his mood inclines him,*
> *And when he finds a player loose,*
> *He forthwith up and signs him.*

Barrow's disappointment with the season carried over into his dealings with his opponents. In late August, Buffalo was in a tight battle with Jersey City for the pennant. Buffalo manager George Stallings asked if a game in Toronto could be postponed until later in the week because of travel diffi-culties. Barrow replied that unless Buffalo appeared Monday afternoon as scheduled, they would forfeit the game. His response was technically within the rules, but the position reflected his angry mood at the overall direction of the season and possibly his personal life as well. Toronto finished the season dead last at 46-88, an embarrassing and humiliating end for a man who had long ago dedicated his career to baseball and whose self-worth was wrapped up in his ability to manage and administer a baseball team.

As the season collapsed around him, Barrow decided to buy the fourteen-room Windsor Hotel at the corner of Richmond and Church streets in To-ronto. He originally planned to operate the hotel as a side business while managing the Maple Leafs. He would not have contemplated returning to the hotel business, however, if he had still felt confident in his future as a baseball manager and executive. And given that he paid twenty-five thousand dollars to acquire the hotel with additional funds required to improve it, he could not afford to neglect it. Moreover, with his history in the business, Barrow must have known that managing the operations and renovation of a hotel required more than part-time oversight. Nevertheless, Barrow spent several months trying to juggle both jobs.

In the fall he continued to reshuffle his team and bring in a new and more talented club for 1907. Of particular note he secured Dick Rudolph, who would later star in the National League with Boston. Barrow shrewdly recognized his potential, remarking that if Rudolph was not the sensation of the Eastern League, "I am a bad guesser." In January, Barrow finally accepted that he could not handle the managerial duties in both baseball and the hotel business simultaneously and resigned his position with the ball club.

Ironically, the 1907 Maple Leafs went on to win the pennant with key players almost exclusively acquired by Barrow. He had assembled the entire pitching staff along with all three outfielders. He was also responsible for the backup catcher and at least two, and possibly more, of the starting infielders. New manager Joe Kelley acknowledged Barrow's influence. At the season-ending party celebrating the pennant, Kelley deferred some of his own congratulations by generously acknowledging Barrow's role in assembling the championship squad. He further showed his appreciation by pinning a diamond pin on Barrow's tie. The 1907 pennant restored much of Barrow's self-assurance in his team-building and player-evaluation abilities. When Boston acquired Jack Thoney for the 1908 season, Barrow confidently predicted that he would star in the Majors, a forecast that proved optimistic.

During his self-imposed exile from Organized Baseball, Barrow remained active in the local baseball scene. In addition to his participation in the pennant celebration, he took part in a number of civic events. For example, in both 1908 and 1909 Barrow officiated at the opening ceremonies of the Toronto Senior Baseball League. Barrow continued to attend games at Diamond Park and stayed close to the players. He often let players stay at his hotel; he remembers charging them only a dollar a day.

By late summer 1909, Barrow was tiring of the hotel business and itched to get back into baseball. Not surprisingly he also rediscovered that managing hotel employees could be at least as exasperating as managing ballplayers, especially for an authoritarian person like Barrow. When he spotted a recently fired bartender drinking at the hotel bar, he confronted his ex-bartender regarding a five-dollar bill he had given him before his discharge.

"You owe me five dollars," Barrow declared.

"You mean you owe me seven dollars for discharging me without due notice," retorted the ex-bartender.

When the former employee then further provoked Barrow with abusive language, Barrow tossed a beer in his face.

The aggrieved ex-bartender brought suit against Barrow for his action, leading to the following exchange in court.

"I don't deny it, but I had sufficient provocation," Barrow testified. "Anyway, it's just the Bartender's Union that's sore, and they are responsible for this action against me."

"You don't know what you're talking about," the attorney for his accuser replied.

"Well, I know you're their lawyer," Barrow responded.

The judge agreed Barrow had been justifiably provoked and fined him a token one dollar.

Throughout the summer Barrow had remained in contact with several Eastern League owners and sensed a new dissatisfaction with President Pat Powers. Powers had many interests and distractions outside running the league. Also, Powers had been president for many years, and antagonisms had naturally evolved with several owners. Some were critical of Powers's refusal to ratify the new National Agreement after achieving several concessions from the Major Leagues. Four of the league's eight teams reportedly favored a change, with Montreal on the fence.

Barrow believed an opportunity existed to maneuver himself into the league presidency, and he publicly announced his interest. His candidacy once again showed Barrow at his most politically inept. He was unable to generate sufficient support, and a couple of owners sought out New York sportswriter Jim Price as a compromise candidate. As the annual meeting neared, Barrow had mustered the support of only Toronto. Three teams, Buffalo, Baltimore, and Newark, favored Price, and the other four, Jersey

City, Rochester, Providence, and Montreal, remained loyal to Powers. The apparent stalemate was broken after some backroom negotiation: Powers agreed to serve only one more year and nominate Buffalo president Jacob Stein for the league's presidency the next year. Once it became clear that this outcome was prearranged, Barrow and Price withdrew their nominations, and Powers was unanimously retained. Joe McGinnity of Newark still hoped to limit Powers's authority and proposed Barrow as an assistant to the president, with the main responsibility of overseeing the umpires. This suggestion had little hope of approval, and a strong objection from Buffalo quickly squashed any lingering hopes Barrow harbored of an executive position in the Eastern League offices.

Despite his three-year absence, Barrow remained generally well regarded within the baseball community. As he campaigned to return to baseball, he uncovered a couple of intriguing leads. For one, the Boston Red Sox offered him a position as their chief scout. But Barrow chose to stay in Canada, and for 1910 he again accepted the manager's job in Montreal, perennially one the league's most financially strapped franchises. Barrow's new boss, owner Sam Lichtenhein, was a well-regarded sportsman about town. One story told about Lichtenhein when he later owned the Montreal Wanderers in the National Hockey Association, a forerunner of the National Hockey League, illustrates the mind-set of these undercapitalized sportsmen. The hockey association wanted to adopt six-man hockey—that is, reduce the number of players on the ice from seven to the now-standard six—but Lichtenhein objected.

"We'll offend everybody in Canada. . . . Hockey is a seven-man game, everybody in Canada knows it. We can't buck tradition."

To change the rule, the league needed unanimous consent.

So one owner pointed out to Lichtenhein, "Did it ever occur to you, Sam, . . . that with six-man hockey you would have one less salary to pay?"

"I never thought of that," Lichtenhein responded. "By George, this is a great idea, this six-man hockey. I'm for it."

The team Barrow inherited had finished in sixth place at 68–83 in 1909. In spite of this mediocre record, Barrow made fewer changes to his roster than in the past. It was not for lack of trying. In January Barrow embarked on a two-week scouting trip throughout the eastern seaboard that took him to New York, Philadelphia, and Washington. He was most likely hampered in his ability to secure new players by the team's limited financial resources. One player on the roster, catcher Paul Krichell, would later become Barrow's right-hand man for twenty-five years as the Yankees' chief scout.

Barrow's club began the season on a long road trip and lost several close games. He anticipated strengthening his club by acquiring two future fringe Major Leaguers, outfielder Fred Kommers and infielder Roxey Roach. Unfortunately, he could secure neither. The team returned home 4-10 and was forced to stew on its record for four days as bad weather delayed the home opener. In mid-May Barrow finally bolstered his outfield by purchasing the St. Louis Browns' Ray Demmitt. Demmitt proved especially valuable because Barrow had run into difficulties with outfielder Mickey Corcoran in early June. Corcoran refused to play the infield when Barrow needed him to sub for injured shortstop William Nattress and then failed to show up at the park the following day. Barrow suspended Corcoran and then sold the sulking outfielder to Buffalo.

During a home game in early June, the fans "roasted" Barrow and his slumping players, particularly Nattress. In a letter to the *Montreal Gazette*, Barrow publicly defended his players from what he considered unfair attacks, especially those leveled against his shortstop, who was playing hurt. Barrow tried several expedients to get his team back on track. He moved Krichell to third base and Yeager to shortstop to shake up his lineup. He also publicly continued his pursuit of better players. Neither strategy worked: Barrow soon returned to his regular lineup, while a potential Major League player purchase fell through. Late in the month, Barrow released aging second baseman George Smith amid allegations of dissension. Both Barrow and the players denied the rumors, which they attributed to the disgruntled Smith.

In July Barrow was hospitalized because of blood poisoning from an infected finger, a potentially serious condition. At first it looked as if the infection might spread, but Barrow quickly recovered. His run of bad luck continued later that summer when President Powers issued an edict that seemed to target his old nemesis. His ruling limited the right to contest an umpire's decision to the players on the field. Specifically, a nonplaying manager "must confine himself to the bench. . . . He ha[d] no right to dispute a decision of the umpire or in any other way to delay the game." As the only nonplaying manager in the league, Barrow must have seethed when he learned of this decree.

As the season advanced, the team rebounded somewhat from its horrible start. Overall, Barrow improved Montreal's record by three games over 1909 and finished fifth. Before the final game, the players presented Barrow with a diamond-studded gold watch charm. Afterward Lichtenhein threw an end-of-season party for Barrow and the players. Although the team's improvement had been marginal, Barrow had impressed Lichtenhein, who stated that Barrow could manage in Montreal as long as he wanted to. He added, however, that he would sacrifice his club's interest for the greater good and support Barrow for the league presidency if he was again a candidate. Barrow clearly harbored ambition beyond the manager's job at a financially strapped Minor League franchise. He would now have another chance to realize it.

7. League President

Over the course of the 1910 season, Barrow, now forty-two years old, continued to lobby for the Eastern League presidency. Because longtime president Pat Powers had stated he would retire at the end of the season, the position appeared open. Initially the field appeared limited, as only *Sporting News* editor Joe Cummings had announced his candidacy. After many years as the league president, Powers had worn out his welcome with a majority of the league's owners. A number of outside distractions cut into his focus on league business. Also, the league's magnates chafed under the existing Major League–Minor League draft rules and were growing frustrated that a tentatively agreed-upon classification system had not been ratified.

As the annual meeting neared, Powers began having second thoughts about surrendering the presidency and resuscitated his own candidacy. For this challenge, however, Barrow overcame much of his customary ineptitude in persuading decision-making bodies. He had spent the year smartly electioneering the owners and secured the support of five teams: Montreal, Toronto, Newark, Baltimore, and, less definitively, Buffalo. The Rochester franchise backed Powers, and Jersey City and Providence also supported him, if less solidly. During a contentious December meeting, the Eastern League owners elected Barrow by a 5–3 vote along those lines. The outcome infuriated Powers. He later sent Barrow a scathing letter accusing him of running an underhanded campaign and, once in office, of bullying players and umpires.

The league owners also agreed to increase the league president's salary from $5,000 to $7,500, a substantial salary for the era. Barrow discussed transferring the league office to Buffalo but was dissuaded. He set up his New York office in the St. James building at Twenty-sixth and Broadway. Upon his election, he declared he would devote all his energies to league business and would deal "harshly with chronic kickers," players who insulted and abused umpires.

As president of a Minor League with the highest classification, Barrow was responsible for three distinct duties. On the most basic level, Barrow

managed the league's day-to-day operations. He hired and scheduled umpires, adjudicated protested games, fined players for abusive behavior, and
performed ceremonial duties. Barrow also oversaw league affairs and monitored the health and ownership of his franchises. Finally, he led the Eastern League as it wrestled with the Major Leagues for a higher classification
and more advantageous drafting rules.

Organized Baseball's top governing body was the three-member National
Commission, consisting of the National and American League presidents
and, as chairman, Garry Herrmann, the Cincinnati Reds president. Herrmann was a compromise choice between the leagues: a National League
owner, but a friend of Ban Johnson, the American League founder and president. In the Cincinnati ownership hierarchy, Herrmann was the front man
for the predominant owners who had little interest in baseball: George Cox,
the political boss of Hamilton County, and the wealthy Fleischmanns. Herrmann took his responsibilities seriously, but he enjoyed the trappings of
the office more than the decision making. In disputes between franchises
Herrmann often shied away from conflict and unrealistically wished for a
compromise to materialize.

   With the assistance of a few American League owners, notably Charles
Comiskey in Chicago and Charles Somers in Cleveland, Johnson had established his league against fierce National League opposition. Because of his
powerful personality and near autocratic jurisdiction over his own league,
Johnson was clearly the first among equals on the commission. The National
League presidency changed often, inhibiting the sort of deference that the
longer-serving Johnson and Herrmann received. Also, the National League
owners were not as beholden to their president and less compliant than their
American League counterparts were with Johnson.

   The Minor Leagues had organized themselves into the National Association of Professional Baseball Leagues. This entity addressed purely Minor
League matters, but on issues involving Major League interests—broadly
defined—the National Association was subordinate to the National Commission. The rules and regulations governing Organized Baseball were set
forth in the National Agreement. This second-class status irritated the higher
Minor Leagues, but nothing caused as much consternation as the Major
League–Minor League draft.

The draft allowed teams to select players from teams in a lower classification. The exact rules fluctuated well into the establishment of the farm
systems many years later, but, as a generalization, teams could draft from
teams one or two levels below and lose one or two players to the leagues
above. The Majors, of course, sat at the top of the food chain and could
draft players from the top Minor Leagues. Teams selecting players owed the
draft price to the team from which they selected the player; this price rose
steadily throughout the early twentieth century. When Barrow assumed the
Eastern League helm, assigned the highest Minor League classification, the
cost of drafting one of its players stood at only one thousand dollars. Overall, Minor League teams sold many players to the Major Leagues during
these years but also earned a significant portion of their income through
the draft, despite the relatively lower draft prices. Major League teams at
the time spent around sixteen thousand dollars per team per year to acquire
Minor League talent. Table 3 summarizes the total amounts paid to the Minors by the Majors from 1909 through 1914.

Each level of Organized Baseball had different perspectives on the desir-
ability of the draft. Nearly all the best players who advanced from the Minors to the Majors did so outside the draft. These players moved upward
usually via an outright cash purchase, which sometimes involved trades of
other players as well. Although few top players arrived through the draft,
its very threat provided an incentive for the leading Minor Leagues to sell
their best players to the Major Leagues. In this way they could receive more
for the players than just the draft price.

The lower-level Minor Leagues liked the draft because it provided a systematic way for them to earn money by having their players advance. Because the low Minors controlled players who were typically less skilled and
less widely scouted, fewer opportunities existed to sell their players for large
amounts. An organized draft gave them a profitable outlet for their assets.
The Major Leagues also liked the draft. The theoretical right to draft players gave the Majors access to all the best Minor League talent.

The draft also benefited the players. It offered players ready to advance to
the next level a systematic, institutional procedure for doing so (although
the process worked far from perfectly). In most circumstances, the magnates within Organized Baseball did not evince any particular concern for

the welfare of their players. When defending the draft, however, the Majors often invoked the players' cause in their argument.

It was the high-classification Minor Leagues that consistently and fervently fought against the draft. For these leagues the draft reduced the prices they could command from the Major Leagues for their best players. The consequent loss of players to the Majors also prevented Minor League owners who wanted to keep their best players from doing so (although the draft did offer these teams an opportunity to restock their talent by drafting from the lower Minors). Also, many of these owners operated in large cities and liked to think of themselves and their teams as being near-Major League. The draft accentuated their second-class status compared to the Majors.

After the 1908 season the Eastern League and the American Association, two of the top Minor Leagues, threatened to withdraw from the National Agreement if certain demands were not met, the most important relating to the draft. After several contentious meetings, the National Commission supported the two high Minor Leagues, and they were given special privileges with respect to several issues. In the end, however, the compromise failed to satisfy the two high Minor Leagues on all counts, and the negotiated reforms were never ratified.

By the time Barrow assumed the Eastern League presidency, his owners and, even more so, those in the American Association, were again agitating for a restructuring of the relationship between the high Minors and the Majors. At first the Majors overreacted to the American Association rhetoric, to which Barrow responded: "The Eastern League and, I presume, the American Association have a few reasonable requests to make to the National Commission regarding classification and drafting rules. We shall try to present our case in a manner to command a respectful hearing, and whatever the commissioners may see fit to do for us we shall try to be satisfied with. At any rate, this talk of war and withdrawal from Organized Baseball is silly and unauthorized by any member of the Eastern League."

Late in the 1910 season, the American Association presented a sweeping set of demands, all of which were rejected by the National Commission. During the winter meetings Barrow joined with the American Association, and together they lobbied for a scaled-down set of changes to the National Agreement. The two leagues succeeded in achieving their key aim: the Eastern League, the American Association, and the Pacific Coast League were promoted to a new class AA league (the Western League and the Southern Association remained at the old class A). The cost to the Majors of drafting a player from a class AA team increased from $1,000 to $2,500. In return, the new class AA teams agreed to immediate delivery for any player sold to the Majors. This last concession was in response to a complaint from the Majors that centered on Marty O'Toole.

Over the previous few years, a couple of players had been purchased for what had then been viewed as exorbitant prices: in 1908 the Giants paid $11,000 for pitcher Rube Marquard, and two years later the Athletics paid $12,000 for pitcher Lefty Russell. Therefore, Pittsburgh Pirates owner Barney Dreyfuss shocked the baseball world on July 20, 1911, when he purchased hurler Marty O'Toole from St. Paul of the American Association for $22,500. After the sale the *Chicago Tribune* reported that St. Paul kept O'Toole "for some weeks and [he] was so overworked that his arm went lame, and he was of little use to Pittsburgh after he joined it." O'Toole's purchase price remained the high-water mark for the dead-ball era. The fact that he never recovered sufficiently to benefit the Pirates may have discouraged some teams from making expensive purchases of Minor Leaguers. More importantly, however, the price of Minor League stars stagnated because of the economic hardship imposed on baseball by the Federal League war and America's entry into the First World War shortly thereafter.

Most of Barrow's job entailed handling the day-to-day operations of the office and overseeing league business. Over the next several years, he capably and aggressively handled routine business as a number of unique challenges arose. One of Barrow's first tasks was to line up eight umpires for the upcoming season. After his years of abusing incompetent (as he saw it) umpires, Barrow appreciated the importance of a professional umpiring crew, and once the umps were hired, he held them to high standards. Much to their chagrin, Barrow instituted a system of daily reports from his umpires on various aspects of the game. In return for his demand of professionalism, Barrow did his utmost to stand up for his umpiring crew against the offensive behavior of managers and players. To improve the fan experience, he began posting the batting orders for both the home and the visiting teams on a "secure board" so that fans could correct preprinted score cards. Also, he hired *New York Press* baseball writer Ernest Lanigan as his secretary and assistant. Lanigan later gained recognition as a *Sporting News* columnist and Baseball Hall of Fame historian. Midway through the 1911 season, however, Lanigan resigned when his wife became seriously ill. An independent thinker with an acerbic wit, Lanigan had chafed under Barrow's authoritarian style, and the two could not have coexisted for long in any case.

For his replacement, Lanigan recommended William Manley, another young sportswriter for the *New York Press*. Barrow accepted Lanigan's suggestion, and Manley stayed with Barrow throughout his tenure. Manley's duties as secretary ranged from the usual league affairs, to sending Barrow copies of newspapers, to checking on Barrow's wife's needs while he was away (as will be expanded later, Barrow remarried in 1912). The league office fostered romance as well: Manley married Barrow's stenographer, Margaret Connelly.

Barrow addressed his first game-related difficulty on opening day in Newark. With fifteen thousand fans in attendance, many pushed their way to spots near the field. In the eighth inning with Montreal leading 7–6, Newark put two on with only one out. John Kelly hit a ball into the throng, but a Montreal player retrieved the ball and threw him out at third. Newark manager Joe McGinnity protested to Barrow, who was sitting behind the Montreal bench. McGinnity claimed that the ground rules explained before the game defined any ball that went into the crowd was a triple. While McGinnity complained to Barrow, a couple of Barrow's old Montreal players caused a ruckus. Barrow's former shortstop William Nattress jumped in front of McGinnity, cursed him, and may have spit in his face. McGinnity retaliated with a punch to Nattress's face. Another Royal, Jack Hardy, joined the fray, and all three men rolled on the ground as they fought.

Barrow handled the situation shrewdly. He had heard the pregame ground-rule discussion and agreed with McGinnity's interpretation. The home plate umpire also understood the rule (the base umpire had apparently missed it) and with a nod from Barrow made the correct call, putting Kelly safely at third. Barrow had arrived at the correct solution, while his umpires saved face and appeared in charge. Barrow fined McGinnity fifty dollars and suspended him for five days. The two Montreal players also received five-day suspensions and were fined twenty-five dollars each.

In late May, Barrow defended his umpires against abusive behavior in two separate incidents. He fined McGinnity and another Newark player after a near riot ensued after a close play at home plate. Barrow also fined Buffalo manager George Stallings and five players fifty dollars each for umpire baiting and suspended one of the five, a pitcher, five games for throwing the ball at the umpire. "No umpire who is abused and insulted over every close play can be expected to show good judgment," Barrow said. "It is a wonder players are not killed for the names and insults they have used." Barrow's crackdown seems to have produced results, and cases of abusive behavior declined.

With his owners' blessing, in 1911 Barrow instituted a postseason series, specifying that the pennant winner (Rochester) play a best-of-seven series against a team made up of the best players from the other seven teams. The participants would share in 80 percent of the receipts from the first four games; the remaining 20 percent would be allocated for expenses. Of the participants' allocation, the winning team would receive 60 percent and the loser 40 percent. This pot was to be divided equally among the players and manager of each team.

As it approached, this series received a surprising buildup in the press. Unfortunately for Barrow's brainchild, the series ended prematurely amid controversy. The schedule called for the third and fourth games to be played in parks other than the league champion's. Pennant-winning Rochester manager John Ganzel, All-Star manager Jack Dunn, and Barrow all agreed to play the fourth game in Rochester anyway after the third game in Buffalo ended in a tie. Rochester owner (and Powers loyalist) C. T. Chapin embarrassed both Barrow and his own manager by refusing to open the stadium for the game. With this rejection, Barrow called off the series, declaring he would never hold another similar postseason series. The All-Stars each received $130.40, and the Rochester Hustlers, $77.02. Barrow later fined Chapin $1,400 to cover expenses, an action his owners backed by a six to two vote.

A workaholic, Barrow had few hobbies other than hunting. After his first season as league president, he anticipated spending much of the fall hunting and fishing in Canada. For his first getaway, he headed to Rice Lake for a week of fishing. Later Barrow planned to spend three weeks at Lake Rosseau hunting, but he had to return home early when, as will be examined later, four franchises almost simultaneously announced they were in financial trouble or on the market.

At the 1911 winter meetings, the Eastern League's magnates rewarded Barrow for his excellent service. Despite rumors that Chapin might attempt to organize opposition after the postseason series fiasco, the owners unanimously voted Barrow a five-year contract at $7,500 per year. They also approved Barrow's suggestion that in recognition of the Toronto and Montreal franchises the league officially change its name to the International League. In other business the league considered the claim of ex-manager Jack Ryan against the Jersey City owners. He argued they owed him two years' salary for the balance of his contract. The league's magnates upheld Ryan and awarded him $3,500.

On January 4, 1912, Barrow remarried, tying the knot with his longtime girlfriend, Frances Taylor. Alice had died in April 1911 in St. Joseph, Missouri, which would have freed Barrow to marry again (if, in fact, they were never formally divorced). Fannie, too, was now free to marry. She also brought five-year-old Audrey into the family, and Barrow would raise the girl as if she were his own daughter. Fannie and Barrow were married in Buffalo at the Church of the Covenant, only a few blocks from the baseball stadium. After the ceremony Barrow, his bride, and friends headed to the Hotel Statler for a wedding breakfast.

As opening day approached, Barrow took an opportunity to crow about his league: "The International League is conceded by all baseball men to be stronger in every way than the American Association. We not only have double the population to draw from, but we have bigger and better plants in all our cities."

When Barrow distributed the preliminary 1912 schedule to the clubs, Lichtenhein apparently sent the schedule to the press but asked them to hold it until officially released. When one paper jumped the gun, Barrow fined his old boss five hundred dollars for the slip-up.

In 1912 Barrow again emphasized controlling abusive behavior, to the extent of trying to limit profanity between players on the field. In a game at Baltimore, Orioles batter Charles Schmidt swore at Providence pitcher Ed Lafitte, whom he felt was trying to bean him. Barrow defended the umpire who ejected Schmidt for cursing. On July 8 he ordered a game replayed in which Baltimore protested Toronto's use of a player under suspension. Barrow successfully navigated the remainder of his second season as league president, justifying the confidence of his owners.

For one of his off-season hunting excursions, Barrow spent two weeks shooting quail and snipe on the Haddock, Georgia, hunting grounds of George Stallings. Stallings also introduced Barrow and other baseball heavyweights to nearby Dover Hall, a large hunting estate. In August 1915, Barrow, along with forty-nine other baseball luminaries, purchased the estate for fifty thousand dollars, each partner investing one thousand dollars. Barrow and his new hunting partners, including New York Yankees owners Tillinghast L'Hommedieu Huston and Jacob Ruppert, Ban Johnson, National League president John Tener, Barrow's old nemesis Frank Navin, Detroit star Ty Cobb, and Stallings himself, named themselves the Dover Hall Club.

In 1913 Barrow needed to rule on a rather bizarre appeal. At the start of the eleventh inning of a game between Baltimore and Providence, the two umpires left early to catch the last train to Montreal. Prior to their departure, the umpires had arranged with the two managers to leave one player from each team in charge of the umpiring. Not surprisingly, the game ended on a disputed play. Baltimore won 5–4 when a base runner at third bumped the third baseman, forcing a bad throw. The home plate umpire called the runner out for interference, preserving Baltimore's lead and the win. Barrow denied Providence's protest and upheld the authority of the emergency umpire to make the call.

In June 1913 a case of food poisoning sidelined Barrow at home. He recovered quickly, and a month later in Brooklyn he attended the formal opening and dedication of Ebbets Field. After the game 150 or so dignitaries, including Barrow, traveled to the Brighton Beach Hotel by automobile, an extravagance for the time.

For the Major League World Series, Minor League presidents were authorized to request an allotment of tickets to distribute among their league's franchises. Typically the parties kept the specific ticket allotments private. In 1913, however, the allotment of tickets became public when a large block fell into the hands of scalpers. As a side note to the investigation into the scandal, it came out that Barrow had requested two hundred tickets for the 1913 Series; the Majors had allotted him one hundred.

During Barrow's initial tenure as league president, the league's franchises were generally profitable. Nevertheless, Minor League baseball remained an unstable enough venture that franchises were bound to experience some financial distress or ownership squabbles. Barrow often found himself defending the league against rumored incursions of the other leagues into Eastern League cities. For example, in mid-1911 stories circulated that the Boston Braves might be contemplating a move to Baltimore. Barrow quickly counterattacked, stating that any incursion into Baltimore would precipitate a baseball war.

Barrow's first season as league president was a financial success, as no team lost money, and a few set financial records. Toronto led the league in attendance, drawing as many as 17,000 patrons to several games. Buffalo and Baltimore also drew well, averaging crowds of nearly 4,000. These averages imply a season attendance of around 300,000, on par with the weaker Major League teams.

Barrow's euphoria was short lived. As noted earlier, in the fall of 1911 disturbing league news forced him to return early from a Canadian hunting trip. Newark owners Joe McGinnity and financial partner Henry Clay Smith announced that they wanted out and were looking to sell. At the same time, the owners of the Providence and Jersey City clubs revealed that they also hoped to sell. The latter two clubs sensed an opportunity to sell at a good price after profitable seasons. An offer of thirty thousand dollars was rumored for Jersey City, a franchise that in the past had struggled financially. Providence set an asking price of thirty-five thousand dollars.

Barrow's old Montreal club, owned by Sam Lichtenhein, was in nearly constant financial difficulty. Soon after assuming the presidency, Barrow found himself denying rumors that he was considering relocating the Montreal franchise. At the end of his inaugural season, stories circulated that the team was about to relocate to Richmond, Virginia.

Ever since the National Agreement of 1903 had ratified the existing hierarchy, competition from leagues outside Organized Baseball's jurisdiction was rare. So-called outlaw leagues were typically short lived, undercapitalized, geographically narrow, and manned with mostly local talent. Beginning in 1912, this situation began to change with the formation of the United States League. A group of mostly undercapitalized entrepreneurs launched the league, placing clubs in Major League cities and briefly scaring Organized Baseball. The league opened on May 1, 1912, with teams in New York, Washington, Reading, Richmond, Chicago, Cleveland, Cincinnati, and Pittsburgh. Opening day attracted ample curious crowds, but by the end of May it was obvious the venture had failed. One postmortem in the *Sporting News* summarized that the league "bit off more than it [could] chew with a Major League circuit for an organization of class B minor league strength." Nevertheless, the undertaking underscored the fact that many businessmen remained convinced there was profit to be made outside Organized Baseball, and that the magnates had not yet shuttered all barriers to entry.

With the Jersey City franchise struggling, in July 1912 Barrow secretly traveled to Pittsburgh to meet with William McCullough, recently president of the Pittsburgh team in the defunct United States League, to discuss the possibility of relocating the Jersey City club to Pittsburgh. Barrow and McCullough called on Pirates owner Barney Dreyfuss to beg permission to share his territory. Not surprisingly, Dreyfuss refused. (This was not quite as preposterous a request as it sounds. Games would have been staggered so that both teams would not play home games on the same day.) McCullough and Barrow carried the appeal to Garry Herrmann, who agreed to use his influence if McCullough would promise another outlaw league would not be started. McCullough could not go that far but did grant there would not be a team in Pittsburgh. How hard Herrmann pushed remains unknown, but Dreyfuss remained adamant. A little more than a year later, McCullough became the catalyst for placing an outlaw Federal League franchise in his city.

A dilemma still unresolved in the twenty-first century emerged in the International League during the 1912–13 off-season. Several of the "small-market" teams became disenchanted that the "larger-market" teams were signing the best players. At the same time, Barrow revealed that the granting of class AA status by the National Commission was linked to some sort of salary curtailment. At the league meetings the small-market teams forced through a six-thousand-dollar-per-month salary cap by a five to three vote. Toronto, Buffalo, and Jersey City opposed the cap, arguing that each club should be allowed to set its own limit. They did, however, prevent adoption of a four-hundred-dollar-per-month individual player cap. Barrow later disclosed that before settling for the cap the small-market clubs proposed a fifty-fifty split of the gate with visiting teams—a large increase for the visitors—for all games in Toronto, Rochester, Buffalo, and Baltimore. This proposal failed because it necessitated amendment of the league constitution, which required six votes.

When player unrest over the salary retrenchment became apparent in the spring, Barrow defended the action: "Not only were the players getting all the money but several of the teams had become so much stronger than the others that it was necessary to make some move to equalize playing strength." Barrow later discussed the impact of the cap at some length: "The fact is indisputable that four of the clubs could not hope to succeed without the limit. Toronto, Rochester, Buffalo, and Baltimore are great ball towns. They can afford to pay salaries which the others could not afford to duplicate. The result is a league anything but well balanced. Under the new arrangement the teams will be well balanced, and all will have a chance to win the pennant and recoup the attendant profits."

In a 1913 interview Barrow demonstrated how far his thinking on this issue had evolved. He put forward a collectivist proposal requiring that prior to each season the league's players be placed under a contract not specific to any particular club. The league would hold a draft to allocate the players. Barrow believed this would offer every team a chance for the pennant, closer pennant races, better attendance, and higher profits. He did not mention the additional hardship to the players. Obviously no league adopted this scheme, but it testified to the tensions inherent in the existing system.

8. "Fight These Fellows to the Finish"

In 1913 a new outlaw league, the six-team Federal League, began operation in several larger cities in the Midwest, including four inhabited by Major League teams: Cleveland, St. Louis, Pittsburgh, and Chicago. Organized Baseball initially remained aloof. Because the new league's players came from outside Organized Baseball, the teams consisted predominately of local semipro players, aging former Major Leaguers, and journeyman Minor League veterans.

Late that first season, the Federal League's owners met in Indianapolis and decided to challenge the existing order as a third Major League. In their first and most decisive step, they named James Gilmore, part owner of the Chicago franchise, league president. The dynamic, glib Gilmore possessed the attributes the new league most needed: contacts with wealthy capitalists who had an interest in baseball and the ability to persuade them of the viability of his new league. "Gilmore could not only convince you the moon is made of green cheese," it was said, "but he could sell you a slice of it." Gilmore promptly set about reorganizing the league to include some of his wealthy connections. Subsequently, the Federal League relocated several franchises to the eastern United States—including Baltimore and Buffalo, two of Barrow's International League cities—and expanded to eight teams, all of which were surprisingly well capitalized. Gilmore's success in lining up wealthy American industrialists as baseball owners testified to the industry's transition from small businesses to large, complex financial operations. It further demonstrated that much of the stigma attached to baseball ownership by the upper class had dissipated. In their estimations of an owner's wealth, the press often failed to make a distinction between total assets and net worth (which subtracts debt and other liabilities from assets); thus the following estimates must be viewed as approximations of financial strength, not as specific values:

St. Louis—Principal financial backer Philip DeCatesby Ball constructed and operated artificial ice plants. The press estimated Ball's wealth at $2 million.

Brooklyn—In one of his greatest coups, Gilmore lined up Robert Ward, a wealthy bakery owner with a reputed wealth of $6 million.

Chicago—Lead owner Charles Weeghman owned a chain of Chicago lunchrooms; his wealth was estimated at $1 million.

Pittsburgh—Ward introduced railroad contractor Edward Gwinner to Gilmore, who promptly transferred the franchise to the wealthy industrialist from its financially strapped ownership. Gwinner's wealth was estimated alternatively at $500,000 and $1 million. William McCullough became the team's secretary.

Indianapolis—Decently capitalized but with no particularly wealthy backer.

Kansas City—Locally capitalized with a number of stockholders.

Buffalo—Described in a *Boston Post* report as "having no millionaires back of them, but they seem[ed] to have plenty of money."

Baltimore—Capitalized with around $200,000, including $164,400 in equity from about six hundred local citizens desirous of landing a Major League team and approximately $36,000 in debt. The lead shareholder and managing partner was Ned Hanlon, the manager and strategist of the great Orioles National League championship teams of the 1890s.

Any upstart organization planning to challenge well-established, entrenched interests needs both emotionally committed leaders and financially strong backing. The Federal League had both and would wreak havoc on Organized Baseball over the next two years. The Federal League challenged the International League in two markets (Baltimore and Buffalo), the National League in four (Brooklyn, Pittsburgh, Chicago, and St. Louis), the American League in two (Chicago and St. Louis), and the Class AA American Association in two (Indianapolis and Kansas City).

The financial wherewithal of the Federals compared favorably with Major League baseball. Among the owners of the established sixteen teams, only Detroit's Bill Yawkey was a top-tier wealthy industrialist. Cincinnati was backed by the wealthy Fleischmanns and the Cubs by Charles Taft, but neither investor was committed enough to baseball to tolerate his franchise absorbing large losses. National Commission chairman Herrmann fronted in Cincinnati, and the obnoxious, indiscreet Charles Murphy was the ostensible decision maker for the Cubs. Several other teams were owned by successful businessmen or their heirs but none with the resources of Yawkey or Ward. Red Sox owner Joseph Lannin, Athletics owner Ben Shibe, and the Brush heirs in New York fell into this category. Charles Comiskey of the White Sox and Barney Dreyfuss were both wealthy men who effectively made their fortunes through the ownership of their franchise. They possessed only limited outside wealth. The capitalization of the remaining eight teams left little margin for error. These teams possessed only minimal reserves or deep-pocketed backers from which to cover losses.

If the Majors were at a slight financial disadvantage compared to the Federals, Barrow's International League was significantly worse off, especially in the two markets competing directly with the Federals. In Baltimore the team was owned by Jack Dunn, a brilliant baseball operator with few financial resources outside his franchise. Buffalo president J. J. Stein headed up one of the league's most poorly capitalized franchises. Providence and Newark were owned by Major League interests; a Detroit group including Yawkey, Frank Navin, Ty Cobb, and Hugh Jennings owned the former, while a Charles Ebbets–led syndicate owned the latter. Because of the impact of the Federals on their Major League teams, neither—particularly Ebbets—had extra funds available to expend in defense of their International League franchises. A corporation that included Bill Devery, part owner of the Yankees and a shady ex–New York police chief, controlled the Jersey City club. The other three franchises, Toronto, Montreal, and Rochester, were principally owned by baseball men of moderate means.

During the winter of 1913–14 the Federal League made its first big player splash when Weeghman signed star Cubs shortstop Joe Tinker to a twelve-thousand-dollar-per-year contract to manage the Chicago Federals. Shortly thereafter, the St. Louis Federals inked another one-time Cubs star, Mordecai Brown, as its manager. Many in the Federal League remained hopeful that they could force an accommodation with Organized Baseball short of a full-scale baseball war. The Federals initially refrained from pursuing players already under contract, although they refused to honor the reserve clause.

Barrow was at his fiery best when confronting an adversary he viewed in black and white. When it became clear that the Federal League would be invading International League cities and tempting their players, Barrow issued one of his typical forceful statements. Note also, however, Barrow's lack of tact and impulsiveness in denigrating three cities in his own league.

> *In the first place, they're trying to masquerade as a Major League when they never can become one. They will have about four Major League players to a team, but that will not make them a Major League. They have a Minor League circuit. Toronto [the Federals initially looked at Toronto before landing Ward for Brooklyn], Baltimore, and Buffalo turn out good crowds, but they do not turn out Major League crowds.*
>
> *The players who jumped to the Federals were disloyal to their employers. Men like Tinker, Brown, and [Otto] Knabe have been around Organized Baseball long enough to know that loyalty to the reserve clause is one of the foundations of Organized Baseball, and as much a part of their contract as their salary.*
>
> *I will say that the International League will fight these fellows to a finish in any of our cities where they intend to place teams. So far I have not heard of them signing any of our men, though I have three letters which the Pittsburgh Federals have sent to my players. I might add that these players were not offered as much as they are getting in Organized Baseball.*

At their December meetings, Barrow and his owners began discussing ways of countering the threat from the Federal League. The American Association advocated a plan to end the regular season after 112 games and then play an interleague series with the International League. Some International League owners expressed interest, but the plan never materialized because of resistance led by Jack Dunn, who feared that fans would have little interest in a bunch of exhibition games after the regular season.

To counter the anticipated Federal League invasion, Brooklyn Dodgers owner Charles Ebbets proposed moving the Jersey City International League franchise to Brooklyn. The team would play in Ebbets Field when the Dodgers were on the road. He hoped that staging baseball competition every day during the summer would either scare the Federals off or decrease their attendance to unacceptable levels. Although not a forceful advocate of the move, Barrow tried to accommodate Ebbets and facilitate his plan. During a late-night meeting in February involving Ebbets, Jersey

City president Thomas Fogarty, and Barrow, Ebbets tried to convince the recalcitrant, skeptical Fogarty of its benefits. Ebbets, however, would not yield on particular conditions he intended to impose on Fogarty's use of Ebbets's park, particularly the rent he hoped to charge. The National Commission discouraged the move as well, mainly because of the perceived (if not real) conflict of interest caused by Ebbets and his partner owning the league's Newark franchise.

Ebbets next proposed moving his Newark team—the 1913 pennant winner, reputed to be profitable—to Brooklyn and then shifting the Jersey City team to Newark. While trying to assist this move, Barrow used his habitual sarcasm to ridicule the Federals: "I am positive that our league can give Brooklyn as good a ball club as the Federal League can. The Federals say they have about one hundred former Major League players. Nearly every player in our league has been up in the Majors at some time, if only for a training trip, yet we do not try to masquerade as a Major League." Ebbets's second scheme died as well when he demanded fifty thousand dollars from Jersey City for the privilege of moving to Newark and using its stadium.

During this preseason controversy, rumors of expansion or contraction of his league flourished because Barrow, incapacitated in his home for several days with tonsillitis, was in no condition to quell them. The league eventually decided to stay the course but never formally dropped the Ebbets matter, pending the Brooklyn Federals final schedule. Another Major League owner did, however, adopt the strategy. Cleveland Indians owner Charles Somers, who also owned the Toledo team in the American Association, shifted that franchise to Cleveland for the 1914 season to provide continuous games throughout the summer as a disincentive for the Federals to place a team there.

Another strategy the International League and the American Association employed to fight the new league was to petition the Major Leagues to eliminate the Major League–Minor League draft. As discussed in the previous chapter, the draft had long been a sore spot between the high Minors and the Major Leagues. Owners and fans in the high Minors often resented being cast as second best, a status accentuated by the forced surrender of players to the Majors. The bitter confrontation with the Federals, who promoted themselves as Major, exacerbated this problem. On the other side, the Players Fraternity—the players union, which was not yet as impotent

as it would be several years later—opposed any change to the draft rules
that would further stifle player advancement.

Barrow spent a considerable portion of his energy over the next two
years lobbying the National Commission and the owners individually to
rescind the draft, at least during the battle with the Federal League. Although sympathetic to the plight of the Minors, the Major League magnates never agreed to Barrow's request. Many felt that eliminating the draft
was tantamount to conferring Major League status, further diluting their
own monopoly. Also, the draft provided a source of relatively inexpensive,
well-trained talent. Barrow saw the world in black and white and was not
a man who liked to ask for favors. The multiple rejections of a request he
viewed as imperative for the survival of his league angered the already apprehensive Barrow.

Much of the war with the Federal League took place in the courts. With
players jumping back and forth between Organized Baseball and the Federal League, it should not be surprising that numerous lawsuits were instigated by teams on both sides claiming unfair or illegal interference with
their players. At one point in the spring of 1914, Barrow predicted that five
or more lawsuits would be instituted within a very short time over defecting
players. These suits would name the Federal League, the individual teams,
and the players as defendants. This threatened litigation, however, appears
not to have materialized or produced any material results.

Organized Baseball also attempted to close ranks against the Federal
League by blacklisting any player who jumped to the new venture. Barrow
considered any player who signed with the Federals nothing short of a traitor
and was at the vanguard of the blacklist initiative. By early March the International League had already lost some thirty players to the Federal League,
and Barrow hoped publicly proclaiming a blacklist could stanch this exodus:
"International League players who have taken part in any Federal League
games are through with our league for all time and cannot come back under
any conditions. They have preferred the Federal League to the International
and they must win or fall with it. In the event that the Federal League blows
up, not a single player who jumped either his reserve clause or his contract
will be permitted to take part in an International League contest."

Barrow also maintained a martial public stance: "We will meet them with our dukes up. The best way to deal with the new league is to let it go ahead on its own hook, and it will come to grief quick enough."

Unfortunately for Barrow and his owners, a Baltimore exhibition game showed that grief would come to the International League as well. Baltimore had a long and successful history as a Major League city. The Baltimore National League franchise had won three consecutive pennants in the 1890s, and the city had later been a charter member of the American League. Baltimore fans felt they were a big league city and should have a big league team. That the principal owner of the Federal League venture was Ned Hanlon, manager of those great 1890s teams, further cemented the city's eager acceptance of the Federals. As a harbinger of the summer in Baltimore, on April 13 the Federal League team drew about twenty-five thousand fans for its opener. At the same time, an exhibition game against the New York Giants by Dunn's International League squad drew only one thousand.

In a further attempt to counter the Federals, Barrow instituted stricter guidelines for his umpires. Daily reports were again required, and Barrow issued a thirty-six-paragraph code of conduct memorandum. The directive included such rules as "Cultivate an even temperament and do not be severe one day and easy-going the next; late hours and drinking and gambling will not be tolerated; and do not talk baseball on streetcars or around your hotel." Barrow further instructed his umpires to fine a player or manager five dollars for discoloring a new ball, and ten dollars for being ejected from the game. Umpires were asked to keep games moving along and were required to file a written report with the league office if a game went longer than two hours.

Despite Barrow's best efforts, by June it was clear that the International League was in big trouble. Not only was Barrow battling the Federals, but the country was in a mild recession as well. Jersey City, though not in direct competition with the Federals, was drawing only 200–500 fans per game. In Montreal the players were so disgusted with poor attendance they sent a delegation to petition owner Sam Lichtenhein to either trade them or sell the club. The players later complained that they could not "play winning ball in that city" and warned they might strike if the franchise was not transferred. In Newark, President Charles Ebbets Jr. had to borrow two thousand dollars from his father to meet payroll. Rochester's weekday games drew only 800–1,200 patrons, versus 2,000–3,000 in previous years.

But it was in Baltimore that the crisis manifested itself most acutely. Despite Dunn's first-place showing, at the gate the fans overwhelmingly chose the putative Major League Federals over the International League. Dunn claimed to have lost $20,000 over the first half of the season, a considerable amount for a Minor League operator without outside means. Dunn weighed a couple of strategies to recoup his losses if help from Organized Baseball was not forthcoming. Interests in Richmond, Virginia, had offered $62,500 for a 49 percent share of the team if he would move the club there. Alternatively, White Sox owner Charles Comiskey had reputedly offered $60,000 for his top five position players and Babe Ruth (then a pitcher). From Barrow's standpoint, neither of these options was particularly appealing. The former would likely require payment to the Virginia League for invading their territory and abandon the league's largest market; the latter would mean the loss of some of the league's best players.

On June 20 Barrow led a delegation that included Dunn, J. J. Stein from Buffalo, and J. J. McCaffrey and Joe Kelley from Toronto to a meeting at New York's Waldorf-Astoria Hotel with the National Commission. The mission of Barrow and his owners was to obtain some relief for the league's mounting financial woes. Barrow advocated either financial support or some type of quasi–Major League status for his league through the elimination of the draft and other changes. Barrow, Dunn, and company were surprisingly successful in getting support from the commission to create a third Major League within the Organized Baseball structure. After the meeting American League president Johnson announced, "There will be a third Major League, and I think it will be a good thing for the peace of Organized Baseball. It is true that the commission has not formally ratified the new project. But that is only a question of formality. We will now see how far the Federal League can go against real Major League opposition on every hand. Let me tell you the new circuit will soon prove its merits over the so-called class of Gilmore's league."

The principal scheme for the third Major League involved peeling off the four strongest markets from the International League—Baltimore, Buffalo, Toronto, and Newark—and merging them into a new league with four from the American Association, most likely Indianapolis, Cleveland/Toledo, Milwaukee, and either Minneapolis, Louisville, or Columbus. The remaining franchises in the two class AA leagues would then be formed into a new Minor League. An alternative proposal floated from the meeting had the new league placing new, Organized Baseball–sanctioned teams in existing Major League cities. In this version Baltimore, Buffalo, and Toronto would be joined by other International League and American Association franchises transferring into the Major League cities of Detroit, Cincinnati, Pittsburgh, and Cleveland, with Newark potentially moving to Washington.

The latter alternative never had any chance of success. No Major League owner would voluntarily permit another Major League in his city. Unfortunately for Barrow and Dunn, the entire third Major League scheme died quickly over the next couple of weeks. As the plan reached a wider audience of baseball magnates, strong opposition developed among several interested parties. Although a few Major League owners were lukewarm, most were hostile to adding a third Major League to the already fierce competition for fans and players. Furthermore, the American Association had little interest in the proposal. Indianapolis and Kansas City had both fared tolerably. And while some of the other franchises were certainly losing money, most owners felt the situation was not dire enough to warrant the dissolution of their league.

Barrow and the representatives from the three International League cities felt betrayed and sorely disappointed. Barrow naturally had hoped to found a new, solvent Major League of which he would be president. The other members of Barrow's delegation had thought they were on their way to becoming Major League owners. In retrospect, it is hard to gauge whether the third Major League option was ever feasible. In any case, Barrow and Johnson failed to manage the political side of the issue with any sensitivity. Such a radical step required backroom lobbying with both Major League and American Association owners prior to any announcement. Consensus building was not a strength of either Barrow or Johnson, dooming any new third Major League scheme.

With the collapse of his reorganization plan, Barrow continued to lobby the Majors and eventually secured limited financial support. Each Major League lent the International League $5,000, and the National Commission provided another $5,500. Ban Johnson sent Barrow an additional $3,219 specifically to bolster the beleaguered Buffalo franchise.

By the time the International League convened a special meeting on July 3, it was obvious that no significant outside help was imminent. In the face of the Federal League challenge, the owners could do little more than state that they intended to weather the losses and stand together.

When Jack Dunn finally realized that no assistance was forthcoming, he sold six of his players, including Babe Ruth, to three different Major League teams for total of about forty thousand dollars. Barrow demanded that a portion of the price be deposited with the league as security that Dunn would finish out the season and not fold his team. Dunn refused, and Barrow eventually backed down after Dunn assured him he would finish the season. Dunn's first-place team dropped quickly in the standings after he dismantled his club. His attendance problems soon reached absurd proportions, highlighted one day when roughly nine thousand fans crowded in to watch the Federals play a doubleheader, while Dunn's International League team drew only twenty-six paying fans.

Over the remainder of the season, Barrow continued the struggle to preserve his league. On September 1 he announced that the league would not fold and the season would run through its scheduled completion on September 27. Because of Canada's entry into the Great War in August 1914, Toronto proposed ending the season on Labor Day, and several other money-losing teams felt similarly. Barrow, however, successfully reined in this sentiment. Late in the season he transferred four games from Jersey City to Providence because of depressed attendance.

Barrow also helped broker the sale of the Providence franchise from Detroit interests to Joseph Lannin, owner of the Boston Red Sox, for $30,000. (Barrow hoped to then sell the struggling Buffalo franchise to the Detroit group, a plan that unfortunately never materialized.) Providence was one of the stronger franchises in the International League; the fall in value from its sale price of $72,500 in January 1912 attests to the financial impact of the Federals.

When the disastrous 1914 season finally ended, Barrow was depressed and discouraged. As table 4 highlights, International League franchises combined to lose close to two hundred thousand dollars, more than any other league (with the possible exception of the Federals). With Canada now at war and two markets flailing against the Federals, Barrow foresaw a bleak future for his league. He was long past the blustery pronouncements he had issued earlier in the season.

In late October, Barrow proposed a peace plan to the Federal League, which had struggled at the gate as well (see table 5 for an analysis of comparative attendance and market sizes). In Barrow's plan the Brooklyn, Baltimore, Buffalo, and Pittsburgh Federal League teams would take over struggling International League franchises from owners Barrow believed eager to sell. Pittsburgh would acquire Montreal and move the franchise to Pittsburgh, while Brooklyn would purchase the Jersey City team and move it to Washington Park in Brooklyn. The scheme had little chance of success and reflects Barrow's state of mind more than any rational initiative. The National League owners in Pittsburgh and Brooklyn would never have willingly allowed a second team in their market. Also, the Federal League owners had little incentive to purchase International League teams when they already had a Federal League team in the same market. Furthermore, the Federal League owners excluded by Barrow's plan would have fought the plan.

By November Barrow was back to his old belligerent self and eager to fight. In consultation with his owners, Barrow devised a multipronged strategy. One component involved relocating his two weakest franchises, Baltimore and Jersey City. Barrow angled for Dunn's Baltimore franchise to move to Richmond, Virginia, and he targeted Syracuse for Jersey City. The key sticking point for both moves was the demand for compensation by the existing, lower classification Minor Leagues, which controlled the territory. Richmond was the property of the Virginia League, a league in the midst of its own difficulties. Many believed that the loss of Richmond would doom the rest of the Virginia League. Within the Richmond business community, however, there was strong interest in bringing in a higher-level franchise. Barrow found local investors willing to purchase half of Dunn's franchise, allowing him to recapitalize it to seventy thousand dollars. Furthermore, they were willing to pay the ten thousand dollars or so necessary to appease the Virginia League.

The Jersey City situation was more problematic. The New York State League, which controlled the Syracuse territory, demanded more than the Virginia League did. The league initially asked for twenty-five thousand dollars, well beyond what a Minor League owner could afford in troubled times. Jersey City owners Devery and Fogarty complicated matters by demanding an above-market price. Even had he surmounted these difficulties, Barrow was having little success lining up interested Syracuse investors to purchase the club.

The league planned to retrench financially as well. The owners voted to reduce the schedule to 140 games, delaying the start of the season to April 27. A late start obviated the need for a spring training trip south, significantly reducing expenses. Roster sizes were reduced from twenty to seventeen, including the manager. Although not rigidly enforced, the league's teams had been operating under the monthly six-thousand-dollar salary cap established several years earlier. Some owners favored a lower, harder cap, but the majority rejected this extreme position for fear they would be forced to jettison some higher-priced stars. Barrow also vigorously lobbied his owners to create a capital reserve, which would be funded by each owner posting a bond of ten thousand dollars as guarantee of his contract obligations. Barrow convinced the owners of its necessity at a meeting on February 15, with the bond due by March 15. It is unlikely, however, that any team ever posted a bond with the league office.

With the failure to relocate Jersey City to Syracuse, Barrow alternatively proposed moving the franchise to the Bronx (the Yankees had not yet moved to the Bronx). Barrow lobbied hard for this move and thought he had lined up the necessary support. Pittsburgh owner Barney Dreyfuss and Brooklyn owner Charles Ebbets both supported the transfer. New York Giants president Harry Hempstead, however, controlled the territory for the National League and rejected the request. The *New York Times* reported: "Experienced baseball men are somewhat surprised at the action of the National League in refusing the request of the International League." The frustrated Barrow remarked: "We have always been loyal to baseball, and I think the National League is making a mistake. However, we will not quit, but will keep the Jersey City team in that city. We are in this fight to stay." Even after Hempstead's veto, Barrow continued a futile push for a transfer to the Bronx.

Despite Barrow's best efforts, the International League remained on the verge of collapse as the season approached. President C. T. Chapin of Rochester thought the league should contract by two teams, although he did not identify which two. An article in the *Washington Post* reported: "Do not be surprised to hear that the International League has decided to suspend operations indefinitely. Unless a miracle is performed by President Edward G. Barrow, the announcement will soon be made that the league will not attempt to play a championship schedule this year. . . . It was learned from a reliable source yesterday that the International League has reached a crisis. The National Commission has been forced to refuse financial assistance to the Buffalo club."

Four of his owners also secretly contacted Brooklyn Federals owner Robert Ward regarding a separate peace accord. The proposal was actually similar to that earlier entertained by Barrow, although at this late date the proposal would have meant abandoning the remaining owners. The new scheme entailed amalgamating International League franchises with Federal League teams in Pittsburgh, Brooklyn, Newark, and Baltimore. The Federal League, though, assumed that the International League was failing and saw no reason to agree to any settlement that did not include the Major Leagues.

To work his miracle Barrow needed to shore up several teams, most urgently the faltering Buffalo and recalcitrant Jersey City franchises. He traveled to Buffalo, searched out new owners and investors to reorganize the troubled club, and brought in Patsy Donovan to manage. Barrow also declared the Jersey City franchise forfeit to the league when Fogarty defaulted on several obligations totaling roughly ten thousand dollars. To help recapitalize the club, Barrow sold shares to the Jersey City general public at one hundred dollars per share. In his sales pitch Barrow clearly showed his frustration with the previous administration: "I cannot, of course, absolutely guarantee the club against loss, but I will surely do my best to prevent it. The business will be conducted on entirely different lines than in the past. A popular and competent Major League manager will be engaged, and every effort will be made to give the fans a team to be proud of." Never one to forget past obligations, Barrow pursued Fogarty for several years in an effort to recover his debts to the league.

While Barrow struggled for survival, the Federals did not remain idle. In January 1915 the Federal League filed suit in the court of Judge Kenesaw Mountain Landis (the future baseball commissioner) against Organized Baseball for violation of the antitrust laws. They named the sixteen Organized Baseball league presidents and the members of the National Commission as defendants. The Federals hoped to take advantage of Landis's reputation as a "trust buster." Given the merits of the case and the interpretation of antitrust law at the time, baseball's owners had good reason to be nervous. A huge baseball fan, prone to displaying whim and personal bias, Judge Landis delayed a decision and let the 1915 season play out.

Federal League president Gilmore landed another blow against Organized Baseball during the off-season when he lined up millionaire oilman Harry Sinclair as a new league owner. Gilmore's initial plan called for Sinclair to purchase the Kansas City franchise, move it east to Newark, and bring in Barrow's old antagonist Pat Powers to help run it. The Kansas City ownership spoiled this strategy by obtaining an injunction and preventing this sale and transfer. Sinclair then switched his focus to Indianapolis, the 1914 Federal League champion, which he successfully acquired and moved to Newark. The International League's Newark franchise was owned by Charles Ebbets and partners, owners of the Brooklyn Dodgers. Already competing with better-capitalized Federal League owners in Brooklyn, the partnership had little capital or emotional energy for this new battle.

Barrow looked forward to the 1915 season with a sense of both pride and trepidation. He had held his eight-team league together, restructured the ownership in Buffalo, and relocated the Baltimore team to a more stable Minor League baseball city. However, with Canada now actively engaged in World War I and in the process of creating and sending an expeditionary force to Europe, the Toronto and Montreal clubs both operated under wartime conditions. Two other teams, Buffalo and Newark, competed directly with the Federals; the latter in particular pitted a beleaguered ownership against one of the nation's wealthiest men. And despite Barrow's efforts, Jersey City remained capitalized on a shoestring. Moreover, his players were defecting as well: according to one report, the International League lost "some fifty-odd players" to the Federals.

The season opened as Barrow had feared. Richmond drew 9,425 fans for its opener, but Newark and Jersey City struggled. The league still controlled the hapless Jersey City franchise, and a couple of months into the season Barrow released manager George Wiltse. The Brooklyn Dodgers owners soon abandoned the Newark franchise to the league as well. Prior to the 1914 season, Ebbets had asked $132,000 for the franchise and reportedly turned down an $80,000 offer. Now the franchise was virtually worthless.

At the International League meeting on June 30, the league voted to transfer the Newark franchise to Harrisburg, Pennsylvania. Barrow was not particularly pleased with this decision. He believed that if the club could hold out in Newark, there was a good chance the Federal League would shift their Newark franchise to a larger market after the season. This decision, along with the league's well-publicized struggles, led Barrow to release a statement after the meeting denying that the season would be canceled after July 4. In Harrisburg the club actually drew adequately: 8,000 for the opener, and an average of 2,200 over the first eighteen games. Barrow moved to quell rumors of further franchise shifts by declaring on August 6 that the league would remain intact through the remainder of the season. Over the second half of the season, Barrow not only had to manage his league's affairs but was essentially running the Jersey City and Harrisburg franchises. When the season finally ended, the reorganized Buffalo club was still afloat and possibly even turned a small profit. Barrow was rightfully credited by many owners, both Major and Minor League, and many in the press with holding the league together.

After the season most observers felt that a settlement with the Federal League was a strong possibility. Federal League attendance had unquestionably fallen below its 1914 figure. Kansas City drew the largest gate with approximately 180,000 fans, while Brooklyn attracted only 50,000 patrons. And despite its league leading attendance, Kansas City lost $35,332. Furthermore, the death of Robert Ward in October eliminated one of the Federals' wealthiest and most passionate supporters. During the fall Barrow and his owners assumed a wait-and-see attitude toward the league's problems. They were aware of clandestine meetings that fall between various Major League and Federal League owners. The International League adjourned its December 13 meeting without taking any actions as they awaited pending settlement negotiations between the National League and the Federals.

The Federal League war affected the National League much more than the American. In 1915 seven of the National League's eight franchises competed head-to-head with another Major League team (granting the Federal League was Major) in its home city. Only the money-losing Cincinnati Reds did not have to contend with a Major League competitor. Active maneuvering by the Federal League to place a team in New York—later portrayed by Gilmore as a giant bluff—further alarmed the Major Leagues.

Yankee co-owner Tillinghast L'Hommedieu Huston sent a nervous telegram to Johnson on December 3 informing him that the Federals were actively securing potential sites in New York. Although he acknowledged it might "all be bluff," he requested Johnson travel to New York to discuss countermeasures.

The Federals and the National Leaguers reached a tentative accord in mid-December calling for the dissolution of the Federal League but providing its owners with a significant buyout. The Federals challenged the American League in only two of its cities; consequently, it had suffered much less during the baseball war. Because of their stronger position vis-à-vis the Federals, the American League only reluctantly acceded to the accord struck by the Nationals. Once the two Major Leagues and the Federals reached a provisional agreement on the major issues, all sides needed to hammer out the details. For these concluding negotiations, Barrow and other representatives from the Minors joined the conference.

Barrow was at the center of the final negotiating session on December 22 because the outstanding unresolved issues focused on the Buffalo and Baltimore Federal League franchises. Barrow, who had struggled for two years to hold his league together, was unforgiving and uncompromising. The Baltimore Federals opened negotiations by claiming they wanted to buy the St. Louis Cardinals and move the team to Baltimore. Their offer of $250,000 was almost certainly negotiating bluster; the marginally capitalized ownership would have been hard pressed to raise the necessary funds. However, it did not really matter: the Major League magnates had little interest in accepting so little for a franchise, especially given the additional complication of the International League's claim to that city. As negotiations continued, the Baltimore Federals asserted that they should be allowed to keep their franchise and have it transferred to the International League. Dunn, who was also in attendance, vigorously objected, claiming he should be allowed to return to Baltimore. Barrow backed Dunn's position, at least as it pertained to the Federal League franchise. After being rebuffed, the Federals offered to sell the team to Dunn for one hundred thousand dollars, a proposal Dunn quickly rejected, maintaining he still controlled the franchise rights to Baltimore. The Baltimore Federals then refused a counter of fifty thousand dollars from Organized Baseball. Finally, the Baltimore owners offered Dunn the manager's position if he would acquiesce. Not surprisingly, Dunn expressed little interest in this idea.

The Buffalo Federal League owner also wanted to join the International League. The team had lost about $170,000 during its two years and hoped to recoup some of it by joining Barrow's circuit. Because the wealthier Federal League owners had financially propped up the Buffalo franchise, and the International League team had stuck it out, the Buffalo position generated less sympathy among the participants. Barrow forcefully objected to a proposal advocating a merger of the leagues' two franchises.

Neither the Major Leagues nor the wealthiest Federal League negotiators wished the agreement stalled by what they felt to be peripheral Minor League concerns. The final settlement resolved all issues except the two involving Baltimore and Buffalo and the International League. A committee of seven, naturally including Barrow, was formed to settle these matters at a meeting in early January. With these two complications tabled until January, the key negotiators, including Barrow, signed the settlement document.

The major provisions of the settlement affecting the other six Federal League teams and other stipulations are summarized here.

Brooklyn—The Ward heirs received $400,000, $20,000 a year for twenty years.

Chicago—The Chicago Cubs were sold to the Chicago Federal League ownership group led by Charles Weeghman for $500,000, of which the National League contributed $50,000. The agreement permitted Weeghman to keep the rights to his players. Thus his 1916 Cubs represented an amalgamation of two teams.

Kansas City—The owners received nothing in the settlement.

Newark—Owner Harry Sinclair received $100,000: $10,000 per year for ten years. He was also awarded the rights to most players not controlled by another owner (an exclusion that applied mainly to the Chicago and St. Louis franchises). These rights proved a valuable commodity when several Major League teams bid aggressively to purchase the Federal League's stars, most notably Benny Kauff and Lee Magee.

Pittsburgh—Owner Ed Gwinner hoped to purchase the Cleveland Indians but would not meet the $560,000 price mandated by the bankers controlling the team for the financially strapped Charles Somers. He settled for a $50,000 payment to be paid over five years.

St. Louis—Owner Phil Ball was allowed to purchase the St. Louis Browns for $525,000. The agreement also permitted Ball to keep the rights to his players. Thus his 1916 Browns represented an amalgamation of two teams.

Players—All were reinstated into the good graces of Organized Baseball. Barrow disliked this provision but did not actively object.

Lawsuit—The Federals agreed to ask Judge Landis to dismiss the lawsuit, and Landis complied.

Ballparks—The settlement granted Organized Baseball the Federal League's ballparks in Pittsburgh, Brooklyn, and Newark. Only the last was ever used by Organized Baseball. (Weeghman also controlled the ballpark—eventually renamed Wrigley Field—in Chicago.)

On January 4, 1916, Barrow traveled to Cincinnati to meet with Federal League owners Carrol Rasin of Baltimore and William Robertson of Buffalo to settle the remaining issues. When he arrived, however, he found the Federals stalling in the hopes of sweetening the negotiations. After first postponing the meeting a few days, the Federals then advocated rescheduling in New York on the nineteenth. Barrow's mood was not helped by a threatened attack of appendicitis while he was in Cincinnati chasing the reluctant negotiators. Upon his return to New York, Barrow announced his resignation from the peace committee (which included the three National Commission members, the two Federal League owners, and Gilmore): "I have resigned from this committee as there does not seem to be any attempt made by the Federal League to get together. We shall go on with our plans for next season without further considering them."

Gilmore may have angled for this outcome, believing that the National Commission alone would be more pliant than the inflexible Barrow. Gilmore supposed he still had some negotiating leverage because the Federals had not yet formally requested Landis to dismiss the lawsuit, and the signed settlement anticipated a resolution of all the Federal League franchises.

It rapidly became evident, however, that the settlement satisfied the wealthier Federal League owners, and they had no interest in reopening the battle. Furthermore, the Major League owners believed they had paid more than enough and had little patience for additional demands. In fact, upon reflection, Ban Johnson and several American League magnates disliked the settlement so much that for a while they threatened to replace Cincinnati owner Garry Herrmann as National Commission chairman or restructure the commission entirely. This posturing soon waned, but the final accord dissolving the Federal League was not inexpensive for Organized Baseball.

Barrow's intransigence and unwillingness to either admit the Federals into Baltimore or pay them off led to consequences well beyond the International League. In March the Baltimore Federal League owners filed a new lawsuit against Organized Baseball alleging violations of the national antitrust laws and asking for nine hundred thousand dollars. After several appeals, the U.S. Supreme Court eventually heard this case. The high court ruled, in a decision that now seems quixotic at best, that baseball was not subject to the national antitrust laws. Despite many challenges, the exemption remains today as neither the court nor Congress has seen fit to materially reverse this decision.

9. No Respite

With the demise of the Federal League, Barrow set about reorganizing his own league. The dispositions of the Richmond and Harrisburg franchises topped the list of immediate concerns. Jack Dunn naturally wanted to return to Baltimore, but Richmond had supported the team and argued for its continued residence. During the peace negotiations Barrow put forward the notion that Baltimore should be without baseball for a year as punishment for not supporting its International League team. Dunn quickly disabused him of this idea, but it testifies to the depth of Barrow's feelings toward the Federals and their supporters.

After some shuttle diplomacy, Barrow allowed Dunn to take over the Jersey City franchise and transfer it to Baltimore. The Richmond interests bought out Dunn's half-interest, and that franchise remained in Richmond. The Federals in Baltimore pressured Dunn to purchase their stadium. Dunn resisted, but Barrow encouraged him to buy their more modern structure. Dunn and Carol Rasin eventually worked out a sale agreement on the stadium—originally built for around fifty thousand dollars—for thirty thousand dollars. To appease the fans who still wanted their "Major League" Federals, Dunn assumed their flag and colors.

Barrow moved the Harrisburg franchise back to Newark and announced it was available for a relatively modest twenty-five thousand dollars. He soon received his asking price from an investment group made up of Jim Price, the former New York boxing commissioner and one-time rival for the league presidency; Fred Tenney (a former Major League player); and Henry Clay Smith, a wealthy Chicago businessman, one-time money partner in the franchise, and friend of Ban Johnson. Also during the spring Joseph Lannin sold the Providence franchise for thirty thousand dollars. Lannin subsequently acquired a large minority interest in the Buffalo team, which was heavily indebted to him for loans he had advanced during the battle with the Federals.

At a league meeting the owners rewarded Barrow for his leadership during the Federal League war by increasing his powers. The *Sporting News* reported that his "executive functions" were now, "final, irrevocable and un-impeachable." The owners also chose to keep the season at 140 games. To scale back expenses, the International League reduced its unofficial salary limit to only $3,500 per month. Even though this was not honored in many instances, salaries fell dramatically. Not surprisingly, the players actively objected to the pay reduction, but with the demise of the Federal League and consequent elimination of meaningful competition for their services, they had little recourse.

Unfortunately, the demise of the Federal League did not lead to a prosperous year for the International. The Baltimore opener drew only 3,000 fans, and in Richmond only 4,500 braved a drizzle to attend opening day. Other teams complained of poor attendance as well, although lousy weather accounted for some of the disappointing turnouts. Rochester, on the other hand, had a strong opener, attracting 10,000 fans.

By season's end, none of the teams banked more than a token profit. In aggregate, the league's franchises lost nearly one hundred thousand dollars in 1916, and many were in severe financial distress. Newark and Rochester each lost around twenty thousand dollars, Baltimore almost as much, and Richmond approximately five thousand dollars. Operating under Canadian wartime restrictions, Montreal and probably Toronto lost money. Only Buffalo and Rochester approached breaking even. With these losses, the Minor League magnates were more restless than ever regarding the Major League–Minor League draft. As the Major Leagues' attendance recovered, the high Minor Leagues strongly resented the price-damping effect that the draft placed on player sales. The Minor League owners further lamented Major League control of many of their players through outright ownership and working agreements, which limited their ability to sell players for a profit.

In late January 1916, after the demise of the Federal League, a new and potentially costly controversy confronted Barrow. The Brooklyn Dodgers owners, Charles Ebbets and his partners, Ed and Steve McKeever, claimed the Newark franchise owed them $75,293.81. During the Federal League war the same individuals owned both the Brooklyn Dodgers and Newark, but they were technically owned by two different corporate entities. Ebbets alleged the Dodgers corporation had loaned money to the Newark corporation during 1913, 1914, and 1915, totaling $75,293.81 with interest. The demand for the International League to honor this debt infuriated Barrow and his owners, whom Ebbets had just deserted in the middle of the Federal League conflict.

When Barrow refused to pay Ebbets the loan repayment he demanded, Ebbets elevated the issue to the National Commission, the deciding body for intrabaseball disputes. Ebbets expressed a willingness to accept a compromise well below his stated demand. As payment, he would accept the difference between the sale price of the franchise to Price's group ($25,000) and the expense incurred by the league in moving and operating the franchise after its forfeiture. The commission finally ruled in July. It first chastised Ebbets for not selling the franchise (several years earlier the commission had issued a confidential memorandum declaring the ownership of a Minor League franchise by Major League owners "antagonistic to the fundamental principles of the National Agreement") after it emerged in the hearing that the team had earned a $26,000 profit in 1913, and Ebbets had subsequently turned down an offer of $60,400 for the franchise. In its final ruling, however, by a two to one vote, the commission ruled in favor of Ebbets's suggested compromise. Barrow estimated the loss associated with running the club at roughly $16,000, leaving the amount due Ebbets at $9,000. The commission's ruling in favor of Ebbets surprised many observers.

The commission advanced two reasons for its ruling. First, when the International League assumed operation of the ball club, few unpaid debts were outstanding. Any unpaid salary claims or other obligations would have become liabilities of the league, and thus the league was not saddled with additional liabilities. Second, the financial support of the club by Ebbets and the McKeevers up until they forfeited the franchise deserved to be recognized.

The decision incensed Barrow, and he immediately demanded a rehearing. Barrow took the quite logical position that the alleged debts between two corporations with the same owners were really nothing more than a single owner covering his losses. Any equity in the club would obviously be lost when the club was forfeited to the league. American League president Ban Johnson, the dissenting member of the commission, agreed that Ebbets deserved nothing. Johnson further pointed out that Ebbets had made no claim for the money until after the Federal League was eliminated.

On August 31, 1916, the National Commission issued a ruling denying the appeal from Barrow and the International League. It further directed Barrow to forward an official statement showing the difference between the price received for the Newark franchise and the amount expended in operating it. Ban Johnson sympathized with Barrow but advised Barrow to withdraw the appeal and abide by the commission's ruling. Barrow delayed any response until the December 11 International League meeting at which the league voted to defy the National Commission, unanimously agreeing to refuse payment. Barrow feared a possible civil suit by Ebbets to recover the money but remained defiant. During the latter half of December, Barrow had to briefly curtail his wrangling due to a bout with pneumonia.

As discussed elsewhere, professional baseball players were becoming increasingly restive at the salary retrenchment, and what appeared to be a major act of insubordination by the International League lost significance in the face of a potential player strike. With the need for owner solidarity and no wish to open old wounds, the commission postponed any action on the International League's defiance until mid-January. In January 1917, with the players still on edge and facing the possibility of a strike, Barrow and the commission worked out an undisclosed compromise on the nine-thousand-dollar obligation.

At the end of the nineteenth century, American industrial workers labored in appalling conditions. Never subject to the ghastly conditions of factory life, ballplayers nevertheless toiled in an environment that today seems quite callous and unfair. Some of the worst abuses in other industries began to be corrected during the "progressive" era of the first fifteen years of the twentieth century. Ballplayers also hoped to improve the onerous work rules to which they were subjected.

In May 1912 Ty Cobb jumped into the stands and brutally attacked a disabled fan who had been viciously heckling him. Ban Johnson suspended Cobb, leading to a spontaneous one-day Detroit Tigers players' strike in his support. Buoyed by this apparent player solidarity and a general sense of player discontentment, in July 1912 Dave Fultz, a former Major League outfielder, organized the Players Fraternity to represent players in the Majors and the high Minors.

By this time American labor unions had begun to diverge in two directions. One philosophy, as espoused by Samuel Gompers and the American Federation of Labor (AFL), targeted material improvements and disdained much of the moralistic and societal reform tendencies of nineteenth-century unionism. On this more conservative side of trade unionism, leadership believed in a strong central authority that negotiated within the framework of the existing order. The more radical unions and socialists such as the Industrial Workers of the World occupied the other end of labor's political spectrum.

Fultz and his union clearly fell into the former camp. (Fultz did, however, exhibit a streak of nineteenth-century moralizing; for example, at one point he admonished the players not to buy cars.) He hoped to alleviate some of the more egregious provisions to which the players were subject. He pressed for such basic conditions as "when a player is transferred, he shall be transferred subject to all the terms of his contract," and "each team shall pay the actual traveling expenses of its players from their home to the training camps." Like owners and bosses in other industries, the baseball magnates were hostile to unionism and organized player action. On the other hand, some of the arbitrary actions by individual owners—particularly in the Minors—were so egregious that many felt some minimal redress was in order; they just did not want it to appear that an organized players' union had achieved these improved conditions.

In late 1913, as the anxiety over the Federal League's impact grew, Fultz astutely pushed his demands. At a large gathering in Cincinnati in January, the fraternity pushed seventeen demands similar in nature to the two noted. Fultz successfully obtained Organized Baseball's agreement to most of the demands. The baseball owners clearly hoped that any goodwill they could earn with the players and the union would benefit them in the upcoming battle with the new league.

In July 1914 Barrow became tangentially involved in an imbroglio surrounding the status of Clarence Kraft. When Brooklyn tried to assign Kraft to Newark, Nashville, in a lower league, asserted it had a prior claim in the event Kraft was returned to the Minors. In addition to Kraft's playing in a lower classification, his assignment to Nashville would result in a $150 pay reduction. Kraft protested to the National Commission, arguing that the Cincinnati agreement stipulated that a player should be allowed to play in the highest securable league. The commission ruled in favor of Nashville, whereupon Kraft appealed to Fultz for support.

Fultz sensed his opportunity and threatened an open break: he warned that unless the Kraft ruling was reversed, all players in the fraternity would no longer consider themselves under contract; that is, they would strike. Johnson perceived an opportunity to break the union and looked forward to a confrontation. He consulted with Barrow and National League president John Tener to plan their strategy. The Nationals, however, chose to defuse the situation and brokered a compromise in which Ebbets paid Nashville $2,500 for the rights to Kraft. When asked, Barrow expressed satisfaction with the outcome, but given the losses his teams were enduring, he probably itched for a showdown as well. In this first crisis since the Cincinnati agreement, Organized Baseball had backed down. Unfortunately for the players, Fultz misinterpreted the outcome, believing that he could threaten the owners and they would yield—and the magnates, especially Johnson, would not again be humiliated by Fultz.

For the first time in many years, the environment in the United States during World War I provided favorable conditions for unions. The demand for goods from the belligerent European powers increased the demand for labor. Simultaneously, the war shut off the huge supply of cheap immigrant labor from eastern and southern Europe, contributing to the labor shortage. Furthermore, as inflation accelerated and unemployment fell, workers grew emboldened. Union membership surged and strikes increased. Also, Gompers worked with the Wilson administration to build support for the war effort. This collaboration, at a time when many in the labor movement still opposed the war, earned Gompers and the more conformist unions a measure of government goodwill they had not previously received.

Similarly, the Players Fraternity began hoping for an increased role in baseball. The remainder of the 1914 season and 1915 were relatively calm. But it was a false calm, because the existence of the Federal League and competition for player talent artificially restrained the magnates. With the demise of the Federals and the associated salary retrenchment, the players became increasingly restless. On October 30, 1916, Fultz presented Organized Baseball with a list of four demands, which by today's standards seem eminently reasonable. Three addressed working conditions almost exclusively in the Minor Leagues.

1. End the practice of not paying players under contract who were injured while playing. (This situation was limited almost exclusively to the Minor Leagues.)
2. When a Minor League player was given his five-day notice and released, he should be immediately free to sign with any other team.
3. Minor League players should have traveling expenses to spring training camps paid.
4. The Players Fraternity should receive copies of the club's defenses in actions brought by players.

Organized Baseball united in opposition to any compromise with the Players Fraternity. The Minors rejected the demands at their annual meeting. The Majors demurred that most of the issues dealt with the Minors. Fultz and the players naturally grew impatient with the lack of willingness to negotiate. Fultz again threatened a strike—the players would not sign their contracts until their demands were met. This time, however, Organized Baseball responded forcefully and quickly. Barrow stated that many Minor League clubs were losing money, with some on the verge of bankruptcy, and could not grant the players any concessions that would add expenses. Under the current economic conditions, he claimed that many owners were in favor of locking the players out in the event of a strike.

In early January Fultz heated up the rhetoric. When pitcher Slim Sallee signed a contract in violation of the fraternity's edict, Fultz expelled him. Fultz asserted that this was simply an aberration and that between six hundred and seven hundred players remained loyal to the fraternity. He further added that no more than one-sixth of the International League's players would report. Fultz also approached Gompers about joining his AFL. Gompers initially voiced encouragement for Fultz's appeal and said he favored a strike by ballplayers if they felt it was necessary.

During January the rhetoric escalated on both sides. Johnson recognized an opportunity to break the union and vigorously denounced Fultz. Barrow reiterated that if the International League players did not sign their contracts, his owners would be happy to close their parks. He also echoed Johnson's line that there would be no compromise with the players. Barrow further declared, "The vast majority of clubs do now and always have paid transportation expenses to their respective players to report." But he went on to add that the Minor League clubs could not make it an "iron-clad" rule, because during years in which they used between sixty and ninety players over the course of a season, the cost would be prohibitive for the lower Minor League teams. This last argument simply shows that Barrow could dissemble with the best of baseball's leadership.

By early February Fultz could see his player's solidarity eroding, and the AFL affiliation discussions had petered out. Recognizing his predicament, Fultz began looking for a face-saving exit. The magnates, however, were not in an obliging mood. In mid-February the baseball owners severed all relations with the fraternity and, claiming the union had violated the Cincinnati agreement of 1914, abrogated it. Organized Baseball would no longer recognize, tolerate, or negotiate with any organization of players. This action effectively ended the Players Fraternity. The players promptly signed contracts, and without the threat of organized action, the union had no leverage for bargaining on any future issues. And so the players lost their last best chance until the 1960s for a union that could collectively deal with their grievances.

After reassessing Fultz's approach, we can clearly see that he misplayed his hand. First, while his list of four demands was reasonable, these issues were hardly inspiring. To expect the players, unaccustomed to collective action, to strike against motivated and better-organized employers for such benefits was naive. Moreover, Fultz erred in expecting Major League players and stars to be willing to strike over what were essentially Minor League work rules. Even a more cohesive Major League union would have experienced difficulty garnering support for collective action in areas that barely affected its members. Finally, he underestimated the intransigence of the owners. With the threat of the Federal League gone, the owners could bring the full weight of their societal and financial position to bear without fear of consequences.

In retrospect it seems unlikely that the Players Fraternity could have survived much longer even if it had been run by a master tactician. As the history of the modern players' union demonstrates, because of an ingrained loyalty to team and a sense of individual accomplishment, players need a sustained internal organizing campaign to prepare them for the rigors of collective action. With the end of World War I, many of the more labor friendly (at least relative to the war years) policies of the federal government receded, leaving unions unprotected from employer abuses.

During the 1916–17 off-season Barrow once again lobbied to have the draft ended or least modified. He proposed requiring a player to spend at least two years in a class AA league before becoming eligible for the draft, raising the price for drafted players, and limiting the draft to every other year. Once again the Majors had no interest in limiting their access to players or raising the cost.

Barrow also spent time that winter searching for a buyer for the Providence franchise. New owner William Draper wanted out after only one year and sought to recoup his initial investment of thirty thousand dollars; with some effort, Barrow found a twenty-six thousand dollar offer, which Draper turned down. Barrow also again traveled to Syracuse for a meeting with New York State League officials to negotiate that city's territorial release to the International League for a possible franchise shift. His efforts met with no more success than two years earlier, and despite rumors to the contrary, he could not acquire Syracuse's rights for his league.

The International League also agreed to a postseason series with the American Association. The plan called for a 112-game regular season followed by a long postseason interleague series. Each team would post five hundred dollars to create an eight-thousand-dollar pot. American Association president Thomas Hickey drew up a proposed schedule and traveled to New York to present it to Barrow. Barrow intended to discuss the schedule at the upcoming International League meeting. The United States declaration of war against Germany on April 6, 1917, however, added uncertainty to an already tenuous situation in the Minor Leagues. In May the two leagues called off the postseason series and added regular league games to the end of the schedule.

As the International League struggled financially, Barrow oversaw an underfunded league office; his shoestring budget can be seen on table 6. To bolster his league's finances he tried unconventional means to generate additional revenue. In one effort, Barrow fell back on his boxing roots and attempted to arrange a match at the Toronto ballpark, offering fifteen thousand dollars to stage the bout. Despite Barrow's efforts and a close four-team pennant race, the season again proved unprofitable.

The league's precarious financial position also led Barrow to again consider establishing business interests outside baseball. While league president
prior to the Federal League war, Barrow had turned down the Canadian
distribution rights for Dodge and the accompanying career change. In early
1917 he uncovered another automotive business opportunity. After a ride
in the Dey Electric, Barrow telegraphed his one-time employer Larry Solman, raving about his ride in a "wonderful car." The two teamed up with
a Dr. Muir, becoming equal partners in the electric-car venture. The business ended in disaster. The investment never paid off, and Dr. Muir landed
himself in trouble. Barrow lamented not fully vetting Muir before bringing him into the partnership. To protect themselves and what remained of
the car venture, Barrow assured Solman that in the event Muir's troubles
became public, he would claim Muir was an old friend.

The ongoing financial troubles of the International League led to revived
discussions of a third Major League, consisting of some amalgamation of
the International League and the American Association. On top of running his league, Barrow spent much of the two years after the demise of
the Federals caught up in these conversations and negotiations. In an interview after the 1916 season, American League president Ban Johnson remarked that he "rather liked the idea" of a third Major League. Johnson
was simply offering his opinion and may have been posturing because of
the Baltimore Federals lawsuit. As the most powerful man in baseball, his
comments received publicity beyond what he had probably intended. The
teams tentatively proposed for the new league were Baltimore, Newark,
Toronto, Buffalo, Toledo, Indianapolis, Louisville, and Milwaukee. With
the Federal League war over, Barrow was in the midst of trying to organize
his clubs for the upcoming 1917 season, and he remained generally upbeat.
He did not want any distracting rumors of impending Major League status for select teams. Barrow called the idea of a third Major League "preposterous" and stated that the International League would operate in 1917
as a class AA league. Barrow did squeeze in the caveat, however, that a third
Major League would come about only as a last resort in the event of a disastrous 1917 season.

By the start of the 1917 season, as the country mobilized for war, the outlook appeared bleak enough to justify Barrow's qualification. By July 1917

a couple of International League teams were considering disbanding after the season. Furthermore, as the league struggled, there was some sentiment to cut Barrow's salary. With the connivance of Johnson and the National Commission, over the summer Barrow enlisted several American Association teams and again cooked up a third Major League scheme. Named the Union League, this new league would consist of four International League franchises (Baltimore, Buffalo, Toronto, and probably Newark) and four from the American Association (Indianapolis, Louisville, Toledo, and possibly Columbus) with Barrow as president.

The politics of the proposed Union League were quite complex. The Major Leagues supported its creation as a way of helping the Minors survive without requiring their active financial support. Also, several reports suggested that the Baltimore franchise in the new league would go to the Baltimore Federal League owners as a compromise to settle their lawsuit. Many Major League owners also did not envision the Union League as true third Major but, at least initially, as a step below. The new league would likely be exempt from the Major League–Minor League draft, but it would not have a member on the National Commission. Johnson also viewed it mainly as an act of wartime expediency. The plan contemplated that those International League and American Association franchises not included in the Union League would join lower-classification Minor Leagues in their geographic area.

Accreditation of the Union League by the Minor Leagues necessitated territorial restructuring to authorize the abandoned teams to join existing leagues; this would drive out some teams in those leagues, which would in turn need to be relocated themselves. The lower Minor Leagues had no interest in significantly disrupting their operations by restructuring along the lines Barrow suggested. Also, American Association president Thomas Hickey and the four leftover franchises in the two merging leagues had no desire to see their dissolution. At the National Association meetings in mid-November, only the Three-I League sided with Barrow, and the Minor Leagues decisively voted down the restructuring proposal eleven to two, effectively ending Barrow's hopes for the Union League.

Straightforward and blunt as always, Barrow, unfortunately, had not learned the correct lessons from his failed attempt to establish a third Major League in 1914. Once again his strength of will, the active support of several teams (in this case mostly from the teams jumping the American Association), and lukewarm support from the National Commission were not sufficient to compel the baseball establishment to submit to considerable restructuring. Barrow again displayed a surprising disregard for the behind-the-scenes politicking that such a substantial project demanded.

At the close of the 1917 season, the forty-nine-year-old Barrow had led the International League through seven seasons, the last few of which had been particularly arduous and unrewarding. The 1917 season had drained much of his remaining confidence in the survival of either his league in particular or the Minors in general. Also, Barrow harbored ambitions beyond a Minor League presidency. His $7,500 salary was excellent for the time, but after close to twenty years in baseball, he needed a new challenge. In October, American League president Ban Johnson was rumored to be close to accepting a commission in the army, and league sources identified Barrow as his likely successor. One American League owner lauded his leadership ability: "Barrow is one of the shrewdest men of the game. He won the spurs in the most successful fight which the International League put up against Jim Gilmore's outlaw ring. The Barrow circuit had to bear the brunt of that battle. No one on the outside can appreciate what powers of executive ability Barrow wielded to keep his organization together in the most distressing circumstances."

The talk of Johnson entering the army soon died, and Barrow returned to contemplating the future of his job and league. The Union League scheme had created a rift between the proposed participants and those left behind. At the upcoming annual meeting in New York on December 10, Barrow expected and deserved a hostile reception from his gloomy, pessimistic owners. One rumor on the eve of the meeting intimated that the league might downsize to only six teams for the 1918 season. Another hinted that because Boston Red Sox owner Harry Frazee wished to spend more time on his theatrical interests, he was looking for someone to run his team, and Johnson reportedly backed Barrow for the job.

At the meeting Barrow assumed the offensive and declared the Buffalo franchise, now under the control of Joseph Lannin (who had become disillusioned with Barrow because of the Union League fiasco), forfeited to the league. The team owed roughly eighteen thousand dollars, including player's salaries, league fees, and guarantees to visiting clubs. With Lannin neutered, the owners addressed two issues: whether to suspend operations for 1918 and Barrow's future as league president. In a sign of the league's distress, the former failed by only a four to three vote; Rochester, Richmond, and Providence voted to put the league on ice for a year; Lannin's Buffalo club was now ineligible to vote.

Barrow had underestimated the lingering resentment generated by his abortive effort to establish the Union League. The four franchises not included in the Union League allied with Dunn (who—probably believed correctly—that the Union League would have squeezed him out for the Federals in Baltimore) to force Barrow's resignation. These offended owners voted four to three to reduce Barrow's salary from $7,500 to $2,500 (Montreal owner Lichtenhein—his old boss—was willing to reduce Barrow's salary only to $5,000), an insult they correctly perceived would oblige Barrow to resign. At the end of the meeting, Barrow and Lannin nearly came to blows. Barrow's two staunchest supporters, Toronto's McCaffery and Newark's Price, held Barrow back, telling him, "Don't hit him, Ed. He's got a bad heart." Barrow remained bitter after the meeting, saying that if the league chose to degenerate to the level of a class B league, he was happy not to be a party to it.

Effectively finished with the job that had consumed him for the last seven years, Barrow was too ornery to simply resign outright. Although he had announced his dissatisfaction with the pay cut at the end of the annual meeting, he nominally remained league president because his resignation did not become official until the next league meeting in mid-February 1918. Until then Barrow bided his time while lining up his next challenge. Almost immediately after the rancorous meeting, Barrow was approached by Harry Frazee, a theater mogul and fellow New York resident.

On the surface, Frazee and Barrow would seem to have little in common beyond being born in small Illinois towns. But though the two had very different personalities, they eventually became close friends. Both were highly competitive and had scraped their way out of poverty into the booming, raw, capitalist economy of the late nineteenth and early twentieth centuries. Frazee also prized Barrow's willingness to play the tough guy in dealing with the players. He even jokingly called Barrow "Simon Legree," after the cruel slave overseer in Harriet Beecher Stowe's *Uncle Tom's Cabin*.

As a sixteen-year-old boy, Frazee had traveled as an advance agent for a small theater company. By age twenty-two he had produced his first show, and several more fairly successful ones, mostly musical comedies, soon followed. Like Barrow he also dabbled in the boxing world to generate publicity, once taking James Jeffries and Jim Corbett, Barrow's two celebrity boxers, on a tour. Around 1909, and still in his twenties, Frazee moved his operations to New York and became a successful producer in America's theater capital.

After the 1916 season, along with theater pal Hugh Ward, Frazee purchased the reigning champion Boston Red Sox from Barrow's future nemesis Joseph Lannin. Frazee recognized that owning the Red Sox not only could be profitable but also would place him in the limelight. According to one account, "he had taken over the Boston franchise in order to make money for himself and from the moment the ink was dry on the official documents the gentleman proceeded to operate with this and no other purpose in mind." Perhaps so, but initially he behaved as if maintaining a winning ball club was the best way to generate profits. With a youthful cockiness and the drive of a self-made man, Frazee easily assumed the aura and stature of a baseball magnate.

Almost immediately after his acquisition, Frazee and American League president Ban Johnson developed a mutual loathing. Frazee showed none of the deference that the domineering Johnson believed he deserved and indeed received from most owners. Since the founding of his league, Johnson had watched over it like a mother hen. He monitored team finances and ownerships, and if problems developed, he orchestrated the team's transition to new owners. Frazee's purchase of the Red Sox surprised Johnson and represented the first franchise sale in American League history negotiated without his involvement. Johnson resented the new Red Sox owner both for his brashness and his lack of allegiance. For his part Frazee never really understood the full weight of influence Johnson held over the league. Beyond the powers conferred by his office, Johnson had accumulated a reservoir of political capital and goodwill from the league's owners both for his skillful management of the league and because they owed their ownership positions to Johnson.

Frazee hoped to lift his team back to the pennant after a dip to second place and an attendance slide in 1917. Accordingly, he sent sixty thousand dollars and three marginal ballplayers to the Philadelphia Athletics for catcher Wally Schang, pitcher Bullet Joe Bush, and center fielder Amos Strunk. Still relatively young, Schang and Strunk were two of only three starters remaining from Connie Mack's 1914 pennant winners that Mack and co-owner Ben Shibe dismantled for cash over the next three years. Schang was the best catcher of the era, while outfielder Strunk went on to several more fine seasons. As a twenty-one-year-old right-hander, Bush led the 1914 Philadelphia club with seventeen victories. Still only twenty-four, Bush also had many fine seasons remaining.

By early 1918 Frazee wished to devote more of his time to his theater interests; in the recently unemployed Barrow, Frazee believed he had found the excellent executive he needed to run his club. He valued his franchise equity at $500,000 and offered Barrow an opportunity to purchase either a one-quarter share for $125,000 or a one-fifth share for $100,000. Barrow also would be required to assume a pro-rata share of the team's liabilities, which totaled $679,000 (setting the enterprise value of the team at $1,179,000). While Frazee concentrated on his outside interests, Barrow would run the team with a title of either president or vice president and general manager, at a "good" salary.

Forty-nine years old, unemployed, and without any real wealth, Barrow desperately wanted to buy into the Red Sox. He also viewed Frazee's offer as an excellent financial opportunity, although this belief was likely colored by his desire to enter baseball ownership. In his campaign to raise capital, Barrow argued that the Boston franchise was baseball's most profitable after the Chicago White Sox and the New York Giants, and that the team's real-estate holdings, consisting mainly of Fenway Park, were increasing in value. By late December he had raised fifty thousand dollars and anticipated another twenty-five thousand from contacts in Toronto. He also received a commitment from his old employer and friend Larry Solman. Barrow next approached White Sox owner Charles Comiskey for a loan. In a surprisingly plaintive and supplicating letter, he asked Comiskey if he would personally (or jointly with Johnson) lend him twenty-five thousand dollars while taking a proportionate amount of his stock in the Red Sox as collateral. He even went so far as to write, "[I] never tried to be friendly with the National League crowd so naturally I turned to the league that I have always got along with, when I needed help."

Despite a desperate search to raise capital, Barrow could not come up with the requisite one hundred thousand dollars. Rumors of Frazee's interest in Barrow persisted, and it seems likely the two reached an agreement that Barrow would join the Red Sox, though in a still-to-be-determined capacity. Barrow was a longtime associate of Johnson's—some even referred to him as a protégé—and his joining the Red Sox without an ownership position may well have been part of an attempt at détente between Johnson and Frazee. According to one newspaper account, Johnson engineered Schang's acquisition by Boston as a quid pro quo for Frazee's hiring of Barrow.

This speculation is not all that far-fetched. Mack and Johnson were longtime allies, and it is highly unlikely that Mack would have arranged this sixty-thousand-dollar transaction—the largest dollar transaction ever up to that point—without Johnson's knowledge and involvement. Johnson hardly would have helped Frazee when both New York and Chicago reportedly would have been interested had they known of the players' availability. Chicago owner Charles Comiskey did not publicly criticize Mack but intimated that he should have had a shot at the three ballplayers. From Frazee's point of view, too, this supposition is reasonable. Barrow was a dozen years older than Frazee and had a lifetime of baseball experience. Despite his inability to raise the funds to purchase an ownership stake, he still fit Frazee's requirements perfectly.

While Barrow was trying to raise the capital to buy into the Red Sox, he acted as an unofficial advisor to Frazee. During this period, Boston made another significant trade: when first baseman Dick Hoblitzel appeared destined for military service, Frazee went back to Mack to pry loose slick-fielding first baseman Stuffy McInnis, Mack's final remaining starter from his 1914 American League championship club. For McInnis, however, Mack refused Frazee's offer of additional cash and received an option on three players from a list of seven. At the end of February, Mack completed the deal by making his three selections, which included Tilly Walker, who would tie Babe Ruth for the 1918 home run title, and third baseman Larry Gardner.

On February 11, 1918, Barrow's resignation as International League president became official, and the next day Frazee named him manager of the Red Sox. After his failure to raise an ownership stake, Barrow expressed surprise that Frazee offered him the manager's position.

"Say, Ed, I have just selected you as manager of the 1918 Red Sox. Want the job?" Frazee asked him.

"Well, Harry," Barrow replied, "I wanted that job ever since I knew Jack Barry couldn't return, but I was afraid that if I asked for it, you might say, 'Get out of this opera house.'"

Frazee retained control over the finances, but delegated to Barrow the modern general manger functions and control over players that most owners reserved for themselves. In fact, as Frazee concentrated on his theater interests, he delegated some ownership functions to Barrow and on occasion even empowered him to respond to ownership inquiries.

Barrow took over a talented team of veterans that had won back-to-back World Series championships in 1915 and 1916 and finished second to a great Chicago White Sox club in 1917. To bolster the squad for the upcoming 1918 season, the Red Sox had just made the two blockbuster off-

season trades noted earlier. Barrow now possessed a deep and talented rotation of Babe Ruth, Carl Mays, Dutch Leonard, and the recently acquired
Bush. The first three, however, were also managerial challenges: the childlike Ruth loved indulging in life's physical pleasures; Mays and Leonard
were dour and mean. Barrow also inherited Herb Pennock and Sam Jones,
two young pitchers yet to establish themselves, who under Barrow would
blossom into stars.

The position players were a little more unsettled. In catcher Schang and
first baseman McInnis, the Red Sox had landed two of the better players at
their respective positions. Unfortunately, surrendering Gardner to acquire
McInnis opened a hole at third base. Two other spots were also open after
the loss of solid veterans, second baseman (and 1917 manager) Jack Barry
and left fielder Duffy Lewis, to military service. Strunk adequately replaced
Walker in center field. The remaining two positions were manned by excellent holdovers: young, slick-fielding Everett Scott played shortstop; and
veteran future Hall of Famer Harry Hooper anchored right field.

Upon officially taking over the managerial duties, Barrow immediately
began recasting his team to address its weaknesses. With Gardner gone,
Barrow brought up Fred Thomas from Providence to help at third. He purchased thirty-five-year-old left fielder George Whiteman from Toronto to
partially compensate for losing Lewis. To offset the loss of Barry, Barrow
acquired forty-year-old second baseman Dave Shean from Cincinnati for
pitcher Rube Foster, whose career was effectively over. After these moves,
Barrow oversaw a team in which six of his eight projected regulars had not
been with the team in 1917: catcher Schang, first baseman McInnis, second
baseman Shean, third baseman Thomas, left fielder Whiteman, and center
fielder Strunk. Scott and Hooper were the only holdovers from 1917.

The off-season changes produced a solid squad in spite of the war-related losses (which included pitcher Herb Pennock along with those already noted). With so many new faces, one of Barrow's biggest challenges
for the season was integrating the new and the holdover players into a cohesive unit. According to one report, manager Connie Mack "did not have
a rosy path in handling" the four newcomers from Philadelphia, but Barrow managed them without any serious altercations. He proved surprisingly skilled at integrating his new players into the team. Unlike his in-
teractions with equals, Barrow could successfully impose his vision on a

group of subordinates, even if several were reputed to have prickly or challenging personalities.

Barrow had not run a team in seven years, and he was over thirteen years removed from his Major League seasons in Detroit. He hoped to hide some of his anxieties behind his natural bluster and the authority that develops from control of more than just the managerial reins. He also planned to rely on his veteran coaches: holdover Heinie Wagner, longtime second baseman Johnny Evers, and former Montreal manager Dan Howley. Barrow signed Evers, known as a smart but irritable player, to help with the on-field tactical part of the game. He brought in Howley to work with the pitchers. Barrow's structure did not come together as planned: he released Evers prior to the start of the season because of his prickly disposition, his agitated, hyperactive manner with the players, and disagreements over the handling of pitchers. Howley left as well, accepting the manager position in Toronto. Barrow's domineering personality was partly to blame for his inability to incorporate these veteran baseball men into his staff. With the season starting, Barrow desperately needed reinforcement in the coaching department.

To bolster his on-field coaches, Barrow turned to star right fielder Harry Hooper. The thirty-year-old Hooper debuted with Boston in 1909 and had been a member of the team's three World Championship teams in 1912, 1915, and 1916. A bright, Saint Mary's College (California)–educated player, Hooper had schooled himself on the nuances of American League players and tactics. To help the new manager, Hooper joined with coach Wagner and shortstop Scott to form what they called a "strategy board." Hooper generally sat next to Barrow on the bench when the Sox were at bat, assuming a role somewhat akin to a modern-day bench coach. Although the two never became particularly close, the relationship benefited both men. Hooper provided Barrow a knowledgeable baseball man to help him during the game, while Barrow allowed Hooper to exert his influence beyond that typically afforded a player.

Barrow's first exposure to Babe Ruth came when Ruth pitched for Baltimore in Barrow's International League. Upon his becoming Ruth's manager in 1918, a complex relationship began that would continually evolve until Ruth's death many years later. The twenty-three-year-old Ruth of 1918 was a trim, tremendous all-around athlete, nothing like the fat, spindly-legged caricature filmed in his final years. The Ruth of 1918 could behave as immaturely as ever, but he was developing a sophisticated awareness of his celebrity and its impact. Barrow was not particularly subtle or multifaceted in his dealings with players; he was typically blunt and aggressive. Nevertheless, he handled his rambunctious superstar as well as possible.

Ruth had an enormous appetite for all of life's corporeal pleasures, and Barrow became of aware of his love of food soon after taking over the club. Sometime before the team left for spring training, Barrow gave team secretary Larry Graver five dollars to take Ruth and McInnis to lunch. Two hours later Graver came back and told Barrow that he needed another $2.85. When Barrow, himself no stranger to a large meal, asked how this was possible, Graver replied that Ruth had eaten a whole custard pie for desert. The cook at a North Carolina hunting camp frequented by baseball people once remarked that Ruth had about "the biggest appetite of any man [he had] ever cooked for," then added, "not even excepting Mr. Ed Barrow."

At spring training in Hot Springs, Arkansas, Barrow worked his team into playing shape. Barrow and his coaches pushed the team hard in the morning, typically finishing the drills with a sprint around the park. To scrimmage, Barrow often played the regulars against the rookies. For more challenging opposition, Boston played several games against the Brooklyn Dodgers, who also trained in Arkansas.

Up to this point in his career, Ruth had been used strictly as a pitcher. But he liked hitting, and in spring training Barrow let him play the field in several games. Ruth further enjoyed himself that spring at the nearby racetrack and casinos.

As the season approached, Barrow recognized his team's lingering weakness at third base and left field and continued to tinker with his roster. When first baseman Hoblitzel briefly remained available while awaiting his officer assignment, Barrow experimented with McInnis, regarded as one of the league's top fielding first basemen, at third base. As for the rest of his starting infield, Shean filled in capably at second, and Everett Scott starred at short. The outfield consisted of the well-regarded Harry Hooper in right, recently acquired Strunk in center, and stopgap Whiteman in left. Schang was the team's best catcher, although he occasionally helped out in left field. Barrow also used fine defender (but overmatched with the bat) Sam Agnew behind the plate. On the mound he settled on a rotation of Babe Ruth, Carl Mays, Joe Bush, and Dutch Leonard.

A number of people selected the Red Sox to again finish second to the great White Sox. A *Sporting News* editorial doubted Barrow could lead his charges to such a high finish. "Under the circumstances the baseball prophets who pick the Red Sox to run second in such smart company and such experienced company as they are in are taking a long chance with Barrow. If their dope works out right and the Hub Hose do prove close contenders, then it will be nothing else than a splendid individual triumph for Ed Barrow—mark him indeed a real Napoleon of baseball."

Barrow opened the season with an outstanding, well-defined pitching rotation. Through the first twenty-eight games, the starting pitchers lined up as Ruth, Mays, Leonard, and Bush, with each receiving seven starts in that same sequence. At this point Barrow's team stood 18-10, two and a half games in front of the second-place Indians. Despite sitting atop the American League, Barrow removed Ruth from the rotation and repositioned him as a first baseman/outfielder.

After three full years in the Majors, Ruth, despite being limited to pitching duties, had sufficiently demonstrated his hitting talent. Ruth was an exceptional pitcher: in 1916 he completed the season 23-12 while leading the league with a 1.75 ERA; the next year he finished second in the league in wins with a 24-13 record and seventh in ERA at 2.01. Despite these impressive statistics, Harry Hooper believed that Ruth's prodigious hitting would make him more valuable as a regular in the field. Although Barrow often deferred to Hooper in matters of in-game tactics, he naturally felt such a decision was for the manager to make. Early in the season Hooper encouraged Barrow to put Ruth in the outfield, but Barrow was predictably apprehensive about doing so with one of the league's best pitchers.

On May 6, with Hoblitzel nursing an injured finger, Barrow succumbed to Hooper's pleas and started Ruth at first base, his first nonpitching appearance in the field after more than three years in the Majors. Ruth made Barrow and Hooper look like geniuses, going two for four with a home run. Over the next several weeks Barrow often used Ruth in the field when he was not pitching, mostly in left field after Hoblitzel returned. Barrow rode his star hard, pushing him into this double duty, but Ruth continued to pound the ball. On May 15 he was leading the league with a .476 (20 for 42) batting average. In an era when striking out was considered a major drawback, Barrow could see past that particular problem with Ruth: "If a batter doesn't hit safely it usually makes no difference whether he strikes out or pops up a fly. At least when he strikes out he doesn't hit into a double play."

Barrow has rightfully received widespread credit for converting Ruth to the field. While Hooper deserves recognition for realizing Ruth's potential as a regular and pushing for it, Barrow warrants the bulk of the acclaim. When a decision has a clearly identifiable decision maker who has both the authority and the responsibility to make it, that person deserves most of the credit for a successful outcome and the blame for an unsuccessful one. Obviously the specific circumstances surrounding any particular decision affect how one evaluates the decision maker—given Barrow's reluctance to make the move and Hooper's persistence, Hooper merits more than the usual share of the credit—but it does not change the fundamental basis for apportioning credit or blame. Had the second-best pitcher in baseball (to Walter Johnson) underperformed in his new role and then returned to the mound at anything but his previous ability, it would have been Barrow who suffered the condemnation and abuse from the fans, the press, and, perhaps most importantly, his players.

Ruth's heavy workload soon began to take its toll, and he did not help matters with his regular enjoyment of the nightlife. When Ruth came down with a severe cold and sore throat in mid-May, Barrow became concerned and rested him a game. Ruth was next scheduled to pitch the twenty-ninth game of the season on May 20, but his temperature soared. Incompetent treatment by the team's trainer landed Ruth in the hospital for a week. After Ruth returned, he told his manager that he would no longer pitch, that performing both duties was simply too exhausting. The hard-charging Barrow had little sympathy and had to force the stubborn, unenthusiastic Ruth to the mound for a start on June 2. This confrontation abated only because Barrow had begun using Sam Jones during Ruth's illness. The young pitcher responded beautifully, surrendering only one run in his first three starts. As long as a solid four-man rotation held up, Barrow acquiesced to Ruth's request to stay off the mound.

In the field Barrow played Ruth mostly in left. Hoblitzel started the season in a horrible slump and was soon commissioned into the army dental corps. Barrow wisely moved McInnis back to his natural position of first base and played Fred Thomas at third. Barrow also occasionally experimented with Ruth in center when resting Strunk. Unfortunately, Thomas would miss much of the season, first with an injury and later with diabetes complications. His draft board initially rejected him, telling him to rest away from baseball for a while.

Without Thomas, the level of play at the hot corner deteriorated dramatically. Barrow tried several Minor Leaguers. Everett Scott remembers playing against the Tigers with Ty Cobb, one of baseball's great base runners, on second. Cobb turned to Scott to ask him about the new third baseman.

"He's a marvel, the best infielder I ever saw tag a base runner," Scott responded. "If you're hitting out for third, Ty, you'd better watch yourself. He'll cut you down if you come in too rough."

"Oh, yeah?" came the retort. "Well I'm going on the next pitch and we'll see."

As Scott remembered, Schang threw the ball to third in time for the out, but Cobb slid under the tag, which missed by about two feet. The third baseman believed he had made the tag and blamed the umpire. When he came to the bench, he continued complaining to Barrow.

"Whattya know about that decision," he grumbled. "Why, I had Ty by five feet."

"Wally did, but you didn't," Barrow teased. "You haven't tagged Ty yet."

In 1918 baseball felt the impact of America's massive, if belated, mobilization for World War I. Although not quite to the same degree as in the final years of World War II, the war disrupted all aspects of American life, including baseball. The creation of the vast American Expeditionary Force demanded many of the country's young men, and those not required for the armed forces were needed in the factories producing war materials. Naturally, the country looked to America's healthy, fit, young ballplayers as a ready source of manpower. As one of the few baseball executives in an executive position during the last wartime season in 1898, Barrow foresaw the impending disruption better than most.

The April 1917 war declaration only modestly impinged on baseball for that season. Conscription was introduced in July, although few Major League ballplayers were selected. The situation became much more complicated in 1918. A number of players had enlisted in the armed services, but not enough to significantly disrupt the start of the 1918 season. In late May, however, U.S. Provost Marshall Enoch Crowder issued a "work or fight" order. This edict required all military-age men (defined as ages twenty-one to thirty-one) to either enlist, find employment in an "essential" industry, or become subject to immediate conscription.

Baseball appealed the decree's application to the national pastime, using Washington catcher Eddie Ainsmith as the test case. On July 20 Secretary of War Newton Baker ruled against Ainsmith and baseball, affirming that baseball players were subject to the work or fight order. Altogether the ruling affected some 237 players in the Major Leagues, all but between two and seven players for each of the American League ball clubs. Not surprisingly, what had formerly been a trickle of players out of the game became a flood, throwing baseball into chaos. Many took jobs with the large defense contractors, most of which sponsored baseball teams in highly competitive leagues. Players who opted for war-related work (as opposed to the armed services) were often pilloried by the press.

Although Baker did not require that baseball cease operations, a number of baseball executives panicked and declared an immediate end to the season. The American Association canceled the remainder of its season. More damaging to Barrow, Johnson ordered the American League season canceled. National League president John Tener and National Commission chairman Garry Herrmann felt likewise but did not assume the same unilateral authority. They offered no public ruling without first consulting their league's owners. Johnson's hasty proclamation terminating the season prompted the first real questioning of his authority and judgment by the league's owners. Except for the sycophantic James Dunn in Cleveland, no other owners wanted to take this drastic step. The owners simply ignored Johnson and played the scheduled games over the next few days. With Frazee unavailable, Barrow spoke for his team, angrily denouncing Johnson's proclamation: "The Boston American League club does not propose to abide by that arbitrary ruling." The fired-up manager confided that in his view the National Commission—whose dominant member was Johnson—had poorly represented baseball with the federal authorities.

National League owners also had no desire to stop playing and kept to their schedule. Once Johnson realized the owners were ignoring him, he backtracked, advising White Sox owner Charles Comiskey to keep playing until notified to stop. Even though the season was continuing, the magnates still had no overall strategy on how to conclude the schedule. Frazee proposed a one-hundred-game season (eighty-six games had been played at that point) followed by the World Series.

Frustrated with Johnson's leadership, a large delegation of owners traveled to Washington for another appeal to Crowder and Baker to exempt the players until October 15. Baker compromised, extending the deadline to September 1. Johnson now wanted to end the season August 20 to allow time to play a World Series before September 1. Herrmann favored playing the season through September 1 and hoping for an extension for the World Series players.

Many National League owners were willing to scrap the Series; they reasoned that the team rosters would be so unrecognizable that a World Series would be meaningless and garner little public interest. Johnson, chastened from his earlier embarrassment at having been ignored by his owners, polled them before issuing any more edicts. He still could not resist grandstanding a bit, declaring: "I will not be party to a baseball game played after September 1. I think the owners of the American League will unanimously agree with my views after the situation is thoroughly discussed."

On August 2 the National League met and decided to play the season through Labor Day, September 2, with the World Series to follow, provided an agreement could be reached with the American League. The group deputized Pittsburgh Pirates owner Barney Dreyfuss to work out an arrangement with the American League and agreed to abide by whatever he negotiated. Johnson, Frazee, and the rest of the American League owners met the following day in Cleveland to hash out their schedule. Johnson vehemently advocated ending the regular season August 20, with the World Series to follow. Frazee, joined by Comiskey, Washington's owner, Clark Griffith, and the Yankees, strongly favored the National League plan; more games meant more revenue, a crucial consideration in this money-losing season. Frazee and his allies prevailed, and the American League concurred with the National League's plan. Johnson, never one to lose gracefully, issued the following statement: "If the clubs wish to take a chance on acting contrary to the ruling of the War Department, that is their business."

Frazee responded with his own statement, purportedly signed by Comiskey and Griffith as well.

The declaration by President Johnson that we were taking a chance on continuing the season, inferring we were defying the War Department, is an unwarranted misstatement of the facts. We have no wish to antagonize the War Department, for which we have every respect.

We defy any person, however, to show us where Secretary Baker has said he was opposed to baseball. To the contrary, in every statement he has made he has said he hoped that baseball would be able to continue regardless of the enforcement of the work or fight order.

If any members of the two teams which will take part in the World Series are cited to go to work they will obey the order forthwith, but we trust we will have enough players left to continue the Series to its completion on or about September 12. We certainly do not expect to meet with the displeasure of either Secretary Baker or General Crowder.

Just why President Johnson should take the stand he did in this matter is beyond our comprehension. We believe he always has acted honestly and in a desire to act for the interests of the American League, but he has bungled the affairs of his league in this particular case.

From now on the club owners are going to run the American League.

We criticize Mr. Johnson merely as an official. We have nothing against him personally, but from now on we intend to take a hand in the management of the league. His rule or ruin policy is shelved.

Several days later Comiskey and Griffith repudiated the statement. Neither wanted an open break with the league president. Comiskey claimed he had never seen it, and Griffith said it had been issued without his authority. Both denied ever signing it. Some dispute existed over whether the document contained the purported signatures of Comiskey and Griffith. Frazee later professed that no signed statement had ever been released, but he never backed off his endorsement of its contents.

The final resolution was the perfect solution from the owners' vantage point: it extended season revenues as far as possible, while placing the burden of adhering to the work or fight order squarely on the players. The players would be forced to choose between playing in the World Series and subjecting themselves to the draft, or leaving their teammates on the brink of the World Series. The owners advised the players to either petition their draft boards for a ten-day extension or secure defense employment but receive dispensation from their new employer allowing them to report seven to ten days late. Not surprisingly, neither of these suggestions reassured the players. With player dissatisfaction mounting, the magnates again petitioned Secretary Baker, this time to extend the deadline for World Series players. At the end of August, Baker granted this exemption, relieving the anxiety of the players involved.

To save paying their last month's salary, the owners released their players as of September 1, technically making them all free agents. The owners further agreed not to sign one another's players, a discreditable gentlemen's agreement that the magnates honored.

In early June the top American League teams remained bunched close together. On June 2, after Barrow cajoled Ruth back to the mound, the Red Sox led by one game over New York, but three other teams were within four games. The favored White Sox were four games back but quickly slipped out of the race; no team was more disadvantaged by war losses. On a relative basis the Red Sox suffered fewer significant losses to the war than most other teams. Nevertheless, in late June Barrow was forced to deal with a critical loss when star lefty Dutch Leonard took a job at the Fore River shipbuilding plant near Boston. Frazee, Barrow, the press, and the fans all grew resentful when they realized Leonard was pitching nearby for the company team and not for the Sox. The press typically criticized players who chose war work over the military. The added irritation of his pitching nearby elicited a press attack so bitter that Leonard announced he might enlist just to quiet the condemnation.

Leonard left the team in the midst of a tightening pennant race. On June 29 Boston was in a three-way tie for first with Cleveland and New York. Leonard's absence meant that Barrow needed another hurler, in particular a left-hander. Fortunately, in Babe Ruth he had one of the best in the game playing in his outfield. Unfortunately, Ruth had no desire to return to the mound and challenged Barrow's order to pitch. He pushed the angry Barrow to the limit by constantly dodging Barrow's requests, often complaining of a sore wrist, which he had aggravated again in Philadelphia. Barrow

was under tremendous pressure because the pennant race was tight and minor injuries on the club were taking a toll. With the Red Sox tied with New
York and one game ahead of Cleveland, the situation came to a boil on July
2 in Washington. Barrow wanted Ruth to take a few pitches during his at
bat in the sixth inning, but the slugger ignored his skipper and swung away.
At this point almost anything Ruth did would have set Barrow off, so it is
not surprising that Barrow lit into him and fined him five hundred dollars
on the spot. Ruth, never one to take criticism lightly, claimed he was quit-
ting the Red Sox, dressed, and went home to Baltimore.

Barrow knew Ruth well and assumed his hot-headed young star would
be back the next day. So it came as an embarrassing shock the following
day when, while sitting with Frazee, he was told by reporters that Ruth had
enrolled with the Chester Shipyards Company and was playing for their
baseball team. Frazee recognized the impact of losing his drawing card
and took the offensive against Ruth and the company, threatening to sue
the shipyard for damages and loudly demanding Ruth's return. The club
sent coach Wagner down to Baltimore to talk Ruth into returning. Ruth
had never really wanted to quit the Red Sox in the first place, so the vehemence of Frazee's statement and the soothing words of his old coach convinced him to return. Barrow was still smarting after Ruth had embarrassed him in front of the press and his boss—he had obviously been caught
off guard by the news of Ruth's apparent walkout. Upon his return, Barrow gave Ruth the silent treatment and kept him out of the lineup for his
first game back (the first of a doubleheader). The dismayed Ruth, who expected an enthusiastic welcome upon his return, again threatened to quit.
Ruth's teammates, who naturally resented his leaving in the middle of a
pennant race, talked him into staying, and Barrow started Ruth in center
field in the second game.

On July 5 Barrow finally hauled Ruth to the mound—his first pitching
start since June 2—and the young lefty led the team to a 4–3 victory in ten
innings, moving Boston back into a three-way tie for first. Having imposed
his will on his young phenom, Barrow conceded the demands of pitching
and playing the field. He did not pitch Ruth again until the seventeenth in
the second game of a doubleheader. While quarreling with Ruth over his
refusal to pitch, Barrow had been using Lore Bader as his fourth starter.
Barrow never felt confident in this erratic thirty-year-old hurler, and for the

last half of July, scraped by with a three man rotation. The short rotation pitched well, and by July 28 the Red Sox had forged a four-and-a-half-game lead. Nevertheless, Barrow feared overworking his starters; on July 29, with Ruth's acquiescence, Barrow moved his star back into the rotation

By grudgingly acknowledging the strenuousness of pitching and playing the field, Barrow earned a measure of deference from Ruth. After the Babe's return, he actually accepted batting tips from Barrow. At one point Barrow proposed that Ruth step back with his left foot and turn toward left field to hit the ball that way. Teams had been overplaying Ruth to pull, and in a subsequent series against the White Sox, Barrow's advice paid off against the overshift.

Ruth demonstrated he still had a sense of humor as well. One morning in mid-July he walked by the hotel where Carl Mays and several other ballplayers were staying, carrying a suitcase.

"Where are you going, Babe?" Mays shouted.

"Baltimore," Ruth replied and hurried along.

Mays then quickly called Barrow to forestall another flight by Ruth. Barrow doubted that Ruth was leaving, and as expected Ruth showed up at the ballpark on time.

As he had during his tenure in Detroit, Barrow could not find a satisfactory third baseman and obsessed over it. In early July, he dipped into the defunct Southern Association and acquired two more third base hopefuls, Walter Barbare and Jack Stansbury. Both ended up playing just a few games at the hot corner, and neither did anything to distinguish himself as a player of Major League caliber. At one point Barrow became so desperate that he played coach Heinie Wagner for a game at third.

On August 2, when the American League met to discuss the schedule, the Red Sox stood at 60-38 and enjoyed a four-and-a-half-game lead over second-place Cleveland. When the Indians came to Boston for a three-game series on August 16, the lead had been cut to two games. Ruth pitched the first game and won in front of 15,129 fans, the largest crowd of the season. The Red Sox won one of the two remaining games and were on their way to the pennant. In mid-August Boston fans received a scare when news reports suggested Ruth, Strunk, and Agnew had received notices from their draft boards to find essential war work by September 1. Frazee later disclaimed these reports, and, in any case, Baker's ruling granted a reprieve.

When the season officially closed, Boston stood at 75-51, two and a half games ahead of Cleveland. Barrow's pitchers and fielders had allowed just over three runs per game, the best mark in the league. Mays, Bush, Jones, and Ruth all recorded ERAs of 2.25 or below. Ruth also paced the batters; he led the league in slugging percentage and tied for the league lead in home runs. Hooper chipped in with one of his better seasons. The team finished third in runs per game on offense mostly on the strength of these two corner outfielders. Dave Shean and Fred Thomas played better than might have been expected, but Everett Scott turned in one of his worst seasons. For the upcoming World Series against the Chicago Cubs, Barrow would have his full complement of regulars available.

With the World Series on deck, Frazee managed to get into yet another spat with Johnson. When he received the Series schedule from Johnson, with the first three games scheduled for Chicago and the necessary remainder in Boston, Frazee again disparaged the league president's leadership. Frazee intimated he might not participate in the Series unless the schedule was revamped. Barrow and the players, of course, were eager to play anywhere. This time Frazee acted rashly; the schedule had been determined by the National Commission based on an agreement between the leagues, and Herrmann defended the arrangement.

> *Had Mr. Frazee waited until he had received his official bulletin with respect to the matter, possibly nothing would have been said by him. The schedule as arranged was made by the National Commission as an entirety and not by Mr. Johnson.*
>
> *The first thought we had in mind was to conserve transportation and for that reason it was agreed that whatever league won the toss that the first three games would be played in the city of such league and the other four games, if it was necessary to play that many, in the city of the opposite league.*

Johnson could not resist getting in his own dig at Frazee: "I do not believe Frazee understood the facts or he would have raised no protest, for I do not think even he is such a poor sportsman as to want to welch on a straight out and out proposition like that." In the midst of this latest controversy, Frazee may have been temporarily distracted by the opening of a new show in Pittsburgh.

Barrow felt optimistic heading into his first World Series, which was scheduled to start on September 4. After a season of nagging injuries, he now had a relatively healthy squad. Thomas, who had eventually joined the navy but received a furlough for the Series, was back at third. One purported weakness was a susceptibility to left-handed pitching. Barrow's top three sluggers, Ruth, Hooper, and Strunk, all hit from the left side, and the Chicago Cubs' top two starters, Hippo Vaughn and Lefty Tyler, both hurled that way. Barrow played coy over his Game 1 starting pitcher, hinting it could be either Ruth or Bush. He gave no further indications after the first game was postponed by rain.

The next day, to throw Chicago off track, he had the right-hander Bush warming up before the first game, but when the game began, he sent Ruth to the mound. The strategy paid off: Boston won 1–0 in a game pitched equally well by Vaughn. Barrow assessed the game: "Ruth and Vaughn each gave a great exhibition of pitching, but Ruth was better in the crucial spots. He was in three dangerous places and got out. Vaughn was in three rather tight places and once he failed to get out. The players on both sides were sure and accurate in the field."

Before the game, while going over the Cubs' batting order for Ruth, Barrow told Ruth to be careful with right-handed slugger Les Mann: "This fellow is apt to get a hold of one any old time, so if you're in a jam and he comes up, put one kinda close to him so he won't crowd you." Ruth seemingly acknowledged the warning and took the mound.

In the fifth inning with two out and the bases empty, Max Flack, a left-handed batter who had struck out in the first and then singled in the third, came to the plate. Ruth hit him with the pitch. After inducing the third out and returning to the bench, he grabbed a seat next to Barrow and told him, "Well, we fixed that Mann, didn't we?"

Barrow sent Bush to the mound in the second game against Tyler. With a lefty on the mound, Barrow started Whiteman in left field, relegating Ruth to the bench. Again the Cubs pitcher threw a stellar game, and this time Tyler beat Boston 3–1. Barrow offered his thoughts on this second game that tied the Series 1–1: "Today's game was a tough one to lose, especially as we nearly broke it up in the ninth inning. The Cubs had the better of the breaks, I think, and piled up a lead in the second inning too great for us to overcome. I do not mean to take credit away from Tyler, who pitched great ball and deserved to win. I expect to start Mays tomorrow and hope to make it two and one."

Despite the presence of twenty-game winner Claude Hendrix, Chicago Cubs manager Fred Mitchell wanted to stay with the lefties to neutralize Boston's left-handed hitters, most obviously Ruth. He shocked Barrow by coming back with Vaughn on one day's rest. Barrow sent Mays to the mound, and in another pitching duel, the Red Sox eked out a 2–1 victory. The Sox scored both runs in the fourth inning after Whiteman was hit with a pitch, and the team followed with four consecutive singles.

After the game, at 8:00 p.m. on September 7, both teams boarded a special train scheduled to arrive in Boston at 10:50 p.m. the following evening. During the long train ride the players had an opportunity to mingle and discuss the state of the Series. It turned out that Frazee had promised to pay several Red Sox players through September 15. When the rest of the team discovered this, they wanted the same. The Cubs players, too, learned of the extra two weeks' pay and confronted owner Charles Weeghman, who acquiesced to their demand.

The players were also angry about the reduced World Series shares they would receive. At the previous year's winter meetings, the owners had decided to allocate a portion of the players' World Series shares to players on the other first division teams (second through fourth place). The owners had estimated that if receipts from the first four games (which the players shared in) totaled $150,000, the winners would each receive $2,000 and the losers $1,400—still well below recent World Series shares. Based on attendance at the first three games, it was clear that receipts from the first four games would fall well short of $150,000. The players organized a delegation led by Boston's Harry Hooper and Chicago's Les Mann to discuss their concerns with the National Commission. The player delegation wanted to meet before Game 4 but was put off by the commissioners, who hoped the controversy would just go away.

For Game 4 Barrow sent Ruth back to the mound, while Mitchell countered with Tyler. With Boston ahead 2–0 in the eighth inning, Chicago tied the game on a walk and two singles (also ending Ruth's twenty-nine-inning scoreless streak, a World Series record that stood until 1961). Boston regained the lead by scoring one run in the bottom of the inning. In the ninth, Chicago put their first two men on, at which point Barrow pulled

Ruth (moving him to left field) and brought in Bush. When the next batter bunted, McInnis threw out the lead runner at third. Bush ended the game by inducing a 6-4-3 double play, and Boston now had a 3–1 Series edge.

The next morning, on September 10, the commission reluctantly granted Hooper and Mann an audience at their hotel. After the two players presented their case, Johnson responded: "Well, it's too late now. It's all been decided. Nothing you can do about it. You'll have to go out and play." The disappointed and frustrated players returned to the ballpark to join their respective clubs. After being informed of the upshot of the meeting, the players on both teams agreed they would not play, stating they would just as soon give their shares to charity and cancel the Series. The players refused to start the game until they had a follow-up meeting with the National Commission.

When the commissioners arrived at Fenway Park and realized the players were not coming out to play, they hastily called a meeting in the umpires' dressing room. A confused assemblage jammed into the tiny quarters. The participants and onlookers included Hooper and Mann; American League president Johnson, Commission chairman Herrmann, and acting National League president John Heydler (Tener had resigned earlier in the season); Barrow; Boston's mayor; assorted reporters; and curious fans. In front of this hodgepodge, Hooper again argued that the players should receive the $2,000 and $1,400 shares estimated earlier, and that the new formula including the nonparticipant teams should be shelved until after the war.

Herrmann and Johnson had both arrived well oiled after a morning of imbibing with friends at the hotel. Herrmann began by recounting the National Commission's glorious history. The sloppy, teary Johnson interrupted Herrmann, threw his arm around Hooper, made a rambling appeal to the players' patriotism, and then told them to get out on the field. Hooper and Mann eventually realized there was little opportunity for compromise with the commission in its incapacitated state. The disgusted Hooper returned to the Red Sox clubhouse and discussed the bleak situation with his teammates. The players unhappily concluded that they had little option but to back down. Before capitulating, however, Hooper went back to the umpires' dressing room and asked for a promise of no retaliation against the players. Johnson replied, "Everything will be all right." When Herrmann tried to get into the act by shaking Hooper's hand and making his own speech, Barrow barged in, saying: "We've wasted enough time. To the field everybody."

Barrow had long ago identified himself with management. While sympathetic to the merits of the case, he detested organized player actions.

During the strike negotiations, Barrow also had to ready his team for the game. Mitchell gave Vaughn his third start, while Barrow countered with Sam Jones. The Red Sox managed only five hits and were shut out 3–0, and the Cubs cut the Series margin to three games to two. Despite three starts in six days, Vaughn had given up only three runs over his twenty-seven innings pitched.

Mitchell, determined to counter Barrow's sluggers with left-handed pitchers, started Tyler on only one day's rest in Game 6. Barrow elected to skip Bush and award Mays his second start of the Series. Although he had relieved for one inning two days earlier, according to Barrow, "[Bush] was sore because I wouldn't let him pitch that game. I wanted to make sure so I pitched Carl Mays. So Bush refused to sit for his picture [the after-game photo of the World Champions] and I had to go in and haul him out of the clubhouse." In this final game Tyler dominated the Red Sox, but Flack dropped a fly ball in the third, allowing two runners to score. Mays and the Red Sox held on to win another close game, 2–1, and capture the World Series title. The Red Sox scored only six earned runs (nine overall) during the six-game Series, but great pitching, timely hitting, and stellar fielding provided the edge for Barrow's club. The magnates left a final sour taste with the Red Sox players by breaching Johnson's assurance of no retaliation. They withheld the World Series emblems, the equivalent of today's World Series rings.

In the end 1918 proved extremely satisfying for Barrow. Essentially fired from a position he had held for many years, he had accepted a job many claimed he was unsuited for after so many years away from the field. He had successfully assimilated a host of new players and dealt with numerous distractions. The Red Sox did not lose as many key contributors to the war effort as the 1917 pennant-winning White Sox, but Barrow still had to overcome significant losses. Barrow had successfully molded the functions of his managerial position to best suit his strengths. He had accepted overall direction of the team on the field while relying on Hooper and Wagner to refresh him on in-game tactics. At the same time, he had assumed many of a general manager's duties for an owner distracted by another career and an ongoing feud with the league president.

Harry Frazee and Hugh Ward had purchased the Red Sox along with Fenway Park in November 1916 for a total capital obligation of $1 million. The duo paid $662,000 for the club itself: $300,000 in cash to Joe Lannin; an additional $100,000 in cash, which Lannin still owed to parties from whom he had purchased the club; and a note for $262,000. The purchase was also subject to $150,000 of outstanding preferred stock. Finally, Frazee assumed a mortgage of roughly $188,000 as part of the Fenway Park acquisition. The stadium was technically owned through an entity called Fenway Realty Trust; the stock of this company (i.e., Frazee's ownership of Fenway Park) was pledged as security for the $262,000 note. The team was obligated to pay $30,000 per year to the Fenway Realty Trust under an existing lease. With his purchase, Frazee now controlled both entities, but the lease technically remained in effect.

Unfortunately for Frazee, profits from the club declined sharply after 1916 due to a sharp drop in attendance. The total gate decreased from 496,397 in 1916, to 387,856 in 1917, and 249,513 in the war-shortened 1918 season. Furthermore, although some recent scholarship contends that Frazee's theatrical shows were generally successful at this time, most sources maintain that his productions were likely a drain on his financial resources. In any case, he was clearly going to have difficulty servicing the three notes (including the preferred stock) given the reduced income from his ball club. Barrow's ability to sustain his championship team was materially curtailed by Frazee's emergent financial difficulties.

The Red Sox were further hindered by Frazee's ugly feud with American League president Ban Johnson. Johnson hated Frazee. For many years Johnson had ruled the American League with dictatorial authority, earned through his successes at the birth of the league and long-term bonds forged with the league's early owners. Newcomer Frazee felt little allegiance to Johnson and showed none of the deference Johnson had come to expect. The two strong-willed men had disliked each other from the start, and Johnson seized on the gambling problem in Fenway Park in 1917 as a pretext (with some legitimacy) to condemn Frazee. Frazee's outspoken criticism of Johnson's mismanagement of the 1918 season only made matters worse. With the season over, Johnson began actively campaigning to oust Frazee from ownership of the Red Sox and was enthusiastically searching for a buyer.

Never one to shrink from a battle, Frazee retaliated by attempting to curb Johnson's authority. With New York Giants owner Harry Hempstead, Frazee approached former U.S. president William Howard Taft about becoming a "one-man National Baseball Commission," an administrator who would oversee all of baseball. The idea was premature and accomplished little except to further infuriate Johnson. The baseball magnates would not conclude they needed a single commissioner until a couple of years later. Johnson never succeeded in forcing Frazee from the game, but for several years he acted both subtly and openly against Frazee's—and hence Barrow's—interests.

The off-season began with Barrow and Frazee contemplating sharing Braves Field. The value of the Fenway Park site had been increasing, and Frazee wanted to capture this value by selling the park for its redevelopment possibilities. In late October Frazee journeyed to Boston from New York. He and Barrow toured Braves Field with James Gaffney, the former owner of the Braves who still owned the stadium. No move ever materialized, but finding additional capital sources had taken on new urgency. Frazee was not the only owner concerned with baseball's economic outlook. After the financially disastrous 1918 season, the league's magnates became cautious, reducing the schedule to only 140 games and roster sizes from twenty-five to twenty-one.

In mid-December after a final conference between Barrow and Frazee, the Red Sox consummated a blockbuster trade with the Yankees. Boston received Ray Caldwell, a decent right-handed pitcher with a drinking problem, three journeymen, and twenty-five thousand dollars. In return the Sox surrendered three once-celebrated players: left-hander Dutch Leonard, right-hander Ernie Shore (who would never produce for the Yankees), and left field mainstay Duffy Lewis. The Yankees naturally felt they had received the better end of this transaction, going so far as to "predict that this [would] prove the best trade made by the New York Club since the American League invaded New York." The trade turned out to be much less significant than envisaged at the time. None of the players involved remained effective Major Leaguers much longer. (When Leonard failed to report, the Red Sox refunded ten thousand dollars, and he was later sent to Detroit.)

From Boston's perspective one can see the merits of the Yankees deal. With players returning to baseball after a year away, the Red Sox seemed to be in the enviable position of being overburdened with capable ballplayers. Even after this trade, the *New York Times* opined, "The Red Sox, as it stands today, is the greatest collection of baseball talent in either league." The trade allowed Frazee to unload a few excess players (and, not unimportantly, their large salaries) plus receive some welcome cash.

Barrow traveled south with generally the same lineup as had played most of the 1918 season, plus he had filled the third base void by acquiring Ossie Vitt from Detroit. The pitching staff also looked strong and deep. In Sam Jones, Joe Bush, and Carl Mays, Boston had three excellent veteran hurlers still in their midtwenties. The staff looked to be further bolstered by the acquisition of Ray Caldwell and the spot duty of Ruth. In discussing the upcoming season, Barrow remarked: "Baseball is about to enter its greatest year. The Red Sox will be stronger than last summer, when we won the pennant. With the White Sox back in harness [their stars were back from the armed forces and the essential industries], the race will be a corker. It'll be a big year."

Despite a generally optimistic outlook on the season, Barrow faced two potential difficulties that spring. Jack Barry, manager and second baseman of the ninety-win 1917 team, had now returned to the team after his stint in the navy. Concern naturally existed about how Barry would accept Barrow's authority and leadership in the clubhouse. A salary dispute with Ruth caused Barrow further agitation. Ruth was well on his way to developing into the larger-than-life personality for which he would become legendary and was looking for a salary commensurate with his ability. Even with Ruth's phenomenal 1918 season—he led the league in slugging and home runs with the bat and went 13-7 in 166 innings on the mound—Barrow remained coy (and possibly uncertain) about how he planned to use Ruth in 1919:

> *Chances are that Babe Ruth, if he plays with the Red Sox this season, will pitch and act as a pinch-hitter. One thing I am convinced*

of, Ruth will play only one position. He will not be switched from
first to left field, and then back to the box. He will not be worked
that way again. I hope there never is any occasion to call upon him
for so much and varied work as was the case last season. Right now
it appears as if we need him in the box. He is our best left-hander,
and one of the best in the business. The American League's most
dangerous batters are left-handers. Then it is a good idea to have
him there in the box.

If we find that our outfield situation is bad and our pitching de-
partment strong, it will be Ruth for left field. But at this stage of the
game it does not seem that we will have such a strong pitching de-
partment or such strength in left-handed pitching that we can afford
to play Ruth anywhere but in the box and as a pinch-hitter.

The team will be stronger offensively than last season. I expect
both [Del] Gainer and [Frank] Gilhooley to come through in the
outfield [neither ever did]. We have until April 1 to hear definitely
from owner [James] Dunn of Cleveland about outfielder Bobby
Roth. If we get a good outfielder there is no chance at all of Ruth
playing anywhere but in the box.

It is unlikely, however, that Barrow actually anticipated using Ruth anywhere but in left field. He had just traded Lewis, his best left fielder, and
both Del Gainer and Frank Gilhooley had played for several years without
ever accomplishing much. And as noted, the Red Sox staff of starting pitchers was surely the team's strength. Furthermore, Barrow did not acquire any
additional outfield help before the start of the season.

For 1919, at the suggestion of New York Giants manager John McGraw,
the Red Sox moved their spring training to Tampa and lined up a number
of exhibition games with the Giants, who trained farther north in Gaines-
ville. For the journey to Tampa, the Red Sox arranged to travel by the SS
Arapahoe, without holdouts Ruth, Mays, and Bush. The steamship started
in Boston with several players and secretary/business manager Larry Graver;
along the way it stopped in New York to pick up Barrow and additional players. Barrow sailed with his players to Jacksonville, at which point the team
disembarked and traveled by train to Tampa. Not all players enjoyed their
time on the water. Sam Jones complained: "If I can put as much on the ball

this season as I put on the briny all the way down here I ought to go unde-feated." Players who did not live on the eastern seaboard made their own arrangements to get to training camp.

Not long after camp opened, Babe Ruth signed a three-year contract at ten thousand dollars per year, eliminating one of Barrow's worries, yet add-ing another. The irrepressible Ruth began infuriating Barrow with his be-havior almost immediately and started his high living as soon as he reported to camp. "Gee, a guy can have a heck of a time in this town," Ruth soon re-alized. He also quickly made his presence felt on the field. For the first ex-hibition game against the Giants in Tampa, playing in left field, Ruth hit a massive home run. Barrow claimed it was 579 feet; Boston writers Mel Webb and Paul Shannon measured it at 605 feet.

Ruth's mammoth shot was one of the longest anyone at the time had ever seen and probably one of the longest ever. The actual distances reported, however, are certainly apocryphal. Physicist Robert Adair addresses home run distances at some length in his book *The Physics of Baseball*. He notes that of approximately two thousand home-team home runs (measured for about two-thirds of the teams) in 1988 and 1989, only two went further than 460 feet (one traveled 478 and the other 473). He specifically evaluated a Mickey Mantle blast in Washington that reportedly went 565 feet and is sometimes credited as the longest ever. Adair calculates that this shot actually traveled between 500 and 510 feet. He concludes by writing: "If someone tells me that a ball was hit 550 feet anywhere in the Majors but Denver, I won't be-lieve it—but I won't bet the farm against it." Adair also claims "450 feet is about the maximum that ballplayers can hit the ball under standard con-ditions." And spring in Tampa does not offer many of the home run length boosters that Adair mentions, such as high altitude, high temperatures, or low humidity. Finally, Ruth was hitting a 1919-vintage baseball, which, even if one doubts a livelier ball was introduced in 1920, was typically softened, darkened, and despoiled through repeated use and pitcher actions. Others have also recently begun to scientifically evaluate home run distances and have come to conclusions similar to Adair's. In sum, Ruth's home run may have equaled or surpassed Mantle's clout, but it is extremely unlikely that it traveled close to the 579 feet Barrow estimated.

At the close of spring training, teams typically traveled back north with another team with whom they played exhibitions along the way. The Red

Sox journeyed north with the Giants and played about ten exhibition games in various southern cities. In Spartanburg, South Carolina, Barrow was surprised when the police chief approached him on the bench to tell him one of his players was in jail. The chief advised Barrow to get someone down there quickly to post bail if he wanted to take the player with him when they left town. Barrow checked, but all his players were accounted for. At the police chief's insistence, Barrow decided he needed to investigate further. In fact, the police had arrested team secretary Larry Graver for pushing a Spartanburg physician who had failed to pay a ten-cent fee at the press gate. When the doctor pressed charges, Graver found himself in police custody. Eventually released on one hundred dollars bail, Graver never returned to stand trial.

As the 1919 season drew near, Barrow remained upbeat about his team. His infield appeared solid and settled at three positions. The aging but still effective Stuffy McInnis would play first. Newcomer Vitt inherited third, and fielding star Everett Scott held down short. Second base remained unsettled between aging Dave Shean, journeyman Mike McNally, and Jack Barry. Barrow hoped to have Barry available, but his injured knee limited his effectiveness, while sapping his trade value. Barrow returned his stellar outfield. Skilled veterans Harry Hooper and Amos Strunk were slotted for right field and center field respectively, and Barrow had resigned himself to the fact that Ruth was most valuable in left field. Veteran Wally Schang and the recently acquired Al Walters shared the catching duties.

With the re-signing of Mays, the pitching staff appeared set as well. In addition to Bush, Jones, and Caldwell, Barrow wisely recognized that his roster contained Herb Pennock, at the time a twenty-five-year-old undistinguished lefty. Pennock had turned in one of his best performances in 1916, when he recorded an ERA of 1.67 in a partial season in Barrow's International League. He had then played sparingly for Boston in 1917 and missed the entire 1918 season in military service. To open the season, Barrow inserted Pennock into his rotation, and the young left-hander would go on to a Hall of Fame career.

The Red Sox started quickly, winning four of their first five games, but the season soon unraveled. At the end of April, before the fifth game of the season, Barrow suspended Ruth. Ruth's late-night, off-field carousing had not slowed since spring training, despite Barrow's assignment of coach Dan Howley to restrain him. When Howley accepted the challenge, he had proclaimed: "I'll take care of that guy if I have to put a ring through his nose." Poor Howley soon came to appreciate the impossibility of his assigned task. While on the road at the Raleigh Hotel in Washington, Barrow decided to catch Ruth at his late-night dalliances. Barrow slipped the hotel porter a couple of dollars and told him to let him know when Ruth showed up. The next day the porter knocked on Barrow's door at 6:00 a.m. to inform him that Ruth had just returned to the hotel.

As Barrow told the story, he went down to Ruth's room, where the lights were on and he could hear voices. After he knocked on the door, the lights quickly went out and the voices fell silent. The door was unlocked, and Barrow entered the room. Ruth was in bed smoking a pipe with the covers pulled up to his neck. Howley was hiding in the bathroom.

"You always smoke a pipe at this time of the morning?" Barrow asked Ruth.

"Oh sure, it's very relaxing," Ruth replied.

Barrow then walked over to the bed and pulled the covers back, exposing a fully clothed Ruth.

"I want to see you two at the ballpark!" Barrow told the two roommates.

While Ruth dressed with his teammates in the locker room, Barrow locked the door and lambasted his team for their off-field shenanigans, directing his remarks mainly at Ruth. After tolerating the tongue-lashing for some time, Ruth fired back, threatening to punch Barrow in the nose. This was almost certainly the reaction the physical Barrow was agitating for. He ordered the rest of the players to head out to the field after they finished dressing and told Ruth: "You stay here, Babe, and I'll give you a chance to see whether you can punch me in the nose."

Hooper and Shean tried to talk the riled-up Barrow out of a fight. But there was no need to; Ruth ran out to the field with his teammates. Prior to the start of the game, a chastened Ruth asked Barrow if he would be playing that day. Still angry, Barrow sent Ruth back to the clubhouse, ordered him to take off his uniform, and suspended him. While heading to New York on the train from Washington, the forlorn Ruth approached Barrow. The manager and his incorrigible star had a long heart-to-heart talk and reached an unusual détente. Barrow agreed to Ruth's unique request: "If I leave a note in your box every night when I come in and tell you what time I got home, will you let me play?" For the rest of Ruth's time with the Red Sox, he would leave a note in Barrow's box telling his skipper what time he had returned home. Barrow accepted Ruth's word and never again checked on his impetuous slugger.

Unfortunately, Barrow's public confrontation with Ruth did little to inspire his club. The Red Sox struggled through an 8-14 May and never returned to the pennant race. After his first start, Pennock was sidelined for most of May. Bush missed nearly the entire year with shoulder problems, unexpectedly forcing Barrow to address a depleted pitching staff. He pressed Ruth into mound service, and his home run hitter started fifteen games as a pitcher during 1919. (In his final year of any significant pitching, Ruth acquitted himself admirably with a 9-5 record and a 2.97 ERA.) He also occasionally worked his submarine hurler, Mays, on short rest. On June 28 Mays won the first game of a doubleheader in New York against the Yankees 2–0. When Mays told Barrow, "I think I can lick those birds again," Barrow agreed and sent Mays out to start the second game, despite his just having pitched a complete game. Mays pitched capably in the second game over a full eight innings but lost 4–1. Mays's feat had become unusual by 1919, and he was the first player that season to start both games of a doubleheader.

With the disappointing start—Boston was 24-31 at the end of June—murmurs of criticism were surfacing. In late June, to bolster his club and quiet the critics, Barrow traded Amos Strunk and Jack Barry to the Athletics for outfielder Bobby Roth and second baseman Red Shannon. Roth was a better hitter than Strunk, though not really competent for center field, where Barrow played him. Barry's knee problems, plus his lingering resentment over not being manager, led Barrow to seek a replacement, in this case the twenty-two-year-old switch-hitting Shannon. Though Roth was described as "a tough bird for managers to handle," Barrow hoped his addition and the jettisoning of Barry would both increase the club's talent level and alleviate some friction.

Carl Mays is arguably the best eligible pitcher not in the Hall of Fame, but several unhappy events completely overshadow his career. Best remembered for throwing a pitch that killed Cleveland's Ray Chapman in 1920, Mays was involved in several ill-fated events during his baseball years, both on and off the field. Known for clean living off the field, but brooding, hot-tempered, and selfish, the ornery Mays remained a loner among his team-mates. The aloof Barrow probably coped with Mays's personality quirks as well as anyone on the club.

Bob Shawkey, a pitching teammate on the Yankees several years later, remembered:

> *He was a stinker. One winter I worked for an insurance company in Philadelphia, and I insured his automobile. He went out and hired a guy to steal it in order to collect on the insurance. He promised the guy a certain amount of money to do it and then never paid him. That's how I happened to find out about it—the fellow called me up and told me what Mays had done. Of course we didn't pay Mays anything. Then he went to Cincinnati and did the same thing with somebody else. That's the way he was. A stinker.*

Although Mays had pitched well over the first half of the season, it had emotionally drained him. In the spring his mother's house had burned down; he endured a lengthy holdout to garner his salary of eight thousand dollars; and he was frustrated by the lack of run support—despite a team-best 2.48 ERA, his record stood at only 7-11. In early July, Ban Johnson fined him one hundred dollars for a Memorial Day incident in which Mays threw a ball at a heckler in the grandstand, further ordering that Mays be suspended un-til the fine was paid. Only Barrow's arguing for extenuating circumstances prevented Johnson from levying a more severe penalty. Despite some sym-pathy for Mays, and the pitcher's refusal to pay, Barrow would not go as far as having the club pay it.

Mays soon returned to the mound, and on July 13 his erratic behavior ig-nited a more serious crisis in the American League boardrooms. In the sec-ond inning of a game in Chicago, catcher Wally Schang's throw attempting to catch Eddie Collins stealing hit Mays in the back of the head. After the inning Mays disappeared into the clubhouse. When he failed to return to start the third, Barrow sent Sam Jones to see what was wrong. Jones found Mays having a nervous breakdown, crying and dressing to leave the park. When he reported back to Barrow, the shocked manager could do nothing to keep Mays in the park; moreover he needed to get a pitcher—in this case George Dumont—into the game. Mays returned to Boston by train, picked up his wife and luggage, and headed for his in-laws in Pennsylvania for some rest and relaxation, mostly fishing. In describing his frame of mind, Mays remembered, "I was young, impetuous, hot-tempered, discouraged, frustrated, and in debt over the burning and rebuilding of my mother's home. At that particular moment my whole world was falling down."

Barrow initially declared that the AWOL Mays would not be sold or traded. Frazee, however, directed Barrow to back off his rhetoric because the club was being inundated with purchase and trade offers, and Frazee recognized an opportunity to cash in. Once the other teams in the American League realized Mays was available, they bombarded Frazee and Barrow with offers. As Barrow recalled: "The Chicago, Cleveland, St. Louis, and Detroit clubs negotiated with me regarding a deal for the services of player Carl W. Mays. The Chicago club, on July 13, 14, 15, through President Comiskey and manager Gleason; the Cleveland club, on July 16, 17, 18, 19, through President Dunn and manager Fohl; the St. Louis club through Secretary Quinn, over the long-distance telephone on July 20, and the Detroit club through President Navin and manager Jennings, on July 21, 22, and 23 at Detroit; and also with manager Jennings over the long-distance telephone to Cleveland on July 25."

These clubs and others were offering players, cash, or some combination of the two. Cleveland proposed pitchers Guy Morton and Ed Klepfer along with outfielder Elmer Smith. Washington put forward hurlers Harry Harper and Jim Shaw. Frazee claimed he had asked Detroit for outfielder Bobby Veach and pitcher Howard Ehmke. Probably at Barrow's insistence, Frazee refused Detroit's counteroffer of "a big cash amount and several players of lesser reputations." Comiskey reportedly offered thirty thousand dollars for Mays, but Barrow needed pitchers and refused the offer of just cash. The Yankees actively pursued Mays as well. The Mays negotiations put Barrow in an awkward bargaining position. He naturally wanted to trade for players to help his team, but Frazee remained focused on acquiring a large sum of money. Further complicating trade negotiations, some proposals were directed to Barrow while others went through Frazee.

Barrow had experienced midseason player insubordination involving league president Ban Johnson once before with Kid Elberfeld in 1903. At that time Johnson and the league's owners were battling with the National League for survival and supremacy. When Barrow suspended Elberfeld, Johnson intervened to engineer his trade to the Yankees. Based on the circumstances at that time, Johnson had concluded that strengthening the American League franchise in New York took precedence over player discipline.

Sixteen years later, Johnson was aghast at the wholesale pursuit of a player he believed should be suspended. One of his core beliefs concerned proper player and manager behavior, which was abysmal during the 1890s, when he had developed his convictions. That a player could abandon his team and force a favorable trade offended his principles. Once he realized Boston was not going to suspend Mays and that teams were actively negotiating for his acquisition, Johnson contacted the clubs and instructed them to stop. Those owners still loyal to Johnson pulled back. The Yankees and the White Sox, however, whose deference to the president had waned, ignored Johnson's directive.

Johnson directed all his communications with the Red Sox to Barrow as opposed to Frazee. Johnson, of course, had known Barrow for many years and must have believed he would find a more sympathetic and deferential reaction. Although some dispute exists over whether it was actually received, Johnson claimed to have sent Barrow a telegram demanding, "Please explain why Boston club has neglected to suspend Mays. This must be done immediately or the American League will be forced to take action."

During the first couple of weeks after Mays left the team, Barrow was not only occupied with intensive trade negotiations and attempts to mollify an irate league president; he was also being criticized for both the team's overall underperformance and his handling of the Mays situation. Mays was not well liked by his teammates. Some players, who did not see the justice or benefit to the team in allowing Mays to, in effect, force a trade through objectionable behavior, grumbled to the press. Furthermore, on July 17 the club lost its fifth consecutive game, falling to 31-38. Reports of this dissension reached such intensity in the press that the next day the players felt required to issue a statement denying it:

> Having in view of the many stories and rumors as to the cause of the present low standing of the Boston American League club, stories of dissension among the players and rumors of mismanagement, we, the undersigned, wish to correct an injustice to manager Barrow. We feel that he has treated his players royally, in a manner that could not be improved upon.

The poor showing of the team was caused by a combination of bad breaks. The failure of some of the regulars to perform up to their past standards, weak pitching and continual bad luck on the field has upset the expectations of the management as well as the critics.

The players are in complete harmony with themselves and with the manager and stories to the contrary are untrue. We are for him to the last.

Not surprisingly, this public letter did little to quiet the press. A week later, on July 24, Barrow refused comment when grilled regarding the criticism of his handling of the ball club. Frazee offered a less than wholehearted defense of his manager when he declared that "the criticism of the management, generally was unreasonable, unjust and unfair, and much of it without foundation in fact." Because of his active involvement in the unfolding crisis, many observers mistakenly overestimated Barrow's authority in the matter. Several sources, unaware of Frazee's desire to cash in on the unhappy Mays, criticized Barrow for failing to suspend him. Barrow's old secretary at the International League office, Ernest Lanigan, was particularly critical. In August at the height of the controversy, he wrote in the *Sporting News*:

Barrow's reputation as a disciplinarian has gone—vanished—as a result of the Mays trouble, and he has before him the job of making a new one as a reconstructionist, for the Red Sox will need to be reconstructed thoroughly before they again can have aspirations for the championship. The great pitching staff is gone, Hooper is aging, Schang cannot be counted on to catch as well right along as he has been doing, as the tight infield is more or less a thing of the past, though Stuffy McInnis and Deacon [shortstop Everett] Scott still are on the job.

At the end of July Boston sent Mays to the Yankees for pitchers Allan Russell, Bob McGraw, and forty thousand dollars (reported variously at the time between twenty-five thousand dollars and forty thousand dollars), ranking with the highest prices ever paid for a ballplayer. During the Federal League war and its immediate aftermath, the Athletics had dealt Eddie Collins for fifty thousand dollars, and the Red Sox (pre-Frazee) sold

Tris Speaker for fifty-five thousand dollars. In 1917 the Cubs paid fifty-five thousand dollars to acquire the Phillies battery of Grover Cleveland Alexander and Bill Killefer. These few sales set the high-water mark until the Babe Ruth sale a couple of years later.

The teams that had withdrawn from negotiation at Johnson's request were obviously annoyed with this result, as was Johnson, who had hoped and expected that Boston would suspend their wayward pitcher. With the announcement of the trade, Johnson promptly suspended Mays indefinitely. The Yankees' owners went to court to enjoin Johnson from any action that would prevent Mays from playing in New York. By publicly challenging the league president's authority, the two ignited a bitter feud among the American League owners. Charles Comiskey lined up with the Yankees' owners and Frazee; the other five backed Johnson. The requisite depositions and testimony associated with the court cases would further draw Barrow's time and attention away from his managing duties during the remainder of the season.

The aftermath of the Mays controversy lingered for several years and at times threatened to destroy the league. On August 6 the court issued a temporary injunction that prevented Johnson from suspending Mays. The subsequent court hearings were particularly bitter. There was briefly some talk by the "Loyal Five" of boycotting Yankees games in which Mays pitched, but this threat soon evaporated.

On October 26 the court ruled in favor of the Yankees' owners, permanently enjoining Johnson from interfering with Mays. Not surprisingly, this did not end the battle. Johnson appealed the decision and withheld the Yankees players' third-place share of World Series receipts (Mays was an integral part of New York's second half, contributing an ERA of 1.65 and a record of 9-3). The Insurrectos, as the New York, Boston, and Chicago owners were dubbed, responded by trying to oust Johnson from the league presidency.

The Mays imbroglio also further depleted Barrow's pitching staff. To bolster his mound corps, Barrow introduced Waite Hoyt, a nineteen-year-old future Hall of Famer. Hoyt began 1919 pitching with the Baltimore Drydocks, a company team in a defense contractor league that continued after the war. Drydocks catcher Norman McNeil convinced Barrow that Hoyt was worth a look. Barrow dispatched a scout to Baltimore; Hoyt impressed him, and Barrow offered the young pitcher a contract. Hoyt demanded a clause requiring the Red Sox use him within four days after signing. Barrow, desperately in need of pitching, agreed to this unique request and sent Hoyt to the mound on July 31.

The Hoyt signing landed Barrow in the midst of another controversy. Originally signed by the Giants as a schoolboy, Hoyt had been farmed out to the Minors for a couple of years. In 1919 he balked at being sent down again, this time to Rochester, and jumped to the Drydocks. In the meantime, Rochester had sold his rights to New Orleans, which claimed technical ownership. Now that Barrow was a Major League manager and de facto general manager, his view of player disputes between the Majors and the Minors had conveniently evolved. With a Major League–Minor League confrontation brewing again over the draft, Barrow now had little sympathy for the Minors and their player claims. He ignored New Orleans's entreaties and started Hoyt in eleven games down the stretch. New Orleans challenged Barrow's high-handed attitude and brought the matter before the National Commission for adjudication. The commission offered a compromise solution: it ruled that New Orleans technically owned Hoyt's rights but that Boston be given the opportunity to purchase his release for a reasonable price. The two sides worked out a settlement, later estimated to be about $2,500.

In mid-September Barrow was forced to defend himself for leaving Hoyt on the mound longer than usual. Hoyt believed the eighth inning was a "hoodoo," which he needed to work through. He asked Barrow to leave him in through the eighth inning regardless of what happened. Barrow had grown to respect his precocious young hurler and acquiesced to the request. At a game in New York, Hoyt pitched through the eighth; he was less successful later against Cleveland, but Barrow was clearly thinking toward the future and encouraging Hoyt for the next season.

With Hoyt filling in capably and Ruth pounding home runs on the way to a record twenty-nine, Barrow brought the Red Sox back to .500 at 62-62 on September 11. Of course, the pennant race was long since over for the Red Sox, but the nine-game winning streak that started September 1 to bring the team to .500 must have been rewarding for the embattled Barrow. The club slipped back during the last couple of weeks and finished the season at 66-71. Overall, in 1919 the Red Sox regressed both offensively and defensively. Barrow could never stanch the collapse of his pitching staff, which fell to seventh in the league in ERA. Pennock helped, but Barrow missed Bush; Jones turned in possibly his worst season, and Mays escaped in July. On offense, Ruth was the lone bright spot. No other player had recorded a slugging percentage above .375. And although home runs were less common in 1919, it is still shocking that the rest of the team combined for only four during the entire season.

Prior to the 1919 World Series, Barrow was asked his thoughts on the upcoming Series between the Chicago White Sox and the Cincinnati Reds: "I have no doubt but that it will be an interesting contest, but to my mind the White Sox have the class," Barrow responded. "I do not mean to disparage Pat Moran's team in any way. Moran undoubtedly has a great team, but man for man I believe it is outclassed by the White Sox."

The 1919 season left Barrow drained and frustrated. Expected to compete for the pennant, his club fell off the pace early and finished below .500. Once again he had found himself stuck between his boss and the league president in the season's foremost controversy. He had also become aware that he no longer worked for an organization aggressively pursuing victory. With his mounting financial obligations, Frazee had become a seller of top talent. To Barrow's disappointment and annoyance, he would now be constrained in his pursuit of players and vulnerable to losing those he had.

After the tumultuous 1919 season, Barrow took a little time away from baseball. Generally an intense workaholic, he had few hobbies outside an occasional hunting trip. After the World Series Barrow spent two weeks in Camp Bryan, North Carolina, hunting and relaxing, to refresh and reenergize himself for the upcoming off-season. Back in Boston, the club moved its offices out of frigid Fenway Park to a downtown office for the winter. When Barrow returned, he met with Harry Frazee in New York to discuss strengthening the club for 1920. After finishing fifth in runs scored and seventh in ERA, the Red Sox clearly needed help both on the mound and at the plate. With Ruth now a full-time outfielder, Bush a huge question mark after missing essentially all of 1919 with a sore arm, and Hoyt only twenty years old, Barrow and Frazee rightfully decided to place pitching depth, particularly left-handed, at the top of the list. The two targeted Washington's Harry Harper, a tall, youthful (twenty-four years in old in 1919) lefthander who they felt might come at a reasonable price after a disappointing 1919 season (6-21, 3.72 ERA). His strong 1918 season (11-10, 2.18 ERA) hinted that improvement for 1920 might be possible.

Barrow was willing to surrender Bobby Roth, his midseason outfield acquisition. Roth could not field well enough to justify playing center, and Barrow was no longer inclined to overlook his prickly personality. Washington president and manager Clark Griffith liked Roth. Barrow added Red Shannon and persuaded Griffith to include Eddie Foster, regarded as one of the league's best third basemen several years earlier but now slowing down, and Mike Menosky, a young outfielder. In sum, Barrow traded a pretty good starting outfielder and a young but overmatched second baseman for a starting third baseman (whom Barrow intended to shift to second—a position he had played in the past), a promising young left-hander, and a young outfielder with some potential. Barrow almost surely convinced Frazee to accept the extra players as opposed to cash, and Frazee, on the verge of announcing the Babe Ruth trade, likely concurred because of public opinion.

With his financial squeeze mounting, on December 26, 1919, Frazee consummated and on January 5, 1920, he announced the notorious sale of Babe
Ruth to the New York Yankees. For Ruth, Frazee received the record sum
of one hundred thousand dollars: twenty-five thousand dollars up front and
three promissory notes of twenty-five thousand each at a 6 percent interest rate, due in November 1920, 1921, and 1922. Ruppert also gave Frazee
a three-month commitment that he would lend him three hundred thousand dollars to be secured by a first mortgage on Fenway Park. The Red Sox
would not finish in the first division again until 1934.

Frazee set up a meeting in the café of the Hotel Knickerbocker to tell
Barrow about the deal:

> *"Simon [as noted, Frazee had nicknamed Barrow after Simon
> Legree]," he said, "I am going to sell Ruth to the Yankees."*
>
> *"I thought as much," I said. "I could feel it in my bones. But you
> ought to know you're making a mistake."*
>
> *"Maybe I am," Frazee said, "but I can't help it. Lannin is after
> me to make good on my notes. And my shows aren't going so good.
> Ruppert and Huston will give me $100,000 for Ruth and they've also
> agreed to loan me $350,000 [sic]. I can't afford to turn that down.
> But don't worry. I'll get you some ballplayers, too."*
>
> *"Listen," I said, "losing Ruth is bad enough, but don't make it
> tougher for me by making me show off a lot of ten-cent ballplayers
> that we got in exchange for him. There is nobody on that ball club
> that I want. This has to be a straight cash deal, and you'll have to
> announce it that way."*

That is the way it was and the way it was announced.

Barrow also recounted that Frazee "showed [him] how much he owed,
how much he had lost at Fenway Park, and how urgent it was that he get the
$500,000 which would be made available by the sale of Ruth."

Fred Lieb, a noted longtime baseball writer and author of several baseball
team histories in the 1940s and 1950s, is another primary source for these
details. Lieb wrote that "Harry Frazee once told [him] the rape wasn't pre-
meditated. He didn't plan it that way; it just happened. He needed money,
and the Yankee colonels, Ruppert and Huston, hungry for a winner, had
plenty of it." (Lieb credited sportswriter Burt Whitman with coining the

phrase "the rape of the Red Sox" to describe the sale of Ruth and other players, mostly to the Yankees.) Later Lieb wrote: "'The Ruth deal was the only way I could retain the Red Sox,' Frazee once told the author in a moment of confidence." Others associated with Frazee and the transaction, such as Ruppert and Huston, also stated that Frazee sold Ruth because he needed the funds.

Over the next eighty years the notion that Frazee had sold Ruth and other players because he needed the money moved beyond conventional wisdom and into the realm of historical fact. I am not aware of any serious baseball histories that disputed this view.

Thus it was certainly startling when Glenn Stout and Richard A. Johnson, in their otherwise excellent book *Red Sox Century*, offered the revisionist claim that Frazee did not in fact sell Ruth because he needed the money. Stout and Johnson make three arguments: "It [the sale of Ruth] rid him of a problem, strengthened his coalition with New York in the war with Johnson, and gave him the cash he knew he'd need to rebuild his club."

This revisionist hypothesis is in no way supported by the facts: the money Frazee received for Ruth (and Shore, Lewis, Leonard, and Mays) was not reinvested in the ball club. In fact, the $165,000 Frazee earned in those player sales simply whetted his appetite for more. With further scrutiny the revisionist arguments can be easily dismissed.

The first claim—and the least verifiable because it addresses Frazee's state of mind—is that Frazee's stated reason for the sale, that Ruth was actually a detriment to the team, honestly reflected his sentiment and was somehow a reasonable position. After the sale Frazee released a statement highly critical of Ruth's lack of discipline, poor behavior, and lax training habits. Stout and Johnson concur that "there were plenty of baseball reasons for Frazee to deal Ruth." (Although Frazee did not exactly "deal" Ruth; he sold him.) Not surprisingly, several sycophantic sportswriters toed Frazee's line, while others were highly critical of the sale.

Even from the perspective of January 1920, it is preposterous to suppose that Ruth's absence could possibly have benefited the Red Sox. Only twenty-four at the time, Ruth was already acknowledged as baseball's greatest attraction and an undeniably great player. After three years as one of baseball's best pitchers, he had converted to the outfield. In his two years as a full-time outfielder, he led the Major Leagues in home runs both seasons. In 1919 he hit twenty-nine home runs to set the all-time single-season record; the rest of the Red Sox combined hit four. Furthermore, a successful theater operator would surely have appreciated the marquee value of the Babe.

The Yankees recognized his value and after the purchase quickly made Ruth baseball's highest-paid player. At the time of the sale, Ruth was under contract for two more seasons at ten thousand dollars per year and wanted twenty thousand. The Yankees agreed, although technically they did not renegotiate his contract: his salary remained at ten thousand dollars per year, but the Yankees paid him an additional twenty-one thousand dollars over 1920 and 1921. And the Yankees were not the only team that recognized his ability; Stout and Johnson note that had Ruth been put on the open market, Frazee might well have received even more.

In the end, whether Frazee really believed, contrary to all available evidence, that Ruth was a liability to his club, or was simply trying to put a good face on a bad situation is irrelevant. He sold Ruth for lots of money, and the club quickly declined. The key point is that for all his talk of reinvesting in baseball talent, very little, if any, of the tremendous sum he raised in the Ruth sale (or his previous player-sale income) ever found its way back to the team.

On the second point, Frazee's quarrels with Johnson had been simmering for some time. The Mays case, however, had blown the American League wide open into two warring factions. The battle between Frazee, the two Yankees owners, and Charles Comiskey on the one side and Johnson and the other five owners on the other became especially vicious over the winter of 1919–20. Stout and Johnson therefore reason that the Ruth deal "bolstered the alliance of the Insurrectos and provided him [Frazee] with operating capital and a reserve were Johnson to try to mount a legal challenge to his right to operate the franchise."

This argument is nonsensical. Most obviously, there is no cause and effect between selling Ruth and bolstering the alliance unless one claims that Ruth was sold at a discount in exchange for an agreement from the Yankees' owners to support Frazee against Johnson. One cannot, however, simultaneously argue that Ruth was a liability to his team but worth more than one hundred thousand dollars. More specifically, the Yankees' owners were even more at the forefront of the imbroglio with Johnson than Frazee and therefore needed Frazee even more than he needed them. Any transaction between the Yankees' owners and Frazee was a consequence, not a cause, of their social relationship and alliance against Johnson.

Which leads to the final problem with Stout and Johnson's argument: Frazee, in fact, desperately needed the money. In 1919 Red Sox home attendance had rebounded to 417,291, but this was a smaller increase than for most other American League franchises. By the end of the season, Frazee found himself squeezed not only by the interest on all his debt—the note to Lannin ($262,000), the preferred stock ($150,000), and the mortgage on Fenway Park (roughly $125,000 at the time of the Ruth sale)—but now the principal on Lannin's note was due as well.

Hamstrung by Red Sox revenues well below projections, Frazee could not meet his financial obligations. In 1920, for example, one of the most profitable years in baseball up to that time and the only one for which I could find financial statements, the Boston franchise turned a profit of only $14,970. And while in later years Frazee may have made money from his plays, in the years immediately preceding the Ruth sale, he was struggling financially. According to his 1918 individual income tax return, after deducting for interest payments and expenses associated with a play, Frazee actually had a negative net income of $13,364. The previous year he even had to forgo his salary as president of the Cort Theatre Company because of the company's financial condition. In 1919 Frazee earned all of $721. To support his lifestyle, Frazee drained money from the team. In addition to having the club pay some of his personal expenses, in 1919 he overdrew his salary by $5,850; in 1920 he overdrew his salary by $21,659 and pocketed another $5,000 on a note.

Frazee had quit paying Lannin interest in May 1919, and in November (two months before the sale of Ruth) he defaulted on the principal payment of $262,000. To satisfy his obligation to Lannin, Frazee began looking at various scenarios to refinance and pull some equity out of Fenway Park. He eventually settled on the new mortgage loan from Ruppert as a condition of the Ruth sale. Unfortunately, given the confused state of Frazee's finances, it would take several months to clear up the existing mortgage. To raise funds immediately after the Ruth sale, Frazee began trying to borrow against his three $25,000 notes from the sale. On December 30, 1919, Colonel Huston wrote his partner, Jacob Ruppert, "I told Mr. Frazee that I would try to get him a short term loan at my bank, with one of the notes we gave the Boston Club as collateral."

In February 1920, as Frazee's attorneys worked to untangle legal complications involving the existing mortgage, Lannin sued to have his security, Frazee and Hugh Ward's ownership interest in Fenway Park, auctioned off, with the proceeds going to pay off his note. Frazee claimed he had not paid off the note because he had unexpectedly assumed an obligation of sixty thousand to seventy thousand dollars when he had acquired the club that was rightfully owed by Lannin. This additional obligation resulted from the Federal League settlement, which Frazee argued was Lannin's responsibility under the original purchase contract.

Stout and Johnson believe Johnson urged Lannin to file his suit, using the threat of Fenway Park's sale as a way to force Frazee to sell the team. If true, this further evidences Frazee's financial vulnerability. Ban Johnson knew just about everything that was happening behind baseball's boardroom doors. If he felt Frazee could be forced out, then he was surely aware that Frazee was in financial trouble. Johnson went so far as to come to Boston and try to recruit a group of investors to purchase the team. Regardless of any malicious influence from Johnson, Lannin needed to force an unwilling Frazee to repay his note, making it unsurprising that he sued.

In February 1920 Huston again sent a message to Ruppert on financing the notes: "Mr. Harry Frazee is asking us to aid in getting three $25,000 notes discounted. He says events with Mr. Lannin have made it impossible to follow his original intention of having the notes discounted in Boston." It seems unlikely that a man free of financial problems would have had so much trouble borrowing against the notes.

At a March 3 court appearance, Frazee's attorneys delayed the sale of Fenway Park by agreeing to put up $250,000. One attorney claimed that a syndicate of investors was prepared to put up the money for Frazee. The disagreement was finally settled in a court document on March 8 in favor of Lannin for $265,000; Frazee received no reimbursement for his Federal League offset claim. The settlement also required a rapid payment schedule for the debt: $25,000 was due by March 8; another $25,000 by March 22; and the $215,000 balance by May 3.

Not only did Frazee need upward of $265,000 to save his franchise, but he was also negotiating to purchase the Harris Theater on West Forty-second Street in New York. He closed on the sale at the end of March, although he would not take possession until July. Although no purchase price was reported, when originally developed by William Harris in 1900 the theater had cost $500,000. A nearby theater had sold earlier in the month for $650,000. The acquisition of this theater was surely an expensive undertaking.

Fortunately for the strapped Frazee, he now had access to the money he needed to settle with Lannin and buy the theater: he had finally organized his finances sufficiently to close on the $300,000 mortgage Ruppert had promised as part of the Ruth sale, a loan that would net Frazee roughly $175,000. In April 1920 Frazee sent a letter to Ruppert asking for the loan, to which Ruppert agreed:

> You remember that I phoned you about ten days before the expiration of your agreement to make a loan of $300,000 on Fenway Park and asked you to extend the time, which you advised me you would tell Mr. Grant to do. However, I have received no word from Mr. Grant. I telephoned Col. Huston today, as I could not reach you on the phone, asking the Colonel to see you and advise that I have cleaned up all matters upon the Preferred Stock which your Attorney wanted before making the loan and I am now ready to accept it on May 15.
>
> You can understand how important this is to me as my plans have all been based on my ability to secure this loan. Therefore, will you please send me signed agreement, copy of which Mr. Grant has, stating that you will advance the $300,000 . . . and if possible make the date May 20th. . . . I need this agreement signed by you here very badly to complete the balance of my negotiations. *(my emphasis)*

Stout and Johnson seem to have recognized that Frazee needed the money when they acknowledge that the negotiations he refers to were to "settle his account with Lannin and to conclude a deal he'd agreed to on March 27 to buy the Harris Theater on 42nd Street in New York." The record is clear that the proceeds from the sale of Ruth went to pay off the obligation still outstanding from Frazee's purchase of the Red Sox and to his theater interests, not for rebuilding the team.

At first Barrow echoed (and possibly even believed) the party line, that is, that Frazee planned to reinvest at least a portion of the Ruth proceeds in ballplayers. On January 13, for example, he announced to the press that he was lining up some deals but not to expect anything until the league meetings in February. At the Chicago meetings, however, most of Frazee's time was spent skirmishing with Johnson, and he refused to allocate Barrow any funds with which to purchase players. In fact, Barrow was forced to become a seller, not a buyer. In his only moves of note, he sold two little-used pitchers, George Winn and Paul Muser, to Minor League teams. The league magnates stopped squabbling long enough to recognize the game's prosperity (in 1919 Major League Baseball recorded its highest attendance since 1913 despite a 140-game season) and return the schedule to 154 games, raise ticket prices, and move the in-season roster size back to twenty-five.

Still in need of a center fielder, in early March Barrow sent young outfielder Bill Lamar and a small stipend to Louisville for journeyman center fielder Tim Hendryx. After several years as a Major League utility player, Hendryx spent 1919 in the Minors. Nineteenth-century star and Red Sox scout Hugh Duffy recommended Hendryx as one of the Minors' best prospects—of course, that Hendryx was already twenty-nine years old surely tempered Barrow's optimism.

For 1920 the Red Sox returned to Hot Springs, Arkansas, for spring training. The Sox dispatched Bullet Joe Bush three weeks early to get his arm back into shape, while the rest of the club began to report in early March. As some of the veteran players drifted in, Barrow was concerned with the morale of the club, not to mention his own. Without Ruth, he knew his team was significantly weaker; a more-assured Barrow would never have tolerated the lackadaisical arrivals at camp. Hooper sent Barrow a note as camp was starting that he was just leaving California. Herb Pennock arrived late to camp as well. The club finally reached a contract agreement with newcomer Harper, but Wally Schang and Ozzie Vitt were both holding out, the former despite being signed to a three-year contract. According to the *Chicago Tribune*, some of the veterans were "a bit peeved upon reaching camp and learning the other old timers had been able to stay at home a while longer." On a more serious note, Barrow received a message from Hendryx that his wife had just died and he would be delayed.

Sans Ruth, Barrow anticipated difficulty scoring runs. Barrow brought a number of newcomers and potential rookies to camp, and although none of the options was particularly good, he competently sorted out his best alternatives. At catcher the weak-hitting Al Walters would start until Schang reported. At shortstop Everett Scott fielded well, played every day, and was a capable hitter. Stuffy McInnis, adequate at the plate and generally regarded as an excellent fielder, held down first. Because of Ozzie Vitt's weak hitting, Barrow intended to leave Foster at third and move Vitt into a utility role. At second base this left 1919 utility infielder Mike McNally as the starter. In the outfield newcomer Hendryx started in center, flanked by Hooper in right and Menosky in left. Of the starting eight, only Hooper (and potentially Schang) could be counted on to provide above-average offense at their positions.

To bolster his thin outfield, in early March Barrow signed Cuban Armando Marsans on the recommendation of scout Ed Holly. Marsans, a speedy center fielder who started for several teams during the second decade of the century, had last played for the Yankees in 1918. He jumped the team in July that year to return to Cuba after learning that his mother was sick and had remained in Cuba during the 1919 season. New York still technically owned Marsans's rights, and he was also on the National Commission's suspended list for jumping the Yankees. After receiving New York's permission, Barrow signed him and brought him from Cuba to Hot Springs. Barrow hoped Marsans could earn a roster spot, but his ability remained in doubt. Marsans had never fully recovered his speed after a severe broken leg in 1917 and had not played against Major League competition in nearly two years. Barrow played Marsans extensively during spring training to determine his value, while also trying to rescind his suspension. But the experiment did not pan out, and Barrow cut Marsans prior to the start of the season.

As to the pitchers, Barrow could realistically be sure of only Pennock and Jones. To round out the rotation, Barrow had four viable options. He hoped that twenty-seven-year-old Bullet Joe Bush could rebound from the sore shoulder that had caused him to miss nearly all of 1919. Allan Russell, who had turned in an excellent half season for the Red Sox after coming over in the Mays trade, was also a strong candidate for the rotation. Barrow also had the option of slotting in twenty-year-old Waite Hoyt, who had pitched well after joining the team midway through 1919. Finally, Barrow had his new left-hander, Harry Harper. To help sort out his various pitching options, Barrow hired Paddy Livingston as a pitching coach, but the ex-catcher had a change of heart and retired from baseball.

As spring training drew to a close, Barrow recovered some of his characteristic optimism: "Just give me some regular pitching from that bunch, and then let me turn a deal for a good right-handed-hitting outfielder and the Red Sox will be all right." Unlike the previous season, expectations for this ball club remained relatively low, and few observers expected it to contend for a pennant.

To get his charges in shape for the season, Barrow often sent them on mountain hikes in the Ozarks, sometimes leading the way himself. The players also spent some time horseback riding. (While out riding Mike McNally became the hero of Hot Springs when he rescued a girl on a runaway horse.) As a tune-up for the season, the team barnstormed north with the New York Giants, a trip that agitated Barrow considerably. The weather was terrible, his Red Sox generally played poorly, the players fought each other nearly every day, and he squabbled unnecessarily with Giants manager John McGraw over the umpire choices for a couple of games.

The Yankees regularly approached Barrow all spring trying to pry Schang loose during his holdout. Barrow wanted Ping Bodie, an aging right-handed-hitting outfielder on the Yankees. Yankees manager Miller Huggins, through scout Joe Kelley, proposed Schang, Vitt, and McNally or a pitcher for Bodie, starting second baseman Del Pratt, and a throw-in pitcher. Barrow scoffed at this offer and remained adamant that he would not surrender Schang, who was still under contract. Barrow countered with Vitt for both Bodie and Pratt, an offer that barely deserved a response. Not surprisingly, given how far apart the teams were, no trade was consummated, despite several meetings both during Boston's barnstorming tour north and later in New York.

The Red Sox began the season in surprising fashion, winning their first five games, including three at home against the Yankees. The doubleheader on Monday, April 19, brought out 28,000 fans, a huge early-season crowd. Even at this time, before the Yankees had ever won a pennant, they had become Boston's hated and bitter rival. In 1920 Boston drew a total of 402,445 fans to its home games; astonishingly, the Yankees accounted for 125,581 of them (31.2 percent of the season's total attendance). Looked at another way, Boston averaged 11,416 fans per game against New York; against the rest of the American League, they averaged only 4,260.

With the hot start; a rotation of Russell, Jones, Hoyt, Bush, and Pennock; some timely hitting; and Schang finally reporting on May 5, Barrow led his team to a 21-9 record and first place on May 26. Unfortunately, the team's weak offense soon doomed the club to fall out of contention. With his restricted resources, Barrow could never land the hard-hitting outfielder he desperately wanted. Waite Hoyt had surgery for a pulled groin muscle in midseason, lost twenty-five pounds, and missed a couple of months. Later in the season Hoyt required an operation for an infected nose and upper lip.

Barrow never stopped looking for inexpensive ways to improve his team. For example, while in Cleveland in July, he traveled to Dayton to watch Al Clayton, a six-foot-six semipro pitcher. Barrow signed the huge hurler, but he never appeared in a game for the Red Sox. Later, on a trip to Chicago, he signed pitcher Buck Freeman from the Saginaw, Michigan, club, another longshot who would make the Majors briefly a year later with the Cubs. In early August Barrow claimed pitcher Elmer Myers on waivers from the Indians. Myers was never more than a journeyman, but Barrow coaxed a brilliant two months (9-1, 2.13 ERA) out of his waiver claim. Myers would never again approach this level.

Many years later future Major League pitcher/outfielder Johnny Cooney related the possibly apocryphal story of his experience trying to join the Red Sox that year. At the time Cooney was pitching for the American Thread Company team in Willimantic, Connecticut. On his way to a game, Cooney's train struck a car, killing four occupants. Cooney jumped off the train and tried to rescue the dying motorists. The experience left him queasy and incapable of pitching. Manager Eddie McGinley, however, needed his star hurler, gave him a few whiffs of ammonia, and sent him to the mound. Cooney proceeded to pitch a perfect game—not a single opposing batter reached first base. When the Red Sox learned of this performance, they dispatched scout Paul Krichell to observe Cooney's next game. Cooney walked the first batter and then induced a double play. And over the course of the game, he again faced only twenty-seven batters.

Krichell arranged for Cooney to travel to Boston to sign a contract, and the teenage pitcher brought along McGinley to help negotiate. Barrow and Cooney agreed to a five-hundred-dollar signing bonus and a salary of three hundred dollars per month. Barrow then directed the check to be cut for the five hundred dollars. But McGinley's history in semiprofessional baseball had made him wary of checks.

He announced, "No checks, mister. We're doing business in cash."

To which Barrow angrily replied: "You mean our checks are no good?"

"I'm not saying they are or they ain't, but I always do business in cash," retorted McGinley.

The infuriated Barrow then tossed both McGinley and Cooney out of his office.

The two left quietly and went to the park. After some time McGinley remarked: "I think we should have accepted that check."

To which the forlorn pitcher answered: "I think we should have."

In the spring of 1920 Barrow also had an opportunity to secure future Hall of Fame third baseman Pie Traynor. Ed Hurley, a Boston baseball writer, heard about Traynor, a top baseball player in the Boston area, and contacted Barrow to schedule a tryout. Barrow watched Traynor, then a shortstop, audition alongside a couple of his regulars. Suitably impressed but without a roster spot for him, Barrow recommended Traynor to Portsmouth, Virginia, owner H. P. Dawson with whom he had an informal working relationship. Common at the time, but technically against the rules, in these relationships the Major League club typically had a handshake agreement that it would have first shot at reacquiring players it had recommended. In the case of Traynor, when the Pirates later offered Dawson ten thousand dollars, he happily accepted. Upon discovering his loss, Barrow angrily accused Dawson of breaking his word, claiming Dawson owed him the ten thousand dollars. Because the whole arrangement was technically in violation of baseball's rules, Barrow had little recourse. In fact, Barrow eventually saw the humor in the episode, and after he and the Yankees built their farm system many years later, they even hired Dawson as a Minor League executive.

Carl Mays, Barrow's 1919 midseason headache, would ignite a more tragic controversy in 1920. On Monday, August 16, Mays threw a pitch that hit Cleveland Indians batter Ray Chapman in the head. The tragedy occurred before the introduction of batting helmets, and Chapman died early the next morning. Not popular with other players and with the reputation of a headhunter, Mays became subject to a league-wide backlash, which had been simmering for some time. During the 1919–20 off-season, Barrow and Huggins had both defended Mays against reports that batters were "awaiting an opportunity to 'get' pitcher Carl Mays because of his menacing 'bean ball.'" Barrow asserted that much of the chatter came from players "jealous of his success." Huggins added that Mays "wouldn't harm anybody and that his 'bean ball' look[ed] dangerous because of the particular delivery employed by the pitcher."

On Tuesday, August 17, Boston and Detroit players met in Boston. A number of Boston players still harbored resentment over Mays jumping the team the previous year, and the group discussed having Mays thrown out of baseball. Widespread bitterness against Mays developed on nearly all teams and led to players discussing the merits of boycotting games pitched by Mays. At the meeting the players prepared a petition along these lines but refrained from acting on it until they had consulted with Tris Speaker, Cleveland's player-manager and leader. Speaker responded with restraint and cooled some of the more inflamed passions. On August 27, Barrow reported to the press: "We have received a letter signed by the Cleveland players regarding the Mays-Chapman accident [asking the players to boycott games in which Mays was scheduled to pitch], but as far as I know there has been no action taken by any of the Sox players. I think most of it is merely talk by the newspapers." With President Johnson angling to head off a boycott, the threat slowly subsided, and most players eventually accepted that, in spite of his reputation, Mays had not intentionally tried to bean Chapman with the pitch.

The Red Sox finished the year in fifth place with a record of 72-81. Barrow was able to piece together a respectable pitching staff as all six spring training camp candidates pitched capably. He was not as successful, however, with the offense. Without Ruth, Hooper and Schang alone could not carry the club, which finished seventh in the league in runs scored, ahead of only the hapless Philadelphia Athletics.

After four complete Major League seasons as a manager (including his tenure in Detroit), Barrow's in-game tendencies had become apparent. He liked to force the action on offense—even when he still had Babe Ruth—and he made use of the ways open to managerial discretion to move his runners along. In Barrow's four full seasons of managing in the American League, his teams finished first twice and second once in sacrifice hits per game. And in 1920, the only year for which the data is available, Barrow's Red Sox finished second in stolen base attempts per game.

Barrow handled his pitching staff much less aggressively than his offense. He liked to let his starting pitcher work as long as possible and rarely used his bullpen. Even relative to the unsophisticated bullpen management of this era, Barrow called on his relief pitchers infrequently. Among his American League competitors, Barrow's Tigers hurlers had made the third fewest relief appearances per game. In Boston, Barrow became even more reluctant to use his bullpen; Red Sox hurlers twice made the fewest relief appearances per game.

At the end of the 1920 season, Barrow had spent twenty-three years in professional baseball and had held just about every job except player. Although he did not yet know it, the fifty-two-year-old Barrow was about to embark on a new adventure that would forever cement his place in baseball history. With the monetary shackles removed, he would build baseball's greatest dynasty.

The Yankees Years, 1920–1953

2

13. Business Manager of the Yankees

When New York Yankees business manager Harry Sparrow passed away in May 1920, the team's operations quickly became disorganized. Yankees owners Jacob Ruppert and Tillinghast L'Hommedieu Huston had entrusted Sparrow with more authority than most business managers had at the time. He was not involved in personnel decisions, but he helped oversee the scouts and the relationships with Minor League clubs. Huston initially tried to manage the business operations himself, also leaning on a couple of front-office employees, traveling secretary Mark Roth and Charley McManus (nicknamed by the press "nip and tuck"). But Huston had too many outside interests and little patience for the detailed administrative tasks that the position required. Furthermore, Ruppert wanted an experienced baseball man to help supervise constructing the roster.

As the 1920 season dragged on, the Yankees duo targeted Ed Barrow as an executive who could fill this need. Both men knew Barrow socially, at least since their venture in the Dover Hall hunting lodge about five years earlier. At one point Barrow donated one of his dogs, "Bunk," to the lodge. In 1917 Huston sent Barrow a tongue-in-cheek letter: "[Bunk,] notwithstanding his former International League affiliations, shows such signs of intelligence, as to be considered a Big League prospect, and . . . he should be sent to the bushes for further training. It has been decided he will be farmed out for the season of 1917. The expense of Bunk's instructions may amount to around fifty dollars, and inasmuch as you did not donate to the club a finished article in 'Bunk,' we feel that you will, no doubt, be glad to bear this expense. We will advise you later on where to send your check."

In his reply, Barrow offered some off-color remarks: "Listen here, you old son-of-a-gun, don't you go trying to pull any of that Georgia stuff on me and my dog Bunk. I don't mind your being friendly with him, but if I find out that you have been 'intimate' with him, I will 'have the law' on you." He later added, "You can give me credit on Bunk's board bill for those turkeys and hats I won off you on Wilson's election [President Woodrow in November 1916]."

Ruppert and Huston had developed an appreciation for Barrow's administrative abilities as he guided the International League through its travails in the Federal League war. The owners gained further respect for Barrow's abilities through their frequent dealings since he had joined the Red Sox.

Boston owner Harry Frazee, in the process of dismantling his team, no longer needed a high-profile, highly compensated manager. He willingly let the Yankees hire Barrow away, although with Ruppert as his principal banker, Frazee could scarcely object. In fact, on October 28, 1920, when the Yankees hired Barrow, Frazee—ever close with the Yankees' owners—joined Barrow in the Yankees' offices for an impromptu press conference announcing the move.

Barrow certainly would have had mixed feelings about the job change. While he recognized that his days in Boston were numbered as Frazee scaled back the financial commitment and expectations for his team, moving from manager to business manager would not have been viewed as a promotion. Barrow, however, lived in New York, and the Yankees offered a generous salary and expanded responsibilities that fell within the purview of a modern general manager. Barrow prided himself on both his organizational abilities and his player-evaluation skills; the Yankees position offered him the opportunity to employ both. Also, despite his ego, Barrow felt comfortable as an administrator for a driven but semidetached owner. Many years earlier in Des Moines, he had engineered just this type of arrangement with financial sponsor Ed Moore for his amateur teams. In New York Barrow rightly appreciated that as he proved his competence he could expand his sphere of influence and gain a large measure of control over the team.

Often referred to as the "two colonels," Barrow's new bosses were an original odd couple. Born wealthy, the physically smaller Ruppert dressed nattily and enjoyed several upper-crust hobbies. The bigger Huston was a self-made man, dressed sloppily, and craved adventure. Tillinghast L'Hommedieu Huston was schooled as a civil engineer, but despite the profession's reputation, he was a risk taker, an adventurer who liked to "raise a ruckus." Huston's father was also a civil engineer, and when the Spanish-American War broke out, the younger Huston was working as an engineer for the water works in Cincinnati, Ohio (his home state). In 1899 he organized Company C, Second U.S. Volunteer Engineers, and led them to Cuba in the service of the U.S. government. Designated the rank of captain, Huston would be known as "Cap" the rest of his life; he would not become a colonel until his service in World War I many years later. Upon its arrival in Cuba, Huston's company was assigned the mission of sanitizing some unhygienic hospitals. Huston successfully accomplished this unenviable task, earning the gratitude of the authorities in Cuba.

Huston remained in Cuba after the war and established an engineering and construction company. The reputation he had gained during the war opened a number of contracting opportunities. Most profitably, in 1911 he landed the harbor concession for Cuba's ports, including Havana. He had to dredge and otherwise improve the harbors; in return his venture was awarded port duties for the next thirty years. To raise capital, the venture issued bonds against this future revenue stream. The bond issuance totaled $25 million, of which Huston was allocated bonds valued at $825,000, making him an extremely wealthy man.

In 1914 Huston moved back to the States. With his newfound wealth he wanted to acquire a Major League franchise. Always a baseball fan, Huston had become friendly with John McGraw during one of the latter's trips to Cuba. He even spent some of his vacation over the prior couple of years traveling with the Giants. In the midst of the Federal League War, Huston secured an option to purchase the Cubs for six hundred thousand dollars. He planned to bring along his pal McGraw as manager and part owner. McGraw expressed an interest but claimed he could not get out of his multiyear contract with the Giants—he probably did not want to leave New York and simply needed an excuse to avoid embarrassing his friend. Without McGraw, Huston lost interest and allowed the option to lapse.

Jacob Ruppert Jr. was a wealthy, perfectionist brewer who often lapsed into a German accent (although he was a native-born New Yorker) when agitated. Less than one year older than Barrow, Ruppert graduated from Columbia Grammar School and passed the entrance exam for Columbia College. His parents, however, guided him into the family brewery, where he started at the bottom at age nineteen. The personable and determined Ruppert rapidly learned the business, and the family promoted him through the company ranks. Successful at his various postings, Ruppert quickly ascended to the top. He proved a skilled chief executive and expanded the operation considerably.

Ruppert also dabbled in several exotic hobbies; the perfectionist in him craved to be preeminent in anything he tackled. He collected jade, Chinese porcelain, and oil paintings. At his country estate in Garrison, New York, he kept a collection of small monkeys and raised St. Bernards for a time. Like many members of the upper class at the turn of the last century, he enjoyed horses as well. Before he abandoned the hobby, Ruppert purchased and raced top horses and managed the Ruppert Stables. He never married and throughout his life remained one of New York's most eligible bachelors.

Popular, wealthy, and well-connected to the German-American community, Ruppert was a natural for politics. He joined an upper-class regiment of the National Guard in 1886. Several years later he was appointed aide-de-camp to Governor David Hill and received the rank of colonel. Ruppert took great pleasure in this title and for the rest of his life liked to be addressed with it.

Late in the 1880s Ruppert joined Tammany Hall, the political machine that controlled much of New York politics. Tammany tapped him to run for city council president but was forced to withdraw his candidacy due to various political machinations and miscalculations. Instead, the Democratic organization sponsored Ruppert for Congress in 1898 in a generally Republican district. Ruppert won in a mild upset and served a total of four terms. After his eight years in Congress, he concentrated most of his energies—aside from all his hobbies—on the brewery business.

Ruppert had loved baseball since his youth. Late in the 1890s he ran into a couple of Major League owners including Harry Von der Horst, fellow brewer and owner of the National League Baltimore franchise. The National League owners were hoping to rid themselves of Andrew Freedman, the disruptive owner of the New York Giants, and they suggested to Ruppert that the Giants might be available for purchase. If Ruppert acquired the team, he was told, the league would give him four players as a gift. When Ruppert contacted Freedman, however, the owner feigned surprise at the inquiry. Nevertheless, Freedman asked how much Ruppert would offer, to which Ruppert replied he would pay $150,000. Freedman refused the offer, saying the club was not for sale, but added that if he decided to sell, he would call Ruppert first. Freedman disappointed Ruppert by selling the franchise several years later in 1903 for only $125,000 without ever contacting him.

In 1914 both Ruppert and Huston were separately poking around baseball, rummaging for a team to buy. American League president Ban Johnson hoped to find a franchise for these two well-heeled prospectors before the Federal League enticed them. Other Major League owners recruited the two as well. Ruppert and Huston did not know each other prior to being introduced while on their separate franchise hunts. When McGraw suggested that the New York Yankees might be available, the two reluctantly agreed to look into what was generally regarded as one of baseball's most hapless teams. As an inducement, their fellow American League magnates-to-be promised to make some decent players available to the Yankees immediately after the two purchased the club. In January 1915 the two colonels created a fifty-fifty partnership, closed on the franchise for about $460,000, and assumed $20,000 in debt. Only Detroit president Frank Navin honored the promise of players: he allowed the Yankees to purchase two reserves, outfielder Hugh High and first baseman Wally Pipp, for $5,500. In July the team purchased budding star pitcher Bob Shawkey for $3,000 from Philadelphia Athletics owner Connie Mack, who, in a financial bind because of the Federal League, was selling his stars.

Resentful but determined, the two colonels hoped to purchase some of baseball's better players in the aftermath of the Federal League war. They spent $40,000 to buy four mediocre players controlled by Federal League owner Harry Sinclair. More successfully, they paid Mack $37,500 for Hall of Fame third baseman Frank "Home Run" Baker, who had held out all of 1915 while demanding his contract be renegotiated. The Yankees' owners felt frustrated and betrayed that same off-season when Ban Johnson engineered the sale of the great center fielder Tris Speaker from Boston to Cleveland for $55,000.

Huston hoped to prove his baseball acumen by actively supervising personnel decisions on the model of Charles Comiskey in Chicago and Barney Dreyfuss in Pittsburgh. Unfortunately, in one of his first high-dollar recommendations, the Yankees purchased pitcher Dan Tipple from Indianapolis for nine thousand dollars—a considerable sum for the time, particularly in the midst of the Federal League war. Tipple's failure to perform and progress as expected quickly led to Huston's eclipse as a baseball insider.

Shortly after acquiring the team, Ruppert and Huston hired Sparrow on the recommendation of John McGraw, manager of the rival New York Giants. Sparrow and McGraw were close friends. McGraw had introduced Sparrow to baseball administration in 1913 when he recruited Sparrow to manage the business end of his world baseball tour. In 1917 Sparrow was hospitalized for several days with a severe attack of indigestion and never fully recovered his health. Sparrow was an adequate administrator, but his tenure with the Yankees was undistinguished. He may have been too close to McGraw and lacked the necessary baseball expertise and, for the last couple of years, the good health to provide the support the Yankees' owners needed.

Sparrow certainly had to negotiate an awkward working relationship between his owners. The partnership of the two colonels was strained from the start. Neither Ruppert nor Huston had the temperament or the desire to share authority. Nevertheless, the two colonels both tried hard—and with surprising success—to make the marriage work. Both were extremely competitive. Ruppert played the hard-driving perfectionist, while Huston was the high-spirited, socially active partner.

The Yankees brought in Barrow's old Detroit hurler, Wild Bill Donovan, as manager. After three years at the helm, New York let Donovan go on the heels of a 71-82 finish in 1917. Huston wanted to hire his friend Wilbert Robinson, the current Brooklyn Dodgers manager. Ruppert, who did not really know Robinson, interviewed him and came away unimpressed.

In 1917 Huston joined the war effort and headed off to France (he would return a lieutenant colonel). Ruppert remained resistant to Robinson and consulted Ban Johnson for advice. Johnson reportedly recommended the St. Louis Cardinals' diminutive manager, Miller Huggins, whom he considered the best manager in the National League behind John McGraw. Ruppert was favorably impressed with Huggins and hired him on October 15, 1917, without consulting Huston. Huston was naturally furious that Ruppert had spurned his candidate and signed another. Ruppert's unilateral hiring of Huggins led to the most serious and long-lasting disagreement between the two men. Huston's anger at the hiring ripened into an excessive dislike of Huggins and a hatred of Johnson for his perceived interference with his team's affairs. Even after he returned from France, Huston never reconciled himself to Huggins. Until he sold his interest in the Yankees several years later, Huston unrelentingly worked to undermine and replace his manager.

Barrow, a friend of Huston's, felt the need to defend himself against the notion that he may have been part of a conspiracy to plant Huggins on the Yankees. He wrote to Huston that while he considered Huggins a great manager, he felt the same about Wilbert Robinson. Barrow denied any involvement in directing Ruppert to Huggins. He further added that he had no knowledge of any involvement by Ban Johnson in the process.

After his arrival Huggins controlled player personnel decisions. In his first significant move, Huggins traded five players, including his starting second baseman and catcher, young hurler Urban Shocker, and $15,000 for star second baseman Del Pratt and aging hurler Eddie Plank (when Plank failed to report, the Browns refunded $2,500). The two regulars were no great loss, but Shocker developed into one of the league's better pitchers. Pratt was an excellent fielder who helped solidify the Yankees' infield defense. Following his first season at the helm in 1918, Huggins concocted the trade with Barrow and the Red Sox, which brought Ernie Shore, Duffy Lewis, and Dutch Leonard to New York for a few journeymen and $25,000. Several months later, as discussed at length earlier, the Yankees purchased Carl Mays.

The Eighteenth Amendment to the U.S. Constitution banning intoxicating liquors—commonly referred to as Prohibition—was ratified in January 1919 and took effect one year later in January 1920. The amendment obviously would have a significant impact on Ruppert's brewery operation, his main source of income. To remain in business during Prohibition, Ruppert shifted to producing near beer (nonalcoholic beer), a much less desirable and less profitable beverage. The purchase of Ruth and the large loan to Frazee testified to Ruppert's willingness to take considerable financial risks—amid uncertainty and declining revenues in his main business—in order to construct a winner.

Babe Ruth's first season in New York cemented his legend. Ruth was an undeniably great player in Boston and had established himself as perhaps the game's best hitter in 1919, when he set the all-time record of twenty-nine home runs. He broke that record in July 1920 on his way to a phenomenal fifty-four—an astonishing total, surpassing all other teams in the American League. This accomplishment combined with his other statistics (.376 AVG, 137 RBI, 150 walks, .532 OBP, .847 SLG) made Ruth seem like something from another planet and forever changed the game.

Many suspected, and most believe today, that the ball was purposely made livelier to increase offense around this time. Barrow claimed no change had been made to the baseball. The elimination of the spitball and other "trick" pitches, along with a concerted effort to keep clean baseballs in play, were sufficient to increase offensive production.

In 1920 the Yankees finished 95-59, their best record to date. Along with Ruth's heroics, Mays won twenty-six games, and Huggins led the Yankees to a third-place finish. There were some setbacks, however. Frank Baker missed the season due to the illness and death of his wife, and the pitching staff was little better than average after Mays and Bob Shawkey. Huggins received a strong performance from his bench, and the team likely outplayed its talent level. The Yankees biggest in-season upgrade was the acquisition of outfielder Bob Meusel from the Vernon, California, club in the Pacific Coast League for four players valued at ten thousand dollars. Barrow had joined a franchise with some obvious strengths; if he could upgrade its talent at several infield positions and add some pitching, it could be great.

Ed Barrow took the reins in October 1920. As he evaluated his new team, Ruppert and Huston were spearheading one of the most contentious baseball ownership controversies since the founding of the American League. Hiring Barrow testified to their competitiveness: even while challenging baseball's hierarchy, they remained focused on improving their team on the field.

The relationship between Ban Johnson and three of his clubs had continued to sour since the Carl Mays controversy in 1919. The Insurrectos— the Yankees (Ruppert and Huston), the Red Sox (Harry Frazee), and the Chicago White Sox (Charles Comiskey)—had been maneuvering to reduce Johnson's authority, even to oust him as president of the American League. The other five American League owners remained loyal to Johnson, creating a precarious stalemate. In the meantime, National Commission chairman Garry Herrmann had been forced out of office before the 1920 season. Already dysfunctional, with his exit the National Commission effectively ceased operation. Amplifying the American League's internal clash and leadership crisis, the Major and the Minor leagues were also in the midst of acrimoniously revamping the draft and other rules. The Black Sox scandal, which became public in late September 1920, added a sense of urgency to filling the leadership void.

Albert Lasker, a Chicago Cubs minority stockholder and prominent Chicago businessman, proposed a plan to replace the old commission system with a triumvirate of neutrals with no financial interest in baseball. The National League generally supported the plan, but the five Johnson loyalists in the American League objected, mainly because Johnson would be forced to relinquish his position as first among equals on the National Commission. After much posturing and politicking, the issue came to a head in November 1920. At a meeting in Chicago on November 8, the three disgruntled American League franchises threatened to jump to the National League, forming a twelve-team circuit (another team would be added later). The new league agreed to adopt the Lasker plan and offer the chairmanship of the triumvirate to Kenesaw Mountain Landis, a federal judge from Chicago.

For several days thereafter Johnson blustered that the American League would form new teams in New York, Chicago, and Boston, gain the support of the Minors, and rejuvenate itself to become stronger than ever. Except for Phil Ball in St. Louis, Johnson's loyalists had neither the resources nor the desire for a drawn-out battle with the New National League. On November 12, the owners of the sixteen Major League teams met. They agreed to adopt a modified Lasker plan: the triumvirate was abandoned in favor of a sole commissioner. A delegation of owners then hustled over to offer the commissionership to Judge Landis, which he accepted after being assured that his authority would be close to absolute.

Player acquisition and development prior to World War II, by which time the Minor Leagues had more thoroughly evolved into a Major League farm system (at least for the wealthier franchises), was much more haphazard and less efficiently regulated than today. Teams acquired talent through basically four methods:

> From other Major League teams in exchange for players and/or money (i.e., trades and purchases or some combination of the two).
> From the Minor Leagues, again in exchange for players and/or money, but most typically as an outright purchase.

By signing an amateur as a free agent (the amateur draft did not
take effect until 1965).

From the Minor Leagues through the Major League–Minor
League draft (the remnants of which exist today as the
occasionally relevant Rule 5 draft).

For the most part, Minor League franchises in 1920 were independent
and not formally affiliated with a Major League team. Local owner-oper-
ators ran the clubs to make a profit and, if possible, win as well. Many of
the top Minor League teams played in large cities with enthusiastic follow-
ers who cared as much about winning as Major League fans. Over the first
three decades of the twentieth century, a complex set of ever-changing rules
and informal arrangements evolved to govern player movement between
the Major and the Minor Leagues. In terms of the actual number of quality Major League players acquired, the draft was probably the least important of the four methods. But unstable draft rules prior to 1931 strongly influenced the relative importance and cost of the other three.

After the financially disastrous 1918 season, the high Minor Leagues
had again challenged the draft. The National Association (i.e., the Minor
Leagues) officially declared itself opposed to the draft and other sections
of the National Agreement it found distasteful. Not surprisingly, when the
association presented its demands, the Majors rejected them. The two sides
agreed to let the National Agreement lapse but separately and informally
arranged to mutually respect each other's territorial and player reservation
rights. But the high Minors had finally obtained their key demand: the Major League–Minor League draft would be abolished for those leagues that
wanted to opt out.

Nevertheless, both sides recognized that a comprehensive agreement between them was important for the prosperity and management of Organized Baseball. Over the next few years representatives from each group
continued to meet after each season to try to hammer out a new National
Agreement. But with baseball's other significant issues still unresolved—
the Black Sox scandal, the dismantling of the National Commission and
the selection of a commissioner, litigation with the Baltimore Federal Leaguers, and the near civil war among the American League owners and president—the relationship with the Minor Leagues did not receive the attention it needed.

The appointment of Commissioner Landis in November 1920 brought some stability back to the baseball hierarchy, and in early 1921 a new National Agreement was finally signed. The new agreement reestablished the draft but included a provision allowing leagues to withdraw from it. Not surprisingly, the three class AA leagues (along with two others) chose to do so. Now that the Minors could hold on to their best players, the early 1920s featured some of baseball's greatest Minor League teams. The great Baltimore Orioles of this era could not have enjoyed their extended success had players like Lefty Grove been subject to the draft.

After the 1923 season a modified draft was introduced that again included all leagues, except for the International League, which continued to hold out. This modified draft, however, still strongly favored the Minors. The only eligible players were those who had once been the property of the Major Leagues, so the high Minors retained full control of many of their best players. After the 1924 season the International League also became subject to this modified draft. The high Minors agreed to the modified draft because they themselves wished to draft from the lower Minors.

Ed Barrow recognized the critical importance of his scouting department for uncovering talent in the Minor Leagues and colleges. The Yankees at Barrow's arrival employed three principal scouts, including ex-outfielder Joe Kelley, one of Barrow's old acquaintances from Kelley's days managing in the International League, and Bob Connery. Teams also used "bird-dog" scouts, locally connected baseball men, often college coaches or managers in the low Minor Leagues. These informants were typically compensated with a commission check or stipend when a team signed a recommended player. Extensive contacts and relationships with these local bird dogs were essential for finding the top young talent before a competitor did.

One of Barrow's most significant and lasting influences was the emphasis and resources he put into scouting. He reorganized the existing scouts to a more regionally based system. By concentrating on a region, the scouts could develop stronger relationships with the local sources. From Boston, Barrow brought over Paul Krichell, his most trusted scout and assistant. Initially focused on college ballplayers, Krichell became one of the greatest of all baseball scouts.

A stocky catcher, Krichell grew up in the Bronx long before the Yankees played there. He broke into Organized Baseball in 1903, and over the next fifty years developed one of the widest ranges of contacts of anyone in the game. After catching for Barrow in Montreal in 1910, Krichell played his only two years in the Majors for the St. Louis Browns. He then spent several years back in the Minors, before he became the manager of Bridgeport in the Eastern League. In 1919 Krichell left Organized Baseball for a year to manage the New York University team. In 1920 Barrow brought him onto his coaching staff in Boston. At the time most coaches also doubled as scouts, and Krichell proved highly proficient in both roles.

At the same time the Yankees hired Barrow, Ruppert also inked Huggins to a contract extension, in effect offering—in spite of Huston's animosity—a vote of confidence in his manager. Physically small, constitutionally frail, and well read, Huggins did not fit the mold of a ballplayer or a manager. He succeeded first as a player and later as a manager through intelligence and force of will. Many accounts of his life conjecture that the ceaseless struggle required to enforce his policies and instructions led to his premature health problems.

Born in 1878, Huggins grew up in Cincinnati playing baseball with his older brother Clarence, often against their father's wishes. To circumvent his parent, Huggins played semiprofessional baseball under an assumed name while attending law school at the University of Cincinnati. His sister later recalled that future U.S. president William Howard Taft, then a law professor at the university, recommended that Huggins concentrate on baseball, which he seemed to enjoy more. Nevertheless, Huggins honored his father's wishes and earned admission to the Ohio bar.

While playing semiprofessionally, Huggins became acquainted with Max Fleischmann, who owned one of the teams Huggins played for. The Fleischmanns were a prominent Cincinnati family involved with city government and had an interest in the National League's Cincinnati Reds. Possibly through a Fleischmann connection, in 1901 Huggins landed the second base job for St. Paul in the Western League. Huggins, despite being only five feet four and 140 pounds, more than held his own in this high Minor League. After Huggins had played three years at St. Paul, owner George Lennon recognized that he had a marketable player. Huggins wanted to go back to Cincinnati and engineered his sale to the Reds for around three thousand dollars.

In Cincinnati Huggins earned the nickname "Mr. Everywhere" for his range at second base. Although he possessed little power, he was valuable at the plate as well. He taught himself to punch hit and at one point played in 364 consecutive games. He often led the league in walks and finished with a career .382 OBP. In 1910 the Reds traded Huggins to the St. Louis Cardinals. After owner Helene Britton fired Roger Bresnahan in 1913, she hired Huggins as player-manager at a salary of eight thousand dollars. In his five years at the helm, Huggins guided the Cardinals to two third-place finishes, their best standing ever until 1921. On the recommendation of close friend Bob Connery (a future Yankees scout), he convinced his cash-strapped owners to purchase future great Rogers Hornsby from a Texas Minor League club for six hundred dollars. Hornsby debuted in 1915 as a nineteen-year-old shortstop, and Huggins successfully launched him on his way to a Hall of Fame career.

Though Huggins certainly recognized that good teams need good players, he also, probably because of his own exertions, believed in the importance of guts and character: "To be successful a manager must be a student of human nature; must be an executive, a diplomat and an aggressive fighter. I don't care how good a team is, it will lose 25% of its efficiency if it doesn't fight. By a fighting team I don't mean a team that is at swords' points with the umpires all the time. A fighting team, to my mind, is a team with individual and collective pluck and never-say-die spirit."

Meanwhile, Ed Barrow, newly minted Yankees boss, enjoyed a short vacation in Canada before taking up his duties in time for the contentious November 8 league meetings. Barrow's name also surfaced that winter as a possible leading executive in the prospective Continental League, a potential new competitor to the Major Leagues. Both the league's prospects and the talk linking Barrow to it quickly faded.

Upon assuming his new role with the Yankees, Barrow did not immediately take a leading role in building the Major League roster. In mid-December Miller Huggins, with Ruppert's and Barrow's approval, swapped catcher Muddy Ruel, pitcher Hank Thormahlen, outfielder Sammy Vick, and Pratt along with fifty thousand dollars to Boston for catcher Wally Schang, infielder Mike McNally, and pitchers Waite Hoyt and Harry Harper. Most observers rated Pratt as the only player of value the Yankees had surrendered, although Ruel soon developed into a quality regular as well. Schang was one of baseball's top catchers, and Barrow had liked Hoyt ever since he put him in Boston's rotation as a teenager. A month later Barrow secured another of his old Boston players, dealing George Mogridge and Duffy Lewis to Washington for Bobby Roth. As the winter advanced, Barrow increasingly began to assert his authority over the player-acquisition side of the business. When rumors surfaced that Baker was to be dealt to Washington, it was Barrow—not Huggins, Huston, or Ruppert—who denied them.

Before he could get his team onto the field, Barrow needed to find a new spring training site. According to the *Sporting News*, the year before Barrow's arrival, "virtually the entire New York club went on a three-day binge while playing a series of three games with the Reds in Miami and Palm Beach." On the heels of this unruly behavior, Ruppert banned future exhibitions in South Florida, a policy Barrow continued. In 1920 the team had trained in Jacksonville, but Barrow wanted a new site for 1921 to create a different atmosphere. At his direction Bob Connery toured the South over the winter. As they would today, the prospective cities and towns rolled out the red carpet when Connery came through, boosting their merits. Barrow and Connery eventually settled on Shreveport, Louisiana.

Business manager Barrow also lined up exhibition games with National and Minor League teams for regular season open dates, a common practice at the time that resulted in teams actually playing well more than the scheduled 154 games. For example, in February Barrow lined up an exhibition game at Cincinnati for July 25. A week later when the American League made changes to its schedule, Barrow needed to either reschedule this exhibition game or obtain league consent for switching a scheduled regular season date. (Because of Ruth, the Yankees were a top draw for these games, and Barrow could often command 50 percent of the gross receipts, more than typical for the road team.)

Barrow grew increasingly excited over his new team's chances as the 1921 season neared. The infield was solid with the return of third baseman Frank Baker, whose comeback allowed Huggins to shift 1920 third baseman Aaron Ward to second. Skillful veterans Roger Peckinpaugh and Wally Pipp held down shortstop and first base, respectively. Ruth and Meusel anchored the outfield corners, while several journeymen, including the recently acquired Roth, patrolled center. In Schang the Yankees boasted the league's best-hitting catcher. Shawkey, Mays, and Hoyt anchored the pitching staff (no other hurler would start more than sixteen games).

Barrow inherited a talented club filled with hard-drinking veterans. Ruth and Mays, the team's two best players, were both complex, sensitive personalities who were a challenge to manage and keep focused on the team's welfare. Prohibition did little to inhibit the drinking habits of some of the team's wilder players, but they did retain their competitive drive and craving for a title. This competitiveness proved sufficient inducement for the players to submit, however halfheartedly, to Huggins's discipline.

The most dysfunctional aspect of the Ruppert-Huston-Barrow-Huggins quartet was the obvious animosity Huston directed at Huggins. Rather than subsiding over time, Huston's unhappiness with Huggins's stewardship festered and grew more bitter. Though Ruppert's support kept Huggins in his job, having one owner opposed to his employment undermined Huggins's authority with the players. Huston occasionally went so far as to overrule or lessen Huggins's disciplinary actions, further inhibiting his control over the strong personalities on his team.

Barrow tried, with only moderate success, to interpose himself between owner and manager. He hoped to partially insulate Huggins from Huston's constant criticisms and allow Huggins to reassert managerial authority over his ball club. Barrow affirmed his support to Huggins, while simultaneously asserting his own dominion over personnel decisions: "You're the manager, and you'll not be second guessed by me. Your job is to win; mine is to get you the players you need to win. I'll take responsibility for every deal I make."

Given the strong personalities on the club and the hatred of one of the owners for his manager, Barrow's inaugural season as business manager proved surprisingly devoid of controversy. The 1921 baseball season witnessed a fairly tight race between the Yankees and the Cleveland Indians, the 1920 champions. Ruth had another phenomenal season, smacking a record fifty-nine home runs accompanied by 171 RBI. Because of the team's formidable hitting attack, the Yankees became known in the press as "Murderers' Row." This epithet was first used in reference to the Yankees as early as 1918 to describe the team's powerful batting order, but it became commonplace in the 1920s after Ruth and his fellow sluggers joined the club. Carl Mays again anchored the pitching staff, winning a league-leading twenty-seven games. Not until September, however, did the Yankees pull away from the Indians. The closeness of the race and the anticipation of their first pennant may have helped restrain some of the players' most raucous behavior.

Barrow made only one significant player move during the season, acquiring outfielder Elmer Miller from St. Paul in July to bolster his weak center field. In one humorous anecdote that season, Barrow informed the press that he had anonymously received $2.50 in the mail. The enclosed letter noted that it was in payment for "a ball I caught in the stands at one of your games." Barrow, the handwriting connoisseur, announced that he owed the sender $1.12 in change and would pay it upon receiving a follow-up letter; he professed he would verify the sender based on his handwriting.

For the 1921 World Series, the Yankees faced off against their hometown rivals, the New York Giants. For the third straight season the Series would be a best of nine format. All the games would be played at the Polo Grounds, which the Yankees and the Giants shared during the season. (The Giants owned the stadium and since 1913 had leased it to the Yankees.) Betting on the Series approached $1 million, with half wagered in New York City alone. One well-known gambler speculated that this total exceeded the previous record of $750,000 bet on the 1917 Series between the Giants and the White Sox. Unfortunately for Barrow and his new organization, the Yankees lost five games to three, despite a tremendous pitching performance from Waite Hoyt, who pitched three complete games without yielding an earned run. He lost the eighth game of the Series, however, when short-stop Roger Peckinpaugh let a ball roll between his legs, allowing the game's only run to score. After the World Series Hoyt was the beneficiary of a big party honoring his performance; the guest list included Barrow and Ruppert, along with a number of his teammates.

More serious matters soon intervened. In January 1921 the commissioner's office had announced its intention to enforce a standing rule prohibiting participants in the World Series from earning additional money playing in exhibition games after the season. Ruth, who earned a lot of money "barnstorming," had no intention of adhering to the new edict; he and several of his teammates planned to earn extra income touring after the World Series ended. When Landis unequivocally prohibited any trip by the players, most of them backed out. Ruth approached Barrow for special permission to stick to his plans. Barrow had no objections to Ruth's winter tour but told Ruth that he needed Judge Landis's approval. Landis invited Ruth to come see him. When Ruth declined to attend a party instead, the vain commissioner fumed at the snub. Ruth and Bob Meusel embarked on the barnstorming tour without Landis's sanction.

As Landis bided his time, Barrow and the two colonels realized that their star was in trouble and began lobbying to keep any punishment as light as possible. Barrow traveled to Chicago to soften Landis, with whom he had become quite friendly.

"Well, what do you want?" Landis demanded, feigning indignation and pugnaciousness.

"I guess you know what I want," Barrow responded.

"Yes, I do. It's about those two lawbreakers. Come here, Ed," Landis told him and directed him toward the window.

"See those kids. I suppose they're saying to each other, 'That big white haired so-and-so in that office up there is the one who's keeping Babe Ruth out of the ball game.' But tell me: what would you do?"

Barrow could do little but hope for leniency. "I'd suspend him too."

Several weeks later Landis ruled that Ruth and Meusel would be suspended until May 20, well into the 1922 season.

The fall of 1921 also brought the more typical off-season administrative chores. In November Barrow took his customary vacation and journeyed down to New Bern, North Carolina, for two weeks of fishing and relaxing. When he returned, Barrow again had to select a site for spring training, as Huggins did not wish to return to Shreveport. After some deliberation, the Yankees' brain trust—Ruppert, Huston, Barrow, and Huggins—opted for Mineral Wells, Texas, only to learn that the Cincinnati Reds had beaten them to it. Eventually, Barrow and the Yankees settled on New Orleans.

Barrow spent much of the winter searching for a stopgap to man the outfield for the first six weeks of the season during Ruth's and Meusel's suspensions. Salt Lake City reportedly turned down Barrow's offer of twenty-five thousand dollars to use their player-manager (and former Yankee), Duffy Lewis, until June 1. Rumors also linked Barrow to Bobby Veach, Amos Strunk, and his old right fielder in Boston, Harry Hooper. Eventually Barrow landed some outfield assistance when he purchased Whitey Witt from the Athletics at the end of spring training. He also learned that veteran lefty Harry Harper would be leaving the team to concentrate on some big contracts awarded to his trucking company.

A standard off-season headache for all clubs was negotiating player contracts for the upcoming season. Because of the reserve clause in all contracts, players had virtually no negotiating leverage beyond threatening to sit out the upcoming season. Typically, each spring the teams sent out contracts to all their players with a salary for the coming season and instructed the player to sign and return it. Inevitably a few players would decide the contract was unacceptable and refuse the proffered salary. These holdouts were usually symbolic: most players had no intention of sitting out a season or switching to another line of work. "How many players ever quit baseball because they couldn't make their employers give them more money than they were worth?" Barrow observed. "Offhand I can name only two—Mike Donlin and Eddie Roush. [There were a couple of others over the years, but Barrow's gist is correct.] Yet both of them came back after one year of idleness." Nevertheless, teams did occasionally increase their offers to holdouts to minimize uncertainty and limit negative publicity.

When Waite Hoyt received his 1922 contract from Barrow, he angrily denounced the $200 pay cut, a natural reaction after his strong season and a stellar World Series. Barrow denied he had requested the pay cut, claiming that in fact Hoyt's contract included a hefty raise. Huston cleared up the muddle when he disclosed that Hoyt had been sent another player's contract by mistake. In 1921 Hoyt had earned a salary of $4,200 plus a $1,000 bonus for the first-place finish. In 1922 the Yankees bumped his salary up to $10,000, and Waite and his wife came down to sign in the Yankees' offices.

After a pretty good season, second baseman Aaron Ward publicly agitated for a bigger raise as well. In 1921 he had earned $5,000, and the Yankees offered him a raise to $6,500. Ward announced that he would not sign for less than $10,000, and his name began popping up in trade rumors for various outfielders. Yankees records indicate that Ward eventually settled for an additional $500, at $7,000.

Despite the impact of Prohibition on Ruppert's brewery income and the sizable costs associated with a planned new stadium, the two colonels remained committed to building a champion at any cost. Amid postwar prosperity and with attendance rebounding, relatively few teams were now selling their stars. Fortunately for the Yankees, Huston and Barrow remained fast friends with money-hungry Boston owner Harry Frazee. It was not difficult to stay "close" to the New York–based Frazee; he sometimes even used the Yankees' offices to conduct Red Sox business.

By 1921 the Red Sox no longer boasted the talent of previous years, but they finished just below .500 and still had some stars remaining from Barrow's tenure. With Ruppert's and Huston's blessing, Barrow acquired two of the league's best pitchers, Sam Jones and Joe Bush, along with star shortstop Everett Scott for four players (Roger Peckinpaugh was the only one of note) and $150,000—the highest dollar amount ever included in a player transaction up to that point, and one that would not be exceeded until the Cubs bought Rogers Hornsby from the Boston Braves near the end of the decade. Unlike the Ruth transaction, the full extent of the dollar amount never became public. Once again Frazee—although by this time no one took him seriously—ridiculously declared that in fact he had made this trade to strengthen the team: "I feel I have considerably strengthened the team and see no reason for discontent."

When the two colonels purchased the Yankees in 1915, they inherited a lease for the Polo Grounds with the Giants, the facility's primary tenant. As part of the Federal League settlement, Ruppert maintained that the Yankees were permitted to acquire a share of the underlying ground lease with the Coogan estate. (The estate owned the land; the Giants owned the stadium itself and leased the site for a twenty-five-year term.) Documents were drawn up but never executed. When Charles Stoneham purchased the Giants in 1919, Ruppert approached him about finally signing the lease agreements. Stoneham, one of baseball's slickest operators, claimed he knew nothing about the arrangement. For an able businessman and former politician, Ruppert's lack of follow-through on the lease with the Coogan estate seems inexcusable, casting some doubt on the validity of Ruppert's assertion. Of course, it may have been Sparrow's responsibility to finalize the document, and given his close relationship with McGraw, he may have been overly nonchalant regarding its execution. In any case, after first threatening to evict the Yankees, Stoneham extended the lease for one year to cover the 1920 season.

As long as the Yankees were New York's second most popular team, Giants manager John McGraw was happy to allow his friends Huston and Ruppert to lease his home park. And Stoneham liked the income generated by the lease. With the arrival of Ruth, however, the Yankees now boasted baseball's biggest attraction, and they were also winning. McGraw and Stoneham now had second thoughts regarding the stadium arrangement and decided they wanted the Yankees out. The death of McGraw's close friend Harry Sparrow had further weakened the ties between the two clubs. Ruppert also suspected that Ban Johnson hoped to see the Yankees evicted—this was at the height of the Johnson-Yankees feud—as a way to revoke their league charter, which required having a venue in which to play. Stoneham eventually extended the lease for another two years through 1922. He made it clear, though, that this was only a short-term accommodation unless the Yankees were willing to pay an exorbitant rent of at least one hundred thousand dollars per year.

Ruppert and Huston naturally recognized that they needed their own ballpark, and needed it soon—by opening day 1923. The site search proved difficult as several additional potential sites fell by the wayside for various reasons; the Yankees eventually struggled through six alternatives before finally settling on a site in the Bronx. Ruppert and Huston purchased most of the site from Vincent Astor, spending a total of close to six hundred thousand dollars to acquire the entire parcel.

As business manager, Barrow was only tangentially involved in the construction of Yankee Stadium. Once work began in April 1922, Huston, the engineer, oversaw the twelve-month project. Barrow managed the expenses and helped with some of the details, including the selection of seats. The cost to construct Yankee Stadium totaled roughly $1.6 million, bringing the all-in expenditure to $2.2 million. To help defray a portion of the cost, the American League lent the Yankees' owners $400,000 on a ten-year term at 7 percent interest. The new stadium was clearly the preeminent and most majestic baseball venue in America and would hold this distinction for many years. Despite his lack of direct involvement in its construction, Barrow would later spend much of his time as business manager patrolling and overseeing the stadium.

On March 18, 1922, Barrow and Ruppert, along with Bridgeport manager Gene McCann, left for spring training in New Orleans. McCann tagged along in hope of finding some youngsters unable to make the Yankees' Major League roster for his Eastern League club. With all the difficult personalities on the team, an indignant Ruth angered by his suspension, and the added pressure of the fast-track construction of Yankee Stadium, Barrow sensed that the upcoming season would be explosive. He was not wrong.

Throughout the spring Huggins had trouble keeping his players from enjoying the charms of New Orleans. His difficulties came to a head on April 5 during an exhibition game against Brooklyn when Carl Mays hurled the ball over the grandstand after Huggins came to the mound to remove him. The club fined Mays two hundred dollars. An angry Mays responded: "There are other players on the club who have done as much as I did, and I told Huggins so. I also told him I don't think he is a good manager, and I've always thought so." He also threatened to quit baseball and jump to an outlaw league if the fine were not rescinded.

To further complicate matters, the Yankees' front office and manager looked dysfunctional in the fining process. At first Huggins claimed that he did not fine Mays and neither did Barrow, implying it came directly from the owners. A day later Huston put the onus back on Huggins, asserting that the manager had in fact ordered the fine but that the club should "back him up." Huggins then publicly issued a revised version of events: "When Mays learned in Bristol that he had been fined, he charged that Barrow had done it and said I was not the manager of the club. Well, nobody in New York had anything to do with it. I'm the manager and I ordered the fine and it will be paid." Mays quickly backed off his threat to leave, but the publicly aired discord set the tone for the remainder of the season. The muddle precipitated by Huston's distaste for Huggins and the latter's difficulties in disciplining his team frustrated Barrow immensely. He had little tolerance for a loosely run ship and struggled to insulate Huggins from Huston's interference. As the Mays incident illustrated, he was only partially successful.

Less than a month later, Huggins was again embarrassed by a player. In the top of the fourteenth inning of a 2–2 game with two on and one out, Huggins ordered Hoyt to walk Boston's Elmer Miller. Hoyt grudgingly complied but then unraveled and surrendered three runs. When the angry and frustrated Hoyt reached the bench, he began cursing Huggins. After a short quarrel, Hoyt punched Huggins in the stomach. The players quickly intervened, reducing the tension from a boil to a simmer. Huggins sent Hoyt back to the clubhouse and Lefty O'Doul up to pinch hit. Huggins's uncertainty regarding his authority is clear from his response to this incident: "As far as I know, I will not finc or suspend Hoyt."

With the players running amok, the Yankees hired a detective, identified only as Kelly, to track the team. The impetus for the idea came from Huston, who probably hoped to demonstrate Huggins's lack of control—a problem exacerbated by Huston's own interference. A seasoned undercover operator, Kelly ingratiated himself with Schang on the team's first western road trip while posing as a racetrack commissioner. Schang introduced Kelly to the Yankees, who quickly took to their new companion after he produced cases of illegal beer and accepted bets on horses.

Many players quickly grew to trust Kelly and welcomed him at various points along the road trip. To further alleviate any suspicion, Kelly pointed out a young reporter—alternatively identified retrospectively as Marshall Hunt or Bob Boyd—as a management spy. For many months the young reporter could not figure out why many players gave him the cold shoulder. When Kelly invited the players to a big party thrown by a brewery friend in Joliet, Illinois, many players eagerly accepted. At the party Kelly convinced the players to pose for a picture, which he persuaded them to autograph for him.

Kelly submitted a full report to Ruppert, Huston, and Barrow, who locked the picture away in his safe. To scare the players into behaving, they passed much of the report on to Landis and asked him to lecture the players on the consequences and dangers associated with gambling and carousing. Landis chose to impersonalize his diatribe and not direct it at any specific players. On June 26, with the Yankees in Boston, he called the players of both teams together. He challenged them with the accusations in Kelly's report and blistered them for their behavior.

Around the same time, veteran New York sportswriter Joe Vila disclosed a rumor that "certain players had aroused a suspicion that they were trying to double-cross Huggins again," that is, purposely trying to lose to discredit their manager. Vila took the rumors seriously enough to demand that "if the alleged conspiracy turn[ed] out to be a fact, Commissioner Landis should conduct a thorough investigation." Given the lack of any tangible evidence, though, no further action was taken. The Yankees were in a slump—the team lost eleven of thirteen in mid-June—and in the aftermath of the exposure of the Black Sox scandal, observers often saw purposeful actions in coincidences.

Other incidents tested Barrow and Huggins as well. Wally Pipp punched Ruth in the dugout after Ruth questioned an error by Pipp; Ward and Roth fought in the dugout; backup catcher Al DeVormer wrestled with Mays and later took on another backup catcher, Fred Hofmann; Meusel and Schang engaged in some dugout fisticuffs; and Ruth was suspended more than once for his run-ins with umpires. To restore at least some semblance of order, Barrow managed to prohibit Ruppert and Huston from barging into the locker room after games. Despite all the brawling and mayhem, the Yankees remained in the pennant hunt. As the season moved into the summer, Barrow's Yankees were in a tight race with the St. Louis Browns, a team built by the American League's other de facto general manager, Bob Quinn.

While confusion reigned on disciplinary matters, Barrow had assumed control over the roster. When rumors circulated in early July that the Yankees might trade Ruth, it was Barrow who fronted for the team, forcefully and derisively denying the hearsay. As the season passed its midpoint, Barrow concluded he needed a replacement for aging and hobbled third baseman Frank Baker. Predictably, at the end of July Barrow went back to his old friend Harry Frazee, who had very little talent left other than, fortunately for the Yankees, third baseman Joe Dugan. Frazee once again proved pliable. On July 23 Barrow sent fifty thousand dollars of the two colonels' money, along with three reserves and a pitcher to be named later for Joe Dugan and outfielder Elmer Smith. As with every previous trade in which Frazee received large sums from the Yankees, he again defended the trade on its merits, proclaiming, "I consider that my club is strengthened." Frazee also asserted, falsely, "If there is any money lying around here for me, I haven't seen it. It was a straight trade." He may even have said this with a straight face.

While not prohibited, these late July transactions by contenders were generally frowned upon. The previous season the National League had witnessed a similar episode when in late July the Giants found themselves running second behind the Pirates, and manager John McGraw wanted to add a third capable outfielder. Never shy about midseason transactions, McGraw purchased star left fielder Emil "Irish" Meusel (brother of the Yankees' Bob) from Philadelphia owner William Baker for thirty thousand dollars and three players. Like the Pirates' reaction to the Meusel acquisition, the St. Louis Browns' organization and fans understandably went berserk when the Dugan trade was announced. The uproar led to the magnates finally voting to ban these late-season trades at a joint league meeting in August.

At the wire the Yankees edged the Browns by a single game. By repeating their American League title, the Yankees again earned the right to face the Giants in the World Series, now back to its traditional best-of-seven format.

Once the 1922 Series started, the many frustrations of the Yankees came to a head, leading to the most embarrassing World Series in franchise history. The Yankees lost a close first game 3–2, when starter Bullet Joe Bush, who finished the regular season 26-7, gave up four straight hits to start the eighth. Bush was bothered slightly by a minor injury, and Huston criticized Huggins for leaving Bush in the game too long. The second game concluded with the strangest non-ending in World Series history. With the score 3–3 after ten innings, umpire-in-chief George Hildebrand called the game due to darkness at 4:45. Inconveniently, it was not yet dark, but Hildebrand called the game on the not unreasonable assumption that it might get dark before the conclusion of the next inning. Veteran umpire Bill Klem, at third base, concurred with the decision. Not surprisingly, the record-sized crowd did not, and they began jeering Commissioner Landis, whom they blamed for the postponement, and catcalled that the magnates were just trying to grab an extra day's receipts.

The heckling cast in his direction incensed the vain and pompous Landis. His embarrassment was magnified by the fact that at the very moment the heckling began, Ruppert was introducing Landis to his celebrity guests, Lord Louis Mountbatten and his wife. Landis exploded after the game, "The blankety-blank fools! The blankety-blank fools! They think that I was the one who called the game. I don't pretend to be the smartest person in the United States, but at least I can tell daylight from night." As proof of his integrity, Landis ordered the $120,554 proceeds from the game to be distributed to charity (the money was not technically his to distribute, but neither the Yankees nor the Giants challenged Landis on the matter).

The Yankees lost the next two games, putting themselves in a 3–0 hole. For the fifth game, Huggins came back with Bush. In the fifth inning, Everett Scott was thrown out trying to get back to third base after ignoring the stop sign from Huggins, then coaching third. But the big blowoff came in the bottom of the eighth with the Yankees leading 3–2. The Giants began hitting Bush, getting men on second and third with two out. Huggins ordered Bush to walk the left-handed-hitting Ross Youngs to face the right-handed-hitting George Kelly. Bush did not like this instruction and yelled into the dugout, cursing Huggins loud enough to be heard by many observers. After issuing the walk, the angry and flustered Bush threw a weak pitch to Kelly, who singled home two runs. The Giants scored one more to win the final game 5–3 and take the Series.

Huston stewed angrily after the game, unhappy with Huggins's managing and angry that he could not control the players. He and his pal Frazee shared a cab with sportswriter Fred Lieb for the ride back to the Commodore Hotel, where the press gathered for the postgame wrap up. While Lieb and Frazee discussed the game, Huston silently fumed. When he reached the main bar at the Commodore Hotel, he finally exploded. He let out a wild yell, sent drinks and glasses flying with a wide sweep of his right hand, and bellowed: "Miller Huggins has managed his last Yankee ball game. He's through! Through! Through!" When found for comment, Ruppert backed Huggins, announcing, "I won't fire a man who has just brought the Yankees two pennants."

Ed Barrow was growing increasingly disenchanted with the dysfunctional Yankees organization. He neither enjoyed nor excelled in such a politically charged atmosphere. Barrow told several versions—with only minor variations—of finally confronting his bosses to let them know he was tired of the feuding and confusion. In what may be the most plausible version, he approached Ruppert after learning that American League president Ban Johnson—frustrated with the loss of power and prestige to Commissioner Landis—was contemplating retirement and that he (Barrow) was a strong candidate for the position. Barrow informed Ruppert that he had decided to quit to pursue the opportunity. Ruppert confided to Barrow that he was contemplating buying Huston out and asked Barrow if he would stay in that case. Barrow, who generally liked his position with the Yankees and recognized the uncertainty surrounding Johnson's status and successor, agreed to remain if Ruppert could gain sole control of the franchise. As it turned out, Johnson remained in office for several more years.

Prior to his conversation with Barrow, Ruppert (and Huston) considered selling the team outright for $2.5 million, but the sale fell through after lengthy negotiations. Huston wanted out as badly as Ruppert wanted him out. He was extremely frustrated by his inability to bring in a manager he respected; he and Ruppert disagreed on where to send the charity proceeds from World Series Game 2; and maybe most importantly, Huston felt nervous having essentially his entire net worth tied up in the new Yankee Stadium. After negotiations broke off for the sale of the team, Huston found a buyer for his half interest. Ruppert, not interested in a new partner, decided to buy Huston out himself. Using the franchise value established in the prior sale negotiations, in December the two agreed on a buyout price of $1,250,000 for Huston's half: $500,000 in cash and $75,000 a year for ten years. Due to several complications, the transaction was not finalized until May 1923, with a turnover date of June 1. After the closing, Barrow was promoted to team secretary and awarded a spot on the board of directors. Ruppert's brother George was named vice president and another relative, John Gillig, treasurer.

With the buyout completed, Ruppert offered Barrow the opportunity to buy a 10 percent share of the Yankees for three hundred thousand dollars. Barrow desperately wanted the prestige and financial benefits of ownership. Unlike his difficulties raising the funds to buy into the Red Sox sev-

eral years earlier, this time he convinced his old friend and partner Harry
Stevens to lend him the money. Barrow intended to repay much of the loan
out of the club's dividends. In the final analysis, this investment turned out
to be surprisingly unprofitable.

Meanwhile, Barrow fine-tuned the Yankees for another run at the championship in 1923. Right after the World Series, the Yankees sent Lefty O'Doul
(then a pitcher) to the Red Sox to complete the Dugan trade. Neither club
recognized that O'Doul would eventually transform himself into a great
offensive player. Barrow also pursued White Sox star second baseman Eddie Collins. Collins was thirty-five years old but had several strong seasons
remaining. As negotiations dragged on, Barrow grew increasingly bitter at
Chicago's apparent intransigence: "How are you going to make a deal when
other people want the whole earth? They expect us to weaken two positions
while we are strengthening one." In the end, despite discussing several possible permutations, Barrow could not pry Collins loose.

   Barrow also targeted Vernon pitcher Jakie May, who in 1922 had won
thirty-five games in the long-season Pacific Coast League. Vernon manager
Bill Essick and owner Ed Maier drove a hard bargain, demanding a large
cash payment and a several players, including a couple not controlled by
the Yankees: "Why, if we could get these two players, we would keep them
ourselves, they are so good," Barrow complained. "It is something for a Minor League club to insist that we get them certain players from other teams
in the American League. Even if we did buy these players it is doubtful if
they should be waived out of the organization." Although Vernon held out
for more than Barrow thought reasonable, he hoped to ensure first crack
at May should Essick reduce his price at a later date. As in his Toronto and
Detroit days, Barrow still operated near—and sometimes over—the line
when manipulating player-control issues.

   Notwithstanding the flare-up over May, Barrow still cultivated a close
relationship with the Vernon club. Shortstop Ray French and pitcher Jess
Doyle toiled for Vernon in 1922 but were controlled by the Yankees under
an optional assignment. No spot existed on the Yankees for either, so Barrow reportedly gave up his option and turned them over to Vernon for future considerations, a legal and acceptable maneuver. On January 22, 1923,
after these players were putatively the property of Vernon, Barrow sent a

telegram to several other Pacific Coast League clubs offering French and Doyle in trade, primarily as a way to force Vernon to loosen up on May. Oakland sent a copy of the telegram to Commissioner Landis, who ruled that Vernon and New York had illegally conspired to control the two players and declared them free agents.

In January Barrow returned to Boston and Frazee, securing Minor League pitcher George Pipgras and outfielder Harvey Hendrick for reserve catcher Al DeVormer. Later in the month he acquired veteran lefty Herb Pennock from Boston for three marginal players. Most current sources indicate the Yankees included fifty thousand dollars in the Pennock transaction, but the reality is more complex and elusive. As has been detailed in the last few chapters, the relationship between the Yankees brain trust and Harry Frazee was extremely tight at both the professional and the personal level. Leslie O'Connor, secretary-treasurer of the commissioner's office and Landis's right-hand man during his lengthy reign as commissioner, testified to Congress many years later that "there was a lot of talk and suspicion that the Boston American League Club was under the domination of the New York Yankees . . . and a lot of people, in and out of baseball, thought the Boston Club was under the domination of the Yankee Club."

In addition to the obvious sale of all of Frazee's top players to New York, there is much evidence for the truth of O'Connor's testimony. Yankees records contain a 1921 note that when Pipgras was drafted by Boston, he was "drafted by Boston for us." This obviously implies that Frazee was using his position in the draft to help his friends running the Yankees. Not as damning, but certainly suggestive, is a comment Huggins made to Pennock after he was obtained: "I could have had you before this but did not figure you had the endurance."

The Yankees' financial records for 1923 do not show a specific cash outlay for the purchase of Pennock and Pipgras. On September 5, 1922, however, the Yankees gave Boston two notes, totaling fifty thousand dollars, with no apparent rationale. The Yankees paid the first of these on January 5, 1923, and the second on May 5, 1923. Given that the two teams had no known transactions between the Dugan and the Pipgras deals, the most probable scenario is that these two notes were issued for future player consideration. Boston finished last in 1922 and had few quality players remaining. With

only limited players to choose from, Barrow appropriated Pennock and retrieved Pipgras in return for the Yankees' outlay.

In the spring of 1923, Barrow's most trusted scout and confidant, Paul
Krichell, still concentrated on the college ranks. Unless on a specific assignment for Barrow, Krichell had the latitude to use his best judgment regarding how and where to track down ballplayers. One particular morning, on a
serendipitous whim, Krichell attended a game between Columbia and Rutgers in New Brunswick, New Jersey, to take a look at the Rutgers players.
Krichell rode back to New York on the train with Columbia manager Andy
Coakley, an old pal. The two talked about Lou Gehrig, the right fielder who
had belted two home runs. Gehrig was mainly a pitcher, and Krichell became more intrigued now that he showed promise as a hitter as well. Still
not entirely convinced, he called in Bob Connery for a second opinion. To
Krichell's delight, in a game against New York University, Connery and
Krichell watched the future legend smack a tape-measure home run. Afterward, Krichell quickly shepherded Gehrig down to the Yankees' offices,
where Barrow signed him for a bonus of about $1,500 and a salary of $400
per month. It would prove to be a bargain.

During the off-season Barrow was again linked to a new league scheme.
Exasperated by the unwillingness of the upper Minor Leagues to reinstate
a comprehensive Major League–Minor League draft, several owners floated
the idea of sponsoring a new high Minor League to compete with the existing Minors. Barrow was provisionally offered its presidency. Vain and something of a blowhard, Barrow liked to tout the demand for his services and
publicly announced his recruitment to the papers. The new organization
was to be named either the Continental League or the Interallied League
and consist of Toronto, Montreal, Buffalo, Newark, Baltimore, Brooklyn,
Washington, and Providence. Barrow had overseen franchises in a number
of these cities during his tenure as president of the International League,
making him a natural for the position. Several owners publicly expressed
lukewarm interest, but without active advocacy the scheme quickly died.

As the 1923 season approached, anticipation for the unveiling of Yankee Stadium grew palpable. The club offered public tours in March, and on one
Sunday ten thousand people showed up. The team Barrow assembled for
1923 boasted one of the deepest pitching rotations ever assembled. In Jones,

Pennock, Bush, Hoyt, Shawkey, and Mays (five of whom had been acquired from Harry Frazee), the Yankees carried six of the league's best pitchers. Anchored by Babe Ruth, the Yankees returned the same great starting lineup that had finished the previous season: Schang at catcher; Pipp, Ward, Scott, and Dugan in the infield; and Meusel, Witt, and Ruth in the outfield.

For opening day on April 18, Barrow arranged to have forty ticket windows and thirty-six turnstiles to handle the huge crowd. Opening ceremonies started at 1:00 p.m. with the game scheduled for 3:30. Barrow's pugnacious personality and lack of tact were on full display that afternoon. Yale basketball coach Joe Fogarty had reserved a box for himself and several minor dignitaries. When they arrived about 1:15, they learned their tickets were no longer available. Fogarty requested an audience with Barrow, who, harried with opening day headaches, arrived in a foul mood.

Barrow told Fogarty: "When you didn't show up sooner, I sold the box. There's nothing doing."

A nearby policeman, sensing Barrow's aggravation, asked, "Are you through with these men?"

"All through," Barrow replied.

And with that the policeman and Barrow sent Fogarty and his party on their way.

Barrow announced official attendance of 74,217 for the inaugural game. Shortly thereafter Barrow and Ruppert leased the stadium to boxing promoter Tex Rickard to stage a fight card. When the attendance figures from the boxing match were announced, it became clear the seating capacity of the Stadium could not be as high as 74,217. When confronted, Barrow admitted that the capacity of Yankee Stadium was really around 62,000, and that the 74,217 was actually an estimate and not an official count (although he never really explained why he had estimated the attendance to the last digit). Barrow went on to state that the paid attendance was 52,000; 10,000 additional invitations had been sent out permitting the free admittance of two people each; and 4,000–5,000 patrons had season tickets. Assuming this revised explanation was correct, about 14,000 patrons must have squeezed into the stadium without a seat.

With the distraction of Huston removed, discipline on the team improved, but the clubhouse was still far from tranquil. Unfortunately, the lines of communication had not been fully resolved. When Ruth missed an exhibition game on June 24 in New Haven because he had overslept, Barrow and Ruppert reportedly met to decide on an appropriate fine. Barrow denied this and said any fine needed to emanate from Huggins. When later told that Huggins had fined Ruth a thousand dollars, Barrow pleaded ignorance, saying he knew nothing about it.

The Yankees' main source of Major League talent dried up when Frazee finally sold the Red Sox in July, although the club was now so bad that little talent remained. Frazee sold the Red Sox to a syndicate headed by St. Louis general manager Bob Quinn for $1,150,000, less than half the value of the Yankees but significantly more than that of some of the other weak franchises. Conveniently, Frazee had significantly enhanced his return from the team by spending the last few years milking the club of all its best players. Ruppert stated that he had spent about $600,000—more than half the eventual purchase price of the Boston franchise—buying players from Frazee. Based on the information available in the Yankees' financial records, this estimate is probably quite accurate. Of the seven pitchers who started at least one game for the 1923 Yankees, six came from Boston, as did four of the Yankees' starting position players.

Much of Barrow's time over the summer was also spent lining up football games for Yankee Stadium in the fall. Renting the stadium out for college football games would prove an extremely lucrative venture for the Yankees' ownership. For example, a game on October 30 between Syracuse and Pittsburgh that drew around twenty-one thousand fans netted $43,440, of which the Yankees' cut was 25 percent, or $10,860. With ten or so games a season, the Yankees earned significant revenue from college football in the fall.

By late July the Yankees were playing near .700 ball and ran away with the pennant race. Ruth batted .393 and again led the league in home runs and RBI. The pitching staff also dominated as expected, leading the league in ERA. Huggins finally benched the sullen Carl Mays, but the other five starters won at least sixteen games—the first time this feat was ever achieved and later matched only by the 1998 Atlanta Braves.

The team cooled slightly over the last couple of months, but interest in the team and the new stadium remained sky high. For a doubleheader in September against the Indians, the Yankees drew 60,331 paid admissions, the second-largest baseball crowd ever—opening day was the largest—and a record number of paid admissions.

At a pre–World Series meeting, Landis favored moving the starting time of the games back to 1:30 from 2:00 p.m. to minimize the risk of the darkness debacle of the previous year. Barrow and Ruppert and the Giants preferred the 2:00 p.m. start time, and Landis backed off. The Yankees would host Games 1, 3, and 5, the first World Series games ever in Yankee Stadium. As the Series neared, Barrow announced the ticket prices: $6.60 for box seats, $5.50 for reserved seats, $3.30 for general admission, and $1.10 for the bleachers. New Yorkers besieged Barrow with ticket requests, and he personally scanned the multitude of ticket requests to keep them out of the hands of known scalpers.

In the Series itself the Yankees started slowly, losing two of the first three games. (In Game 3, Barrow squeezed a record 62,430 patrons into the stadium.) In the fourth game the Yankees' bats finally came alive. Over the last three games the team scored twenty-two runs, winning all three games and capturing their first World Championship, four games to two.

15. Collapse

Never one to rest on his laurels, after the World Championship Barrow recognized the Yankees' weaknesses and hoped to bolster them during the off-season. Now that Harry Frazee had sold the Red Sox to Bob Quinn, however, Barrow's chief talent pipeline was closed off. Moreover, the other American League teams were all satisfactorily capitalized and also looking to win, not to make quick cash. Barrow would have to find his players elsewhere.

With Huggins's input, Barrow pursued a number of targeted players. In Huggins's view the team needed "a southpaw to help out Herb Pennock. Next a right-handed hitting outfielder who [could] step up to the plate and sock the left-handers." The manager also hoped to replace the slumping Everett Scott at shortstop. Huggins was open to shifting Aaron Ward, one of his favorites, to shortstop if another capable second baseman could be acquired. Barrow had several discussions with St. Louis regarding their disgruntled right-handed hurler Urban Shocker. Shocker had been suspended in September 1923 after he threw a temper tantrum when the club had refused to allow his wife to travel with him. In the end, despite offering various permutations of players, Barrow could not pry Shocker loose.

In what had become an annual hot-stove dance, the Yankees again pursued Eddie Collins with the White Sox. The Yankees were reportedly willing to surrender Waite Hoyt in the deal, one of the obstacles the previous season. Even so, the trade again failed to materialize. As Barrow remarked during the negotiation, "There are four players on the Yanks who won't be traded in any deal for Collins. They are Babe Ruth, Joe Dugan, Aaron Ward, and Sam Jones. You can erase those names right now. But we will trade anyone else on the team, and I make no reservations on that statement." No doubt Ward was only included on Barrow's list because of Huggins.

In a move that brought no players, Barrow finally disposed of Huggins's nemesis, Carl Mays, by selling him to the Cincinnati Reds for twenty thousand dollars. Huggins and Mays hated each other; once Huggins possessed enough pitching depth to make Mays less important, he shunned his one-time ace, pitching him only eighty-one innings during the 1923 season.

The Yankees brass were also understandably concerned that Mays might have been involved in thrown games. Sportswriter Fred Lieb was a first-person witness to a "prominent player in a number of Broadway shows" telling Commissioner Landis that Mays had "let up in the last two innings" of Game 4 of the 1921 World Series. Landis investigated and later told Lieb that the detectives he hired had found no evidence of foul play. Sometime later, however, Lieb was enjoying a drunken evening with Huston and several other baseball magnates and their wives. Finally, everyone was asleep or had passed out, except Lieb and Huston. After some prodding the latter revealed: "I wanted to tell you that some of our pitchers threw World Series games on us in both 1921 and 1922."

Lieb followed up. "You mean that Mays matter of the 1921 World Series?"

Huston clarified cryptically, "Yes, but there were others—other times, other pitchers."

But Lieb could pry no more out of Huston before he stumbled off to bed.

Several years later, Ruppert revealed that the report from detective Kelly charged that Mays had bet on a baseball game in Boston. Mays was still an outstanding pitcher, who had a couple of excellent seasons remaining, but the Yankees gladly bid him farewell.

Without American League teams willing to sell their stars, Barrow and the Yankees concentrated their efforts on the more uncertain market of high-priced Minor League talent. In this pursuit the Yankees had two significant advantages: a well-heeled owner willing to spend and an excellent network of scouts managed by Barrow. Barrow recognized the importance of an influx of young talent, even for a world champion, and harassed his scouts to uncover the best players in the Minors.

The prices for Minor League players had leapt because of the change in the draft rules and the upsurge in profits earned by Major League teams after World War I. This sudden increase can be illustrated by tracking the sales of select players. As discussed earlier, on July 20, 1911, Pittsburgh Pirates owner Barney Dreyfuss purchased hurler Marty O'Toole from St. Paul of the American Association for $22,500, an unheard-of sum that shocked the baseball establishment. In this era Minor League teams sold many players to the Major Leagues but also earned a significant portion of their income through the draft, despite the relatively lower draft prices. Major League teams at the time spent around $16,000 per team per year to acquire Minor League talent.

O'Toole's purchase price almost surely remained the high-water mark for the dead-ball era. The fact that he never panned out was much less a factor in holding prices down than the economic hardship imposed by the Federal League war and America's entry into the First World War shortly thereafter. In the early 1920s the end of the draft from the class AA leagues coupled with postwar prosperity caused player purchase prices to explode past those of O'Toole and the dead-ball era. From 1922 to 1924 the average price paid per year by each Major League team for Minor League players jumped to just over $50,000 per year. Estimates of the proceeds from player sales by Dunn's Baltimore Orioles alone during the 1920s ranged from $400,000 all the way up to $1 million.

The first high-dollar purchases occurred after the 1921 season when two of the better-capitalized teams paid previously unheard-of prices: the White Sox spent one hundred thousand dollars to acquire third baseman Willie Kamm from San Francisco (to help offset the loss of the eight "Black Sox"), and the Giants paid San Francisco seventy-five thousand dollars for outfielder Jimmy O'Connell. Over the next couple of years, Detroit joined these two clubs, though at prices below those established for Kamm and O'Connell.

Teams often exaggerated some of the prices for the press. In their purchase of Minor Leaguers, Major League clubs commonly included lesser Major League players or Minor League players whom they controlled in addition to cash. To assure maximum publicity for their new acquisition, teams often assigned an excessive dollar value to the players included with the cash and summed it all together when announcing the "price." In fact, any Major League players sent to a Minor League club as part of a transaction were required under the rules to clear Major League waivers. (A waived player is made available to all other fifteen clubs, who are given the right to claim him for the waiver price.) That no other team claimed the players involved in these sales implied that they had minimal value. On the other hand, gentleman's agreements on occasion led to a team passing on a player who might have benefited it.

After the 1923 season Barrow and his scouts targeted several top Minor Leaguers. He pursued Baltimore's star shortstop Joe Boley but came to no agreement with has old friend Jack Dunn, who wanted close to one hundred thousand dollars. Barrow also again turned down Jakie May—a disappointment in 1923—for whom Vernon was now seeking thirty-five thousand dollars and five players. In January the Yankees purchased outfielder Earle Combs from Louisville for fifty thousand dollars plus outfielder Elmer Smith (many observers were surprised that a nine-year veteran with ability could clear waivers). Ruppert strongly advocated this acquisition and encouraged Barrow to spend the money. Around the same time Louisville sold their other star, pitcher Wayland Dean, to the Giants for a similar amount. The fifty thousand dollars spent for each represented the highest price ever paid for an American Association player up to that time. After landing Combs, Barrow left for Atlantic City and his vacation, which had been delayed by the Louisville negotiations.

For Major League trades and purchases, Barrow worked closely with Huggins. Often the two would decide on a trade strategy, and Huggins would be responsible for trying to execute it with his opposite number. But Barrow had clearly become the senior partner. Sportswriter John Kieran amusingly wrote of a scene in the Yankees' offices in December 1923 as Huggins held forth to reporters on some Yankees plans for the off-season. He told them that all the American League teams passed on waivers on Mays, discussed the team's interest in acquiring Shocker, noted the acquisition of pitcher Benny Karr, and answered several other questions on Yankees player personnel strategy. When asked about someone named Autrey, Huggins pleaded ignorance and told them to ask Barrow. One reporter traipsed down the hall and returned to the impromptu press conference with Barrow in tow. When Barrow arrived, he found Huggins still sharing their plans with the press. Huggins's public disclosures maddened Barrow, and he quickly chastened Huggins for his openness.

Barrow demanded of Huggins, "What do you know about Autrey?"

"I don't even know his first name," admitted Huggins.

"Who told you to say anything about Benny Karr," Barrow further interrogated.

Huggins backpedaled. "I didn't even know we had him until today."

Barrow finally chided him and ended the press conference (as Kieran humorously reconstructed for the reader): "What do you mean by coming to town and spilling all this information that I have been saving for judicious distribution through the next three months?" Kieran obviously took poetic license with this exchange, but Barrow clearly disliked his manager enlightening the sportswriters.

During the off-season Barrow also turned his attention to several new business matters. Ban Johnson had issued an edict banning boxing in American League stadiums, potentially eliminating a revenue stream for the Yankees. As a sign of how far Johnson's power had fallen, such a decree now required the approval of the owners. At the league meeting that winter, no team even brought it up for a vote. Barrow also needed to decide on a spring training site. Huggins did not like training in New Orleans, but the lateness of the date and the superstition associated with following the same pattern after winning the World Series militated against leaving New Orleans for 1924. To reduce off-field temptations, the veterans did not report until March 10, near the close of the horse-racing season.

By the end of the 1923 season, Washington owner Clark Griffith had assembled a solid group of regulars and some promising youngsters to go along with ace pitcher Walter Johnson. But Griffith became dissatisfied with manager Donie Bush, whom he jettisoned after the season. Griffith sought a tough, aggressive, proven winner to take over as manager and approached Barrow, whom he had tried to recruit twice previously. Griffith offered a hefty salary, but Barrow once again refused Washington's offer. With the opportunity to buy into ownership and consolidation of his control over player procurement, Barrow had little incentive to leave New York. Griffith next targeted Eddie Collins (to be a player-manager) but experienced the same intransigence with White Sox owner Charles Comiskey as had Barrow. With Barrow and Collins unavailable, Griffith promoted young second baseman Bucky Harris to the position; with this selection he chose to concentrate on the aggressive, intense part of his job description rather than the veteran, proven-winner criterion.

Other than losing Mays and gaining Combs, Barrow returned basically the identical squad in 1924. Naturally, after the Yankees fine 1923 season, he expected the team to again capture the pennant. At the start of the season, he predicted Detroit for second and Cleveland for third.

But defending the title proved difficult. When Combs broke his ankle early in the season, the team again needed the barely adequate Whitey Witt to patrol center field. Unfortunately, the Yankees could not defend their pennant for a fourth straight year. As the season deteriorated, the patrons grew increasingly restless. At one point Barrow was forced to ban the throwing of what the *New York Times* called paper "darts and other missiles" lest someone get hurt; apparently fans were tossing them from high in the stands at the field and other spectators. On the positive side of the ledger, Barrow had to adjudicate fewer disciplinary issues as Huggins seemed to be solidifying his hold over the players.

One unusual request during the season came from the Los Angeles Angels of the Pacific Coast League. The Angels were battling for a pennant, but their first baseman was struggling. The club president sent an emissary east to find a first sacker for the remainder of the season. The Angels' president first met with Cleveland manager Tris Speaker during a series with the Yankees to ask about Frank Brower. Speaker told him no, but Huggins suggested a slugging first baseman the Yankees had in Hartford named Lou Gehrig. When the emissary followed up with Ruppert, the owner extended permission subject to Barrow's approval. Barrow quickly vetoed the transfer. The Hartford club was in a pennant race, and Barrow did not want to strain his relationship with that club by plucking one of their star players at midseason.

Ruth remained a constant management headache for Barrow and Huggins. Sportswriter Marshall Hunt recalled an evening in St. Louis when Ruth decided to spend the night at an establishment that served generous portions of both spareribs and female companionship. Ruth called Barrow to tell him he would be unable to return with the team, surely fibbing a little about the reason. When Barrow demanded to know how he would get back, Ruth calmly told him that he would fly back with Hunt, a good pal, whom he often hung out with on the road. Barrow reluctantly accepted this situation. When he called Hunt to find out what was really going on, Hunt begged off any blame: "This is his own and he's invited me."

After three straight pennants, the Yankees finished three games behind the Washington team managed by Harris. Except for Pennock, the pitching slipped from its 1923 level, and the team dropped to eighty-nine wins. Barrow attended the World Series with Ruppert. He must have felt at least a twinge of remorse about passing up the opportunity to manage the Senators. Naturally, he betrayed none of this publicly. While Ruppert visibly rooted on the American League entrant, Barrow was more nonchalant and "seemed more interested in counting the gate," cockily observing that he was just "getting in shape for next season."

In the mid-1920s, in addition to his investment in the Yankees, Barrow joined many other Americans by investing in Florida land. Skyrocketing prices quickly turned into a bubble about to burst as more and more Americans hoped to buy into the dream of quick wealth. The frenzy was exacerbated by shady operators who sold undevelopable land to unsuspecting purchasers. Barrow, who had never given up his search for the next great investment, purchased a piece of Florida real estate in April 1924 for $8,667. Like the holdings of many other speculators, Barrow's piece turned out to be virtually worthless. Barrow held on until 1944, when he finally sold for only $1,000.

Barrow had a little better luck in the residential housing market. In April 1924 he bought a house at the corner of Pelhamdale Avenue and Mt. Tom Road in Pelham Manor, just over the Westchester County line from New York. He paid forty thousand dollars, a substantial amount for a house in the 1920s. Only a year later he resold the house for forty-five thousand. Soon thereafter Barrow moved to 6 Howard Street in Larchmont, New York, where he would live for many years.

On the heels of their second-place finish in 1924, Barrow and Huggins sat down several times to discuss the team's needs for the forthcoming season. Huggins was still dissatisfied with Scott at shortstop and hoped for another starting pitcher. Both also felt that Schang was slipping behind the plate. To get Huggins his pitcher, Barrow finally landed Urban Shocker from the Browns. In exchange he surrendered Bush, two lesser players, and fifteen thousand dollars. Barrow had now jettisoned both pitchers, Mays and Bush, who had posed the greatest challenges to Huggins's authority. The Shocker acquisition enhanced the pitching rotation, but Barrow failed to address the team's weaknesses at catcher and shortstop.

For spring training in 1925, the Yankees settled on St. Petersburg, Florida, where they would remain until World War II. Huggins wintered there, making him a strong advocate. As a further enticement, Barrow negotiated a new, thirty-thousand-dollar spring ballpark for the team. The city also agreed to later erect a concrete stadium and practice facility for the Yankees.

As a stopgap at catcher, Barrow claimed Steve O'Neill, a one-time star but now well past his productive years. During the season ahead Huggins would rotate Schang, O'Neill, and Benny Bengough, picked up a couple of years previously from Buffalo for ten thousand dollars; none anchored the position to Huggins's satisfaction. At short Huggins would finally bench Everett Scott after a record 1,307 consecutive games, inserting overmatched rookie Pee-Wee Wanninger into the starting lineup. These limited moves fell well short of those necessary to salvage the upcoming season.

The 1925 Yankees season belonged to Babe Ruth but for all the wrong reasons. As the team traveled the South playing exhibition games at the end of spring training, Ruth became ill, running a high fever. On April 7, as he got off the train in Asheville, North Carolina, he collapsed with stomach problems. The team hurried the unconscious Ruth to the hotel, where he was examined by the hotel physician. Barrow dispatched Krichell— but no doctor—to pick up Ruth and accompany him on the train back to New York. When they reached Washington, the train was met by a flock of reporters who had heard rumors that the Babe was dead. Ruth felt better during the train ride, and Krichell could assure the reporters that Ruth was functioning just fine. As the train neared New York, however, Ruth suffered a relapse.

The scene as Ruth arrived at Pennsylvania Station in New York can only be imagined: hundreds of well-wishers gathered at the station to welcome home the nation's ailing, superstar celebrity. As the train approached the station, Ruth again seemed to regain some strength. To clean him up a little, Krichell left Ruth for a moment to get his comb. When he returned, Krichell found Ruth semiconscious on the floor. Once the train pulled in, Barrow, Charley McManus (who ran Yankee Stadium and doubled as Barrow's assistant), scout Ed Holly, Ruth's wife, Helen, and her friend, and the stationmaster boarded the train to help with Ruth. Based on the last update from Krichell, Barrow expected to find a sick but recovering Babe.

Upon seeing Ruth, the shocked greeters quickly sent for the station's doctor. Because of the stretcher's length, Barrow and Krichell realized that to get Ruth off the train he would have to be passed through the window. The window had bars, which further delayed Ruth's departure while everyone waited for a mechanic to come remove the bars.

Meanwhile, station guards were attempting to hold back the anxious, pressing crowd of concerned well-wishers. While this chaos unfolded, a train carrying the Boston Braves arrived at the station, and manager Dave Bancroft and veteran hurler Rube Marquard hiked over to Ruth's train to wish him well—but they too were denied access to Ruth's car. Barrow, Krichell, and Holly finally got Ruth off the train and carried him to the baggage room and up the freight elevator to where an ambulance was supposedly waiting. But no ambulance appeared; it later turned out that the ambulance had broken its steering wheel. Ruth, Barrow, and the rest of the stretcher party were forced to wait while another was dispatched. During this delay, to the horror of his wife and other onlookers close enough to follow the action, Ruth suffered three seizures. Eventually another ambulance arrived to rush the group to St. Vincent's Hospital. This ambulance, too, was defective—its siren was broken—so the streets had to be cleared in advance by the police.

At St. Vincent's Hospital Ruth was examined by his doctor and seemed slightly improved. Ruth remained there in a generally improving condition until a week later when, as the *Washington Post* reported, "the appearance of abscesses on his back made surgical attendance necessary." The surgery confined Ruth to the hospital until late May. For the first few weeks of his hospitalization, Barrow banned everyone but Ruth's wife, himself, and hospital staff from Ruth's room. Not surprisingly, this flustered the ailing and bored Ruth, who missed his girlfriend. Exactly what disease afflicted Ruth remains unknown. The press called it an attack of influenza. Others have suggested some type of venereal disease. In any case, Ruth was hospitalized for close to two months.

Without Ruth, the Yankees' offense faltered; at the end of May the team's record stood at a pedestrian 15-25. Ruth returned to the lineup on June 1, and the next day, as part of a lineup shake up, Huggins replaced Wally Pipp with Lou Gehrig. Pipp would never reclaim his position, and Gehrig would not miss a game for fourteen years. Surprisingly—or maybe not so surprisingly—Ruth's illness did not slow his late-night drinking, carousing, and general merriment. Huggins was growing increasingly irritated with his slugger, who was provocatively flouting the team's training rules.

Finally, Huggins summoned Ruth to his hotel room for a man-to-man talk on the importance—both to his own well-being and the team's—of scaling back his escapades. One can only imagine Ruth's colorfully vulgar reaction from Huggins's own admission that it left the manager "chalk white, trembling and ashamed, not of himself but of human nature." After the disappointing heart-to-heart, Huggins resigned himself to fining and suspending Ruth at the next opportunity. He telephoned the Yankees' offices to explain himself to Ruppert but got Barrow instead.

"Hello, put Colonel Ruppert on."

"He's not here right now," Barrow replied. "What do you want?"

Huggins told him: "I want Colonel Ruppert. I'm going to fine the big fellow and I want it to stick."

Barrow reassured Huggins. "That's all right. Go ahead. It'll stick."

Huggins, who knew how fatherly Ruppert felt toward the Babe, persisted. "But you better get the Colonel. I'm going to fine him $5,000 [a huge amount for the time] and I don't want Colonel Ruppert to back down on it."

Barrow again pledged Ruppert's support: "If you think it's important enough to fine him $5,000, the Colonel will think it important enough to back you up. Go ahead and I'll tell him about it." Barrow's resolve was further fortified by a recently received detective's report detailing Ruth's escapades—one night in Chicago he had "entertained" six different women.

When Ruth showed up late on August 29, Huggins slapped him with the fine and suspension. The huge fine made national news, and the childlike Ruth threw the equivalent of a temper tantrum, threatening to quit unless Huggins was fired. But Barrow held up his end and convinced Ruppert of the importance of backing Huggins. Against a united front from management, Ruth quickly became contrite. Huggins let him dangle a little longer before reinstating the chastened Ruth back into the lineup.

With the Yankees struggling throughout the summer, rumors persisted of an impending shake-up. Some had Huggins about to be fired—some even had Barrow stepping into his shoes—another held that the Yankees were about to spend $250,000 to purchase five Pacific Coast League stars.

In fact, Barrow and Huggins both recognized the team needed shaking up. Barrow purchased only one of the five named Minor League stars, but he was on the verge of retooling the Yankees around younger, hungrier players. In mid-May Barrow had bought aging veteran outfielder Bobby Veach (to mitigate the loss of Ruth during his illness) and Alex Ferguson, a competent midrotation starter, from Boston for $12,000 and Ray Francis. Out of the race by mid-August, the Yankees agreed to send the two to Washington, the eventual pennant winner. Because the trade deadline had passed, the transfer to Washington required the players to first clear waivers. That is, all the teams below them in the standings had to first pass on the two. Fortunately for Griffith, no other team was willing to pay the waiver price. The Senators eventually lost the World Series in seven games, but Ferguson was a key contributor with two starts in the Series.

The 1925 season stands as the nadir of Barrow's tenure at the helm of the Yankees organization. The team won only sixty-nine games and finished seventh in the eight-team league. They would not finish that low again until 1966. At the baseball writers' annual dinner, attended by Barrow, Ruppert, and Huggins, the writers presented Ruppert with a little ditty titled "My Wonderful Two":

> *My wonderful two, how I dote upon you—*
> *Ed Barrow so handsome and tall*
> *And wee little Hug, just as small as a bug,*
> *There are thousands can't see him at all.*
> *Although I am blue, I give credit to you;*
> *With my bankroll you've made me a dub.*
> *As I am a sinner, instead of a winner*
> *You gave me a seventh place club.*

To recuperate after the disappointing season, Barrow vacationed at a Canadian hunting lodge with Ty Cobb and Toronto manager Dan Howley. After Christmas he embarked on a trip to Bermuda, presumably with Fannie as opposed to Cobb. The Barrows announced at least one piece of good news that winter: Audrey, who had recently graduated from the Barnard School for Girls, was engaged to be married to Frederick Campbell. A Cornell graduate and member of the New York Athletic Club, Campbell certainly traveled in the correct New York social circles.

Both Huggins and Barrow felt the 1925 debacle could be traced to lackadaisical play and poor training habits on the part of several veterans who had lost their starting roles. During and after the season, Barrow jettisoned one-time stars Everett Scott, Whitey Witt, Wally Pipp, and Wally Schang. Barrow sent Scott to the Senators in June for five thousand dollars. To clear the starting first base spot for Gehrig, Barrow coaxed twenty thousand dollars out of the Cincinnati Reds for Pipp. He traded Schang to St. Louis for four thousand dollars and pitcher George Mogridge. Barrow thought he needed Mogridge as partial payment for Tony Lazzeri, a top Minor League infielder he wanted. When Mogridge proved unnecessary for the Lazzeri acquisition, Barrow turned around and sold him to the Boston Braves for four thousand dollars. Huggins had also grown disenchanted with the personal habits and regression of his one-time protégé, second baseman Aaron Ward. Barrow deputized Huggins to negotiate a trade with the St. Louis Browns for their young second base star, Marty McManus, but St. Louis held out for Waite Hoyt, and McManus remained a Brown.

Barrow also continued to refine his scouting staff. In January he brought in two new scouts: Eddie Herr, another Huggins confederate from his St. Louis days and now in the Detroit organization; and ex-Vernon manager "Vinegar" Bill Essick. The latter would become one of baseball's most successful scouts and a key member of the Yankees organization for decades. Barrow put Essick in charge of the West Coast and Herr the Midwest. Bob Gilks retained oversight of the South, Ed Holly (another player from Barrow's 1910 Montreal team) the East, and Paul Krichell the college ranks. Barrow trusted his scouts, and for many years they would deliver him more than his fair share of baseball's top young talent, both from the Minor Leagues and the amateur ranks.

1. Barrow in his twenties, nattily dressed for a night on the town. National Baseball Hall of Fame Library, Cooperstown, New York.

2. Barrow in 1903. National Baseball Hall of Fame Library, Cooperstown, New York.

3. 1902 Toronto Maple Leafs (Barrow *center*). Courtesy David Eskenazi Collection.

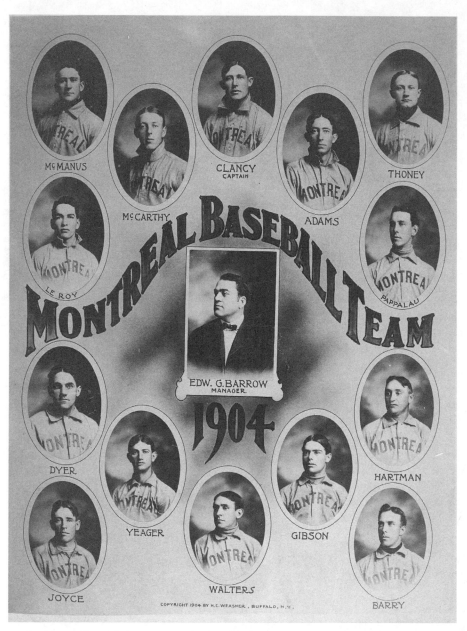

4. 1904 Montreal Royals (Barrow *center*). Courtesy David Eskenazi Collection.

5. 1905 Indianapolis Indians (Barrow *back row, center*). Courtesy David Eskenazi Collection.

EDW. G. BARROW
PRES., SEC'Y AND TREAS.

CIRCUIT:

TORONTO   BALTIMORE
MONTREAL   PROVIDENCE
BUFFALO   NEWARK
ROCHESTER   JERSEY CITY

THE

INTERNATIONAL LEAGUE

OF

PROFESSIONAL BASE BALL CLUBS

OFFICES: ST. JAMES BUILDING

26TH ST. AND BROADWAY   NEW YORK

6. Barrow's International League business card. Courtesy David Eskenazi Collection.

7. Barrow (*far right*), league president, with (*from left*) International League umpires John Mullen, William Finneran, Gerald Hayes, Richard Nallin, William Carpenter, and Ernie Quigley, circa 1913. Courtesy Private Collection of Michael Mumby.

8. Barrow at spring training in 1918 with Billy Sunday and Babe Ruth. Courtesy Transcendental Graphics.

9. Barrow with Harry Hooper, ca. 1919. Courtesy Private Collection of Michael Mumby.

10. Owners' meeting, 1919 (Barrow *middle row, second from left*). Courtesy Private Collection of Michael Mumby.

11. Well dressed as usual. National Baseball Hall of Fame Library, Cooperstown, New York.

12. In his straw hat in 1930. National Baseball Hall of Fame Library, Cooperstown, New York.

13. Barrow and Joe McCarthy in Barrow's office. AP/Wide World Photos.

14. Barrow with George Weiss and Joe McCarthy, late 1930s. Courtesy Private Collection of Michael Mumby.

15. Barrow at the Major League–Minor League Baseball meeting, December 11, 1944, with Boston Red Sox president Tom Yawkey, Chicago White Sox vice president Harry Grabiner, and American League president William Harridge. AP/Wide World Photos.

16. Even at eighty-four years old Barrow still attended old-timers' day. Here he is in 1952 with (*from left*) Charlie Keller, Red Rolfe, Red Ruffing, Joe Gordon, Earle Combs, and Lefty Gomez. AP/Wide World Photos.

17. Barrow with Joe McCarthy in 1940. National Baseball Hall of Fame Library, Cooperstown, New York.

18. Old-timers' day, May 13, 1950, honoring Barrow. *From right*: Bob Meusel, Tom Zachary, Spud Chandler, Roger Peckinpaugh, Wally Pipp, Ben Chapman, Bill Dickey, Whitey Witt, Joe Sewell, Frank "Home Run" Baker, and Lefty Gomez. AP/Wide World Photos.

19. Barrow in retirement holding a shotgun given to him by Babe Ruth and a picture of Ruth from the ceremony retiring the Babe's number, three. AP/Wide World Photos.

20. Sitting for a portrait after becoming president of the Yankees in January 1939. National Baseball Hall of Fame Library, Cooperstown, New York.

16. Rebuilding a Dynasty

As he argued in the story of his years running General Motors, American industrialist Alfred Sloan understood that "the big work behind business judgment is in finding and acknowledging the facts and circumstances . . . in their continuously changing forms." The success of the Yankees' dynasty resulted in large part from Ruppert and Barrow adapting their Yankees player acquisition and development strategies to best fit the prevalent conditions. At the start of the 1920s, Barrow improved the Yankees roster by buying up Major League talent from the league's only willing seller, Huston's needy friend Harry Frazee. With the exhaustion of this source, the Yankees moved on to the other most fertile source of Major League–ready talent, the high Minor Leagues. As has been mentioned, the circumstances surrounding the high Minors changed around 1920 with the elimination of the draft. The Minor Leagues now effectively controlled the promotion of their ballplayers, and the subsequent bidding wars favored the big-spending clubs.

The situation facing a team needing to rejuvenate its roster was surprisingly analogous to the modern system of free agency. Through successful scouting a club first needed to establish which players could help it the most. Once identified, the team needed to be willing and able to spend the money necessary to acquire them. Building a relationship—either with the player in the case of modern free agency or with the Minor League operator in the 1920s—also offered an opportunity for competitive advantage. The Yankees excelled in all areas: Barrow had assembled an excellent team of scouts, the team was profitable, and ownership was willing to spend; and Barrow, Huggins, and the scouts had an extraordinary depth of relationships with Minor League baseball owners and managers.

Despite the influx of better-heeled owners in the aftermath of the Federal League war, Ruppert remained one of the handful with significant assets outside their franchise's value. Of course, a number of owners, such as Charles Comiskey, Charles Ebbets, and Frank Navin, had accumulated substantial wealth simply through their team ownership.

As table 7 demonstrates, the Yankees had more to spend because the team earned more than any other franchise, and the Yankees' owners did not distribute their profits; they reinvested them in the club. Four American League clubs distributed at least $200,000, reducing the funds available for investing in Minor League talent. From 1920 through 1924, the Yankees plowed over $1.6 million back into the franchise; no other American League team retained even $700,000 and no National League club over $900,000. Ruppert made this capital available to Barrow, who spent much of it acquiring Minor League talent.

In early 1925 Huggins's close friend and Yankees scout Bob Connery purchased a controlling interest in the St. Paul American Association franchise. Connery brought in Huggins as a partner, and the latter purchased a one-third interest in the team in his sister's name. The precise relationship between the Yankees and the St. Paul Saints remains murky. Connery naturally retained his close relationship with the Yankees and happily accepted New York players on option. He also typically offered the Yankees a first look at his players. But the relationship benefited Connery much more than the Yankees; New York paid him huge prices for his players, and none became top stars. Ruppert later grumbled that he spent around three hundred thousand dollars buying players from St. Paul—the Yankees' financial records support this assertion—for very little return. Barrow and his scouts did not distinguish themselves when buying players from the Saints, and one can only wonder at Huggins's influence in these acquisitions. He had an obvious conflict of interest, and Barrow must have known of his ownership stake.

Following the success of the Earle Combs purchase, Barrow looked to reenergize his squad by infusing additional young stars. In 1925 he traveled to St. Paul to negotiate with Connery for the purchase of shortstop Mark Koenig. Connery drove a hard bargain; Barrow eventually agreed to a price of fifty thousand dollars and six players (the Yankees valued the players at a total of twenty-five thousand dollars: the six consisted principally of players the Yankees controlled but who were not on their active roster). Barrow also purchased right-handed pitcher Herb McQuaid for around thirty thousand dollars. Koenig developed into a capable regular, and his purchase seems relatively defensible: in 1925 as a twenty-two-year-old he had hit over .300

with eleven home runs. McQuaid, however, never panned out. In 1925 he was already twenty-six, and although he finished 14-5, his ERA was a more mundane 3.81 (and in 1924 it had exceeded 5.00). In his final notable purchase from St. Paul that season, Barrow acquired catcher Pat Collins for fifteen thousand dollars. Collins had spent the early 1920s as a backup for the Browns before St. Paul acquired his rights. With the Yankees, Collins provided two years of adequate service.

Much more significantly, Barrow bought second baseman Tony Lazzeri from Salt Lake City for fifty thousand dollars and five players. Lazzeri had hit sixty home runs in the long-season Pacific Coast League, but Krichell remembered watching him struggle when he had scouted him. Nevertheless, Krichell was convinced he would be a star in the Major Leagues and called Barrow with the news.

"How in hell can you like him when you've just told me he strikes out fourteen times in six games?" Barrow demanded.

Krichell defended his recommendation. "Sure he strikes out. So does Babe Ruth. But I got to like him even when he's swinging. All he needs is an education on where the strike zone is and what constitutes it. He's a sucker for high inside stuff. Balls I mean. When he swings at a true strike—well, up in this thin air he rides it a sleeper jump. Incidentally, Ed, he's big and he's strong and active, but he takes fits . . ."

Barrow interrupted. "What are you talking about?"

"Fits," Krichell told him. "This wop is an epileptic. But there's nothing says he's gotta take 'em between two and six in the afternoon—when we play ball."

Barrow wanted confirmation before he agreed to Salt Lake's exorbitant price. He practically ordered Bob Connery—no longer a Yankees employee but still receiving large payments for his players—to cross-check Lazzeri. Barrow also sent Ed Holly to validate Krichell's enthusiasm. Both backed him up, and Barrow anted up to secure him. Lazzeri proved an excellent investment and turned in a Hall of Fame career for the Yankees. As insurance for Lazzeri, Barrow claimed reserve infielder Spencer Adams on waivers from Washington. Barrow also picked up a lesser-known Minor League infielder from Hartford for $7,500, shortstop Leo Durocher. Durocher was generally regarded as one of the Minor Leagues' best fielders but not yet ready for the Majors. Barrow optioned him to Atlanta for 1926.

Barrow and Huggins had intelligently and successfully, albeit expensively, turned over much of the offense since the team's last pennant in 1923. Off-season purchases Collins, Lazzeri, and Koenig now manned catcher, second base, and shortstop, respectively. After taking over at first base midway through 1925, Gehrig launched his legendary career. The outfield consisted of veterans Ruth and Meusel flanking sophomore star Combs. Barrow did not feel the need to revamp the pitching rotation, which still consisted of 1923 mainstays Hoyt, Jones, Pennock, and Shawkey, along with Shocker, the previous off-season's acquisition.

For several years the Yankees had been sending some of their veteran players, including Ruth, to Hot Springs, Arkansas, for a couple of weeks of "boiling out" prior to the start of spring training. Over the winter Barrow announced that the club was suspending this policy and perk. In concept, the baths and hot springs were to help the players recover from a winter of inactivity. But Ruth's bout with illness at the start of 1925 and the overall poor showing of the team's veterans made the Yankees' brain trust doubt their supposed health benefits.

Many sportswriters expressed their skepticism of the Yankees' off-season makeover. Barrow had a complex relationship with the New York press, who often referred to him as "Cousin Ed" or "Cousin Egbert." He was habitually depicted as mean, caustic, and domineering by the press, some of whom grew to dislike and resent his presence. Others readily ingratiated themselves to remain closer to the story. On March 14, 1926, sports columnist Westbrook Pegler wrote a syndicated story that absolutely incensed Barrow, opening in the vernacular of the day: "If Miller Huggins knew how to manage a ball team, he might manage a pretty good club this year if he had a ball team to manage." He concluded: "They aren't a ball team, they're just a lot of ball players who think their manager is a sap." Barrow clipped it and sent it to Huggins, telling him to put it on the clubhouse bulletin board for motivation. Barrow later recalled that the article, which also upset the players, "made the team."

The rejuvenated Yankees jumped out to a quick start and soon threatened to runaway win the pennant. The team stood at 12-3 at the end of April and maintained a strong pace through July, which they wrapped up at 66-34. The Yankees slumped to 25-29 during August and September, allowing some semblance of a pennant race to develop. In early September, Barrow and Huggins arranged to pick up veteran pitcher Dutch Ruether on waivers from Washington for the four-thousand-dollar waiver price plus two players to be named later (one, Garland Braxton, would lead the league in ERA in 1928 before fading away). With Ruether on board, the Yankees held on to capture their fourth pennant on Barrow's watch. The season was not without a couple of interplayer scrapes. In September during an exhibition game with Baltimore, Ruth and Koenig traded punches, but the squabble had no lasting effect. For the upcoming World Series, the Yankees would face the St. Louis Cardinals, who under Branch Rickey, another de facto general manager, had just won their first pennant.

One of Barrow's biggest headaches, which he fortunately dealt with fairly often, was managing the distribution of World Series tickets. At that time baseball clubs made a conscious effort to keep tickets out of the hands of scalpers, usually with only limited success. After selling the twenty-five thousand reserved and box seats, Barrow warned that the team knew who had received them and it would trace those that fell into the hands of speculators. Another ticket problem surfaced when the Series went to a seventh game. The Yankees' initial book of tickets contained tickets for Games 1, 2, and 6. Most of the boxes for Game 7 were already reserved for baseball executives and other dignitaries, but Barrow and his staff had to supervise the distribution of nearly sixty thousand tickets for the game.

The Series itself was highly suspenseful. The teams split the first two games in New York. The Yankees won two of the next three in St. Louis to bring the Series back to Yankee Stadium with a 3–2 lead. The Yankees lost Game 6, setting up the deciding game on October 10. Game 7 ended with the Yankees behind 3–2: with two out in the ninth, Babe Ruth was caught trying to steal second base. Herb Pennock, who had won Games 1 and 5 was the Yankees' star, but Grover Cleveland Alexander, the aging legend who had won two games and saved the last, stole the spotlight in leading the Cardinals to their first world championship.

When the players divvied up their World Series shares, they voted reserve third baseman Mike Gazella, who had been active most of the season but played only sparingly, a one-quarter share. Gazella protested this slap and complained to Huggins. After Huggins begged off getting involved, Gazella approached Barrow. Barrow saw the merit in Gazella's complaint and revisited the issue with the players, whom he persuaded to increase Gazella's share to one-half. Barrow advised Gazella to accept this compromise, but Gazella, believing he deserved a full share, still balked and further protested to Commissioner Landis. Landis sided with Gazella and ordered the Yankees to allot him a full share. Coincidentally or not, in the future the Yankees became particularly inclusive and generous in the allocation of their World Series money.

Despite the Yankees' return to the American League title in 1926, Barrow and Huggins were typically unsatisfied with the status quo. After the Minor League meetings in December, Huggins announced the team's needs for the upcoming season as "two pitchers, one infielder and one outfielder." Joe Dugan was slowing at third due to knee problems, and Huggins wanted a capable fourth outfielder. Despite their professed desires, the Yankees made surprisingly few moves. During the off-season they made no trades or Minor League purchases of lasting significance. In a couple of minor deals, they sent out-of-favor infielder Aaron Ward to Chicago for a reserve catcher and an infielder, and aging pitcher Sam Jones to St. Louis for a mediocre reserve outfielder and mop-up pitcher. As a potential replacement for Dugan, Barrow shipped forty thousand dollars to St. Paul for Julian Wera, who unfortunately never lived up to expectations.

The Yankees' key acquisition for 1927 came in the midst of the 1926 season. There are multiple stories behind the signing of Wilcy Moore, and their telling sheds light on Barrow's personality. As he aged and assumed a more strictly administrative role, Barrow feared his player-evaluation skills would be forgotten. He constantly reminded baseball writers and enthusiasts of his "discovery" of Honus Wagner. Barrow also liked to claim he had unearthed Moore, who became a vital component of the legendary 1927 team. In his autobiography Barrow relates how he noticed Moore's 30-4 1926 season in the lower Minors at Greenville while researching Minor League records. He supposedly asked scout Bob Gilks about Moore and was told: "He can't pitch. And anyway, he says he's thirty but he must be forty." Barrow, however, insisted the Yankees buy him—anyone who can win thirty games, even in the relatively low Minors must have some potential.

The actual story is much less flattering to Barrow. Yankees bird-dog scout and Minor League umpire Jack Walsh recommended Moore to Barrow in the middle of the 1926 season after Gilks passed on him. Barrow wisely sent

Gilks back for a second look, and in August, with his record at 25-2, the Yankees purchased Moore for four thousand dollars. Barrow, however, refused to honor his agreement to pay Walsh a finder's fee and claimed credit for Moore's discovery. Walsh later appealed to Commissioner Landis, who ducked the controversy by pleading that he did not rule in cases that did not stipulate a specific finder's fee. With this avenue closed, Walsh filed suit after the 1927 World Series asking for a ten-thousand-dollar fee. Prior to trial, Barrow and Walsh reached an undisclosed settlement. The frustrated Walsh claimed he had also recommended several other future big leaguers, including Dale Alexander and Red Mahaffey, to Barrow, but Barrow had failed to follow up.

After the settlement Walsh believed that Barrow blackballed him from baseball. (This is a fairly dubious accusation: Barrow had enough issues of his own to worry about and little control over the business of Minor League operations, in any case.) In 1930 Walsh sent Barrow a letter essentially threatening blackmail: if Barrow did not hire Walsh as a scout—and Walsh argued he was a very good one—he would release the documents from the Moore case to the press, which he claimed would embarrass Barrow. When Barrow brushed him off, Walsh carried his crusade to Ruppert. In a long hand-written diatribe against Barrow, Walsh touted his case and denigrated Barrow as an "untrustworthy wretch." Ruppert also ignored the embittered Walsh. Walsh next tried to generate some newspaper interest in his vendetta, at which point Barrow had had enough. He sent a letter to Walsh with the warning: "[If you do not stop the campaign] in which reflections are cast upon my character and integrity, complaint will be made to the Postal Authorities and your letters turned over to them as evidence for criminal action." Upon receipt of this letter and little reaction from the baseball establishment, Walsh apparently finally gave up the fight.

By January 1927 American League owners had tired of President Ban Johnson. Johnson had never reconciled himself to the prestige and power he had lost when the owners hired Commissioner Landis. After his many lost battles with Landis, it was clear to everyone but Johnson that his authority had been whittled down to little more than managing the umpires and trifling league affairs. In early 1927 he challenged Landis's exoneration of Ty Cobb and Tris Speaker on an old gambling charge, and the league owners finally had enough. Johnson had become an embarrassment, and the magnates agreed that it was time for a new president. Barrow's name immediately emerged as one of the front runners for the position in the event Johnson was forced to resign. He almost surely could have been pressured into the position, but Barrow professed he was not a candidate, adding: "I am thinking of my family in this matter. If I become head of the American League I would be forced to give up my stock in the Yankees. I am not willing to do this. It is a legacy that I have always intended to leave to my family."

When Johnson became ill, the American League owners retreated from their insistence that he step down. Instead they named Barrow's old nemesis, Detroit owner Frank Navin, as acting president. After Johnson recovered, he disappointed the owners by refusing to retire. Under extreme pressure Johnson finally surrendered his position in July, with Navin again assuming an interim role. After the season, when the owners needed to select a new president, Barrow's name was again mentioned prominently, but he did not actively pursue the opportunity. The owners settled on Ernest Barnard, who had been running the Cleveland franchise, as the next president.

Early in Barrow's tenure as business manager, Ruppert handled the contract negotiations with the stars and Barrow those with the lesser players. The Ruth salary negotiations, in particular, were always newsworthy. After four years earning $52,000, Ruth demanded an increase for 1927. When Connie Mack offered Ty Cobb $75,000, Ruth's negotiating leverage increased further. Finally, in March Ruppert and Ruth agreed to a three-year $210,000 contract. The public signing ceremony included Barrow affixing his name as a witness.

Over the winter Barrow and Frances also returned to Bermuda, accompanied by the Frazees, with whom Barrow remained friends. In fact, as rumors of Barrow's possible American League presidency gained traction, a Boston banker wrote Frazee asking if he could use his influence with Barrow to have him transfer a portion of the American League's deposits to his bank. As spring training drew near, in mid-March Barrow and his wife left for Florida. They first traveled to Palm Beach, and from there Barrow headed over to St. Petersburg. He joined the team at their spring camp, mainly to settle the final contract holdouts. While in Florida, Barrow learned of the suicide of his former business partner and friend Jake Wells. Barrow later attended the annual "Al Lang's dinner" at the Jungle Country Club. Lang was one of the area's biggest boosters, and his dinner extravaganza had become an annual bash for over two hundred baseball executives, umpires, players, and managers.

The team started quickly in 1927 and never looked back. They finished 110-44, becoming one of only a handful of teams to play better than .700 ball. Babe Ruth hit his legendary sixty home runs, Gehrig hit forty-seven—no other American League team totaled more than fifty-six—and Lazzeri finished third in the home run race with eighteen. Combs chipped in by hitting .356 and leading the league with twenty-three triples. The pitchers, too, excelled. The team's ERA of 3.20 was well below the next closest at 3.91. The star of the staff was new acquisition Wilcy Moore, who led the league in ERA at 2.28. In the World Series the Yankees swept the Pirates in four straight, the first sweep ever by an American League club. Many still regard the 1927 Yankees as the greatest baseball team of all time.

Huggins used Moore in a role rarely then employed. Moore started twelve games, completed six and won six, while pitching 93 innings as a starter. Less traditionally, Huggins also used Moore in thirty-eight games in relief. In his relief games Moore threw 120 innings (over 3 per relief appearance), registered a 1.95 ERA, and compiled a 13-3 record (and thirteen saves as retroactively calculated; saves were not recognized until many years later). The bullpens of the time were generally made up of pitchers unable to start, not typically key components of a championship pitching staff. For his handling of Moore, Huggins had likely been inspired by Washington manager Bucky Harris's usage of Firpo Marberry in 1924. The Senators won the World Series that year using Marberry in a similar but not quite as extreme role. The first exceptional pitcher used mainly in relief over a period of years, Marberry often started several games each year.

Barrow still actively oversaw his scouts as they scoured the Minor Leagues and colleges. In 1926 the Yankees had earned close to $500,000 in profits, well above any other franchise, and in 1927 they made even more. The ultracompetitive Ruppert advanced a significant portion of these funds to Barrow and his scouts to sign talent. By the middle of the 1927 season, Barrow was ready to spend the money aggressively. In August he effected the single largest cash transaction up to that time involving Minor Leaguers. Barrow paid $125,000 to Oakland for their keystone combo of shortstop Lyn Lary and second baseman Jimmy Reese, the former being the key to the deal. Barrow allowed the players to remain in Oakland during the 1928 season. He also received the right to purchase either or both Pete Daglia and Howard Craghead prior to November 1, 1929, for $35,000 each.

Over the second half of the 1927 season, Barrow spent liberally for a number of other Minor League stars. From St. Paul he purchased third baseman Gene Robertson for twenty-five thousand dollars plus an additional five thousand dollars or a player to be named later and sent another fifteen thousand to Connery for pitcher Al Shealy. Hurler Archie Campbell from Wichita cost fifteen thousand dollars.

Of lesser cost than any of these but of much greater significance, on September 3 the Yankees landed future Hall of Fame catcher Bill Dickey from Little Rock for $12,500. The Chicago White Sox had a working agreement with Little Rock, positioning them for first crack at Dickey. Either they passed or New York scout Johnny Nee simply outmaneuvered the White Sox, allowing the Yankees to purchase him. To persuade Barrow of Dickey's value, Nee telegraphed: "I will quit scouting if this boy does not make good." In January they paid $15,000 to Oklahoma City to acquire Lee Craig; to complete the transaction, St. Paul sent an additional player to Oklahoma City on behalf of New York.

Paul Krichell later illustrated how Barrow pushed his scouts to find Minor League talent with his story of the Dusty Cooke acquisition. Through his scouting contacts, Barrow had learned of Cooke, an outfielder playing in Durham, North Carolina. Barrow wired Krichell, who happened to be in Knoxville, Tennessee, scouting another player: "Durham club now ready to do business on Cooke. Better get there at once, Regards, Barrow." Krichell later joked that every wire from Barrow always required action "at once" or "immediately." So Krichell started out on a 5:25 a.m. train. Later, after a three-hour layover, he had to transfer to a bus. In all the trip took nearly fifteen hours: Krichell arrived in Durham at 8:30 p.m.

The next morning Krichell headed to the Durham team offices and offered $2,500 for Cooke. Team vice president Red Rowe played coy with Krichell, remarking that if the Yankees were interested in Cooke, maybe they weren't quite ready to sell. Undaunted, Krichell followed Cooke for a couple of days on a road trip and liked what he saw. When he returned to Durham, however, he found the town crawling with scouts—the team had put out the word that the Yankees were targeting Cooke. Krichell remembered one in particular, Billy Rapp of the Indians, cozying up to Rowe. After four days in Durham, Krichell realized he needed to do something to shake up the situation. At 7:30 in the morning, he hustled over to the home of Dr. Booker, Durham's president.

Krichell jumped right in with his pitch. "Doc, I couldn't sleep last night. Is it true what they say?"

Booker was obviously confused. "True? Is what true?"

Krichell continued using one of his perfected ploys. "That you have no authority to sell a player on your own club. That it's all up to the manager and the vice president."

Krichell's insinuation worked, and the two headed down to the team's office to consummate the sale. After a little haggling, they agreed on a price of fifteen thousand dollars, for which Krichell needed to call Barrow for approval.

Barrow could not believe the high price. "Who the hell is paying that kind of cash for a ballplayer in class c?" After calming down Barrow asked, "Do you stake your reputation on this?"

Krichell responded, "Ed, that's quite a load to throw on a man when he's in the switches. This Cooke is a Yankee, all the way. Meanwhile, both leagues are kickin' down the door."

Barrow was sold. "Close the deal."

Krichell did. When he and Booker opened the door to the army of scouts waiting to get into the office, Booker announced that he had sold Cooke to the Yankees, much to the dismay of the competition.

As a postscript, Cooke never developed as hoped. Shortly after the signing, the Cubs offered one hundred thousand dollars for Cooke, which Barrow refused. Krichell blamed Cooke's failure to develop into a star on a severely separated shoulder Cooke suffered in Washington in 1931.

Barrow had little tolerance for airing league business in public. In the winter after the Yankees' great season, the new owners in Cleveland rankled Barrow. A January 3, 1928, article in the *Cleveland Plain Dealer* identified the players on whom the Yankees had requested waivers, information that clearly came from the Indians organization. Teams often requested waivers on players for the purpose of sending them to the Minor Leagues or trading them to the other Major League. Teams strove to keep the names of the waived players secret from the public and the players themselves. Because most waivers were revocable, teams commonly withdrew waivers if another team claimed the player. Therefore, they did not want a player distracted by knowing he might be designated for the Minors or a trade.

Barrow angrily denounced the Cleveland owners to new American League president Ernest Barnard regarding their breach of etiquette. Barnard replied with a diplomatically written letter. He noted that the Cleveland ownership had been in place for only six weeks, and that "the Cleveland people talked very frankly with their newspapermen, and it was only natural for them to make some mistakes and permit some things to make it into the conversations which were not proper matters for discussion with the baseball writers." He then noted that the Cleveland owners would "adjust themselves," leaving "no further reason for complaint."

In other, more public business, Barrow announced the planned expansion of Yankee Stadium, scheduled for completion July 1 at a cost of $341,000. The new addition increased the seating capacity to seventy-two thousand for baseball (plus room for an additional eight thousand standing-room-only spaces), seventy-five thousand for football, and nearly one hundred thousand for boxing. The remodeling extended the third base side of the triple-decked segment so that it curved around the left field foul line and into left field. This alteration increased the distance down the left field line by 22 feet to 307, while right field remained at 294 feet 10 inches.

Barrow also spent much of his time on one of his main off-season duties, signing his players to contracts for the forthcoming season. Players often objected to Barrow's opening offer. Sometimes if a star player could not come to a salary agreement with Barrow, he would encourage the player to talk to Ruppert. The players referred to this as getting the "elevated treatment." Of course, Barrow and Ruppert had discussed the player's salary target in advance.

Waite Hoyt remembered the story of his salary negotiations after his stellar 1927 season and World Series championship. He did not like the first proposal from Barrow; after further back and forth, the two remained at loggerheads. Barrow told Hoyt there was nothing more he could offer and suggested Hoyt discuss the matter with Ruppert. After a heated exchange with Ruppert, the owner asked Hoyt to cool down in the outer office. While waiting, Hoyt passed the time by admiring the pictures of buildings hanging on the walls. When Ruppert came out to get him, he caught Hoyt looking at the pictures. Ruppert happily started discussing all the buildings with his captive audience. Ruppert told Hoyt that he owned the buildings, pointed them out individually, and proudly announced how much they were worth. As Hoyt recalled, the Ruppert Building on Fifth Avenue was worth about $4.5 million, and Ruppert's estate at Garrison was worth $750,000. Ruppert went on to show Hoyt several other buildings and noted the value of each as well. Finally, Ruppert asked Hoyt if he was ready to sign at the club's number. When Hoyt still refused, the frustrated Ruppert blurted, "What do you think I am? A millionaire?"

To pressure players into signing, Barrow worked his newspaper contacts to portray holdouts to the club's advantage. Once during a protracted negotiation, Hoyt tipped a reporter that he was asking for twenty-five thousand dollars and had received little response from the Yankees. When Barrow saw the story in print, he called the reporter and blistered him: "Stories like that are subversive. Any story which backs the player against the club on salary is against the best interests of baseball. Besides, what we pay a player is none of your business. Do we dig into your salary relations with your paper?" Of course, Barrow was not above leaking a salary offer to the press if he thought it would help pressure the player to sign.

Barrow also originated a creative way to reach an agreement with players coming off injuries. A player would not want to sign for a reduced salary if he could prove he was healthy, but the team did not want to risk paying for an injury-depleted performance. Barrow introduced the concept of a contract with the salary set to one dollar. The existence of the contract kept the player from becoming a free agent. As spring training drew to a close and the extent of any lingering injury effects emerged, the team and the player could agree to terms that best fit the circumstances. Players generally accepted this as opposed to the alternative of a salary cut based on uncertainty over an injury. Freddie Fitzsimmons, who signed this type of contract with the Giants, summarized the player's view: "Rather than accept a compromise salary that might prove unsatisfactory to both parties, after I've proved that my arm is as good as ever, I know the club will treat me as fairly as it has always done in the past. If I don't come through—but that's a possibility I'm not even considering."

The Yankees lineup in 1928 remained nearly unchanged from the previous season. Huggins hoped that Robertson could take over for Dugan at third, but Dugan held on to the position until severe knee problems finally sidelined him. Barrow and Huggins also wanted to integrate a couple of new pitchers into the rotation. During the off-season Barrow released two pitchers: longtime mainstay Bob Shawkey, seldom used in 1927; and veteran Dutch Ruether, who had supplied twenty-six pretty good starts. The Yankees elevated George Pipgras and Hank Johnson to join Hoyt and Pennock in the rotation. Huggins again designated Moore for a relief role. Barrow also took a flyer on aging free-agent pitcher (and future Hall of Famer) Stan Coveleski.

The pitching rotation was further depleted by the loss of Urban Shocker. Now thirty-seven, Shocker had endured serious heart problems for a couple of years and was contemplating retirement to pursue his radio business interests. His physical ailments caused Huggins to lose confidence in Shocker's ability—he did not use him in the World Series—and Barrow planned to reduce his salary from the $13,500 he earned in 1927. Shocker finally agreed to pitch, but his health problems escalated, and he appeared in only one game in 1928 for the Yankees, who finally released him in July. In his weakened condition, Shocker contracted pneumonia soon after his release and died in September.

During the first half of the season, the Yankees again looked invincible. On July 1 the Yankees' record stood at 52-16; their closest competition, the Philadelphia Athletics, were thirteen and a half games behind. Over the next couple of months, however, the Yankees played around .500 ball, and the Athletics went on a tear. Amid what could have been one of the great comebacks of all time, Philadelphia actually gained first place on September 8 by a half game.

Barrow's staff mismanaged the ticket sales for the September 9 doubleheader with the Athletics. When the box office opened at the Yankees' offices on Forty-second Street, more than five thousand fans had stood in the rain all morning. The Yankees sold out before many had purchased tickets, inciting what the *New York Times* called a "small-size riot." A considerable police presence was required to quell the disturbance. Much of the fiasco was caused by confusion over the number of tickets available. At their offices the team was selling only reserved seats. The grandstand and bleacher seats did not go on sale until 11:00 a.m. Sunday morning. On the field the Yankees won both games to regain a narrow lead, which they held on to through the end of the season.

The Yankees won 101 games in 1928 and again swept their National League opponent, this time the St. Louis Cardinals, in the World Series, gaining a measure of revenge for the 1926 setback. This Series belonged to Ruth and Gehrig. Ruth hit three home runs, batted .625, and slugged 1.375. Gehrig outdid his senior teammate: in the four games he smacked four homers, batted .545, and chalked up a slugging average of 1.727, still the World Series record.

The Yankees' domination in the 1928 World Series—no game was closer than three runs—climaxed three straight pennants and gave New Yorkers little reason to fear a Yankees' drop-off. But small cracks were beginning to appear in the Yankees' juggernaut, particularly on the pitching staff. Waite Hoyt, still only twenty-eight, turned in a strong season, as did Herb Pennock, despite an illness. George Pipgras, also twenty-eight, started thirty-eight games and recorded the best season of his career. Hank Johnson, however, did not develop as anticipated. More importantly, Wilcy Moore's arm appeared dead, and he never again enjoyed a season close to his phenomenal 1927. Sportswriter Dan Daniel wrote that Moore hurt his arm in the off-season when he fell off the roof while building a barn. Moore blamed his loss of effectiveness on his 1927 workload.

Huggins was also dissatisfied with the left side of his infield. Koenig could hit quite well for a shortstop, but Huggins found his fielding erratic. For 1929 the Yankees planned to go with Leo Durocher at short. As Barrow explained: "Durocher is one of the great fielding shortstops in baseball, and we can substitute hitting strength for defensive strength." Dugan's knees had given him trouble for some time, and he had little range left. Barrow initially agreed to give Dugan his unconditional release when he believed Dugan would sign with the Cubs. When Barrow learned that he might sign with an American League team, he placed Dugan on waivers to make sure he received compensation. The Boston Braves claimed him, and Dugan felt betrayed.

For a replacement at third base, Barrow explored trading for Boston Red Sox third baseman Buddy Myer (who was eventually traded to Washington instead) and Washington's Ossie Bluege but could not come to an agreement on either. Without a solution from outside the organization, Barrow was forced to address the situation internally. The Yankees' options included either shifting Koenig to third or hoping a Minor League prospect such as Julian Wera or Gene Robertson would finally deliver. Huggins was also dissatisfied with his catchers. Barrow sold Pat Collins for ten thousand dollars, and Huggins worked twenty-two-year-old Bill Dickey into the starting lineup.

To bolster the pitching staff, the Yankees turned to three relative newcomers. In August 1928 Barrow had purchased two Minor League hurlers: he paid St. Paul twenty thousand dollars and a couple of players for Fred Heimach and Birmingham fifteen thousand dollars and two players for Ed Wells. Both were given extensive action in 1929 with only limited success. Also in August 1928, the Yankees purchased lefty Tom Zachary for the eight-thousand-dollar waiver price from Washington. Zachary would pitch only 120 innings in 1929, but his 2.47 ERA was recognized as the league's best.

Jaded by the nonbaseball promotions necessary to keep his struggling Atlantic League afloat many years earlier, Barrow now disdained such sideshows. Nevertheless, in January 1929 he announced that the team would wear numbers on their uniforms, the first team to do so on a regular basis. As an old scorebook hawker, Barrow recognized the value of easy identification of his stars. He settled on a simple numbering scheme: the first player in the batting order, Earle Combs, would be number 1; Babe Ruth, who hit third, number 3, and so on. When one writer noted that Huggins could try to confuse the opposition by batting the players in an order different from their numbers, Barrow ridiculed the suggestion: "Yeah, I suppose we can give the Babe's number to [Gene] Robertson or Durocher and give one of their numbers to the Babe. Then the other side won't know when Babe comes to bat."

With three straight pennants in tow, Barrow felt optimistic heading into spring training. He recognized the apparent weaknesses of the team's pitchers, but remained upbeat regarding some of his young players—optimism that in retrospect was misguided: "With Pennock, Lazzeri, and Moore back in shape, they'll make the Yankees stronger than last year. Lyn Lary will make good at short and improve the infield, with Koenig shifting to third. Ed Wells, the southpaw from Birmingham, and Gordon Rhodes, the young right-hander from Hollywood, will strengthen the pitching staff." Later in the interview he brazenly predicted the American League order of finish with the Yankees naturally first, followed by the Athletics and Washington.

In early 1929 the Barrows became grandparents when Audrey and Campbell had a daughter, Patricia. The next year the couple added a grandson, John. Campbell worked for Coca-Cola as a junior executive and hoped to move up through the ranks. The young couple—Audrey was twenty-two and Campbell twenty-eight in 1929—appeared to the outside world like an upwardly mobile, happy young family.

To help organize and manage his myriad jobs and responsibilities, Barrow hired Elizabeth King as his executive secretary to handle some of the club's most sensitive correspondence. King would outlast Barrow in the Yankees' front office, serving thirty-one years. Only once during her tenure did Barrow accuse her of breaking a confidence: on one occasion he suspected her of releasing Lou Gehrig's salary to writer Dan Daniel. As he aged, Barrow became much more prudish; he forbade King from attending social events with players or sportswriters. In fact, this may have been the result of Barrow's obsession with secrecy rather than any excessive fatherly concern for King.

Barrow took advantage of the popularity of Ruth and his Yankees by scheduling an extended tour after spring training and prior to the start of the season. Teams typically played a number of exhibition games as they barnstormed north after spring training, but in 1929 Barrow arranged games as far west as Oklahoma. In all he scheduled twenty-seven games between March 12 and April 14 over a wide swath of territory. Security was generally lax. Kids crowded the field, often mobbing players, particularly Ruth, and stealing hats and bats. According to one report, this tour drew close to 270,000 fans, and earned revenues of $65,600. To put this figure in perspective, the Yankees generated receipts of $663,676 for their home games in 1929, meaning that the tour brought in revenues equivalent to nearly 10 percent of the total receipts from their home games that season. The take represented a 66 percent increase over the 1928 training trip receipts.

Around nine thousand fans sat in the bleachers on May 29, 1929, with about half crammed into the right field bleacher area, known as "Ruthville" because of Ruth's preponderance to hit home runs to that section. As the bottom of the fifth inning started, a slight drizzle began. While some fans in the bleachers sought cover, most of those in Ruthville stayed put; they wanted to see their hero, who had hit a home run earlier that day, come to bat. After Ruth grounded out, with Gehrig approaching the plate, the rain became a downpour. The fans rushed for the exits. The southernmost exit from Ruthville was down fourteen narrow steps and then through a dirt passageway walled with chicken wire.

As the fans crowded into the narrow exit, tremendous pressure built up at the bottom of the stairs. When several people tripped and fell, the exit became further constricted. The crush from the top continued unabated, creating a huge heap of bodies at the bottom of the stairs. The mass of humanity grew so large that it knocked out the chicken-wire walls and spilled out of the passageway. In the pile-up two people were killed, a seventeen-year-old girl and a sixty-two-year-old man, and an additional sixty-two people were injured, several of them seriously. The police averted an even greater disaster by getting to the top of the stairs and halting the press of the fleeing fans. The district attorney cleared the team of any negligence, but several witnesses testified to a couple of problems. One suggested that the failure of a security guard to open other gates contributed to the rush for the stairs. Another, a doctor who had helped the injured, claimed the medical facilities within the stadium were inadequate.

Barrow and Ruppert both steadfastly denied any liability. Barrow issued a not particularly sympathetic statement: "As far as I can see there are no changes we could make. The exits at the stadium have always been considered thoroughly adequate to handle even greater crowds than the one we had last Sunday. . . . A bleacher crowd, too, is usually made up of young fellows, and there probably was a lot of shoving and fooling—as youngsters will do—before they realized how serious the matter was."

Not surprisingly, a number of the injured and the estate of the man who had died filed suit against the Yankees alleging a shortage of exits. In 1932 the action brought by thirty-two plaintiffs for thirty thousand dollars each finally came to trial. The jury returned a mixed verdict, which an appellate court later ruled invalid and called for a second trial. Just as the new trial was scheduled to begin in December, the Yankees and the plaintiffs settled for a much-reduced total of forty-five thousand dollars.

During the summer of 1929 the Yankees were one of several teams pursuing Hank Greenberg, a prep phenom from the Bronx, who would go on to a Hall of Fame career. Many assumed that a Jewish kid living in the shadow of Yankee Stadium was a natural for the Yankees. Paul Krichell tracked Greenberg and his family doggedly, making several offers to Hank when he visited their home. The scout even brought both Greenberg and his father, David, to meet with Barrow at the Yankees' offices. Barrow misread

David's personality and warned him not to let Hank go to an out-of-town team because of the temptations away from home. This was not a wise approach; David felt he had raised a son who could look after himself and resented Barrow's impertinence. Furthermore, the advice was patently gratuitous; the attractions of the road existed for any player while traveling with his team regardless of where he lived.

During another game late in the season, Krichell joined Greenberg in the stands to cajole him into signing with the Yankees. Greenberg, a first baseman himself, remembered Krichell telling him that Lou Gehrig was "all washed up." Greenberg, naturally concerned about getting stuck behind Gehrig, was not convinced. Barrow and Krichell did not help themselves by initially offering only a token $1,000 signing bonus. They eventually came up to $7,500, but the Tigers offered $9,000. Once Greenberg accepted Detroit's offer, the Yankees reportedly upped their bid to $10,000, but at that point it was too late.

The Yankees' run of pennants did not survive the powerfully rejuvenated Athletics. The team that had almost overtaken the Bombers in 1928 ran away with the 1929 league title. Philadelphia won 104 games, finishing 18 ahead of the second-place Yankees. The new left side of the Yankees infield was unproductive. Durocher played most of the games at short and Robertson at third, with Lary and Koenig receiving significant time at each position as well. But as Huggins had feared, the disappointing finish was mainly due to the breakdown of the once-vaunted pitching staff. Neither Hoyt nor Pennock could start more than 25 games; Pipgras could not repeat his stellar 1928 season; and newcomers Wells and Rhodes were disappointing. Only Tom Zachary, who finished 12-0 with his league-leading ERA, surprised on the positive side.

The final days of the 1929 season were overshadowed by Huggins's sudden death. In late September Huggins developed a carbuncle below his left eye. He was already run-down from the grind of the season, and the infection quickly spread throughout his body. In those days before antibiotics, the doctors tried blood transfusions to stem the spread, but Huggins died only a few days after the diagnosis and treatment. Barrow and Ruppert spent the morning of September 25 at Huggins bedside before leaving for lunch. Prior to their return, Huggins passed away. He had been only fifty-one years old, and his death shocked Barrow, the Yankees, and the world of baseball. The news so depressed Barrow that he became too ill to attend the funeral a couple of days later. The two men had established a surprisingly strong friendship given their personality differences, and Barrow felt Huggins's loss very personally.

Barrow and his scouts spent lavishly by the standards of the era to land top Minor League Baseball talent. From the purchase of Earle Combs in early 1924 though the end of the decade, the Yankees spent nearly half a million dollars on high-dollar Minor Leaguers. Tables 8 through 11 spotlight the high dollar expenditures by the Yankees and the other clubs from 1920 through 1929. (Note: Care has been taken to count all purchases of at least twenty-five thousand dollars, although it is likely that a few have been overlooked.) The American League was much more aggressive in purchasing Minor League stars, and this more energetic approach to talent acquisition paid off on the field. From 1926 through 1939 the American League won ten of the fourteen World Series. The St. Louis Cardinals captured three of the four won by the National League because they partially outmaneuvered the Minor League monopoly on high-priced players by originating the farm system.

The data for the Philadelphia Athletics is also presented in its own table. Operating partner and manager Connie Mack had famously sold off all his stars in the wake of the financial hardship caused by the Federal League war. Mack and his financial partner, sporting goods magnate Ben Shibe, then allowed the team to languish in the cellar for several years. After Ben died in the early 1920s, the Athletics' purse strings passed from Ben to his son Tom. Connie Mack and the younger Shibe aggressively went after good young ballplayers, spending over four hundred thousand dollars on high-dollar players.

The remaining two tables summarize the rest of the American and National League clubs. White Sox owner Charles Comiskey futilely spent over four hundred thousand dollars as he tried to rebound from losing eight players, including several great ones, to the Black Sox scandal. Late in the decade, Barrow's old rival Frank Navin of the Tigers also went on a spending spree to compete with the Yankees and the Athletics. In the National League only the Giants targeted multiple high-priced Minor Leaguers and only early in the decade. As owner Charles Stoneham's legal troubles mounted, he milked his franchise of its revenues and had little capital available for player acquisition.

During the latter half of the 1920s, the Yankees continued to enjoy a revenue advantage over their rivals. As table 12 highlights, from 1925 through 1929 the Yankees earned a profit of over $1.6 million. In the American League, no other team earned even half the Yankees' total; Philadelphia, at just over $800,000, was the closest. Furthermore, Ruppert again reinvested it all into the ball club. Other profitable teams such as Detroit and Washington distributed nearly $1 million between them.

In the National League several teams earned more than $1 million. Two, the Chicago Cubs and the St. Louis Cardinals, limited their distributions to ownership and retained their earnings in the operation. These two teams were also the only National League franchises run by a de facto general manager: Bill Veeck Sr. in Chicago and Branch Rickey in St. Louis. With smart professional administration and reinvested capital, these two franchises captured seven pennants in the eight years from 1928 through 1935.

The National League's other two most profitable franchises, the Pittsburgh Pirates and the New York Giants, could not sustain their on-field success of the early to mid 1920s. The Pirates, owned by Barney Dreyfuss, paid out large dividends, leaving little to reinvest in player acquisition. The aging Dreyfuss, and later his heirs, could not reconstruct the energy, baseball network, and player-evaluation skills of his younger days. In New York, manager John McGraw spent liberally in the early 1920s, purchasing both Major and Minor League stars. With a large, loyal following and a great manager, the Giants should have remained a strong competitor with Barrow's Yankees. But during the mid to late 1920s, owner Charles Stoneham significantly tightened McGraw's purse strings, siphoning off $1.1 million. The Giants would capture three pennants in the 1930s, but no others over the twenty-six seasons from 1925 to 1950.

A possible rival for the Yankees' financial and on-field dominance in the 1920s and 1930s, the New York Giants were forestalled by the legal troubles of New York Giants owner Charles Stoneham, a backroom operator who today would almost surely be in jail. He had made his fortune operating what was known as a "bucket shop," a sort of cut-rate stockbrokerage that played fast and loose with both the rules and the investor's stocks and money. Also, Stoneham loved horseracing, had part ownership in a racetrack, and enjoyed gambling in general. He cavorted with a number of New York's more unsavory characters, including notorious gangster Arnold Rothstein, who arranged the fix of the 1919 World Series. Rothstein was a secret partner in a couple of ventures with Stoneham and could sometimes be found in Stoneham's box at the Polo Grounds, even after the 1919 Series fix became public.

When Stoneham sold his brokerage business in 1921, the accounts of his clients were transferred to other firms. A couple of these firms failed, costing investors thousands of dollars. Stoneham was charged in two separate criminal cases: for perjury in one, and mail fraud related to the collapse of his original company and one of the failed firms in the other. He was indicted on both charges in 1923. Stoneham was eventually acquitted nearly two years later, but not without plenty of unsavory smoke. Two executives from one of the failed firms pled guilty, received prison sentences, and found themselves in additional trouble for destroying key documents. It was the eventual disclosure of what the records contained that led to Stoneham's perjury indictment. Furthermore, Stoneham's attorney later went into hiding to avoid prosecution after being indicted for trying to bribe a juror in a related case. And one juror involved with Stoneham's acquittal later claimed he had been intimidated into changing his vote. Two other indictments in the case were eventually dropped a couple of years after the acquittal.

Barrow's first order of business for the 1929–30 off-season was the hiring of a new manager. Although it remains unknown whether Barrow ever seriously considered him, Bob Connery quickly took himself out of the running for his best friend's old job. Barrow first targeted Donie Bush, most recently manager of the Pittsburgh Pirates and skipper of the 1927 team that had won the National League pennant. Like Huggins, Bush was small in stature, but a scrapper and aggressive, qualities Barrow valued in a potential manager. Unfortunately, when Barrow finally reached Bush on the phone, Bush informed him that he had just signed that very day to manage the White Sox.

Barrow next sought Eddie Collins, now coaching on the Athletics after a stint as a player-manager for the White Sox. Barrow had long respected Collins's smart, aggressive play (as evidenced by his nearly annual attempt to trade for him during the early 1920s), but Collins elected to remain in

Philadelphia. He probably expected to take over the managerial reins of the current world champion Athletics after his mentor, Connie Mack, retired. Mack was already sixty-six years old, and retirement seemed likely in the near future (of course, Mack would last many more years at the helm).

Among the Yankees family, the most obvious choice was Ruth, who desperately craved the job. Both Barrow and Ruppert believed Ruth lacked the maturity for the position and gave him little consideration for the position. Another logical Yankees candidate turned down Barrow's offer. Third base coach Art Fletcher had learned the game under John McGraw and had managed the Phillies from 1923 to 1926. Unlike his mentor, Fletcher was quiet, reserved, and courteous off the field, while on it he managed with McGraw's ferocity and venom. National League president John Heydler once remarked during Fletcher's tenure as manager of the Phillies: "Fletcher today is my number one problem. He has become far worse than McGraw. I cannot understand how a man can come into my office and speak so politely and sincerely, and then act as he does on the ball field." Fletcher understood the stress that this dual personality caused him and told Barrow he was not interested: "I feel that this is the greatest honor that has ever come to me— but I cannot accept it. I had too many headaches and heartaches in Philadelphia, and I never want to manage a team—even this team—again. If it's all the same to you, I'll stay on the third base coaching line."

Barrow settled, not very enthusiastically, for another capable in-house candidate, the team's 1929 pitching coach, Bob Shawkey. As he told Ruppert when announcing the choice, "I don't know why I didn't think of him at first. I guess he's been around so long and I've gotten so used to looking at him, I just couldn't see him." At a time when managers often earned as much as mid-level stars, Shawkey's new managerial salary attested to Barrow's lack of enthusiasm. At only fifteen thousand dollars (Huggins was reportedly earning twenty-five thousand his last year as manager), it was dwarfed by Ruth's and Gehrig's salaries, slightly below Lazzeri's, and no greater than those of his one-time rotation mates, Pennock and Hoyt. To soothe Ruth, Barrow told him, "Shawkey deserves the chance," hardly a ringing endorsement. Shawkey never campaigned for the job and may not have really wanted it.

Taking over from a highly successful manager who had died on the job, Shawkey was walking into a no-win situation. Ruth tried his best to behave, but there could be no hiding that the Yankees best and most popular player resented his presence. Furthermore, after so many years as a teammate, Shawkey was close friends with many of the players. To ascend from friendship to a position of authority created many uncomfortable moments and frayed friendships.

After a conference with Barrow and Ruppert, manager Shawkey acknowledged that Miller Huggins's concerns of the previous season had not been addressed: "The Yankees need strengthening on the left wing of the infield and the pitching staff also needs bolstering. We must roust up a first-class pitcher somewhere and if possible two." To shore up the revolving door on the left side of the infield, Shawkey indicated he was contemplating shifting Lazzeri to third and reinstalling Koenig as his starter at short. Shawkey and Barrow hoped Jimmy Reese could nail down second. Shawkey correctly recognized that his pitching staff was in a state of transition.

In August 1929, at the recommendation of West Coast scout Bill Essick, Barrow shelled out forty-five thousand dollars to purchase twenty-year-old pitcher Lefty Gomez from the San Francisco Seals. Gomez was a little raw to help immediately but would soon develop into the Yankees lefty ace of the 1930s. The top pitchers of the last pennant were either aging or no longer at the top of their game, and the more recent acquisitions were underperforming Barrow's and his scout's expectations.

Cleveland scout Cy Slapnicka had had the first shot at landing Gomez, but the Yankees got a break because of one of Slapnicka's more bizarre superstitions. Sportswriter Al Kemp happened to be interviewing San Francisco owner Charley Graham at the Seals stadium after a game when Slapnicka joined them and asked to visit Gomez in the locker room. A half-hour later Slapnicka returned and said he had decided to pass on Gomez. A surprised Graham asked why the change of heart. "Well, I'll tell you, Charley," Slapnicka responded. "I saw Gomez undressed in the clubhouse, and anybody who's got as a big a prick as he's got can't pitch winning ball in the Major Leagues."

The loose relationship between Major and Minor League clubs is further illustrated by Essick's pursuit of Myril Hoag, an outfielder for the Sacramento Solons. While duck hunting after the 1929 season, Essick and Sacramento manager Buddy Ryan came to an agreement. The Yankees paid the Solons a fee upfront for Hoag for delivery at the end of the season, but this "deal" was never recorded with the commissioner's office. In 1930 Hoag improved dramatically over his 1929 season; by midseason several clubs wanted Hoag and were willing to pay sixty thousand dollars or more to get him. Some of the Sacramento owners wanted to wriggle out of their manager's deal. In the end Sacramento honored the handshake with Essick, but only after forcing Barrow to ante up a total of forty-five thousand dollars. Later, Barrow may have wished Essick had been less effective in defending his deal; Hoag never developed into a quality Major League regular.

Essick was not as lucky with future Hall of Fame shortstop Arky Vaughan. On his way to Fullerton, California, to sign Vaughan, Essick detoured to Long Beach to scout a player who played only on Sundays. The Pirates meanwhile were also scouting Fullerton, but to see their catcher, Willard Hershberger, another future Major Leaguer. After watching Fullerton play, the Pirates were so impressed with Vaughan they ignored Hershberger and signed Vaughan instead. By the time Essick arrived, it was too late for him to acquire Vaughan. As a consolation prize, Essick signed Hershberger, who eventually made the Majors with the Cincinnati Reds.

To open an outfield spot for one of his younger players, such as Sammy Byrd or Dusty Cooke (in 1929 Krichell's signing had turned in a monster year in St. Paul, leading the league in home runs, RBI, and walks, while hitting .358), Barrow sold Bob Meusel to Cincinnati for twenty-five thousand dollars. Meusel had suffered an ankle injury in 1928 and a down year in 1929, and Barrow rightly concluded that the thirty-three-year-old Meusel's career as an effective regular was just about over. Later in the off-season Barrow sold shortstop Leo Durocher to Cincinnati. Cincinnati owner Sidney Weil later recalled the Durocher negotiations:

> I went to the Yankee offices to see Ed Barrow. He offered to let me have Durocher's contract in exchange for another player whom he required to satisfy the needs of a farm club, and $25,000. [As noted earlier, this was not uncommon: Minor League teams occasionally asked Major League clubs to track down certain players as part of the Major League team's acquisition of a Minor Leaguer.] I suggested $7,500, which was enough for such a hitter. Mr. Barrow didn't say a word. He looked at me hard and then looked out the window. I

sat there for a minute, staring at his back. Then I started to get up,
remarking: "Well, I've been thrown out of better offices than this."
He whirled around in his chair and, before I could recover my bear-
ings, I had bought Durocher for $10,000 and that ballplayer, whose
name I've forgotten. [It was Clarke Pittinger, who never again ap-
peared in the Majors.]

Barrow sold Durocher principally because his excellent fielding could not
compensate for his anemic bat, but other factors were at work as well. Durocher had become a loner on the Yankees team because of his brash, high-
living personality. He owed many New Yorkers money and had gained the
enmity of Ruth. In 1929 Durocher earned five thousand dollars with a one-
thousand-dollar bonus conditional on his behavior. He felt he deserved a
raise for 1930 and confronted Barrow, who told him the offer was final.

Durocher snapped, "Don't hold your breath, because that's never going
to happen."

Barrow then gave Durocher the same treatment he had given Weil: he
turned his back and looked out the window as if to dismiss Durocher. Durocher got up to leave, but as he reached the door, his temperament got the
better of him and he said, just loud enough for Barrow to hear: "Ahhh, go
and f—— yourself."

Barrow chose not to ignore the remark and yelled: "What did you say."

Durocher refused to back down and responded: "Didn't you hear me?"

Barrow yelled back: "Yes, I did hear you."

To get in the last word, Durocher retorted: "And it still goes."

But Barrow never let a player get in the last word and told Durocher: "And
so do you" (meaning Durocher was about to be dealt from the Yankees).

Shortly thereafter Barrow sold him to Cincinnati.

Barrow was actually quite fond of Durocher in a paternalistic sort of
way, and if anything, this exchange strengthened his feelings. When Larry
MacPhail contemplated hiring Durocher as manager many years later, he
called Barrow for a reference, and Barrow gave him a favorable recommendation. He also continued to lecture Durocher on the evils of borrowing
money. Barrow's disillusionment with his own inability to raise funds to buy
into the Red Sox back in 1918 affected his guidance to Durocher: "You think
you have a lot of friends in baseball don't you? Just wait for the day you're

in trouble and you try to borrow some money. That's when you'll find out different. If a man has two real friends in his entire life, he's lucky."

Ruth's three-year contract expired after the 1929 season, leading to a new round of public negotiations for America's top celebrity. Though Barrow consulted with Ruppert in setting Ruth's salary target, once negotiations began the owner handled them himself. In the event, the slugger settled on a record-breaking two-year contract for eighty thousand dollars per season. Ruppert also agreed to return the five-thousand-dollar fine Huggins had leveled in 1925.

Shawkey handled his old teammates about as well as could be expected. At the beginning of the 1930 season he was probably more lenient than he should have been; Ruth generally behaved himself, but Hoyt took advantage of his old rotation mate. Shawkey recalled that Hoyt began hanging out with a theatrical crowd, often staying out well into the night. Despite numerous warnings, Hoyt persisted in his high-living behavior, even on nights before he pitched. Shawkey concluded he needed to trade the veteran Hoyt, who had become uncoachable. Hoyt later insinuated that Barrow "caused more problems" but never elaborated further.

Shawkey also had to deal with previous baggage in his relationship with Koenig. Shawkey had once berated Koenig after the latter misplayed a ball, costing Shawkey a victory. Koenig never forgot this outburst and showed little respect for his new manager. Shawkey wanted to trade the shortstop, and Barrow, who still hoped Lary would justify his earlier price, acquiesced to Shawkey's request. At the end of May, Barrow sent both Hoyt and Koenig to Detroit for veteran outfielder Harry Rice and two throw-ins. Neither Cooke nor Byrd had proven ready for full-time duty, so Shawkey promptly installed Rice in the starting lineup.

In June 1930 Barrow's thin skin and short temper came very close to costing him his job. Veteran sportswriter Bill Slocum mildly chastised Barrow for employing excessive secrecy in demoting catcher Arndt Jorgens to the Minor Leagues. To challenge Slocum, Barrow positioned himself at the entrance to the press gate. When Slocum arrived, Barrow verbally accosted him, and the two began arguing. Barrow, the ex-pugilist, quickly lost his cool and landed a right to Slocum's jaw, knocking him to the ground. Barrow's actions appalled and embarrassed Ruppert, who reportedly would have fired Barrow if Slocum and his newspaper had pushed the issue. Fortunately for Barrow, Slocum and his paper were willing to let the matter slide. Ruppert hoped to avoid a repeat of the incident by installing his confidant and friend George Perry to a newly created press secretary position. He announced that from then on, all Yankees' press contacts would go through Perry. Once the incident blew over, however, Ruppert's edict was soon forgotten, and Barrow was again talking to the press.

Nineteen-thirty was one of the best offensive seasons of all time, yet even factoring in the era, Shawkey oversaw an outstanding offense. The team led the league by scoring 1,062 runs, the third-highest total since 1900. Despite a trial at third, Lazzeri spent most of his time at second, and Lary took over at shortstop. Shawkey installed Ben Chapman, a fiery, young hotshot, signed back in 1927 and seasoned for a couple of years in the Minors, at third.

Unfortunately for Shawkey, the pitching staff disappointed again, and he could bring the team in no higher than third. The pitchers that Barrow and his scouts had delivered over the previous few years could not compare to those purchased from the Red Sox early in the 1920s. Only George Pipgras started more than twenty-five games as Shawkey experimented with fourteen different starters, a large number for the time. On Shawkey's advice, Barrow made one key pitching acquisition during the season. Like Frazee before him, lead owner Bob Quinn was experiencing cash-flow problems in Boston. He had several capable pitchers, including Ed Morris, Danny MacFayden, and Red Ruffing. Barrow asked Shawkey's opinion on the three, and Shawkey strongly recommended the right-handed Ruffing. Barrow agreed, and in early May he sent spare-part Cedric Durst and $17,500 to the Red Sox for pitcher Red Ruffing, who immediately became the Yankees' best pitcher, finishing 15-5 under Shawkey.

During the season Ruppert and Barrow became convinced that Shawkey was not the long-term answer as manager. Shawkey was bitter about the way Barrow and Ruppert handled his dismissal: "Just before our last road trip I had a meeting with Ruppert and Barrow. They told me . . . that they were very happy with the way things were, even if we did come in third. They told me that I was going to be there next year. One day after the season had closed, I went up to the office to talk over some business. I was heading for Barrow's office when the door opened and Joe McCarthy came walking out. I took one look and turned around and got out of there. I knew what had happened."

18. McCarthy

Late in the 1930 season Barrow met with Chicago sportswriter Warren Brown in New York. Brown confidentially knew that Joe McCarthy, a close friend, would not be returning as manager of the Chicago Cubs. At a boxing match Barrow attended with the writer, Brown passed along his scoop on McCarthy's status for 1931. Barrow, in another example of the incredibly close relationship between the press and ball clubs, confided to Brown that the Yankees intended to jettison Shawkey at the end of the season. Brown plugged his friend McCarthy as a potential replacement. Hoping to further advance his McCarthy-for-manager campaign, Brown also tracked down George Perry, Ruppert's confidant, and asked Perry if Ruppert would like to have McCarthy manage the Yankees. Perry checked with Ruppert and reported back that Ruppert had dismissed the question: "He said Wrigley [Chicago owner William] was a great friend of his. He said Wrigley would never let McCarthy go. He said I was crazy. He ran me out." But when it became clear that McCarthy was available, Ruppert and Barrow jumped on the opportunity to hire a great manager (after Wrigley gave Ruppert his blessing).

Rare among baseball managers of the era (and like Barrow), McCarthy never played Major League Baseball. To chase his baseball dream, McCarthy had quit college to play professionally in 1907. Unfortunately, he was released early in the season and quickly jumped to an outlaw league. The next season he caught on with Toledo in the American Association. In 1913 he received his first real taste of managing, when, at age twenty-six, he served as player-manager of Wilkes-Barre in the New York State League. After a successful season both on the bench and as a second baseman, he moved on to Buffalo, just as a player. Barrow became acquainted with the scrappy McCarthy during the latter's two years in Buffalo during the Federal League war.

After the 1915 season Barrow recommended McCarthy, the player, to the Yankees. McCarthy, still aching for a shot at the Major Leagues in almost any capacity, traveled to New York to meet with the Yankees and the Brooklyn Federal League club, which had also expressed an interest. In New York McCarthy first interviewed with Yankees owner Huston and manager Bill Donovan. The two were only mildly interested and unwilling to offer Buffalo an acceptable price. He next met with the Brooklyn Feds, who quickly signed him. Unfortunately for McCarthy, the league soon folded.

With the end of the Federals, McCarthy joined the Louisville Colonels, managed by Billy Clymer, one of McCarthy's old managers and mentors. Barrow may have targeted McCarthy as a potential manager for his league's Jersey City franchise, but its sale to Jack Dunn as part of the league's return to Baltimore obviated this opportunity. Also, while Barrow agreed to take Federal Leaguers back into his league, he may not have been quite as ready to advocate for their move into discretionary positions.

At midseason 1919, McCarthy was promoted to manager of the Colonels. As a player-manager in 1920, he brought Louisville home second. The next season McCarthy virtually retired himself as a player and managed the Colonels to the American Association pennant. In the Little World Series, Louisville upset the International League's heavily favored Baltimore Orioles. McCarthy won a second flag in 1925. His success, despite his youth and lack of Major League credentials, testified to his managerial talents. After suffering through three managers and a last-place finish in 1925, Chicago Cubs owner William Wrigley and President Bill Veeck opted to take a chance on McCarthy, generally regarded as one of the Minor League's best managers. He quickly executed two brilliant player acquisitions, landing hard-hitting outfielders Riggs Stephenson and Hack Wilson.

In the spring of 1926, McCarthy faced the key challenge of his young managerial career: earning the respect and trust of a group of Major League ballplayers. McCarthy fancied himself something of a psychologist and did, in fact, have a unique and effective manner of getting through to his players, demanding and receiving professionalism both on and off the field. And he had a knack for knowing what was going on in the clubhouse. McCarthy rarely berated a player; when he felt it necessary to do so, he often delegated the task to Jimmy Burke, his old Minor League manager and now trusted coach. McCarthy remained wary of reporters. Barrow reinforced this sentiment early in McCarthy's Yankees tenure when he chastised McCarthy for a mostly innocuous reply to a reporter's question regarding a holdout. McCarthy mastered the difficult art—especially in New York—of saying little and giving out even less. His standard response of "let me worry about that" became a running joke with the reporters.

Yankees third baseman Red Rolfe, who later became a manager himself, said that McCarthy's most important trait was his ability to make his players feel important. He noted McCarthy had only two rules, both of which he enforced meticulously: a midnight curfew, and no poker—he worried that teammates might lose the all-important dedication to the team concept if they owed one another money.

McCarthy rarely challenged or criticized a player directly in public, but he often made indirect comments that communicated his message. For example, one time he came upon a postgame card game that included a player who had a missed a sign that day. McCarthy remarked to the card players: "You fellows certainly amaze me. You know every card in the deck, but you don't know a simple hit-and-run sign when you see it." Another time he pulled Frank Crosetti aside, telling him to throw the ball extra hard to Gehrig at first because Gehrig was looking a little lethargic, and he wanted to wake him up. Crosetti dutifully obeyed and began firing the ball to first. In fact, McCarthy felt it was Crosetti who was a little tired and intended to stimulate him by making him think he was helping Gehrig.

Back in 1926, future Hall of Fame pitcher Grover Cleveland Alexander provided a stiff early test for McCarthy in Chicago. Alexander was now thirty-eight years old, probably an alcoholic, and loathe to follow McCarthy's training rules. In June, after Alexander had arrived drunk for a large percentage of recent games, McCarthy suspended him. Soon thereafter, McCarthy dispatched Alexander, one the Cubs' most beloved stars, to the St. Louis Cardinals (where he performed his heroics in the 1926 World Series against the Yankees). This move and Wrigley's backing helped establish McCarthy with the veterans. The fact that his two new outfielders performed well also helped. The resourceful McCarthy handled Wilson's drinking and late-night excursions adroitly. He managed to get several Hall of Fame seasons out of his outfielder, including the all-time single-season RBI record in 1930. When Wilson was no longer partnered with McCarthy—despite being only thirty years old—Wilson's career deteriorated quickly.

After several years of competitive teams, McCarthy finally captured the National League flag in 1929. Wrigley provided some bittersweet help before the season when he purchased superstar second baseman Rogers

Hornsby for five unremarkable players and two hundred thousand dollars—the highest price ever paid for a player up to that time. McCarthy's Cubs won ninety-eight games, earning the right to face the Athletics in the World Series. Trailing two games to one, McCarthy suffered through the longest inning of his life, the seventh inning of Game 4. The Cubs led 8–0 and appeared on their way to evening the Series. But aided by a ball Wilson lost in the sun, the Athletics scored ten runs in the inning and held on to beat the Cubs 10–8. Philadelphia went on to win Game 5 and the World Championship.

Mainly due to injuries, the team fell just short in 1930, and McCarthy's job situation became surprisingly precarious. Wrigley never reconciled himself to the Game 4 debacle and began to blame McCarthy. Furthermore, the prickly Hornsby had managed the 1926 Cardinals to their victory over the Yankees and presumed he could manage better than McCarthy. With his access to Wrigley and Veeck, he subtly worked to undermine McCarthy. When Wrigley refused to give McCarthy a vote of confidence, McCarthy resigned in late September just before the end of the season; Wrigley quickly named Hornsby manager. As recounted earlier, Ruppert and Barrow turned to McCarthy. The awkward and surprising timing of McCarthy's resignation regrettably led to their inconsiderate treatment of Shawkey.

To sign McCarthy, Barrow dispatched Krichell to Philadelphia to find him and bring him to New York. Delighted by their interest, McCarthy met Barrow and Ruppert at Ruppert's apartment in New York to discuss a contract. McCarthy drove a hard bargain, and every so often Ruppert and Barrow would adjourn to another room to discuss the latest counteroffer. As negotiations dragged, McCarthy eventually drew a line in the sand over his final proposal by thanking them and heading for the elevator when Ruppert and Barrow failed to accept it. Before McCarthy could get away, Ruppert called him back and signed him to a two-year contract. Ruppert had needed to act decisively; Boston's Bob Quinn and Pittsburgh's Barney Dreyfuss had also hoped to land McCarthy.

Babe Ruth had grudgingly acquiesced to the hiring of his longtime teammate Bob Shawkey in 1929, but he actively resented the hiring of Joe McCarthy. Barrow dismissed Ruth's desire to manage, believing him too self-absorbed and immature. Ruppert, who liked the affable Ruth, took a more paternalistic approach and equivocated with Ruth on his future managerial possibilities. McCarthy coped with Ruth by simply allowing him to keep his own training rules, while demanding professionalism and discipline from the balance of the squad. Fortunately for McCarthy, he assumed leadership over several mature and talented veterans such as Combs (who had played for McCarthy in Louisville) and Gehrig, both of whom welcomed his approach.

With McCarthy in the fold, the new Yankees brain trust—Barrow, Ruppert, and McCarthy—met in early November to discuss the team's off-season plans. McCarthy reported to the newspapers that the Yankees' top priorities were a backup catcher and a front-line starting pitcher.

Barrow, on the other hand, diagnosed the weaknesses of the Yankees as extending beyond a backup catcher and one pitcher. He persevered in his ongoing effort to rebuild the left side of the infield. Accordingly, he signed free agent Joe Sewell, a one-time star shortstop recently converted to third base, whom Cleveland had just released after a subpar 1930 season. After looking over his talent in the spring, McCarthy returned Lazzeri to second, installed Sewell as his starting third baseman, and moved Ben Chapman, overmatched at third, to the outfield. Not completely satisfied with the arrangement, however, McCarthy continued to experiment with his infield throughout the season. Lazzeri spent thirty-nine games at third, and Reese played sixty-one at second.

Barrow and his scouts continued to pursue top Minor League talent. During the 1931 season Barrow purchased second baseman Jack Saltzgaver from St. Paul for $40,000; this acquisition offered another infield option: shifting Lazzeri back to third and inserting Saltzgaver (who never panned out) at second. As part of the transaction, Barrow sent Connery another $10,000 to acquire pitcher Johnny Murphy. Barrow also sent $7,500 to Jersey City for pitcher Johnny Allen, who had logged a deceptively poor won-lost record of 12-16: his ERA of 3.98 was excellent given the league's offensive levels. Barrow also grabbed another shortstop; on the advice of West Coast scout Bill Essick, he spent $50,000 on Pacific Coast League star Frank Crosetti.

The 1931 season proved both physically painful and a disappointment on the field for Barrow. In May, he underwent surgery for gallstones. Barrow had not been feeling well for some time but had waited until the team left on a road trip before submitting to the surgery. Although he was now sixty-three years old, Barrow recovered surprisingly quickly from the operation. In other business, the death of American League president Ernest Barnard in March put Barrow's name in play once again as a possible replacement. The league's owners, however, initially chose to carry on temporarily with league vice president Frank Navin as acting president. At the end of May the American League's magnates named William Harridge president, a job he would hold until 1959.

The team improved in 1931 but still finished well behind the powerful Athletics. Led by terrific seasons from Ruth and Gehrig, the Yankees set the modern record by scoring 1,067 runs, 182 more than the next closest team that season. The pitching, although improved, could not match Philadelphia's. In his farthest-reaching pitching decision, McCarthy inserted the youthful Lefty Gomez into the starting rotation. He further benefited from a full season from Red Ruffing, though Ruffing did not have one of his better seasons. Aging veteran Pennock turned in another fine season, but Pipgras was limited to 138 innings. Notably, pitching hopefuls such as Hank Johnson and Ed Wells once again failed to deliver.

After the 1931 season Ruppert was three years removed from his last pennant and getting antsy. Barrow and McCarthy both felt pressure to return to the top. When Ruppert had inked McCarthy to his original contract, he told him: "I'll stand for finishing second this year, McCarthy. But remember, I do not like to finish second." McCarthy's mulligan year was now used.

In November 1931 the Yankees purchased a future mainstay, outfielder George Selkirk, from Jersey City. With less success, Barrow spent twenty-five thousand dollars to acquire Jesse Hill, another outfielder. Barrow found his future third baseman when Jeff Tesreau, one-time Major League pitcher and Dartmouth University baseball coach, recommended his shortstop, Red Rolfe. Barrow dispatched scout Gene McCann to assess and sign him, but other scouts had also become aware of Rolfe's potential. In the ensuing frenzy, Barrow outbid his rivals and landed Rolfe for a six-thousand-dollar signing bonus, a fairly hefty amateur bonus for the time. Optioned to the Minors, Rolfe eventually anchored third base for many years.

The Yankees rarely lost a player they coveted. As testified to by the Cooke and Hoag signings, the Yankees' scouts were well connected and resourceful. While Ruppert gave Barrow an essentially open checkbook, in many instances the ingenuity of their scouts put the Yankees in a first position

prior to the bidding process. Their signings were not universally successful. Of particular concern, other than Gomez the team had missed on several starting pitchers. But restocking a Major League organization requires
both quality and quantity. Prospects often fail to develop. By focusing on
landing as many Minor League stars as possible, the Yankees gave themselves a margin of error. For every Hoag and Hill, the Yankees found a Selkirk and a Rolfe.

19. "If You Say I Did It, I Did; but I Did It Asleep"

During the 1920s, the Majors and the high Minors bickered as they struggled to develop a mutually satisfactory working relationship. While Branch Rickey pioneered a rudimentary farm system for the St. Louis Cardinals, other teams remained skeptical that such a scheme was worth its huge cost. The evolution of a more elaborate farm system emerged from the maturing economics of baseball, the slumping national economy, and baseball's changing rules in adapting to both. The two fundamental problems of new talent procurement—how to acquire it and how to develop it once acquired—were particularly acute in this era. As we have seen, the elimination of the draft for the highest Minor Leagues significantly raised the price of prospects and acted as a check on landing top Minor Leaguers for those teams unable or unwilling to meet the high asking prices.

The restrictive option rules were another annoyance to Major League owners, making the long-term development of young prospects more difficult. The 1921 Major League agreement set the player control limit at forty players (an increase from thirty-five) and limited teams to twenty-five active players during the bulk of the season. Thus, a Major League franchise was constrained to controlling only fifteen prospects. These players could play in the Minor Leagues through an "optional assignment," or "option." Under an option, a Major League franchise could assign a player's contact to a receptive Minor League team that would pay a nominal fee for the player's use. The Major League club retained the right to recall the player at a later date for a slightly larger, but still low, dollar amount. A Major League club was allowed to control a player for only two years under option. After the two-year period, the Major League team had to either keep the player on its active roster or place him on Major League waivers. If no other Major League team claimed him off waivers, the team had to either cancel his right of recall (in effect give or sell him cheap to the Minor League team to which he was optioned) or sell him to another Minor League team for the best possible price.

Major League teams often created more extensive "working agreements" with friendly, trusted Minor League owners and directed their optioned players to these teams. The Minor League team occasionally benefited from an under-the-table stipend, but more importantly it often retained the rights to the player if he did not make the Majors at the end of his two-year option period. Not surprisingly, Major League front offices chafed under these restrictive player-development rules. Many tried to increase the number of players under control though clandestine working agreements. Retaining rights after a player's two-year option period expired, such as Barrow tried to maneuver with Ray French and Jess Doyle in Vernon, was one such example. Commissioner Landis objected to these secretive evasions of the player-control rules, but his limited office staff (essentially Leslie O'Connor) could do little more than sporadically police such handshake agreements.

In 1925 the option rules became even more constrictive. The National Agreement between the Majors and the Minors technically allowed only eight players to be placed on option, although neither Commissioner Landis nor Minor League secretary John Farrell felt it necessary to enforce this highly restrictive clause in the Major League–Minor League agreement. During the winter meetings in December 1924, International League president John Toole challenged Farrell on this issue and forced through a resolution to enforce the statute. With the Minors aggressively lobbying to impose the letter of the agreement, Landis eventually complied. It was Barrow who first publicly announced the new restriction in May 1925 while in St. Paul negotiating the purchase of Koenig.

Narrowing the total number of Minor League players a team could control to eight severely constrained the ability of Major League teams to sign and develop young players. During the mid-1920s one team, the New York Giants, carried future Hall of Famers as teenagers on its Major League roster (Travis Jackson, Freddie Lindstrom, and Mel Ott). The reduction so angered Barrow that he actively worked to depose Toole from his position as president of the International League. Once again, however, Barrow's lack of political skill hindered his ability to get what he wanted; Toole won not only reelection but a pay raise as well.

St. Louis Cardinals vice president and baseball pioneer Branch Rickey hoped to overcome these two impediments—the high cost of players and the limited avenues to develop them—by investing directly in Minor League teams. He first purchased an interest in a Minor League franchise in the early 1920s and described his rationale:

> We finished in last place. And I said to myself, "What can I do about it? I have no money." . . . Clubs usually finish last on merit, because they do not have enough good players. . . .
>
> Now, a club in the condition in which the St. Louis club was at that time could buy, for a small price, a part of the club at Fort Smith [Arkansas], or 18 percent at Houston, or 50 percent at Syracuse, and then out of trial and error find that the investments were good or bad, and come to the place where it would own a small Minor League club where it could put its players recommended by a personal friend here or there, or by a limited number of scouts which you could afford to employ, and the farm system was ridiculed; it was made fun of.

In fairness to the skeptics, investment in Minor League teams did not really address a couple of key difficulties posed by the rules. For one, the top Minor League players remained under the control of the high Minors. More importantly, Commissioner Landis did not want Major League teams to control Minor League franchises: he felt such ownership would lead to a restriction on the movement of players and also destroy the legitimacy of Minor League pennant races as Major League teams recalled players without concern for the pennant prospects of the Minor League team. Landis did not attempt to ban outright ownership of Minor League franchises by Major League clubs, but as we will see, he enforced the player movement rules to limit its benefit.

Furthermore, while Rickey's Minor League organization helped restock the team on the field—the Cardinals won the 1931 World Series—owner Sam Breadon was unhappy with his financial return. Despite his championship, in 1932 he pondered a franchise shift to Montreal. He went so far as to twice travel to Montreal to investigate possible ballpark sites. He eventually decided to back off the move once the expense associated with a transfer—purchasing a site, building a ballpark, and all the other ancillary costs—became apparent. Breadon also considered a transfer to Detroit, but this inchoate plan was quickly vetoed by Tigers owner Frank Navin.

As the 1920s dragged on without any relief from the Major League–
Minor League agreement, other teams began experimenting with farm teams
as well. Ruppert grew increasingly frustrated and directed Barrow to evaluate gaining a controlling interest in a couple of Minor League teams. In
late 1928 Barrow sent Krichell to Chambersburg, Pennsylvania, in the Blue
Ridge League to close on the purchase of the Yankees' first farm team. Soon
thereafter Barrow backed off consummating a pending thirty-five-thousand-
dollar purchase of Syracuse in the New York–Penn League.

Excerpts from the minutes of the 1929 winter meetings offer, in the owners' own words, their frustrations with the existing system. For Ruppert
the recent purchase of Lyn Lary and Jimmy Reese now appeared unlikely
to turn out as hoped, and he had failed to win the pennant. At the Major
League meeting on December 12, 1929, in New York, with Barrow in tow,
Ruppert vented his frustration:

> *Mr. Chairman, I own a Minor League ball club, at least the Yan-
> kee Ball Club owns it, the Chambersburg Club. I realize, as [St.
> Louis Cardinals owner] Mr. Breadon said, what are we going to do
> to develop our ballplayers. I do not know whether a Major League
> club owner makes money or loses money on the clubs he owns, and
> I do not care. That is not my business. I know what it costs me to
> run the Chambersburg Ball Club. I know I am going to be forced
> into owning Minor League clubs and so is every other Major League
> owner in this room, for the simple reason, as was stated before by
> Mr. Breadon and Mr. Navin, where are we eventually going to get
> our ballplayers from? I do not know which club—I don't care which
> ball club it is—can afford to pay the prices for the Minor League
> ballplayers that we are paying for them now. The Minor Leagues
> have got us just where they want us. If a man today owns a Major
> League ball club, he is allowed to put out eight men to develop. I
> don't know whether any men in the Majors cheat or not, nor do I
> care whether they do, but I do say one thing: that we come here year
> after year and we all say the same thing. I believe that 75 percent
> of the Major League ball club owners feel that we have no way by
> which we can develop our ballplayers as we wish to bring them up.
> Two or three years ago it was said that we could buy a ballplayer,*

put them out for two years and develop them. I do not think that is enough to develop a ballplayer. Some develop faster than others. We get that ballplayer back, we put that ballplayer on the bench, we want to put somebody else in, and the next time we put him out [send him down to the Minors], he is put out to a Major League ball club [sold to a Major League team], we have no way to get that man back. He must go to the draft first [Ruppert here refers to the exception to the high Minors draft exemption: players whose rights were once held by a Major League team and who were then sent to the high Minors were eligible to be drafted]. That Major League club owner may sell that man for $50,000, but what do we get? Just what we paid for him. . . .

I for one am opposed to owning Minor League ball clubs. As I said repeatedly, and I will say again, I for one am going to own a Minor League ball club, although it is against my own idea, but at the same time I must do something to develop my own players. . . .

There is one thing I did miss. We have a rule in baseball that I could never figure out. We are permitted to carry forty ballplayers up to a certain date, and I think every club has the forty ballplayers. Then after that date, we must cut our players down to twenty-five, and we are allowed to put eight men out on option. That gives us thirty-three. I've often wondered what became of those seven men, but they are gone somewhere. If we're allowed to have forty men up to a certain time, then they are cut down to thirty-three, why can't we have forty all the time? If it is right to have forty before a certain date, why can't we have forty after that certain date?

Therefore I should think we could equalize that thing by taking those players and putting fifteen men out on option instead of eight, and then we have got our forty men, but, no, we must get rid of those seven men. I never know where they go. I have tried to find out, but I cannot.

Also, we should have three years to put out our men instead of two.

Ruppert had obviously struck a nerve. Boston Braves owner Judge Emil Fuchs chimed in:

I agree with Colonel Ruppert that if you have forty players, you can just as well cut down to thirty-three, because the other seven men don't do you any good. The time arrives around the June period when you have got to cut down, and sometimes you have to give them away, practically. I think it does not affect a rich club any more than it does a poor club.

Sam Dreyfuss, son of principal Pittsburgh owner Barney Dreyfuss, added his resentment of the existing rules as well:

I would just like to put the Pittsburgh club on record as being of about the same opinion on the whole matter as Colonel Ruppert. We owned two Minor League clubs last year. We have dropped the Saulsbury club, returning the franchise to the league on December 1, and since the close of the 1929 season we have acquired by purchase the Wichita club of the Western League.

We don't want to own Minor League clubs, we don't believe in owning Minor League clubs, but we feel that we have been forced into it. You can go out and buy ten or twelve new men every fall, then you have to put those same men out two years, which gives you twenty to twenty-four in two years, and you are only limited to eight going out. We have been forced at the end of one or two years to sacrifice them at the small prices that we can get from Minor League clubs, some of these very excellent prospects that we have picked up.

I can name dozens of players in the National and American leagues—the Pittsburgh club secured from B or C clubs or as free agents, had them out two years on option, found they were still not ready for our club. We could see they were big league prospects, but being up in the race we had to have ballplayers who could do us some good at the immediate moment, and we were forced to let these men go, and somebody had the good fortune at the end of one year to buy these men and reap the benefit of the time and money we have put into them.

I could name George Haas, of the Athletics, who played quite a part against the National League this year; Joe Cronin, whom the Washington club picked up—he was only twenty-one years old

when they got him—and the Chicago club has Black, the same con-
dition. I could name lots of others.

That is the only reason that the Pittsburgh club has gone into ac-
quiring Minor League franchises. We feel that we cannot afford to
invest in ten or twelve or fourteen players every fall and then have
to give them out and have to give up seven of those men each year
without any further trial or any further opportunity to realize on
our investment. . . . I am sure that, if there could be any solution
whereby the Major League clubs could put out twelve or fifteen men
for three years on option that the Pittsburgh club would gladly get
rid of all the trouble and the bother and the financial loss that is
entailed in operating a Minor League franchise.

Several other owners chimed in, after which Ruppert proposed an amendment: "that we be permitted to put out fifteen optional players and that the time be extended from two to three years and that we keep a player limit of forty." The motion passed easily. In conclusion Landis noted that the new policy could not be considered by the Minors until the December 1930, twelve months away.

By the end of 1930, as the severity of America's descent into the Great Depression was becoming apparent (during 1930 the unemployment rate exploded from 3.2 percent to 8.7 percent, and the gross national product (GNP) declined 10 percent, one of the worst drops ever in the nation's output of goods and services), the Minor League owners began to tone down much of their previous bluster and demands for complete independence. Tired of being stonewalled, the Majors threatened an open break with the Minors unless given relief from the stringent player-movement rules. The Minors recognized that they needed the support of the deeper-pocketed Major League owners and negotiated a compromise on the draft. The high Minors once again agreed to a draft but managed to exempt a number of their players. A Minor League player was not draftable until he had played in Organized Baseball for a designated period: from two years for those at class D up to four years for those at class AA. Also, the Minors ratified the Majors' resolution at the previous winter meeting: the number of players allowed out on option was increased to fifteen and the years of control to three.

With the change in the draft and option rules, Barrow and Ruppert concluded they probably did not need to develop a farm system. Nevertheless, late in 1931, when Newark owner Paul Block approached Ruppert regarding the sale of his International League franchise, Ruppert showed interest. Without consulting Barrow, he agreed to pay Block $250,000 for his team, the Yankees' second foray into Minor League ownership and the first at a high level. The Yankees had just finished their third consecutive season without a pennant, despite huge cash outlays for players. As Ruppert had made clear in his diatribe at the winter meeting, the current system exasperated him. But two more-recent occurrences likely provided the necessary impetus for Ruppert to buy the Newark team. First, by 1931 the failure of Lary and Reese to develop into Major League stars had become evident. More importantly, the Jack Saltzgaver acquisition in 1931 may have finally tipped the scales. At some point Ruppert had come to believe that the Yankees already owned the rights to Jack Saltzgaver, and therefore, the $40,000 price tag was illegitimate. Paying $40,000 for a player he thought he already controlled reinforced his unwillingness to be held hostage by the arcane, confused, haphazardly enforced Minor League player rules, even if recently modified to the benefit of the Majors. Ruppert timed his Newark purchase fortuitously. The key institutional constraints on the advantages of owning a Minor League team were about to be eliminated.

The Depression deepened during 1931, with the GNP falling another 8 percent and the unemployment rate mushrooming to 15.9 percent. The Minors, particularly those class B and below, were suffering: the number of Minor Leagues fell from twenty-five in 1929 to just sixteen in 1931. The Minors formed a committee, chaired by Judge William Bramham, president of the Piedmont League, to explore avenues of survival. Bramham traveled to the Major League meetings in December 1931, hat in hand, looking for financial support from the Major League magnates. Barrow's sympathies had long since passed from the Minors to the Major Leagues. At the December 1931 meetings, he mostly watched as Ruppert and the other owners debated the confused arena of roster rules, a discussion that at times seems farcical. The transcript of these meetings further testifies to the owners' confusion over the rules and illuminates the limitations of a farm system—limitations that were eliminated at this meeting:

Ruppert: *Mr. Chairman, I would like to ask a question: in the event of a club lending a man, or giving a club at least $3,000, and he gives you an option on his ball club, or an option on one or two players, are those players counted in the player list? [Bramham proposed that the Majors provide financial support to Minor League owners or teams in return for rights to their players.]*

Ruppert was asking for clarification regarding the central question of Major League investment in Minor League franchises: If one bought an interest in a Minor League club as Bramham was suggesting and through that investment acquired the right to purchase one or more players, did those players count against his forty-man player control and fifteen-player option limit? Obviously, if they counted, the value of investing in a Minor League franchise was significantly diminished because it did not increase nonactive player control beyond fifteen.

Landis: *Yes, sir.*

[St. Louis Cardinals vice president Branch] Rickey: *Perhaps I did not understand the question. If I did, I do not understand your answer. If I have the right to purchase one player from the Minneapolis baseball club for the season of 1932, I have a purchase of one unnamed player from that club, who will count in my forty limit over the year, and who will count as one in my fifteen list. That is correct?*

Rickey here was asking for clarification of the method he employed to evade the letter of Landis's restriction. He would secure the right to purchase one player—but anyone he wanted—and this counted as only one option. Clearly an option on any player on a team was more valuable than one tied to a particular player and provided the benefits of a true farm system. So, was Rickey's procedure valid?

O'Connor: *No.*

Landis: *Yes.*

Rickey: *He counts as one of my fifteen.*

One can feel the confusion. O'Connor was Landis's right-hand man and fought the concept of Major League control of Minor League teams at least as tenaciously as Landis. Rickey followed up by trying to clarify the issue to his advantage. Landis then continued:

> **Landis:** *Some of you have received letters on the subject, but it is my recollection—I generally will yield to your (Mr. O'Connor's) memory. It is younger than mine, but it is my recollection that that player is counted in the forty and as an optional player.*

Here Landis was referring to a distinction without a practical difference: whether a player in the forty-man control limit was technically one of the fifteen option players. If a team had a forty-man control limit and a twenty-five-man active roster, it did not matter how the other fifteen were classified (once the option limit was increased from eight to fifteen). A Major League organization could not control more than fifteen nonactive players. Whether they were technically out on option or some other form of control was essentially irrelevant.

> **[Washington owner Clark] Griffith:** *That is how you so ruled.*
>
> **Ruppert:** *Two years ago at Chattanooga, when the Nebraska State League wanted different clubs financed, at that time you remember we were going to finance a club, I believe they had eleven players on that club; and we were then to select from that club one, or as many players as we saw fit. And at that time, Judge, you ruled those eleven men on that club would count in our player limit.*

With this comment Ruppert summarized the main drawback to the ownership or control of Minor League clubs: Landis ruled that it consumed nearly all of one's nonactive player control slots. That is, the eleven players on the Nebraska State League team would count against the fifteen-man option limit.

> **Landis:** *If you wanted to extend your limit, consider the whole club.*
>
> **Ruppert:** *Correct. Your entrance in a class D club, if you loan money and take an option, and they had ten or eleven players, that would*

count in your player limit of forty. That is the way the judge ruled two years ago at Chattanooga.

Rickey: *Did they recite you had the right to select eleven men?*

Ruppert: *Eleven men or one man; you had an option on the club one of each in number, and you said you would take an option, would count as your player. If you take a club and say I will take an option on three of them, they count.*

Rickey: *I think, just a suggestion there, if the commissioner rules and has ruled an option on a club counts as one, an option of one player; if we have an option of two players it counts two of the fifteen options, you will arrive at the same destination. At least I have for several years of taking an option on the club of one man, say $3,000; I have the option on this club to take one man at a certain time, for $3,000.*

I don't believe there has ever been a time that any man who has taken an option on a club in those circumstances has ever lost the second man to anybody else, if he wanted the second man. I have never known of it in my experience.

The importance of Rickey's last statement in this exchange cannot be overemphasized. Rickey sacrificed the secret of his farm system in the hope of having his methods sanctified by Landis and the other owners. When Rickey invested in a club, he typically secured the right to purchase one player—any player—of his choice. As recorded by the league office, this generally counted as only one of his fifteen options. But as a result of his investment and relationship with the Minor League owner, informally Rickey knew he could acquire any other players he wished.

Rickey: *I would present an issue to the commissioner on that point. There is a difference there, I think, Mr. Commissioner, in this way: we have we will say ten men on our club; under our straight-option agreements those ten men are named, are known and definite.*

We have the right of option, to be exercised on or before the first of September, to select a player from Minneapolis, for example. That man is not named; it is not definite. It is far from certain we will ever exercise the option. I see a difference, that that option should not be counted as one of our fifteen, because it is not definite; it is not fixed and not certain, and we do not know it will ever be exercised. I do not think that man should count in our option list.

Seeing the discussion going in his favor, Rickey decided to press his advantage. He further advocated that having the right to purchase a player from a Minor League team should not even count as one option. As the conversation continued, the perplexed owners attempted to reach some common understanding on the roster rules.

[Cleveland general manager Billy] Evans: *Have we still forty men now since we adopted a twenty-three rule? [As a money-saving move, the active rosters were reduced to twenty-three for 1932.]*

Landis: *Yes, you have a right to forty.*

O'Connor: *Forty players; only twenty-three after June 15.*

Evans: *We have to cut down to thirty-eight?*

Landis and O'Connor both told Evans forty, but he did not seem to understand.

O'Connor: *No, that gives leeway for all these other class players.*

By "other class players" O'Connor was referring to other methods occasionally employed for controlling players. One common practice involved the purchase of a player for future delivery (as Barrow did with Lary and Reese). While Major League teams sometimes resorted to this strategy, it was not particularly beneficial: the player counted against the forty-man roster, and as he had already been paid for, the team was obligated to take him regardless of his continuing performance in the Minors.

Rickey: *The effect of the twenty-three rule is to reduce to thirty-eight possible players.*

Evans: *I have thirty-nine right now.*

Rickey: *This is not June 15.*

O'Connor: *You buy a player in June, for instance for delivery next season, he counts in your forty limit, but not your optional limit, or active player limits.*

Evans: *Then there is really a period when we have a thirty-eight limit.*

O'Connor: *No.*

Rickey: *Yes, there is, Mr. O'Connor, unless you say you may buy two players for future delivery who will fill out your thirty-eight to forty.*

You are reduced necessarily so far as your active list and the optional list is concerned, you are reduced to thirty-eight. Right?

O'Connor: *No.*

Evans: *No.*

Rickey: *If you simply say on two lists, your optional list and your active list, those two lists are necessarily limited from June 15 on the thirty-eight men. That is true?*

O'Connor: *If you exercise the full limit in both cases, certainly.*

In this exchange Rickey and O'Connor rehashed the rules, while a confused Evans tried to keep up. Rickey and O'Connor eventually agreed that each team had an active roster of twenty-three; a team could further control fifteen players through options and two other class players (such as players purchased for future delivery). As an owner with a new, expensive Minor League team, Ruppert quickly grew impatient with the confusion over the small stuff. He directed the discussion back to how investments in Minor League teams affected the fifteen-man option limit.

Ruppert: *If a Major League club finances a Minor League, and they in turn say you can take an option on a ballplayer, that would not count on your player limit?*

Landis: *Of course under the existing Major–Minor League rules, he counts in your forty; and my recollection is that I have been counting them in the optional limit players, but Mr. O'Connor's recollection is very definite. I may be wrong about that; the player is counted only in the forty.*

Haven't I written some of you gentlemen on the subject? Haven't any of you received letters raising that question?

Landis had little recollection of how he had actually ruled in the past and asked the owners if they remembered.

Rickey: *I think in my correspondence with your office, I've got that very thing, the man counts in the optional list.*

I am sure that I have correspondence with you that states that very thing; that player counts in the optional limit. That was for the old days under eight, when that thing was up.

Landis: *[Chicago representative Harry] Mr. Grabiner, didn't your club have a case of that sort somewhere with some club?*

Evans: *I had a case where I bought pitcher Stewart from the Springfield club. I took it up with Mr. O'Connor. My recollection is Mr. O'Connor ruled he was one of my forty but not on my optional list. I know he ruled him in the forty.*

Landis: *You're talking about your rulings and not mine.*

Landis was trying to remember how he had adjudicated an earlier dispute and became irritated when Evans brought up one of O'Connor's.

Ruppert: *I think he ruled that in our case with Abbott, Lary, and Riggs, for next year's delivery, they counted in our optional players.*

O'Connor: *That is a different case; it is not Mr. Rickey's case at all.*

Rickey: *No, it is not. That is definite and fixed.*

[National League president John] Heydler: *In our office, an agreement comes in designating John Smith of the Cincinnati Ball Club be secured for future delivery, we count him in the forty.*

The average agreement that two or three ballplayers going down to the Minor League club, then they reserve themselves the right of the pick of one player or two players. He may be the man they send down. In that case, we always count those as optional, one of the fifteen; if two, it is two; three, it is three.

But any man for future delivery payment down we always put them in the forty, never in the optional.

Rickey: *I think that is clear.*

Despite Ruppert's frustration, the owners continued to debate the relatively trivial issue of whether a player counted as an option player in addition to counting against the forty-man player control limit. Amusingly, only Rickey, O'Connor, and Heydler seemed to fully grasp the rules.

> **[Cincinnati owner Sidney] Weil:** *I had two cases of that kind.*
>
> **Landis:** *What were your two?*
>
> **Weil:** *Bartlesville and Davenport.*
>
> **Landis:** *You had an option on each club to pick a player.*
>
> **Weil:** *I had an option on each club to pick a player.*
>
> **Landis:** *And they were not charged?*
>
> **Weil:** *I don't remember you ever writing. You remember I had an agreement; I had not submitted it to you for approval, and you asked that it be put on the regular transfer form.*
>
> **Rickey:** *He overlooked it.*
>
> **Landis:** *If you say I did it, I did; but I did it asleep, although the recollection of my distinguished coadjutor here is with you.*

The muddle in this exchange was palpable. Weil raised the point that he had two players who were not charged against his player limit. Rickey actually appeared to have been keeping better track of the roster rules and player status questions than Landis. It was probable that Rickey did not complain about Weil's two extra players because he himself had several who had slipped by Landis. More generally, the owners and Landis wanted to establish a consistent foundation while trying to remember how he (and occasionally O'Connor in his stead) had ruled in various individual cases to establish precedent. Unfortunately, not only could the magnates not reach consensus on what the rules actually were; they could barely recall the circumstances of the previous rulings. Heydler clarified that the National League interpreted an option to purchase one or two players from a Minor League team as Rickey described; that is, they counted as one or two options respectively against the Major League team's option limit.

Boston Red Sox owner Bob Quinn finally introduced an amendment that would revolutionize the value of a farm system by effectively eliminating all restrictions on the number of players an organization could control.

> **Quinn:** *Under the present condition, say for two years if you will— put it any way you want—that the commissioner will suspend the*

present rules and regulations and not count in the player limit any
of these players that are on the B, C, and D [league classifications]
that this man helped out . . . is that motion all right, Judge?

Rickey: *If I understand Mr. Quinn's motion, I would second. I*
think the commissioner is able to do that, on the point I made a
while ago, without really suspending the rules.

   It can be done so very easily by saying Mr. O'Connor's posi-
tion, if he is correct about it, is well taken; namely, there is a dif-
ference between a man you send out under a well-known optional
agreement and the man you purchase from there for future deliv-
ery. . . . But I second the motion if it will be of any assistance to the
commissioner.

Rickey did not grasp Quinn's true intent. He simply looked at the motion as further clarification of the narrow question of whether a particular
player's control status technically qualified as an option. Quinn, however,
intended a much more drastic overhaul.

   Rickey: *Do you mean the forty-player limit, Mr. Quinn? You do*
mean the forty-player limit?

   Quinn: *Yes.*

   Landis: *You mean they count in neither limit?*

   Quinn: *They count in neither limit until such time as they desig-*
nate what player they're going to take.

   . . .

   Landis: *All in favor of this motion say "Aye"; opposed "No." The*
ayes have it.

Under the new rule, a Major League team could own a Minor League
team, have full rights to all its players, and none would count against the
Major League limits until the Major League team actually designated a
player for call-up. (The exemption was eventually implemented for the
higher-classification Minor Leagues as well.) Whether Landis and Quinn
recognized the far-ranging effect of this proposal remains unknowable, but
Landis offered little opposition to a proposal that surprised and delighted
even Rickey in its scope. Later that winter the Majors further enhanced the

value of a farm system by initiating a policy whereby a team, after it had used up its three options on a player, could send him to an allied club. This rule particularly incensed Landis, who had worked meticulously to enforce the old rule requiring a player to be placed on waivers or released to an unaffiliated Minor League team.

Barrow grudgingly accepted that the rule changes validated Ruppert's determination to develop a farm system. Once Ruppert directed the new approach, Barrow moved quickly: in February 1932 he announced that the Yankees intended to own or control four Minor League franchises in different classifications. Now that they had purchased the Newark franchise, the Yankees needed someone to run it. And with several more Minor League purchases pending, both Barrow and Ruppert appreciated this hire would also oversee the forthcoming farm system.

For this position Barrow recommended his old friend and Yankees scout, Bob Connery, owner of the St. Paul Saints in the American Association. Connery was only forty-eight, but Ruppert claimed to want a younger man; he probably considered the hire for this position as an understudy for the sixty-three-year-old Barrow. More important, though, was Ruppert's dissatisfaction with Connery. He had paid St. Paul around three hundred thousand dollars for players; other than Koenig, none developed into more than a passable Major Leaguer. Furthermore, he suspected he had been treated unfairly in the Saltzgaver acquisition.

After some investigation on his own, Ruppert selected Baltimore general manager George Weiss. A native of New Haven, Connecticut, Weiss was only thirty-six, but he had already spent nearly twenty years in baseball. Like Barrow, Weiss was a workaholic and had begun his career in baseball promotion while still in his teens. In high school he had become the business manager for the school's baseball team to help administer a meager budget. After graduation, Weiss held much of the team together, brought in a couple of new players, and began promoting them as a semipro team. For a venue, he leased the grounds at Lighthouse Point, an amusement park just outside the New Haven city limits. He quickly recognized an opportunity to capitalize on Sunday baseball, then prohibited by the blue laws in New York, Massachusetts, and New Haven proper. By promising a guaranteed purse, Weiss brought in stars such as Ty Cobb and Walter Johnson, with whom he became close friends, to play in Sunday exhibitions with his semipro team.

As a twenty-one-year-old promoter, in 1916 Weiss inadvertently precipitated heartache for a number of Red Sox players. He organized an exhibition game on October 15 between several world champion Boston players, including Babe Ruth, and his semipro team, bolstered with Ty Cobb. The two teams played to a 3–3 tie in front of three thousand fans, a large number for an October exhibition. Unfortunately, the rules at the time prohibited championship teams from barnstorming without the permission of the club owner. This rule was enforced only sporadically during the Federal League war, but the magnates were now reasserting their authority over the players. The National Commission penalized the Boston players who had participated in the exhibition by denying them their World Series emblems, equivalent to today's World Series rings and valued at approximately eighty-five dollars on a wholesale basis. As noted earlier, a couple of these Red Sox players would again be denied their emblems two years later in the aftermath of the abortive protest over their World Series shares.

Weiss's promotional skills made his semipro team so popular that it began siphoning off interest from New Haven's Organized Baseball team in the Eastern League. When the league approached Weiss in 1919 and offered him an opportunity to buy the team for five thousand dollars, Weiss borrowed the money and purchased the franchise. He quickly turned the team's on-field fortunes around, and New Haven won the Eastern League pennant in 1920. In June 1923 Weiss arranged an exhibition game with Barrow for the Yankees to play New Haven. Around ten thousand fans showed up to see Babe Ruth and the Yankees. When Ruth failed to appear, the team announced before the game that they would allocate one thousand dollars of the gate to reimburse the angry fans a portion of the ticket price. This payment came out of the Yankees' guaranteed payment and infuriated Barrow, and for some time thereafter, Barrow carried a grudge against Weiss.

In December 1923 Weiss and New Haven manager Wild Bill Donovan (Barrow's star pitcher during his year and a half managing the Tigers) set out for the winter meetings in Chicago aboard the Twentieth Century Limited. Donovan occupied the lower berth, Weiss the upper. Outside of Erie, Pennsylvania, the train crashed, killing Donovan and eight others in the car. Badly injured, Weiss spent the next four months in the hospital.

Weiss learned quickly that survival as a Minor League owner depended on player sales to Major League and higher-classification Minor League teams. During his decade with New Haven, he sold twenty-six players for around two hundred thousand dollars. By the late 1920s, the interest level in Minor League baseball in New England appeared to be faltering. Thus, when principal Baltimore owner Jack Dunn died, and the stockholders offered the top executive position to Weiss, he sold his New Haven team and took over Baltimore. Weiss spent three seasons in Baltimore before Ruppert plucked him to run his freshly launched farm system.

Once it became effectively organized, the new Yankees' farm system, in combination with Barrow's excellent scouts, laid the foundation for one of the great stretches of sports dominance in American history. For the next couple of years, Barrow continued to direct his scouts to include the high Minors in their quest for talent. Soon, however, the focus shifted almost exclusively to the low Minors and amateur ranks to generate prospects for the burgeoning farm system.

As the Yankees embarked on their farm system experiment in 1932, Barrow remained focused on his usual sources of talent as well. Bob Quinn, struggling financially in Boston, was finally at the end of his meager resources. Quinn had nothing resembling the talent that Harry Frazee had once offered, but Barrow liked a couple of his remaining pitchers. Having acquired Red Ruffing in 1930, Barrow now pressed Quinn to sell him his other two top starting pitchers: Danny MacFayden, a twenty-six-year-old who had finished 1931 16-12 for a weak Boston team; and Ed Morris, a strapping thirty-one-year-old right-hander who had struggled through the past couple of years after strong 1928 and 1929 seasons. Over the winter Barrow negotiated for the purchase of both hurlers, reportedly offering sixty thousand dollars for Morris. Tragically, Morris was killed by a companion during a hunting and fishing outing in Alabama. While drinking around the campfire, Morris attacked another member of the party. When a third hunter jumped in to act as peacemaker, Morris began hitting him as well. As the fight escalated, Morris's second victim feared for his life and stabbed the big hurler.

Barrow was more fortunate with MacFayden but soon regretted the outcome. In June 1932 he paid Quinn fifty thousand dollars plus Ivy Andrews and Hank Johnson to secure MacFayden. Other than bringing a washed-up Wilcy Moore back from Boston in May, it represented the first Major League trade by Barrow since the Hoyt and Koenig deal more than two years earlier. Relative to its cost, the MacFayden acquisition proved the least successful of Barrow's Major League purchases. Barrow called it his worst deal in New York: "I may have gone wrong here or there on a young pitcher, but I think I made only one really bad deal since coming to New York. That was when we purchased Danny MacFayden from the Red Sox in 1932. . . . I really thought MacFayden would prove another pitcher for us like Ruffing, a fellow who could win close to twenty games a year, season after season. But, somehow, he couldn't click in our uniform."

Jumping ahead, MacFayden spent only two and a half nondescript years in New York before Barrow sold him to Cincinnati on December 1, 1934, for $2,500 plus an additional $2,500 by May 15, 1935, or the return of the player. After a slow start, Cincinnati returned MacFayden to the Yankees. Barrow compounded his original mistake of overpaying for MacFayden by almost immediately reselling him to the Boston Braves for $5,000. Back in Boston, MacFayden turned in several quality seasons. MacFayden later attributed his lack of success in New York to McCarthy tinkering with his delivery.

The MacFayden purchase represented the last high-dollar Yankees purchase for some time. Barrow and his scouts exerted the majority of their efforts on amateur players and those in the lower Minors to stock their expanding farm system. To stay current on his players' training habits and injury status during the off-season, Barrow often dispatched his scouts to visit the Yankees players at their homes.

The Yankees exploded out of the gate in 1932. By mid-May the team was 19-6 and playing superbly. At shortstop McCarthy inserted rookie Frank Crosetti into the regular lineup, although Lary still played eighty games there. Gomez and Ruffing anchored the rotation, and the Yankees received strong supporting seasons from rookie Johnny Allen, veteran George Pipgras, and aging star Herb Pennock. With the pennant just about a foregone conclusion, on July 4 Bill Dickey added some tension to the season with ill-considered fisticuffs. In the first game of a doubleheader in Washington, base runner Carl Reynolds crashed into Dickey while he was blocking the plate. Dickey retaliated by punching Reynolds in the jaw, breaking it in two places. American League president William Harridge fined Dickey one thousand dollars (8 percent of his salary) and suspended him for thirty days. Washington owner Clark Griffith protested that the suspension was too lenient; he wanted Dickey banned until Reynolds was ready to return.

Ruppert and Barrow, on the other hand, were incensed at the severity of the suspension. Ruppert demanded a meeting of the American League board of directors, of which he was a member, to review the suspension. Harridge, still relatively insecure in his new post as American League president, acquiesced to a hearing in Cleveland the following Monday. Both Ruppert and Barrow traveled to Cleveland to make their plea to the board. Three of the four league directors—Quinn, Alva Bradley from Cleveland, and Harry Grabiner (representing Louis Comiskey) from Chicago—voted to uphold Harridge's ruling. As the interested party, Ruppert was prohibited from voting. With this defeat, Ruppert decided to let the matter rest.

In early September Ruth became ill and was diagnosed with appendicitis. Some concern existed regarding his availability for the World Series. Barrow, who knew something about the history of Babe's illnesses and his quick recoveries, remained publicly optimistic. After a week or so, Ruth's relatively low fever broke, and no operation was required. By late September Ruth was again ready to play.

Possibly due to the Depression, World Series ticket sales started out slower than in 1928. On September 21 Barrow announced there were still plenty of seats available at nearly all price points. In the games themselves, the Yankees dominated the Cubs, winning four straight contests. In Game 3 Ruth hit a home run—the famous "called shot"—in which he may or may not have pointed to the center field bleachers before he hit it.

After the World Series, Barrow announced that McCarthy had signed a new three-year contract. The terms were not publicly announced, but subsequent government releases revealed McCarthy now earned thirty thousand dollars per year, a hefty salary for a manager. Aside from merely wishing to lock in McCarthy for several years, Barrow likely foresaw the looming trouble caused by Ruth's pleading for the managerial helm. Nearing retirement, Ruth made no secret of his desire to manage after the conclusion of his playing career. Having McCarthy under contract would make it that much easier to rebuff Ruth's blandishments. Barrow probably also feared that Ruppert, who gave Ruth credit for far more maturity and discipline than did Barrow, might succumb to Ruth's entreaties.

As secretary of the Yankees and Ruppert's spokesman on all but Ruppert's pet issues, Barrow became one of the league's leading voices on a number of issues. For example, early in the 1932 season the National League abolished the rule that prohibited players from talking to fans; those guilty were subject to a five-dollar fine. Barrow, ever vigilant against any possibility of gambling improprieties (probably obsessively so), lobbied for its retention in the American League. The edict's obscure purpose was to prevent gamblers in the stands from learning any information about the day's pitcher.

After the World Series, in another minor fuss, Barrow expressed his dissatisfaction with the reduced receipts from only a four-game Series. For the players, the winning player's share was $5,232, while the losing players each received $4,245. Barrow felt the Yankees club did not receive a reasonable return for winning the pennant. He proposed that the formula whereby players received a percentage of the gate receipts from the first four games be eliminated. He recommended that the players on the winning team receive a flat $4,000 and the losing team $2,500. Barrow's proposal found little support and quickly died.

With Barrow's silly proposal off the table, issues relating to radio broadcasts of baseball games became a key topic at winter meetings (in addition to the evolving relationship with the Minor Leagues). Radio broadcasts had always been within the purview of the individual clubs, but the three New York teams generally opposed radio broadcasts and wanted to make broadcasts a league matter, mainly because that would make them easier to prohibit. Because of the potential conflict caused by one team broadcasting a game while another was playing at home, thereby cutting into ticket sales, the three New York clubs agreed among themselves to prohibit the radio broadcast of any games. Thus, although the New York teams could not ban radio broadcasts leaguewide, they did manage to mitigate a development that they feared would reduce attendance.

In other business, now that the Yankees owned the Newark club, Barrow once again had an active interest in the International League. For the first couple of years, before Weiss assumed full control, Barrow often represented Newark in International League affairs. For example, late in 1932 Barrow and the International League owners faced a dilemma when Brooklyn decided not to exercise its option to purchase the Jersey City franchise. By spring, when no other purchasers had come forward, the franchise verged on bankruptcy. With Barrow representing Newark, the league decided to offer financial assistance and players to help keep the club afloat until a more permanent ownership solution could be found.

By the start of the 1933 season, Babe Ruth would be thirty-eight years old. With the full impact of the Depression now being felt nationwide, Barrow and Ruppert intended to drastically reduce Ruth's 1932 salary of $75,000. Negotiations with Ruth were always front-page news in New York, and

Ruth's loud public rejection of Barrow's initial offer of $50,000 caused the usual commotion in the press. Nearly all players were subject to salary cuts during the depths of the Depression; Ruth, though, with his generous but self-indulgent view of the world, saw no reason why the economic squeeze should affect his income. Ruppert, though, held firm, and Ruth ended up signing for $52,000.

Not surprisingly, other star players also objected to Barrow's proffered salaries—often at a reduced rate—while coming off a World Series victory. Lazzeri sent Barrow an angry letter from California threatening he would not return if given a pay cut. As their bottom line turned red, the owners instigated pay reductions that they justified with pleas of financial distress. The players naturally saw little reason to accept salary cuts for the benefit of men wealthier than they. Amid this general player unrest and threats of holdouts leaguewide, Barrow defended baseball against allegations the sport was faltering: "What is the matter with boxing? What is the matter with wrestling, horse racing, and college football? What is the matter with the newspapers, the banks, railroads, trust companies, and other lines of big business? Why, it is absurd to put such a question about the greatest outdoor professional sport in America. There is nothing the matter with it except tremendous overhead expenses, which all clubs are trying to cut down."

Because of the high-profile annual salary negotiations with his star players, Barrow received a reputation as an overzealous negotiator. Actually, however, he conducted negotiations fairly evenhandedly, although he became frustrated with players who did not stop negotiating when he thought they should. Also, he did not try to humiliate or berate players during the standard back-and-forth. Along with Ruppert, he proved surprisingly willing to negotiate with players if they pushed their cause in an intelligent, gracious, and possibly obsequious manner. Barrow's negotiation with Earle Combs over his 1932 salary illustrates his negotiating posture and thoughts on what drives a player's salary. Before the 1930 season—that is, before most observers recognized the onset of the Depression—Combs signed a two-year contract for $13,500 per year, a respectable salary for a star outfielder. After the 1931 season, with the Depression deepening, and Combs coming off a good but not great season, Barrow offered him $12,000 for 1932. Barrow sent a cover letter along with the contract on January 13, 1932. That letter led to a series of correspondence between Barrow and Combs. Excerpts from those letters offer insights into Barrow's style and approach. In the initial cover letter quoted here—best described as a form letter—Barrow used a salutation of "Dear Sir." In the subsequent correspondence Combs addressed Barrow as "Dear Mr. Barrow," and Barrow replied with a salutation of "My dear Combs."

> *We are enclosing herewith a set of contracts covering the season of 1932.*
>
> *The terms named in these contracts are absolutely the best the New York Club can offer you.*
>
> *Trusting that you will understand conditions and will sign and return the contracts without useless delay and argument.*

Combs responded:

> *Your letter and contract for 1932 received. I am not signing and returning as you requested. Heretofore you have listened to my argument very patiently, and I feel you will do so this time.*
>
> *Of course I was surprised when I learned my contract was reduced, but it seems I was not the only one.*
>
> *Mr. Barrow, there are several reasons why I think my salary should not be reduced. I am sure my play the past season does not warrant a cut, and of course that is what we ball players are judged by. . . . For eight years I have given my best to the New York Club and have never had a bad year. I don't see why my salary should be cut when I'm going at top speed. I know I haven't slipped that much.*
>
> *It has always been my policy to try to do the fair thing. I will sign a one-year contract for $13,500 or two-year for $26,000. Don't you think that is fair enough?*

Combs naturally felt that after a season in which he delivered his typical statistics, he should not be subject to a salary cut. He offered to take a five-hundred-dollar pay cut in exchange for the security of another two-year contract.

Barrow replied:

> *Your letter of January 19th received and was quite surprised at its contents. If you knew how hard I had to work to have your salary*

made $12,000 for the coming season, you would not delay in sign-
ing and returning your contract to this office.

Considering business conditions, our offer was a very liberal one
and I am compelled to tell you that there is not a chance in the world
of an increase, nor for a two-year contract on any terms.

If ballplayers could see the idle men on the streets and in the bread
lines here in New York and the number who call at this office ev-
ery day looking for jobs, they would realize how lucky they are, es-
pecially as the coming season does not promise to be a very prosper-
ous one either in baseball or other lines of business.

The New York club does appreciate your efforts and loyalty in
the past. That is the main reason your salary was not given a fur-
ther reduction.

Combs's rejection of his initial offer did not shock Barrow. In reply, he rejected Combs's counter and concluded with what appears to be boilerplate
language—likely sent to many players after they refused Barrow's initial
contract—that emphasized the hardships of the Depression.

Combs, however, persisted:

It seems to me that Baseball had a fair season last year, and are cut-
ting salaries in anticipation of a poor year in 1932. . . . I'm will-
ing to take my reduction along with the others. You will agree that
I have never been exorbitant in my demands regarding salary. Of
course all players are lucky, so is anyone else who makes a success in
his profession regardless of what it may be. . . . I am sure you want
a winner. I feel that I am an important cog in your machine, and
I do not say it boastfully. I want to help bring one more pennant to
the Yankee Stadium. . . .

I am going to make you a proposition which I think is fair. I
will sign a two-year contract for $25,000. That is nearly a 10% re-
duction and no business is recommending a larger cut than that. I
have tried to see both sides and feel I have been very reasonable. If
these terms do not meet your approval I shall have to return your
contracts unsigned.

On January 26 I mailed to the Yankee Stadium by insured par-
cel post the uniform I had. Hope it reached you safely.

Barrow's further explanation did not convince Combs. He lowered his demand but still wanted more than Barrow was offering. He argued for a two-
year contract as a way to bridge the salary gap. As an interesting side note,
Combs mailed back a uniform that he must have kept over the winter.

Barrow fired back a mildly threatening letter at what he viewed as Combs's
unreasonable intransigence:

> *You are making a very serious mistake in the stand you are taking
> on the salary question. I explained the situation fully in my last let
> ter. I will tell you again, however, that there is not a chance in the
> world for either an increase in the terms already offered you or for
> a two-year contract.*
>
> *Players' salaries are being reduced all along the line and Colonel
> Ruppert and Manager McCarthy, who is now here, are both strongly
> opposed to two-year contracts, and, therefore, no more contracts of
> this kind will be made with any player no matter who he may be.*
>
> *If you are foolish enough to become a hold-out by returning your
> contracts unsigned, we will all be very much disappointed in you
> and there is no telling what the final result may be.*

Barrow was now frustrated. He had expected that his plea using the nation's financial woes would induce Combs to sign. In response to Combs's
refusal, he sent a long personal letter both beseeching and threatening. In
it Barrow also invoked McCarthy and Ruppert to support his argument.
This reference may also have subtly opened the door to some salary movement by introducing other potential decision makers.

Combs held firm in his demands and seized on Barrow's opening:

> *I am making one more appeal to you, hoping we can reach an agree
> ment on the 1932 contract. Since you are so opposed to two-year con
> tracts I am perfectly willing to sign for one year. I'm not afraid of
> my ability. At one time you preferred the longer term contracts and
> I didn't know you had changed.*
>
> *You understand I'm willing to take my cut along with the oth
> ers but I think that you have reduced me too much on general prin
> ciples alone. . . .*
>
> *I am fighting for my rights just like I fight for you on the ball
> field. I believe if I could talk with you personally I could convince*

*you that $12,500 is as low as my salary should be reduced. Since that
is impossible we must settle it otherwise.*

*Won't you, Manager McCarthy and Colonel Ruppert reconsider
my contract?*

Once again Combs refused to accept the salary cut offered by Barrow.
In a long heartfelt letter, Combs used the reference to McCarthy and Ruppert to his own advantage. He recognized Barrow's opening and allowed
him an avenue to gracefully back down.

Barrow did:

*Well, old boy, you win! Colonel Ruppert has agreed to give you the
extra $500 you asked for.*

*Have changed the terms of the enclosed contracts to $12,500 for
1932. Kindly sign and return them to us at once.*

*We gave you credit for all of your good points when we decided
to do this. Hope you will try to show us that we have not made a
mistake.*

Whether Barrow actually discussed the matter with Ruppert or made
the decision on his own is unknowable. In any case, Barrow negotiated in
such a way as to make Combs feel good about a one-thousand-dollar pay
cut. To Combs's credit, his persistence won him an additional five hundred
dollars, a not insignificant amount in 1932.

Barrow's miserly reputation is further belied by table 13, which furnishes
payroll information for select years during Barrow's stewardship. In 1933,
for example, the Yankees' payroll of nearly $295,000 dwarfed the next clos-
est American League competitor, the Washington Senators, at just over
$187,000. And this was not merely a function of Ruth and Gehrig: even if
one eliminated Ruth's $52,000 salary and Gehrig's of $23,000, the Yankees
would still top the league with a payroll well above $200,000. As the ta-
ble makes clear, the Yankees consistently paid the highest salaries throughout Barrow's tenure.

The table also illustrates the effect of the Depression on player salaries.
In 1929, the last year before its onset, Major League player salaries totaled
around $3,765,000. By 1933 players' payrolls had fallen about 20 percent

to just over $3 million. Overall club revenue dropped even more dramatically. Gross operating income declined by over 33 percent: from $9.7 million in 1929 to only $6.5 million in 1933. In response, some owners proposed a salary cap, an initiative resisted by the Yankees. Ruppert, who recognized that any cap would naturally affect the highest-spending teams the most, actively opposed efforts to instigate a cap.

Not surprisingly, as table 14 illustrates, during the early 1930s and at the beginning of the Great Depression, profits fell off dramatically for all teams. Staggering losses buffeted several teams. In aggregate, American League teams lost in excess of $1 million in 1933, at the height of the Depression. The Yankees generally remained profitable but at a much lower level. Profits fell from their average of over $300,000 per season during the 1920s to less than $40,000 for the five years from 1930 to 1934. On a relative basis, the Yankees' revenue advantage slipped as well as they fell to fourth in profits. Again, however, they paid out no dividends; Ruppert continued the policy of reinvesting all profits back in the team. Several teams continued to distribute cash flow, despite the lack of profits from which to pay them. Charles Stoneham took a huge payout from the Giants. Interestingly, Ben Shibe and Connie Mack in Philadelphia paid out a large dividend just prior to pleading poverty and selling off their stars.

Barrow stood pat during the 1932–33 off-season. Although he and McCarthy considered a couple of deals, they felt little pressure to make a move after winning close to 70 percent of their games in 1932. The Yankees started the same eight regulars in 1933 and again led the league in runs scored. But the Yankees could win no more than ninety-one games and finished second behind the revamped Washington Senators, mainly because the pitching staff slipped from its 1932 achievements. Gomez had another stellar year, but Ruffing slipped, Allen could not repeat his great rookie campaign, Pennock was finally showing his age, and none of the other young pitchers stepped up. McCarthy analyzed his starting pitching after the season: "Our pitchers in 1934 will not be as bad as they were last season. Johnny Allen was ill, Charley Ruffing had a sore arm, and Lefty Gomez was in love." Both McCarthy and Barrow hoped to land another established hurler for 1934. Barrow balked, however, when teams demanded Lazzeri: "But McCarthy is not letting Lazzeri go at any price and that settles that." Over a weekend in January, Barrow negotiated with the St. Louis Browns for workhorse pitcher George Blaeholder but could not reach an agreement.

To help stabilize the rotation, Barrow next looked to his Minor League system. The team promoted Johnny Broaca, who showed potential and capably joined the rotation. When Krichell had signed Broaca off the Yale campus a year earlier, he knew he was getting a hardheaded lad. Broaca had once refused to pitch in a scrimmage against a semiprofessional team on the grounds that he too should be paid. Krichell remembered signing the argumentative Broaca, who had also boxed while at Yale: "The lights were dim and I was glad of that because he couldn't see to argue over every line in the contract. He had the pen in his hand and he was hesitating, and finally, as he bent over he pointed the pen at me and said very vigorously: 'All right, I'll sign. But remember, if I make good I'm holding out.'"

Meanwhile, Babe Ruth was still agitating for a managerial position. He denigrated McCarthy often, with the hope that Ruppert might actually give him the job. In Detroit Barrow's old rival, Frank Navin, recognized that an icon like Ruth would offer an excellent drawing card in very difficult times. When Navin asked Barrow about Ruth's availability, Barrow stalled until he could consult with Ruppert. Both acknowledged that Ruth was slipping as a player and was a headache in the clubhouse. The two agreed that pawning off Ruth on Navin as a player-manager, especially if they could land a useful player in return, would benefit the Yankees. With Barrow's blessing, Navin summoned Ruth to Detroit to sound him out on the idea.

Ruth, however, was about to depart for Hawaii for a series of exhibition games. He could have stopped in Detroit on the way but told Barrow: "I'll see him when I come back. That'll be plenty of time."

Barrow rightly feared Navin would not wait around for a manager: "I think you're making a mistake," Barrow warned Ruth. "You should see him now." Ruth, underscoring Barrow's already negative impression of his self-discipline, ignored Barrow's counsel and headed for Hawaii. Unfortunately for both Barrow and Ruth, Navin had no intention of waiting around for Ruth to return. When he realized that Connie Mack was selling off more of his stars, he borrowed the money to purchase future Hall of Fame catcher Mickey Cochrane for one hundred thousand dollars to fill the player-manager role.

That off-season Ruppert also offered Ruth the managerial job in Newark. Ruppert probably meant this offer seriously: he felt a genuine obligation and paternalistic friendship toward his star and wanted to help him. Not surprisingly, Ruth's ego would not let him accept a Minor League managerial post. Other star players had jumped right into a big league managerial post, and Ruth saw no reason why he should not be accorded the same treatment. Ruth's stubbornness relieved Barrow. Having Ruth at Newark, one step away from Yankee Stadium, would have added to the already tremendous pressure on McCarthy. Also, Barrow might have been forced to promote him if McCarthy ever departed. When no acceptable managerial position materialized, Barrow and Ruppert re-signed Ruth with mixed feelings for 1934. Still a great drawing card, at thirty-nine years old Ruth had lost much of his bat speed and fielding ability. Fretful over an opportunity to manage and anxious over his declining skills, he was no longer the joyous clubhouse presence of his youth. Ruppert and Barrow were convinced that his thirty-five-thousand-dollar salary would be his last as a Yankee.

Barrow aggressively weighed in on another off-season league controversy. After the high-scoring 1930 season, the National League decided that it needed to deaden the baseball. The American League, however, happily stayed with the existing ball, which encouraged offense. Barrow explained that only the covers of the balls were different; the cores were identical. The National League, he argued, used a horsehide cover that was thicker. As to the way the two balls played, Barrow expounded: "The American League ball traveled faster on the ground, lifted farther. When the National League ball was hit dead center, it traveled just as far as the American League ball. But if it wasn't hit solidly, grounders were easier to handle and fly balls softer." He disliked the divergence and suggested a compromise: "Major League baseball should be played with similar implements in both leagues. Put the American League cover on the ball. Add the thicker stitching now used in the seams of the National League ball. That should satisfy everyone."

To resolve the fuss, the National League reportedly agreed to adopt the American League ball (although the stories behind nearly all controversies regarding the nature of the baseball are ambiguous at best). Washington manager Joe Cronin complained during 1934 that the balls provided by Barrow for games at Yankee Stadium were different from those used at other American League parks. He claimed Barrow had acquired a large cache of

1933 balls that he was still using in 1934. And although the balls were supposed to be technically the same, Cronin grumbled that the ball appeared and felt different to his pitchers.

That winter the Barrows suffered a personal tragedy. One night in December 1933, their daughter's family nurse heard cries from Barrow's grandchildren, Patricia and John, around 5:30 a.m. When she checked on them, she found the young children semiconscious and almost asphyxiated from carbon monoxide fumes that had seeped up from the garage below their room. The nurse quickly woke Audrey. They soon discovered her husband, Frederick Campbell, in his car in the garage with the motor still running. He was fully dressed and slumped over the wheel, dead. The medical examiner ruled his death a suicide, although Barrow and Campbell's relatives objected to the ruling, arguing that his death was an accident. Shortly thereafter Audrey and the children moved back home to live with the Barrows.

On February 21, 1933, his thirtieth birthday, a man named Tom Yawkey came into an inheritance of several million dollars. The nephew and adopted son of William Yawkey, Barrow's old boss in Detroit, the younger Yawkey wanted a baseball team of his own. He had a ready seller in Red Sox owner Bob Quinn, now deeply in debt. After he acquired the stripped-down team from Frazee, the undercapitalized Quinn had been unable to make a success of the Red Sox either on the field or financially. Despite maintaining a low payroll and neglecting necessary repairs to Fenway Park, from 1926 through 1932 the Red Sox lost nearly $340,000. Yawkey, a wealthy sportsman who idolized ball players, bailed Quinn out by purchasing the Red Sox for $1.2 million.

Since the Yankees had purchased Boston's stars in the early 1920s, high-dollar player sales between American League teams had waned. The league's other franchises were all adequately capitalized, and the economic boom of the 1920s mitigated any financial shortcomings. The onset of the Depression changed everything. Yawkey initially hoped to win a pennant by purchasing stars from other teams. He had money; many other owners were feeling pinched. Those struggling financially were happy to unload their players for the enormous sums Yawkey was offering. Although the Depression did not materially affect Ruppert's ability to fund his team and business interests, he was not immune to its effects. Barrow was not directed to sell players, but he understood the importance of augmenting revenue. Thus, when Yawkey and Eddie Collins, the ex-star Yawkey had hired to help with front-office decisions, came calling during the 1933 season, Barrow was happy to sell George Pipgras and young shortstop Billy Werber, two players who had contributed little in 1932, for fifty thousand dollars. More famously, Yawkey purchased several players from Connie Mack's champion Athletics.

Despite the sale of Werber, by the beginning of the 1934 season the Yankees still had three relatively young, highly touted shortstops: Frank Crosetti, Lyn Lary, and Red Rolfe. Because of their huge investment in Lary, the Yankees had naturally given him numerous opportunities to win the starting job. But after he had played five years in the Majors, Barrow and McCarthy concluded he was not the answer. As Yawkey persevered in his quest to buy players—often with only limited regard for quality—Barrow approached him regarding Lary. He convinced Yawkey and Collins that Lary still showed potential. Barrow was pleasantly surprised to recoup a meaningful amount of the Yankees initial investment by enticing Yawkey to pay thirty-five thousand dollars and a Minor League infielder for his third-string shortstop. Despite their difference in age and temperament, Barrow and Yawkey became surprisingly close friends. Whether because of his relationship with William Yawkey, their mutual enjoyment of hunting, or some other factor, they began to spend considerable time together. In fact, Yawkey could often be found in Barrow's box at Yankee Stadium.

The Yankees also needed to replace third baseman Joe Sewell, who had retired to become a Yankees coach. As in previous seasons when he had no obvious third base solution, McCarthy spent much of the summer trying to sort out the infield (other than Gehrig, of course). Overrated, high-dollar acquisition Jack Saltzgaver played third the most in 1934, but McCarthy shifted Lazzeri to third for thirty games, Rolfe played the hot corner twenty-six times, and even Crosetti played twenty three. The regular outfield of Ruth, Combs, and Chapman patrolled for the first half of the season until Combs crashed into the wall in St. Louis, fracturing his skull. Dickey, too, missed the last month of the season with a broken hand and a dislocated finger. Without Combs, and with Ruth well past his prime—in August he announced he would be retiring as a regular but wanted to con-

tinue as manager and occasional pinch hitter—the Yankees did not lead
the league in runs scored for the first time in several years.

In early August 1934, as New York battled the rebuilt Detroit Tigers for
first place, Barrow got into a public spat with Washington owner Clark
Griffith over pitcher Al "General" Crowder. Both Barrow and Navin wanted
the veteran Crowder to bolster their respective pitching staff for the stretch
run. After Griffith sent Crowder to Detroit, Barrow accused Griffith of purposely diverting the pitcher away from New York. Because the trading deadline had passed, a player needed to pass through waivers (meaning every
team had an opportunity to claim him for the $7,500 waiver price) before
they could trade him. Barrow accused Griffith of waiting until the Yankees
took first place—waiver claims occurred in inverse order of the standings—
before placing Crowder on waivers. In other words, Barrow charged that
Griffith engineered the release of Crowder to Navin for $7,500 without giv-
ing the Yankees a shot at him.

Griffith angrily and publicly denied the accusation. He asserted that he
had twice put Crowder on waivers, once early in July and again later, and
neither time had Barrow claimed him. To support his claim, Griffith released further details on discussions with Barrow. If Crowder cleared waivers, Griffith had wanted Minor League hurler Jack LaRocca in exchange for
his pitcher. But Griffith claimed Barrow had offered only MacFayden or a
nonprospect Minor League catcher. He acknowledged that after negotiations with Barrow fell through, he had let Crowder go to Detroit for little
more than the waiver price. Crowder finished 5-1 for the Tigers, and Navin's
club bested the New Yorkers by seven games to win the pennant.

After the 1934 season Connie Mack led an American League All-Star team
on a baseball tour of Japan. During the exhibitions Mack let Ruth do much
of the managing. Many speculated that Mack hoped to land Ruth from New
York and turn the Philadelphia helm over to Ruth when he retired. Barrow
denied he had been approached by anyone from Philadelphia about trading
Ruth. But he did state that he and Ruppert would not demand any compensation should a team want Ruth as manager (as opposed to simply an aging
drawing card as a player). Barrow also publicly complained about Mack's
Japan excursion. Mack had the Yankees two best players, Gehrig and Go-

mez, and Barrow feared the worst: "Suppose the ship sinks? Suppose there is a wreck or something? Where in hell would the Yankees be?"

The question of what to do with Ruth resurfaced with a vengeance after his return from the Japan tour. Ruth publicly declared he would not come back as a player, only as a manager. Such an ultimatum completely misread Ruppert and Barrow. Barrow would never tolerate Ruth—whom he had never really respected beyond his abilities on the field—at the helm. Ruppert, who enjoyed a more-adult relationship with Ruth, might have given in (much to the embarrassment of Barrow) if he had not already had a valued manager in McCarthy. Ruppert and Barrow rightly feared the public-relations nightmare of a vindictive Ruth if they simply released him. Barrow inherited the unenviable task of resolving the situation to everyone's satisfaction. Initially, he promoted Ruth around the Major Leagues as a managerial candidate. Unfortunately, and somewhat surprisingly given Ruth's gate appeal, Barrow could interest no takers.

The Depression had wreaked havoc on the National League's undercapitalized Boston Braves. Nominal owner and operating partner, Judge Emil Fuchs, owed financial partner Charles Adams several large debts that were now coming due. To raise capital, Fuchs proposed turning Braves Field into a dog-racing track and sharing Fenway Park with the Red Sox. Not surprisingly, this idea horrified the other owners, who ever since the Black Sox scandal had shunned gambling—especially in such blatant forms as dog racing—above nearly all else. Under the pressure of his fellow owners and Commissioner Landis, Fuchs backed off his dog-racing scheme. But he was still looking for a money-raising gimmick.

Barrow and Fuchs became convinced that returning Ruth to Boston could offer a solution to both of their problems. Fuchs, however, was determined to remain loyal to his manager, Bill McKechnie. Notwithstanding this concern, the two devised a scheme to move Ruth to Boston anyway. To assuage his ego, Ruth would be given the titles of vice president and assistant manager—much to the dismay of McKechnie—with the assurance (not guaranteed) of additional future authority. Despite Ruth's legitimate expectation, his off-field duties were nonexistent; Fuchs simply hoped he could draw fans and save his franchise as a part-time player. As the Braves stumbled from the gate and financial losses mounted, Ruth grew surly over his status. The cash-strapped Fuchs, focused on just trying to maintain operational control of the franchise, had little energy or ability to rectify Ruth's troubled situation. In the turmoil neither would survive the 1935 season as Boston Braves.

Meanwhile, to relax and discuss the upcoming campaign, Ruppert and Barrow enjoyed their annual off-season sojourn in French Lick, Indiana, for a three-week vacation. For the first time in several years, the pitching appeared more solid than the offense. Led by Gomez and Ruffing, the staff had rebounded in 1934 to lead the league in ERA. After a number of disappointments, two young pitchers finally seemed to be developing: Johnny Murphy finished third in the league in ERA while splitting time between starting and relieving; and Johnny Allen, despite starting only ten games because of arm troubles, remained highly touted. Notwithstanding the apparent improvement, Barrow still believed that a deeper rotation was necessary to ensure a return to the pennant.

With the retirement of Ruth and the possibly career-ending injury to Combs, the Yankees also needed two new outfielders. In November 1934 Barrow authorized the purchase of Joe DiMaggio, a popular youngster from San Francisco playing for his hometown Seals. DiMaggio earned his megaprospect status after debuting in the Pacific Coast League as an eighteen-year-old in 1933, hitting .340 and leading the league with 169 RBI. San Francisco owner Charley Graham, suffering financially from the Depression, envisioned selling his star for one hundred thousand dollars or more to one of the numerous scouts swarming around him. To his horror, Graham's meal ticket mysteriously hurt his knee late one night in May 1934 while out on the town. To protect DiMaggio's high price, Graham tried to hide the injury from his many suitors. In August, however, DiMaggio reinjured his knee, this time on the ball field, and Graham could do little to disguise the extent of the injury. Most teams backed off, but Yankees scout Bill Essick continued to pursue Graham in the hope of purchasing DiMaggio at a reduced price.

Essick finally convinced the cash-hungry Graham to give him an option to buy DiMaggio for twenty-five thousand dollars plus five players to help restock his Depression-depleted team. Essick then persuaded West Coast scouting supervisor Joe Devine to let him take DiMaggio to a Los Angeles doctor for examination. "He pulled my leg and yanked in all directions," DiMaggio remembered. "With every yank, I felt the sharpest pain throughout my entire body. I decided if he yanked once more, I'd get up and punch him in the nose. Then he stopped and turned to Essick saying: 'The leg is all right; your club can pay Graham the money.'" For his advice the doctor charged twenty-five dollars. When he heard the news, Barrow wired, "Close deal," and the Yankees landed one of the all-time greats. As part of the purchase agreement, the Yankees allowed Graham to keep DiMaggio for the 1935 season.

The infield also remained unsettled. Crosetti had won the shortstop position, but the team still had no third baseman, and a switch of Lazzeri to the hot corner remained an option. For another possible solution, Barrow targeted Philadelphia third baseman Pinky Higgins. He offered Mack fifty thousand dollars and five marginal players for Higgins, but Mack, who had been selling his other stars to the lesser American League clubs, demanded one hundred thousand dollars. Barrow wisely had no interest at that level.

The Yankees also pushed forward with the expansion of the farm system. At the end of 1934, the Yankees controlled outright or through working agreements four teams in addition to class AA Newark: Binghamton, in the class A New York–Pennsylvania League; Norfolk in the class B Piedmont League; Wheeling (Barrow's old stomping ground) in the class C Middle Atlantic League; and Washington (Pennsylvania) in the class D Pennsylvania State Association. For 1935 Barrow added Joplin of the class C Western Association and Oakland of the class AA Pacific Coast League. The specific terms of the working agreement with Oakland for 1935 are not available but likely were similar to those for 1936, which called for New York to lend Oakland five thousand dollars interest-free for six months. Oakland could either repay the loan or send the Yankees two previously identified players. Also, New York had the option to purchase any Oakland player for ten thousand dollars, such option to be exercised by September 1, 1936. In only three years, Barrow, with Ruppert's prodding and Weiss's help, had created a farm system larger than any in the league and second only to the Cardinals in all of Organized Baseball.

In 1935 manager Joe McCarthy could finally manage without the distraction of a resentful, surly Babe Ruth. Early in his tenure McCarthy had commanded and earned the respect of the rest of his charges, and he could now let go of any lingering anxieties about his status relative to Babe Ruth. Of course, the pressure to win was still overwhelming. Jacob Ruppert demanded a pennant, not another second-place finish. Barrow, too, felt the onus of two consecutive misses.

For 1935 Barrow would need to dip into the farm system, which was just beginning to bear fruit. Combs had recovered enough from his injury to play part-time, but the Yankees clearly needed two new outfielders to flank Ben Chapman, now shifted to center. To fill one spot, Barrow promoted George Selkirk from Newark after he hit .357 in 1934 (and .313 in limited time up with New York). For the other outfield position, the Yankees promoted Jesse Hill. Both were acquired in 1931 and had spent several years maturing in the new Minors. McCarthy also continued to experiment with the high-priced Myril Hoag, who had filled in for the injured Combs the previous season. To steady his infield, McCarthy finally planted Red Rolfe at third.

The Yankees again battled Detroit for the flag and again came up short, this time by only three games. The offense once more failed to lead the league in runs. The pitching held up well, however, and the Yankees again won the ERA title. Lefty Gomez, Red Ruffing, Johnny Allen, and Johnny Broaca all turned in respectable seasons. McCarthy made another move with his starters that paid dividends for several years: he converted Johnny Murphy into a full-time relief pitcher, a role not filled by an outstanding pitcher since Firpo Marberry and Wilcy Moore several years earlier. Murphy had only one good pitch, a curve ball, although he could dominate hitters with it. McCarthy believed a starting pitcher could not be successful with only one Major League–caliber pitch. McCarthy at his best understood how to find ways his players could help rather than dwelling on their weaknesses. In 1935 Murphy validated McCarthy's approach; he finished with a record of 10-5 in forty games, of which he started only eight.

After three second-place finishes, the Yankees needed to win. When Mc-
Carthy joined Barrow and Ruppert in French Lick prior to the trio heading
to the league meetings in Chicago, he publicly predicted the Yankees team
good enough to win the 1936 pennant. The boldness of this prediction was
mitigated somewhat by the fact that Ruppert was demanding a flag. Anything less would not be acceptable to the boss. Although Ruppert was not
in the most robust health—he had to skip the 1935 All-Star Game in Cleveland because of his rheumatism and sent Barrow in his stead—he was willing to do almost anything to get the necessary players. From the perspective
of the twenty-first century, considering the Yankees' dynasty in retrospect,
the entire 1921 to 1964 period often gets lumped together as one long string
of pennants. But during the seven-year period from 1929 to 1935, the Yankees won only one pennant. They finished second in five of those years. Jacob Ruppert did not like to finish second.

Ruppert, in fact, had become obsessed with winning a pennant. After
the 1932 season, Connie Mack began selling off the star players from his
three straight pennant winners. Unlike in the early 1920s, however, the
Yankees did not benefit from a team liquidating its stars. In his first transaction, Mack sent Al Simmons, Jimmy Dykes, and Mule Haas to the Chicago White Sox for around $150,000. This represented a huge expenditure
for the Comiskey heirs, who were not independently wealthy. Mack seemingly refused to sell his top players to the Yankees, but no other team os-
tensibly had the capital available for much more. Mack's fortune improved
when Tom Yawkey bought the Red Sox and announced at the 1933 winter
meetings that he was ready and able to spend money.

Mack and several other owners fought their way to Yawkey and general
manager Eddie Collins to sell their wares. After the 1934 season, Collins,
on Yawkey's behalf, approached Washington's Clark Griffith regarding his
young star shortstop and manager, who also happened to be his nephew-
in-law. Griffith had no interest in selling Joe Cronin, but when Collins finally upped the ante to $250,000, Griffith could not refuse, nephew-in-law
or not. It is almost impossible to overstate how large a sum $250,000 rep-
resented at the height of the Depression. It was greater than the entire payroll of fourteen of the sixteen Major League teams.

Ruppert had never actively participated in the "trading mart," but in Chicago several reporters commented on seeing him trolling the floor at the win-

ter meetings to help generate a deal. At one point Ruppert copied Yawkey's open checkbook gambit with Griffith, this time to pry loose second baseman and 1935 batting champion, Buddy Myer. Once again Griffith had no interest in selling his star, but Ruppert demanded Griffith name a price anyway. Jokingly, Griffith told Ruppert $500,000. "And do you know that Ruppert almost made a deal with me," Griffith recounted. "He actually was going to give the Washington club $400,000 and second baseman Tony Lazzeri for Myer, until Ed Barrow, his business manager stopped him. If Barrow hadn't been around that night, I'd have made a $400,000 sale."

To regain the heights of the 1920s, Barrow rightly recognized that if the Yankees added one more star hitter they should once again have a dominant team. But he had no intention of overpaying for Myer to get there. In August 1935 Barrow was already thinking about debuting Joe DiMaggio with the Major League club in 1936. Unsatisfied with Chapman's defense in center, Barrow instructed Charley Graham to shift DiMaggio from right to center. When DiMaggio wrapped up the Pacific Coast League season with a .398 batting average, Essick's persistence looked prescient. Graham, who could then have received much more money for his star, was philosophical about the matter: "Barrow took a gamble and won. Barrow is smart, but I like to do business with smart people."

Barrow and McCarthy managed two meaningful trades during the offseason. In December, at McCarthy's urging, the club traded its talented but mercurial pitcher Johnny Allen to the Cleveland Indians for pitchers Monte Pearson and Steve Sundra. Pearson was the key: another young pitcher with a track record of success. While Allen starred in Cleveland, Pearson proved a valuable member of the Yankees' rotation for the next several years. McCarthy did not like southerners in general, and in particular he felt that the volatile personalities of Allen and Ben Chapman were detrimental to the professionalism he had instilled in his troops. The club later sent young outfielder Jesse Hill and a pitching prospect to Washington for two veterans, outfielder Roy Johnson and pitcher Bump Hadley. Like Pearson, Hadley would become a solid midrotation starter for several years.

Barrow had done a nice job of turning the lineup over. Of the position players, Gehrig and Lazzeri were thirty-three and thirty-two, respectively; the other regulars were all twenty-nine years old or younger. With DiMaggio added to the lineup and the pitching staff bolstered by the addition of Hadley and Pearson, the Yankees exploded from the gate. After sweeping a July 4 doubleheader in Washington, the Yankees' record stood at 51-22.

As usual, Barrow remained active during the season, making two more moves of some significance. In May he sold outfielder Dixie Walker to the Chicago White Sox for fifteen thousand dollars. Walker had only recently recovered from a debilitating shoulder injury and seemed superfluous given the number of outfield prospects Barrow and Krichell ranked higher. Over the next few years, Walker passed through several teams before eventually developing into a fine ballplayer. In New York's other significant in-season move, it swapped twenty-seven-year-old outfielders with the Senators, sending Ben Chapman to Washington for Jake Powell. McCarthy disliked the hot-headed, fleet-footed Chapman, and both he and Barrow had targeted Powell for some time. For the second half of the season, Powell assumed Chapman's spot in the Yankees' outfield alongside DiMaggio and George Selkirk.

During the 1936 season, the temperamental Pearson, regarded by management as something of a hypochondriac, complained he was ill. The Yankees sent him home, telling him to remain in bed until they sent the doctor around. Three days later Barrow wondered what had become of his pitcher. He called Pearson, demanding where the heck he was and why he had not returned. Pearson told Barrow that he was still laid up waiting for a doctor to come examine him. Barrow slammed down the phone and quickly dispatched a couple of doctors, who determined, as Pearson remembers it, that he had a bad case of the flu.

The second half consisted of more of the same, and the Yankees ran away with the pennant. The team scored 1,065 runs, the second-highest total in modern baseball history. They slugged 182 home runs; no other team topped 123. The pitching excelled as well, if not to the stratospheric level of the offense. The staff ERA of 4.17 easily led the league, and six pitchers won at least twelve games. For the World Series against the Giants, the odds makers set the line for the Yankees at just better than 1 to 2. The bookmakers correctly gauged the relative strength of the teams: led by Series hitting star Jake Powell, the Yankees captured the World Championship four games to two.

Barrow, who liked to consider and tinker with rule changes, proposed that the need to actually throw four balls to issue an intentional walk should be eliminated. He felt that announcing one's intention to the umpire ought to be sufficient, and it would speed up the game. Eliminating the four-pitch intentional walk is an idea that has been (and still is) proposed every generation or so. The suggestion rarely gathers much support, and Barrow's recommendation generated little interest this time as well.

The Ruppert-Barrow relationship had started on a professional (but friendly basis) and remained that way for many years. By the mid-1930s, however, after many years working together, the two had become close friends. After the World Series the two men took long vacations together, usually to the springs at French Lick, Indiana, accompanied by some of Ruppert's other confidants. McCarthy, too, typically joined the party for some of the time. In October 1936 Ruppert and Barrow traveled to the Adirondacks for a week-long vacation. Afterward they headed to the springs in French Lick for a month of rest and deliberations on their baseball team. Now in their late sixties, both men needed time away from the pressure surrounding the nation's best-known professional sports team; French Lick was the perfect getaway. Neither, of course, ever forgot baseball for long.

The Yankees continued to expand their impressive farm system. During the off-season the team brought the Kansas City franchise in the class AA American Association into the Yankees' fold with a working agreement. The Yankees now possessed a ten-team farm system: four by outright ownership and six by working agreement. Only the St. Louis Cardinals organization could boast a larger chain, and no other organization was comparable. They also aggressively sought top talent with which to stock it. The Yankees jumped on the twenty-four-year-old Tommy Henrich when Commissioner Landis declared him a free agent early in the 1937 season. Cleveland had secretly orchestrated his transfer from New Orleans to Milwaukee. Henrich protested this move to Landis, and Landis sided with the player. Barrow dispatched scout Johnny Nee to lead the bidding for New York. Nee, an excellent salesman for the Yankees organization, enticed Henrich to sign for a twenty-thousand-dollar bonus and five-thousand-dollar salary.

The Yankees' organizational model of a general manager—a baseball executive other than the principal owner or manager responsible for player procurement decisions—slowly caught on throughout the thirties, particularly in the American League. Heading into 1937, Eddie Collins held the position for owner Tom Yawkey in Boston; Cleveland owner Alva Bradley promoted scout Cy Slapnicka to the job; in St. Louis, president Don Barnes hired Bill DeWitt as his general manager; and although he had not yet officially been promoted, the Tigers were grooming scout Jack Zeller for the spot. The National League remained behind the American. Only Branch Rickey in St. Louis, Warren Giles in Cincinnati, and Larry MacPhail in Brooklyn—working for the league's three most successful clubs—operated as general managers.

But despite emulating the general manager concept, no team ever approached the Yankees' dominance. So how did the Yankees re-create their dynasty after several down years? First, the entire Yankees organization was obsessed with winning. Ruppert drove his front office hard but backed up his demands by committing his own resources, primarily financial. Barrow followed Ruppert's lead by hiring the best executives, whether scouts or on-field managers and coaches.

Second, the Yankees' leadership correctly recognized the key strategic issues involved in running a baseball organization. As business historian Alfred Chandler understood, business executives must "coordinate, appraise, and plan." Barrow and Ruppert oversaw these long-term administrative functions diligently and intelligently. Ruppert realized that the changing environment necessitated a farm system; Barrow brilliantly coordinated their great lineup of scouts into supplying the new and growing Minor League organization. He continuously reappraised the status of the Yankees organization, both globally and in terms of specific Major League strengths and weaknesses. Finally, Barrow and Ruppert spent many hours during the off-season, even on their annual vacation to French Lick, planning their future moves. The Yankees' front office constantly maintained its focus on improving the club. As the rules of player procurement and development evolved, Barrow recognized their implications and continually refreshed the Yankees with young talent.

Chandler further recognized that to be successful, an administrator must be concerned with an organization's "smooth and efficient day-to-day operation." Barrow and his staff efficiently managed the many off-field business issues, such as Yankee Stadium operations, the leasing of other stadiums, and the Yankees' business operations. He entrusted the on-field operation to a great manager and generally stayed out of his way after providing the players. A brilliant manager, McCarthy successfully integrated the young stars signed by Barrow's scouts and trained in Weiss's farm system.

Barrow and Ruppert experienced the usual travails in trying to sign the Yankees' stars for 1937. With the World Series victory and the associated increase in media coverage, salary disputes became even bigger stories than usual. Ruppert expressed surprising bitterness at the demands of Gehrig and Gomez. He vented publicly his lingering anger over the 1934 trip to Japan and its perceived negative effects on their performance: "[They] seem to forget that they cost us a pennant in 1935 by going off on their barnstorming tour to Japan. Gehrig comes into my office and says he should get more than $31,000 [his 1936 salary]. But he does not mention that he also had a poor season. So I remind him of it. [In 1935 Gehrig actually had a very good season, but it fell short of his triple crown season in 1934 and MVP season in 1936.] I also reminded him that in 1936 we were only getting back what we dropped on some of the lean years and that both he and Gomez ruined our pennant chances in 1935 with their Japan trip." When Gehrig threatened a holdout, Barrow spent fifteen thousand dollars to purchase slick-fielding first baseman Babe Dahlgren as an insurance policy and potential future replacement. Gehrig's quiet professionalism eventually won out, and he realized a raise to thirty-six thousand dollars. The Yankees thereupon demoted Dahlgren, a one-time (and future) Major League regular, to Newark.

Ruppert saved his real opprobrium for the fun-loving Gomez. In addition to the Japan tour, Gomez slacked off in 1936. When Gomez developed a "bad arm" during the season, Barrow became suspicious of Gomez's training habits. Following his not-atypical practice, he hired a detective to tail Gomez. The detective shadowed him around Broadway for ten very late nights. With the detective's report in hand, Barrow confronted Gomez: "That's what's wrong with your arm. Get wise to yourself." With his subpar 1936 now in the books, Ruppert demanded Gomez's salary be slashed from the $20,000 he had earned in 1936 and initially offered only $7,500. When he received this contract, Gomez sent it back with a note: "Dear Mr. Ed: I have found the enclosed paper in a letter you sent me. It is very plain that you have mailed me the batboy's contract, by mistake. Please rush the McCoy to me at once." Ruppert was in no mood for Gomez's smart-aleck reactions: "He certainly has plenty of nerve comparing what we have offered to a bat boy's salary." After some less-public pleading, Gomez salvaged a salary of $13,500.

By early in the 1937 season, it was clear that Barrow, Ruppert, and Mc-Carthy had created something special in New York. The Yankees' season of 1937 reprised 1936, quashing any hope of their American League rivals that the 1936 runaway had been a fluke. DiMaggio led the league in home runs and hit .346. Barrow's chastisement of Gomez may have helped: he won 21 games and led the league in ERA. Behind the rallying cry, "You sed it," the Yankees once again led the league in runs scored and runs allowed and won 102 games. McCarthy continued his brilliant use of Murphy as an ace reliever. Murphy started only 4 games but finished 13-4 in 110 innings pitched.

In a tragic incident two months into the season, Hadley beaned Detroit's player-manager, Mickey Cochrane, ending his playing career. Cochrane required a considerable stay in the hospital; as an old acquaintance, Barrow scheduled a visit to offer his sympathy.

Barrow also lost Broaca halfway through the season. A rotation regular for the last three years, Broaca struggled early in 1937 because of arm problems and marital difficulties. While in Cleveland in July, he did not report from the hotel to the stadium. The team assumed he was ill, but when they checked on him, he had checked out. Broaca left no note or information regarding his destination and stayed AWOL for the remainder of the season. When his wife sued for divorce in December, Broaca claimed he could not remember what he had done with all his baseball earnings. Broaca ended up sitting out the entire 1938 season as well. Barrow eventually released him on waivers to Cleveland for the $7,500 waiver price. Broaca lasted just one year in Cleveland.

McCarthy later told one of his favorite stories about the enigmatic Broaca. With two out in a game against the Red Sox, the Yankees were up by one run with the tying run on base. Joe Cronin was at the plate with Jimmie Foxx, a great hitter, on deck. Broaca walked Cronin on four pitches, putting the winning run on base. Foxx then launched a bomb to center field. DiMaggio, however, made a tremendous catch to save the game. As McCarthy remembered the incident: "As soon as Broaca comes to the dugout, I shout 'Why did you walk Cronin?' 'To get to Foxx,' he answers. 'I wasn't afraid of him. I just knew I'd get him out.' He got him out all right, but it took one of the greatest catches I ever saw to do it. What do they teach those fellows in college anyway?"

On August 6 in a game against Cleveland, trailing 6–5 with two out in the bottom of the tenth, the Yankees had runners on second and third. DiMaggio hit a line drive down the third base line that went off the glove of diving Indians third baseman Odell Hale and caromed into left field. Home plate umpire Charles Johnston ruled it foul by waving his arms two or three times. Both Yankees runners, off at the crack of the bat, crossed the plate. The runners and McCarthy converged on Johnston pleading that the hit was fair. Johnston began to doubt his call and conferred with third base umpire George Moriarty (Barrow's one-time fight opponent many years earlier). Moriarty ruled the ball fair. The umpires then agreed the two runs counted. At this point the Indians erupted. How could the umpire change the ruling after the play? After all, they thought the ball was foul; if they had known it was fair, they might have been able to hold the trailing runner at third or even throw him out at the plate. Not surprisingly, the Indians filed a formal protest after the Yankees won the game 7–6.

Barrow fired off a message to American League president Harridge arguing that Cleveland was just looking for a cheap victory. Moriarty's report concluded that the Indians left fielder had no chance of either holding the trailing Yankees runner at third or throwing him out at home. Harridge, nevertheless, upheld Cleveland's protest. He ruled that the umpires could have permitted the lead runner to score and continue with the score tied and runners on first and third, but they could not allow both runners to score. He set the makeup game for the next time the Indians played in New York. Barrow vigorously fought this ruling. He further complained that if the game had to be replayed, it ought to be from the point of the tenth inning dispute, that is, with runners on first and third in a tie game. When Barrow believed he had been wronged, his strong sense of self-righteousness often got the better of him. When Harridge disregarded his entreaties, Barrow threatened to present his case to the league board of directors. Barrow's threats, however, were empty and looked foolish. League rules stated that the league president has sole authority over protests, and historically American League protested games were always replayed in their entirety.

The pennant was never really in doubt, and Barrow could organize selling World Series tickets with plenty of lead time. He again sold box and reserved-seat tickets in blocks of three, for Games 1, 2, and 6. He set the price for the block of three at $19.80 for the 4,748 box seats; $16.50 for the

36,579 reserved seats. The 16,000 general admission seats were sold on a single-game basis at $3.30; the 14,000 bleacher seats at $1.10. On the field, the Yankees again faced the Giants; this time they dispatched their cross-town rivals four games to one.

To the dismay of the rest of baseball, the aggregate 1937 season testified to the excellence of the Yankees' player procurement and development organization. New York's top farm team in Newark compiled a winning percentage above .700 and won the International League by a record 25 1/2 games. Newark boasted a number of future Major League regulars including Joe Gordon, Babe Dahlgren, George McQuinn, Charlie Keller, Atley Donald, and Marius Russo.

Paul Krichell, who for many years had concentrated chiefly on the colleges, maintained this predisposition even after becoming the head scout. The Yankees had signed Joe Gordon from the University of Oregon and immediately placed him on the fast track for the Majors. Scout Bill Essick assigned Gordon to Oakland for the 1936 season, and he was soon promoted to Newark. Krichell also signed Marius Russo out of Long Island University.

Charlie Keller and Atley Donald both testify to the high esteem in which prospects held the Yankees. While Donald was attending Louisiana Tech, his coach, L. J. Fox, sent Barrow a letter recommending him. Fox had recommended several players, only a few of whom had panned out. Thus, despite Fox's assurances, Donald received no response from Barrow. Determined to join the Yankees, in December 1933 Donald rode the bus to St. Petersburg for a chance to try out with the Yankees during spring training. He arrived broke and found a job in a grocery store to make ends meet before spring training started. Donald eventually tracked down scout Johnny Nee and convinced him to set up a tryout. Nee and McCarthy liked what they saw, signed him, and sent Donald to the low Minors to begin his Yankees career.

Scout Gene McCann had been tracking University of Maryland star Charlie Keller for some time. By the time he was ready to sign, other scouts had heard of Keller as well. Keller, though, had always wanted to play for New York and in March 1937 agreed to sign with McCann for around $7,500 and the right to select the Minor League team he would debut with. McCann, anxious to land this budding star, agreed without wiring either Barrow or Weiss. After signing Keller, McCann wired Barrow, "I have just signed the greatest prospect I have ever seen." Keller would probably have received more had he waited for other clubs, but the Yankees' mystique and the persistence of their scouts brought him into the fold.

In recognition of the superiority of the Yankees organization, in 1937 the *Sporting News* named Barrow Major League executive of the year. In its acknowledgment, the *Sporting News* summed up his accomplishments and duties:

> *Gruff, quick-tongued, brief, versatile, and punctilious, Barrow as "chief-of-staff" of the Yankees pours oil on troubled waters; arranges the salaries and settlements with all players, except Lou Gehrig (Babe Ruth being the exception before the first baseman); furnishes the technical knowledge; exercises general supervision over the farm system that has grown to equal, if not surpass, that of the St. Louis Cardinals, and is the chief advisor for both Col. Ruppert and those under him. In fact, it is Barrow who keeps all the wheels moving for the Yankees in Gotham, as well as in far off Oakland, Cal., and many points between.*

Once again, Barrow mostly stood pat during the 1937–38 off-season. Right after the World Series, he announced the re-signing of McCarthy to a three-year contract at thirty-five thousand dollars per year, a raise of five-thousand dollars per year over his previous contract. He also announced that the Yankees had unconditionally released Tony Lazzeri. Although only thirty-three years old, Lazzeri had chipped a bone in his finger in August, prompting him to reveal he planned to retire after the season; he hoped to secure a managerial position. He had also regressed at the bat and in the field. McCarthy saw Lazzeri's managerial ambitions as an opportunity to diplomatically replace the longtime second base mainstay. Chicago Cubs owner Philip Wrigley admitted he hoped to negotiate with Lazzeri but needed Lazzeri's discharge by the Yankees first so as not to violate tampering rules. Ruppert agreed and released his letter to Lazzeri to the press. In it he remarked, "[We are] keeping a promise we made to you some time ago [regarding giving him the opportunity to move into coaching]."

The Yankees also lost George McQuinn, who had run out of options, to the hapless St. Louis Browns. A year earlier, new Browns owner Don Barnes had approached Ruppert about buying some of the Yankees' stars. He even asked for a price on Joe DiMaggio. Ruppert, sick in bed at the time, sputtered, "Man, are you crazy? You can't be serious! DiMaggio nor any other members of my ball club are for sale. Go and see Barrow and he may be able to sell you somebody off the Newark club." Barrow, however, had no desire to sell any Major League–ready prospects to the Browns and offered little help when Barnes followed up.

After the season Barrow once again traveled to French Lick for a long vacation and baseball discussions with Ruppert. From French Lick he headed to the winter meetings. Barrow also spent time with Tom Yawkey at his estate in South Carolina. Upon his return to New York, Barrow began his annual salary negotiation battles. By this time in his career, Barrow saw less and less of the players outside salary negotiations and casual meetings at the ballpark. He never actually spoke with DiMaggio during the 1937 season until the World Series, when DiMaggio approached him to buy two extra tickets. Barrow later vetoed DiMaggio's arrangement to play basketball over the winter for a Brooklyn semiprofessional team, reasoning that it would be too risky for his knees.

Barrow's salary negotiation with DiMaggio was especially bitter that winter. Barrow and Ruppert felt that in giving him a raise from fifteen thousand to twenty-five thousand dollars they were being generous. DiMaggio disagreed. He felt he deserved forty thousand dollars after his excellent 1937 season. At one point Barrow called DiMaggio, telling him to come to New York and work out a contract. During the call he reiterated that twenty-five thousand dollars was their top price; DiMaggio demurred and remained in San Francisco. To complicate matters, boxing manager Joe Gould had befriended DiMaggio and reportedly become his unofficial advisor. In fact Gould never became actively involved in the negotiations. In those days before player agents, Barrow had little patience for an advisor. When questioned as to how he would respond if a player used an agent, Barrow barked that he would "toss the bum out."

Barrow was generally willing to negotiate up to the point that he believed was fair. He did not really take holdout threats too seriously because he recognized that ballplayers would always eventually report. But with the DiMaggio stalemate dragging, Barrow and Ruppert publicly challenged DiMaggio to report. DiMaggio finally surrendered on April 20, accepting the Yankees' offer after a brief holdout into the season. Barrow docked DiMaggio's pay until he was ready to play; this amounted to around $1,500.

The Yankees opened the 1938 season with much the same lineup as they had used the previous year. Bill Dickey, the league's top catcher, remained behind the plate. The outfield consisted of Selkirk in left, DiMaggio in center, and Henrich in right. Lou Gehrig anchored first base, Crosetti shortstop, and Rolfe third. The only major change was at second base, where the Yankees broke in Gordon to take over for Lazzeri. The pitching staff also mirrored the previous season. Ruffing and Gomez anchored the rotation, followed by Pearson, Hadley, and Spud Chandler. Chandler was another collegian, who had also starred in football for the University of Georgia. McCarthy retained Johnny Murphy in the role of bullpen ace.

The 1938 home schedule began inauspiciously with a chaotic opening ceremony. It started on time with a military band leading a parade of the players to the flag. Managers McCarthy and Bucky Harris of the visiting Senators stood ready to raise the American flag, while Barrow stood at attention. In their ready positions, the group awaited acting mayor Newbold Morris as the official dignitary. But Morris was not forthcoming. The delegation at the flag waited fifteen to twenty minutes before Morris finally appeared, arriving through left field with a police escort. The fans greeted him with jeers and boos for his tardiness (it turned out Morris had been held up by his refusal to cross a picket line). With the acting mayor finally in attendance, the band played the national anthem, the flag and the 1937 pennant were raised, and Morris threw out the first ball. The Yankees' players then took their positions in the field, but unfortunately, an important part of the ceremony had been omitted. The players were quickly called back and assembled at the plate for presentation of their World Series tokens. Commissioner Landis, however, in attendance for the Yankees' home opener had grown tired of the delay and ordered the Yankees back to their positions and the game to begin. Another dignitary had planned to make a formal presentation of the World's Fair emblem, but this too was abandoned due to the delay. With the pregame confusion out of the way, the Yankees crushed the Senators 7–0 and never really looked back the entire season.

The season did not go entirely smoothly, however. In late July 1938 while on a road trip to Chicago, wgn reporter Bob Elson approached Jake Powell for an on-air interview after he had taken batting practice. Elson casually asked Powell what he had done over the winter to stay in shape. "Oh, that's easy," Powell answered. "I'm a policeman and I beat n—— over the head with my blackjack while on my beat." (wgn did not record the interview, so his exact response is lost to history, but in all reports he clearly used the "N word" and claimed he was a policeman who had hit blacks on the head.) wgn and Elson, to their credit, immediately recognized the inappropriateness of this obscene response and cut off the interview.

Organized Baseball at this time barred black players. Because blacks were denied access to the upper strata of nearly all other sectors of American society as well, neither the owners, the players, the fans, nor the mainstream media much concerned themselves with the issue. Nevertheless, blacks attended Major League games and listened to the radio. Black America, incensed at Powell's response, immediately deluged the Yankees and the commissioner's office demanding punishment for Powell and a statement repudiating his remarks. The vehemence of the reaction surprised and confused the status quo–accustomed baseball establishment. The mainstream press, too, minimized the content and underestimated the ramifications of Powell's comment.

While still in Chicago, McCarthy and Powell met with Commissioner Landis, who quickly suspended Powell for ten days in the hope of defusing the situation. But neither Powell, McCarthy, nor Landis quite recognized the gravity of Powell's remarks nor the depth of feeling it had created in black America. Landis released a statement that read in part: "Although the commissioner believes the remark was carelessly and not purposely made, Powell is suspended for ten days." Powell at first actually tried to deny making the remark: "I don't remember saying anything like that at all, and I certainly would never mean to say anything offensive to the Negroes of Dayton [where he claimed to be a policeman], Chicago, or anywhere else. I have some very good friends among the Negroes in Dayton."

Both McCarthy and Landis blamed not Powell but the media. Despite the innocuousness of Elson's questions, McCarthy ruled that he would no longer allow radio interviews with his players unless from a prepared script. He claimed, somewhat disingenuously: "The ballplayers do not want to en-

gage in these broadcasts. . . . But they are pestered and pestered until finally one of them gives in. Then in an unguarded moment something is
said, maybe only in a joke, but it is taken the wrong way and then there is
trouble. I don't know what Powell said, but whatever it was, I'm pretty sure
he meant no harm. Probably just meant to get off a wisecrack. So the radio
people ran out cold with apologies and I'm out a ballplayer for ten days in
the thick of a pennant race."

The suspension and half-hearted response from baseball and the Yankees
did not quiet the uproar. Powell returned to the lineup in Washington, a
ballpark where black fans were forced to sit in segregated sections. Several
black patrons expressed their continuing anger by hurling bottles and other
objects at Powell. The umpires stopped the game several times to clean up
the debris and with great difficulty kept the disturbance from further de-
generating into uncontrollable chaos.

Barrow no more understood the anger than did the rest of white America. He reiterated that Powell's statements did not represent the views of the
organization, but then went on to profess that there was nothing the Yankees organization could do (the New York black community wanted him
traded or censured). He added that the club had previously repudiated anti-
Semitic comments by Ben Chapman. Unfortunately, Barrow further demonstrated his lack of awareness when he related that his "colored servants"
thought it was a mistake that would not happen again.

In the context of the times, Ruppert and Barrow had a generally good
relationship with the black community. Barrow liked to point out that the
Yankees let the Negro Leagues use Yankee Stadium for their annual East-
West game. To preserve some of this goodwill, Ruppert and Barrow ordered Powell to defuse the situation by making amends through visits to
black newspapers, businesses, and bars. Powell dutifully toured these es-
tablishments and apologized for his remarks. Some accepted his apology as
sincere, but the controversy lingered, with a significant share of the black
community calling for Powell's exile via trade or sale.

The Yankees held onto Powell through the 1938 season. Heading into 1939,
many in New York's black community continued to demand his banish-
ment. After Barrow re-signed Powell for 1939, he addressed the black press,
displaying his own disingenuousness and a continuing lack of appreciation
for the seriousness of the issue: "Yes, he is signed up. But it is not definite

that he will be used. That is up to manager McCarthy. Powell may be retained or he may be traded. Nothing is certain right now. But I think Powell has done about everything he could to prove he meant no harm in that broadcast." Barrow then went on to chastise the black press for keeping alive a controversy he hoped would die: "There has been no outburst of resentment anew. Why keep on stirring the matter up? We played the World Series in Chicago last year, scene of his broadcast, and there were no demonstrations against Powell." Barrow and McCarthy brought Powell back for 1940 as well, but he suffered a severe head injury crashing into a fence in a spring exhibition game and missed considerable time.

Partially to assuage the anger of black fans, in 1939 Barrow introduced the Jacob Ruppert Memorial Cup tournament to Yankee Stadium. The tournament would consist of ten doubleheaders between Negro National League teams. Barrow announced: "Negro baseball can build its own structure right alongside the Majors. Given sufficient opportunity to show their ability, the colored stars will undoubtedly attract thousands of fans and supporters [many of whom would undoubtedly be paying fans in Yankee Stadium] who will help them in their fight to reach the pinnacle of Organized Baseball." This sentiment, while lamentable today, was actually quite enlightened within the baseball establishment. Barrow unfortunately squandered some of the goodwill gained through sponsorship of the tournament when he initiated a "service charge" for black reporters covering games of black teams in Yankee Stadium.

Why Barrow and McCarthy kept Powell for two more seasons remains a mystery. He was rarely used in either 1939 or 1940, and the Yankees certainly had capable replacements in their Minor League system. McCarthy may have simply liked Powell, who was an aggressive, hustling ballplayer. Or Barrow may have felt that he needed to get an adequate return for a player once potentially regarded as a budding star. After the 1940 season Barrow finally sold Powell to San Francisco, reportedly for twelve thousand dollars, a pretty good sum for a baggage-laden journeyman.

Powell, who it turned out had never actually been a policeman in Dayton, was arrested in 1947 for passing bad checks. The police arrested him again a year later on the same charge when he attempted to cash about three hundred dollars in bad checks at a hotel. While in police custody, and before he could be transferred to his cell, Powell shot himself to death. The depressed

Powell and his female traveling companion had reportedly been discussing marriage. Even after death, Powell's handiwork led to distress: upon learning of his death, a wife materialized and revealed he was not divorced.

Despite the Powell debacle, New York cruised to the 1938 pennant, winning ninety-nine games and finishing nine and a half games ahead of second-place Boston. Gordon debuted with a strong season as Lazzeri's replacement. DiMaggio, Gehrig, and Dickey led the offense, which once more topped the league in runs scored. The five-man rotation of Gomez, Ruffing, Pearson, Chandler, and Hadley all pitched well, and the Yankees also again paced the league in runs allowed. In the 1938 World Series the Yankees quickly dispatched the Chicago Cubs four games to one. With the World Series victory, the Yankees became the first team in history to win three consecutive World Series. In 1939 the Yankees would shoot for their record-tying fourth straight pennant—a record shared by the 1880s St. Louis Browns of the old American Association (then overlooked by most writers) and, more importantly, their crosstown rivals, the New York Giants of 1921–24.

When Joe DiMaggio finally signed his contract in the spring of 1938, the Yankees arranged the usual photo and publicity event. Ruppert hurried through the affair—which he usually doted on—begging off that he had some important business to attend to. In fact, Ruppert had a doctor's appointment to treat phlebitis, an inflammation of the veins, in his left leg. Although his ailment was not thought to be serious, Ruppert was confined to his home for several days. The illness forced him to skip the opening day ceremonies he was planning to attend at his newly acquired farm club in Kansas City. Throughout the year Ruppert struggled with the condition and its complications. On January 13, 1939, after drifting in and out of a coma for several days, Ruppert died at the age of seventy-one. One of the last people he spoke with about baseball was Barrow. At one point he emerged from the coma to see Barrow standing by his bed. "Do you think we will win the pennant again?" he asked. Barrow reassured him. "We'll win again, Colonel."

Ruppert's death threw the ownership of the Yankees into turmoil. He left the bulk of his estate in three equal shares to two nieces and Helen Weyant. Upon learning of her inheritance, Weyant expressed surprise and trepidation. The daughter of a deceased friend of Ruppert, she had been a longtime acquaintance; her brother Rex Weyant had been the Yankees' assistant road secretary for the past three years. The *New York Times* reported that full control over the estate fell to the "executors and trustees for the lifetime of the beneficiaries, who are to receive the entire proceeds during their lives." Initially Ruppert's wealth was estimated at $40–45 million, of which about 60 percent would have to be paid in estate taxes. The Yankees organization was roughly valued at $10 million, requiring a tax payment of $5–7 million. Thus, the estate would have to monetize many of its assets to pay the taxes and distribute the value of the estate to the beneficiaries.

Ruppert had designated three trustees for the bulk of his estate: his brother-in-law, H. Garrison Sillick Jr.; his brother, George Ruppert; and his longtime attorney, Byron Clark Jr. Clark also became the estate's executor. Ruppert had added Barrow as a fourth trustee for the Yankees corporation. Although the beneficiaries ultimately would command the proceeds of the estate, Ruppert left the decision-making authority in the hands of the trustees. George Ruppert sought to reassure Yankees fans that Ruppert had provided for the Yankees and that the team's management and operation would not change. The trustees elected Barrow president of the team and released a statement:

> *Colonel Ruppert provided that all such taxes should be paid out of the residuary estate which comprehends all the Colonel's other vast and varied brewery and real-estate interests. And, further, in the realization that unusual demands might be made on the club in the matter of purchasing of players and farm clubs, or even a complete revamping of the Yankees team, the Colonel provided that the trustees, taking in all his holdings, other than the ball club, may make loans and advances to the baseball trust in order to enable it to meet any possible financial contingency that might confront it.*

Ed Barrow was now president of the Yankees. Hard-nosed and persistent, at seventy years old he had reached the pinnacle of his chosen career. Congratulations poured in from the many friends and acquaintances he had developed over his years in baseball. He would now be the Yankees' decision maker for a growing assortment of league-level controversies and squabbles, several of which will be explored in this chapter. Of course, he did not actually own the club. The trustees managed it for the three beneficiaries, and almost immediately rumors of a sale emerged. Despite George Ruppert's assurances regarding the safeguards built into his brother's will, payment of the estate's tax burden weighed heavily on the trustees.

Skipping ahead, as early as July 1939, Clark disclosed that in response to the many sale inquiries Barrow had informally valued the Yankee organization at $7 million. By March 1940 Barrow felt he needed to respond to the many rumors of an impending sale: "I have had several legitimate offers for the sale of the club, which I am not at liberty to mention just now, but this is not one of them. It would take a lot of money to buy the Yankees. I estimate the club to be worth roughly $6 million. Anybody who has that kind of money and is ready to put it up can buy the Yankees."

The price continued to fall as the tax matter persisted. The asking price was actually closer to $4 million, and the Yankees had received no bona fide offers over $2 million. Clark, George Ruppert, and Barrow were all discussing the sale with several potential suitors, including Joseph Kennedy (patriarch of the emerging Kennedy clan), with little success. In July 1940, George Ruppert acknowledged that the franchise had been offered to postmaster general and Democratic Party bigwig James Farley for $4 million. To line up the capital, Farley was struggling to assemble a syndicate of moneyed investors. Under Farley's ownership structure, he would become president, and Barrow would be retained in an administrative capacity similar to his role under Ruppert. The trustees required that Farley muster a down payment of at least $1.5 million. In December 1940, Byron Clark traveled with Barrow to the winter meetings in Chicago, reportedly to facilitate the sale. But raising the initial down payment proved more difficult than expected, and Farley's money-raising road show to various potential investors dragged on for nearly a year. In the end he could not round up the necessary funds.

In the meantime, Ruppert's estate turned out to be worth much less than originally estimated. The trustees placed the overall value at only $7 million, a fraction of the earlier approximation. They valued the brewery stock at $2.5 million, the Yankees organization at $2.4 million, real estate at $600,000, and additional disparate items at $1,450,000, including miscellaneous securities, furniture, jewelry, paintings, and a $50,000 yacht. Of course, the trustees naturally had reason to value the estate as low as possible to minimize taxes. Nevertheless, the value of Ruppert's holdings was clearly below expectations. It turned out that Ruppert owned only a portion of the brewery stock. In the real estate he so prized, he owned only a minority position, and furthermore, the value of many of the properties had declined during the Depression.

Barrow had to sue the estate to preserve the rights to his 10 percent ownership in the team. The original loan from Harry Stevens to purchase his share of the team had been amended in 1938 to reflect a principal amount of $250,000 and an interest rate of 3 1/2 percent. The Yankees had also paid Stevens accrued interest on behalf of Barrow. Ruppert's willingness to forgo dividends and recycle all the profits into the team benefited the Yankees organizationally, but it gave Barrow little return for his 10 percent owner-ship—not even enough to pay the full interest on his note. In his settlement with the estate, the 1938 note was assigned to the team; in other words, the Yankees assumed Barrow's liability. The settlement further provided that Barrow could purchase a 10 percent interest in the team for $305,000 un-der the same terms as the original agreement with Ruppert, dated July 17, 1925.

In 1935 Larry MacPhail and the Cincinnati Reds introduced night base-ball to the Major Leagues, playing seven games under the lights. Most Ma-jor League magnates, however, viewed night baseball as a novelty and re-mained opposed to its expansion, insisting, as *Fortune* noted, "that the quality of the game suffers from too much glare in some parts of the field and too little light in others; that night ball keeps both players and specta-tors up too late; that in many cities it gets too cool for the fan's comfort or the player's welfare; that the game can't be properly reported in the morn-ing papers, with consequent loss of valuable publicity. Further, almost all big league players dislike it."

Despite the hesitancy of his fellow owners, after taking over the Dodg-ers MacPhail installed lights in Ebbets Field. In their seven night games in 1938, Brooklyn drew 178,000 fans, nearly 27 percent of the season's to-tal attendance. Sunday games had long attracted the largest crowds. Night games, due both to their convenience for working people and to their nov-elty, in effect added additional "Sunday" games to the schedule. The other fourteen teams could not help but notice the huge attendance boost from playing games at night. For 1939 three American League clubs—Cleveland, Chicago, and Philadelphia—planned to install lights and introduce night baseball to the junior circuit.

More than forty years earlier a younger Barrow had conspired with Denny Long to add a night game to the standard July 4 doubleheader festivities in Wilmington. Because of the poor lighting and nonregulation baseball, the game had degenerated into a joke. Whether this fiasco many years ear-lier influenced his thinking remains unknowable, but Barrow adamantly opposed night baseball. A believer in the importance of balance and har-mony, Barrow feared night baseball would upset the sense of balance he had created in the Yankees organization: "Our success is built upon harmony on the field, harmony in the clubhouse, and harmony in the home. Night baseball is a terrible disrupter." He further pleaded that lighting Yankee Stadium was simply cost prohibitive: "Putting lights into the stadium will entail a tremendous outlay—at least a quarter of a million dollars [the lighting system for Cincinnati cost only sixty thousand dollars]. It is the hardest of all the parks to light and the big steel towers would cost a fortune." Barrow went so far as to declare that the Yankees would never be involved in night baseball. Detroit owner Walter Briggs also strongly disliked the idea of night baseball, and Barrow and Briggs agreed to act in concert in their opposition. To assuage some of Barrow's and Briggs's recalcitrance, the teams installing lights agreed that no night games would be played on "getaway" days (the last day of a multigame series) in this era when teams still traveled by rail.

Barrow later maintained that he could have mustered enough votes to completely shut down night baseball in the American League but did not push the issue. Barrow and Briggs retreated slightly from their pledge when the three teams added their lights for 1939. Barrow finally agreed to play night games in Philadelphia on June 26 and in Cleveland on August 30. As chief executives of two of the more profitable clubs, the ailing Jacob Ruppert and Briggs recognized that agreeing to play a couple of night games against the less fiscally solid teams offered a relatively painless way to help them financially. Furthermore, Barrow hoped that by agreeing to play these games he could mitigate the "break up the Yankees" sentiment lingering just below the surface among some of his fellow magnates.

When the Giants decided to add lights for the 1940 season, Barrow felt the need to reiterate his opposition: "Please get this straight, once and for all so I am not waked at two in the morning to deny a rumor. As long as I have anything to say about the running of the Yankees, they will not play night ball in the stadium. Night baseball is a passing attraction which will not live long enough to make it wise for the New York club to spend $250,000 on a lighting system in the Stadium." In the American League, the Browns added lights in 1940 and the Senators in 1941. Despite its growing popularity, many clubs remained leery of expanding too quickly and possibly diluting the novelty. In 1941 the owners still restricted the eleven Major League teams with lights to only seven night games each (one against each of the other teams in their league).

America's entry into World War II further boosted the clamor for night baseball. The teams with lights could now argue that baseball had a patriotic duty to offer night baseball to workers in the war industries. President Roosevelt provided a further impetus in his letter to Commissioner Landis encouraging baseball to remain active during the war. He advocated that adding more night games would allow the day-shift workers in the war plants to see an occasional baseball game. In response, each team was allowed up to fourteen night games in 1942. Another early opponent of night baseball, Clark Griffith, spent $220,000 installing arguably the Major Leagues' best lighting system. He now argued that because of the unique circumstances in Washington during the war—nearly full employment and mostly daytime workers—the Senators ought to be allowed additional night games. He asked for twenty-eight and received twenty-one.

Even as the number of night games increased, they continued to outdraw comparable day games. Barrow, however, remained opposed to lighting Yankee Stadium. Both he and Paul Krichell worried that night baseball was corrupting the game: "I will go so far as to call night baseball a fake!" Krichell wailed. "A nothing-ball pitcher under the lights looks like Walter Johnson. Double plays are made with motion-picture speed. Every throw by the catcher looks like a rifle shot. It's an invention based on deception. Sure a lot of folks go for it. But it's not the real thing." Barrow added that its effects went beyond simply Major League baseball: "It has ruined thousands of fine prospects. It has chased our youngsters out of our parks. It has deteriorated the living habits of our players and spectators." The attendance increase from night baseball, though, assured its survival and growth. Once America entered the war, however, the military's material demands mooted any question of adding lights to the five remaining holdout stadiums. In any case, Barrow would have resisted lights as long as possible. When the Yankees finally added lights in 1946, Ed Barrow was no longer in charge.

In 1938 the struggling Brooklyn Dodgers franchise brought in Larry MacPhail to run its organization. Like Barrow, MacPhail was a brilliant baseball executive. He had rebuilt the hapless Cincinnati Reds in the mid-1930s; soon after he departed, they captured two pennants. And he would soon transform the equally hapless Dodgers into a pennant winner. Nevertheless, the iconoclastic MacPhail was the antithesis of Barrow in every way. MacPhail was a maverick among the conservative baseball establishment; he had introduced night baseball to the Major Leagues in 1935 and was now threatening to break the no-radio pledge of the three New York teams.

In December 1938, MacPhail announced that he was pulling out of New York City's no-radio agreement, and that the team would broadcast all its games. Barrow responded, "All I know is that the Giants, Dodgers, and Yankees entered into an agreement, signed by Mr. Stoneham [the Giants' owner], the late Mr. McKeever [the Dodgers' owner], and Colonel Ruppert, not to broadcast and that this arrangement had another year to run." Barrow adamantly opposed radio. He felt that giving the games away free would keep fans away from the ballpark. Because radio broadcast rights were still a relatively small part of team revenue (for those teams that broadcast games), it would not require many fans to choose radio at home over the ballpark experience to diminish net revenues.

In response to MacPhail's unilateral decision, the Giants began to waiver on the radio question. The ailing Ruppert, still obsessed with his baseball team, encouraged Barrow to put the Yankees on radio in 1939 as well. Barrow acquiesced. The Yankees and the Giants had always worked their schedules to minimize conflicting home dates. In the same spirit, the two agreed to team up for their radio broadcast rights in 1939. Each would broadcast only home games to minimize the risk of cutting into the other's stadium attendance. Of course, it remained unknowable how this would affect home attendance of the team actually broadcasting. It is important to remember that at the time no one knew the eventual impact of radio or how best to harness it for baseball. Teams were experimenting with the medium, and the most financially successful teams naturally feared upsetting their winning formula.

Not surprisingly, sponsor demand was intense for the inaugural New York broadcast rights. The two teams executed a two-year contract with General Mills for Wheaties. Proctor and Gamble also signed on to pitch Ivory Soap. For the advertising rights, the Yankees and the Giants each received $110,000. The Dodgers, with a smaller market, received $87,500 despite broadcasting road games as well. (At the time announcers did not travel on the road; they broadcast re-creations based on the wire reports as they came in.) The rights fees received by the New York clubs were significantly more than those received by the other franchises, which typically ranged from

$30,000 to $60,000. By mid-season 1939, the Yankees' attendance lagged 1938 by a significant margin. Barrow blamed both radio and the New York World's Fair for the decrease in patronage. In total the Yankees' attendance fell by over one hundred thousand from 1938 to 1939, despite a dominant team trying for its record-tying fourth consecutive pennant.

The sponsors fared poorly, too. Nationally, baseball had about a 33 percent share between 3 p.m. and 5 p.m. In Chicago the percent of radios tuned to baseball was estimated to be slightly higher. In New York, however, baseball received only a 12 percent share. Some of this was blamed on Yankees announcer Arch McDonald, a capable announcer from the South who may have been a little too laconic for the taste of New Yorkers. Because of low 1939 ratings, the New York teams voluntarily agreed to reduce their 1940 fee to seventy-five thousand dollars. The clubs also brought in Mel Allen to be the lead announcer for both the Yankees' and the Giants' broadcasts. When attendance bounced back in 1940 to the 1936–38 levels, Barrow's reluctance to embrace radio diminished, at least slightly. For 1941 Barrow and his Giants counterparts held out for at least seventy-five thousand dollars per team again. But this time no sponsor could be found at that level. Neither Barrow nor the Giants felt it worthwhile to put the games on for a lesser rights fee and withheld their games from radio in 1941.

The newspapers feared the impending competition from radio, and many resented its newfound influence. Early in the 1941 season, the *Washington Post* reported that some newspapers were accused of "gleefully inferring that the increased attendance at Yankee games this season [was] the result of the broadcast ban." In 1942 the Yankees and the Giants were back on the air, and Mel Allen returned as the lead announcer. In 1943 Barrow again failed to reach an agreement with a sponsor, and neither the Yankees' nor the Giants' games were aired that season. Barrow even managed to get in a gratuitous dig at Washington owner Clark Griffith, with whom he was feuding. Early in the 1943 season, he prohibited Griffith from broadcasting Washington's road games in Yankee Stadium back to Washington. Finally, in 1944 Gillette stepped up as a sponsor. The Yankees would never again play a season without radio coverage.

Like many others of the era, Barrow and his Giants counterparts did not understand the true potential of radio as a medium to build excitement and interest in the teams. Understanding the true impact of a new technology

generally takes many years. Not until the Yankees came under new ownership after World War II did the team end its partnership with the Giants
and began to truly exploit radio's possibilities. At that point, the Yankees
became the first Major League team to have the announcer travel with the
team on the road, eliminating the campy re-creations. With the unsurpassed
Mel Allen as the play-by-play announcer both at home and away, the Yankees jumped to the forefront of capitalizing on the medium.

In his Yankees office Barrow sat at a desk that had once been owned by William Rockefeller. On the walls Barrow displayed only a few pictures: one
showed a seated Barrow and Harry Frazee with Ruth and Stuffy McInnis
standing behind them; another was a team photo of the 1903 Tigers; a third
showed a Paterson club team photo; and a fourth was of Miller Huggins in
St. Petersburg. Barrow clearly prided himself on being more than just a baseball executive; he craved recognition for his well-rounded baseball talents.
He never ceased to tout his managerial history and his scouting abilities, the
latter as testified to by his oft-noted "discovery" of Honus Wagner.

As team president, Barrow maintained his same daily routine, which by
this time was no longer particularly strenuous. He typically caught the 8:30
train in Larchmont and arrived in his office before 9:30. In the morning Barrow conducted business, received reports, and met with staff. When Ruppert was still alive, Barrow talked with him just about every day. If Ruppert was not available in person, Barrow often phoned in the late morning
to give him an update of the day's business. He also usually had his barber come to the office for a shave. On days without a game, Barrow often
met with the press in the afternoon to fill them in on those items he felt
they could be trusted with. The press generally learned much more as well,
but in the spirit of the times, they could not print much of what they uncovered. Barrow usually left the office punctually at 5:00, to catch the 5:13
train back to Larchmont.

On game days, stadium manager Charley McManus would call Barrow to bring him up to date on any issues. About 1:00 p.m. Barrow would
head over to the ballpark and eat lunch with Joe McCarthy at the com-
missary. This was the main opportunity for Barrow and McCarthy to discuss current concerns and issues. After eating, Barrow watched the game
from his box, usually in the company of a couple of friends. Afterward he

would stop by the stadium office and check on the game's attendance and receipts and other events of the day. If no urgent business awaited him, he would then head home.

By the time Barrow ascended to the presidency in early 1939, a number of owners were gunning for the Yankees, both on the field and in the board-room. Many resented the Yankees' deep farm system, which they viewed as a prime source of the Yankees' advantage. Barrow's Yankees owned five Minor League clubs outright and could boast working relationships with another eleven. Weiss's farms were turning many of the players dug up by Krichell's scouts into pretty good Major League ballplayers. A mostly light-hearted feud had been simmering for several years between Barrow and Clark Griffith, a fierce but undercapitalized competitor. To pull the Yankees back to the pack, at the December 1938 winter meetings Griffith proposed lim-iting an organization to one farm team at each Minor League classification level. Because of its sweeping effects on several organizations, the league re-jected Griffith's proposal. A suggestion by Barrow that player contracts be lengthened to eight months (from the existing six) to limit spring training holdouts was also turned down.

Now that he was fully in charge, Barrow traveled to Florida with the team for spring training for the first time in many years. One story attributed his past reluctance to travel to Florida to Ruppert's love of walking. Ruppert did not like to walk alone. Barrow supposedly got so tired of all the walk-ing that he decided to remain in New York and work on Yankees' business, including player holdouts, during the spring. For 1939 Barrow brought his wife and daughter with him, but they stayed in Sebring, Florida. Barrow spent much of his time with his family in Sebring, well away from the Ma-jor League camp.

Barrow nearly regretted his trip south. On a fishing trip with Fannie on a stream near Sebring, he narrowly averted a serious mishap. According to the report, Barrow was attempting to change his spot in the boat when he fell into the tropical waters. Afraid he would capsize the craft if he tried to climb back in, he grabbed a rope tied to the boat and swam, towing the boat behind him, to the nearest land. Unfortunately, when he reached the "land," exhausted, it turned out to be a sandbar composed of quicksand. As he sank up to his knees, his wife cleverly used an oar to leverage the boat over to Barrow so that he could sit on the edge and yank his legs from the muck. To complete his ordeal, Barrow had to row the boat back upstream to the spot where he had left his car. The seventy-year-old Barrow, who prided himself on his physical stamina and strength, naturally woke up early the next morning for another fishing expedition.

That spring training Krichell, with Barrow's approval, introduced a new device to help pitchers with their control. Krichell's device consisted of a painted canvas target with five holes cut into it, which he hoped would improve his pitchers' control. Although not directly related to Krichell's invention, he and Barrow both felt the pitching needed some bolstering after the team lost Spud Chandler to surgery for an arm injury he had sustained while working out at the University of Georgia.

In his effort to replace Chandler, Barrow became a victim of his own success. During the winter meetings, Barrow had successfully lobbied to reset the active roster limit to twenty-five (from twenty-three). While granting the two extra slots, the owners also eliminated the sixty-day involuntary retired list on which teams often stashed injured players. To clear a roster spot for Chandler, Barrow requested waivers on Chandler for the purpose of sending him to the Minor Leagues. Unfortunately, two teams claimed him, so to retain Chandler, Barrow was forced to use one of his precious twenty-five roster spots to carry Chandler until he was available to pitch late in the year. After the 1940 season, possibly in response to the Chandler affair, the owners approved a new sixty-day disabled list at the annual meeting. Under the new designation, a team could place up to two players on the disabled list without affecting their roster limits.

The baseball press—particularly in New York—focused much of their attention during spring training and early in the 1939 season on Lou Gehrig and his mysterious slump and sloppy play. Eight games into the season, after 2,130 consecutive games played, Gehrig removed himself from the lineup. Gehrig's trouble had started a year earlier, and his New York doctor had diagnosed gallbladder problems. During the spring Gehrig was clearly having motor-control problems. "There must be something organically wrong with Gehrig," Barrow observed. "I've been in baseball fifty years and I never saw a great hitter go to pieces all at once before. The last thing the great hitters lose is their ability to hit the ball."

Lou and Eleanor Gehrig and the Barrows lived near each other and had become social friends—especially Fannie and Eleanor—during Gehrig's many years on the Yankees. Eleanor remembers sitting at a table with Fannie when she finally decided to call the Mayo Clinic in Rochester, Minnesota, to make an appointment for Gehrig. The Mayo Clinic ran its tests on Gehrig in mid-June and soon diagnosed him with amyotrophic lateral sclerosis (ALS), later to be known as Lou Gehrig's disease. The Mayo Clinic provided Gehrig with a letter he could release to the public summarizing his condition. In part it read: "This type of illness involves the motor pathways and cells of the central nervous system, and in lay terms is known as a form of chronic poliomyelitis (infantile paralysis)." Gehrig presented the letter to Barrow, who released a statement to the press: "Gentlemen, we have bad news. Gehrig has infantile paralysis."

To mitigate the severity of the diagnosis, the doctors linked the nearly always fatal ALS to polio, a terrible, but often crippling instead of fatal disease. Both the public and Gehrig himself accepted the polio analogy. Amazingly, none of the many reporters covering the issue independently verified the verdict as it related to Gehrig's remaining life span. Or if they did, it remained unacknowledged by the mainstream press. Besides Eleanor, only a few others close to Gehrig learned of the gravity of his illness as his health continued to deteriorate. Barrow and Fannie were both in on the "conspiracy" to minimize its seriousness. Others who knew included longtime teammates Bill Dickey and Frank Crosetti.

For July 4, 1939, Barrow and the Yankees organized Lou Gehrig Appreciation Day. Between games of the doubleheader, many of the all-time Yankees greats came out to raise a 1927 Yankees pennant up the flagpole and then line up on the field. Barrow led Gehrig out to home plate, supporting him all but the last ten yards. After several speeches at the microphone, including one by Babe Ruth, Gehrig finally approached the microphone. When the overcome and nervous Gehrig seemed to hesitate, McCarthy offered a friendly nudge, and Gehrig delivered one of the most memorable and moving speeches in American history. After declaring that he "considered [himself] the luckiest man on the face of the earth," Gehrig acknowledged the important people in his life: "Who wouldn't consider it an honor to have known Jacob Ruppert? Also the builder of baseball's greatest empire, Ed Barrow?"

Barrow and Fannie continued to visit the Gehrigs socially to buoy their spirits. Gehrig biographer Ray Robinson learned from Eleanor's attorney, however, that Eleanor resented Barrow for his failure to offer Gehrig a job in the Yankees organization after his forced retirement (he accepted a job with the New York parole board). Bob Considine of the *Washington Post*, on the other hand, reported that Gehrig could have had any position he wanted with the Yankees organization, but his pride prevented him from accepting a make-work job. And he would not take a junior desk job out of concern he would be depriving a young up-and-comer of a baseball job. Gehrig himself did not reveal any such disappointment or animosity toward Barrow.

The 1939 World's Fair in New York, with its celebration of technological advancement and an unlimited future, captured the imagination of both New Yorkers and the rest of the nation. America was finally putting the Depression behind: real U.S. GNP (the total output of the U.S. economy) in 1939 finally surpassed that of 1929. As Americans at last recovered some of their optimism and spendable income, about 26 million visited the World's Fair prior to the end of the season. That same summer the Yankees hosted the All-Star Game. In the spirit of the World's Fair, Barrow decorated Yankee Stadium with red, white, and blue bunting and organized a festive salute to baseball's centennial. (At the time Organized Baseball still promoted the notion that Abner Doubleday had invented baseball in 1839.) At the end of the year some politicians floated the idea of building a large sports complex on the World's Fair grounds. Barrow opposed this suggestion, arguing that the area's baseball parks could handle any large crowd. He also obviously had the ulterior motive of not wanting any further competition.

Late in the season, a perplexing ruling by American League president Will Harridge incensed Barrow. On Sunday, September 3, in the second game of a doubleheader, the Yankees and the Red Sox stood 5–5 after seven innings. With one out in the top of the eighth, the Yankees took the lead on the Red Sox 7–5. At that time Boston had a 6:30 p.m. curfew on Sunday baseball. The Yankees recognized that because they had taken the lead with only ten minutes before the curfew, they needed to quickly end their half of the inning, then retire the Red Sox in the bottom of the eighth. If the Red Sox were not put out before 6:30, the score would revert to 5–5, and the game would need to be replayed at a later date.

After scoring their seventh run, the Yankees had Selkirk on third and Gordon at second. As Babe Dahlgren approached the plate, Boston manager Joe Cronin grasped the time implications as well. He ordered an intentional walk to Dahlgren to delay the game. Dahlgren, however, swung anyway—strike one—and Selkirk attempted a mock steal of home: he was tagged out at the plate. Umpire Cal Hubbard warned Dahlgren not to swing at the second intentional ball, and Dahlgren complied. Gordon ran in from third base and was tagged for the third out. Cronin ran out to protest the making of intentional outs, and the Boston fans erupted in anger, hurling bottles and other debris onto the field. As the clock wound toward 6:30, it became clear that the field could not be cleared in time to give New York a chance to retire the Red Sox before curfew. Umpire Cal Hubbard held Cronin and the Red Sox fans responsible for the delay and forfeited the game to the Yankees.

Harridge surprisingly overruled his umpire, declaring the game needed to be replayed. This angered Barrow, but Harridge's gratuitous one-hundred-dollar fines of Dahlgren, Selkirk, and Gordon really infuriated him: "We do not mind having the game ordered replayed, but we do consider the action of holding the Yankees entirely responsible and fining three of the players entirely uncalled for." To fine players for legally trying to win a game is absurd. Dahlgren had even complied with Hubbard's directive not to swing. Despite Barrow's protests the tie-game ruling stuck.

Not that it really mattered. Baseball historians Eddie Epstein and Rob Neyer rank the 1939 Yankees as the greatest of all time. For the fourth consecutive season, the Yankees led the league in both runs scored and allowed. The club finished with a winning percentage above .700 and a record of 106-45. Dahlgren adequately replaced Gehrig at first base. The rest of the infield carried over from 1938. The team boasted four excellent outfielders: Joe DiMaggio, George Selkirk, Charlie Keller, and Tommy Henrich. Red Ruffing and Lefty Gomez again anchored an extremely deep pitching staff. Despite the Yankees' dominance, Barrow would later express some concern about his top three pitchers: "Let me confess that until Labor Day last season, Joe McCarthy and I felt we were sitting on a volcano. We didn't know when Ruffing would blow, when [Monte] Pearson's arm would go, and we were not sure about Gomez."

In the World Series the Yankees easily dispatched the Reds in four games. Barrow's only serious headache came before Game 3, the first in Cincinnati. The Yankees' hotel was overbooked, and the hotel contended that the players would have to sleep on cots. A fuming Barrow swiftly rectified the confusion, and the hotel agreed to find his players beds.

A comparison of the 1939 team with previous champions from 1923 and 1927 highlights Barrow's (and Ruppert's) brilliance in adjusting player procurement strategies to the circumstances of the time. As shown in table 15, of the 1923 team's top thirteen players—eight position players and five pitchers—all but two came from other American League teams. The Yankees purchased eight of them, including four of the top pitchers, from Frazee. By 1927 the Yankees had retooled with players purchased at high prices from the high Minor Leagues. Earle Combs, Tony Lazzeri, and Mark Koenig cost the Yankees about $150,000. The team still relied on Major League veterans for its starting rotation, but five of their eight position players debuted as rookies with the Yankees.

The 1939 roster testifies to the success of the Yankees' scouting and farm system. Barrow procured only four of the top fifteen players from other Major League organizations. Six were purchased from the high Minors, and unlike those acquired in the mid-1920s, the majority of these players spent additional time in the Yankees' farm system. Four were signed as college stars and seasoned in the Minor Leagues. Teams at or near the top often hope to hang on or get a final push by bringing in aging Major League veterans. One key to the Yankees' dynasty was its willingness to break in young players. Barrow and McCarthy, and to some extent Huggins before him, eschewed short-term low-risk veterans for higher-risk longer-term solutions. The quality of the Yankees' scouting system and Ruppert's willingness to spend on players made this high-risk, high-reward strategy highly successful.

Although Barrow eventually became a staunch advocate, Ruppert was the father of the Yankees' farm system and Weiss its director. When discussing the 1939 team, Barrow wanted to make sure the farm system was not overcredited for the Yankees' record of success. The scouts were Barrow's pride and joy; he emphasized their importance in finding Major League–ready players: "People overlook the fact that we won six pennants in the first eight years I was in New York when we didn't have a single farm club." Barrow added that Gordon and Keller were the only stars signed as amateurs that the system produced. He expressed concern that they had not yet developed a star pitcher but thought Marius Russo—whom he had also banned from playing basketball—could become one.

As illustrated in table 16, during the second half of the 1930s, with a string of championships on the field, the Yankees' profits also returned to the top. Despite the Depression, the Yankees cleared over $1.2 million, nearly returning to the high profit levels of the 1920s. Of the other clubs, only the Tigers and the Giants recorded profits in the $1 million range. In Boston, owner Tom Yawkey, probably baseball's wealthiest magnate, accepted staggering losses while trying to buy a winner. Although he did not capture a pennant in these years, his purchases turned a laughingstock franchise into a first division team. The Yankees also finally paid out a huge dividend, essentially forced by the short-lived Federal Undistributed Profits Tax in the mid-1930s. In 1935 the team paid out $100,000 and in 1936, $420,000, the only distributions between 1920 and 1940. This payout had little effect on the Yankees competitive situation: even with the dividend the Yankees boasted the highest retained earnings.

Despite his setback at the 1938 meetings, Clark Griffith remained determined to slow the Yankees' juggernaut, one way or another. Rebuffed in his effort to restrict the Yankees' farm system, he decided to curb their ability to trade. At a league meeting just before the 1939 All-Star Game, he presented a proposal to prohibit trades by the previous year's pennant winner—a move clearly directed against the Yankees. The league owners had little interest in debating this suggestion at midseason and tabled it, but Griffith persisted with his scheme and continued to lobby the other owners.

Barrow misjudged Griffith's determination and salesmanship, and Barrow's weakness as a politician again came to the fore. He had acquired many loyal friends in the game, but he also had an abrasive, domineering personality that hindered his ability to deal with other factions. With the more regal and beloved Ruppert now out of the picture, Barrow had no backstop to his bluster. At the winter meetings Griffith successfully forced through a rule: "The championship club in either league [the National League did not adopt the restriction] shall not be permitted to acquire player contracts within its own league except through waiver channels until such time as it is no longer champion." In other words, the Yankees would be limited to trading for players who had cleared waivers. In effect, the Yankees (or the then-current pennant winner) would always operate with respect to the trade market as if the midseason trading deadline had passed. It remains unlikely that Griffith could have forced through this amendment had Ruppert been around to lobby the other owners. Griffith also reintroduced his farm system restriction of no more than one team per classification. Mercifully for Barrow, Harridge tabled any discussion on this proposal by declaring it so drastic that it would require evaluation by a subcommittee.

After losing the vote over the trade ban, Barrow publicly proclaimed that the Yankees would not be affected. He correctly asserted that most of the Yankees' talent came through the Minor Leagues, not through trades. However, Barrow recognized that even if the farm system harbored excellent talent, one often needed a trade to sort it all out, that is, to use duplicate talent in the Minors as trade bait to bolster weaker positions at the Major League level. For example, dissatisfied with the slick-fielding but only adequately hitting Dahlgren at first, Barrow had been hoping to regain first baseman George McQuinn from the St. Louis Browns. He reportedly offered Dahlgren, other players, and cash (reportedly as much as seventy-five thousand dollars) for the Browns first sacker. Griffith's legislation terminated any negotiations. Ironically, the Browns were the American League's weakest franchise and would soon be receiving financial support from the league—in fact, sportswriter Shirley Povich revealed many years later that Griffith confided to him that for several years the Browns received one penny for each American League ticket sold—and this trade would have helped restock the team with players and a little cash.

Skipping ahead, in 1940 the Yankees came back to earth, and Barrow found the ban stifling as he tried to fine-tune his team. He actively lobbied the league's owners to repeal the trade restriction. At the end of May, Barrow announced that he had five owners in favor of repeal, which would occur at the league meetings in July. Barrow had once again misread the political current, and in June he acknowledged it might not be until the end of the year. That season Detroit finally dethroned the Yankees. Barrow admitted, "The rule hurt us this year, but that's something over the dam." Now that the Yankees were no longer league champion, Barrow saw its advantage: "It will hurt any other club that wins this year's pennant, understand?" Most of the owners also recognized the unfairness of the rule, but by a 5–3 vote they failed to repeal it, most likely because to do so after one year would be a tacit admission that the rule was directed specifically at the Yankees—something Griffith and the other owners publicly denied. Finally, in mid-1941 the owners voted to rescind the trade restriction as of the end of that season. Even with its obvious flaws and unfairness, three teams still voted to oppose its repeal.

As the 1930s drew to a close, Commissioner Landis, concerned over the growth of farm systems, increased his vigilance in enforcing the remaining player-control rules. In March 1938 in the sensational "Cedar Rapids case," Landis found that the St. Louis Cardinals controlled more than one team in a league, a clear no-no. As punishment Landis released seventy-four players from their contracts, making them free to sign with any team. This action was less severe than it at first appeared. None of the players released, save for Pete Reiser and Skeeter Webb, was a top prospect. Furthermore, given the size of the Cardinals' farm system, these players represented only a small fraction of the organization's Minor League talent. In another action Landis freed Tommy Henrich, a ruling that benefited Barrow and the Yankees.

Now addicted to the financial support of the Major Leagues, the Minors no longer wanted their independence protected by Landis. Larry MacPhail, looking to develop a farm system for Brooklyn, used the Minors' stance to try to limit Landis's interference in the Major-Minor relationship. In the fall of 1939 the Minor Leagues and MacPhail plotted to pass new rules liberalizing ownership rights by the Majors. At the Minor League meetings in early December, the National Association adopted several amendments, the most significant of which required each Minor League team to be considered a separate unit regardless of ownership or affiliation. Such a rule would completely nullify many of the player-control limitations imposed on Major League organizations by virtue of their control of Minor League teams. The new rules would allow Major League organizations to further restrict player advancement by various subterfuges. For example, a team could release a player and have a sister team in a nearby town resign him as a "free agent" and in the process reset the Organized Baseball service time clock. This unholy alliance between the Minors and the Majors infuriated Landis.

With the Minor League ratification of the new rules, MacPhail lined up his fellow National League magnates in support. Passage in the American League remained more problematic. Despite their mutual antagonism, Barrow was probably MacPhail's best ally in the junior league. Overseeing the American League's most extensive farm system, Barrow naturally favored any legislation that would increase his ability to further restrain player movement. To MacPhail's horror, the rest of the American League feared the Yankees' dominance more than they feared Landis's interference in Major League–Minor League matters. Furthermore, fewer American League teams operated extensive farm organizations: St. Louis, Philadelphia, and Washington administered only the most rudimentary systems.

Barrow's halfhearted lobbying of his fellow owners proved less than successful. Already under pressure related to the trade ban, Barrow had little political capital to expend on the Minor League issue. Furthermore, Weiss's farm system operated successfully under the current rules. Barrow did not feel a burning need to further adjust the Major-Minor relationship. "If he [Landis] goes along in the future as in the past," Barrow remarked, "I can't see where the farm systems have anything to worry about." Once Barrow realized he could not influence his league's decision, he abstained from the vote; the American League voted 7–0 to reject the amendments. In a divisive, bitter joint session, Landis, empowered with the deciding vote in the event of a stalemate between the leagues, cast his tie-breaking vote: no.

MacPhail was furious. "What is the use?" he complained. "Here we've gone to all the trouble of clarifying rules governing farming systems. But the commissioner's mind is made up. He has always been dead set against chain-store baseball, and a group of American Leaguers, determined to tear down the Yankees, are using this as a means toward gaining their end." Another National League executive added, "Certain American League clubs, unwilling to spend the energy the Yankees have to build themselves, now seek to reduce their league champions to their own level."

On January 13, 1940, Landis exercised his authority once more. As in the Cedar Rapids case, he found an organization guilty of illegally controlling players on more than one team in a league. To rectify the situation, Landis granted ninety-one players in the Detroit organization free agency. The emancipated players included four from the Tigers Major League roster. In total the freed players represented about $500,000 in value. Landis further ordered the Tigers and their affiliates to compensate fourteen players with punitive payments totaling $47,250. The Tigers were left with only seventy-eight players in their entire organization, including the Majors. And although the team remained intact, the Minor League system would take many years to rebuild.

Two of the emancipated players, Roy Cullenbine and Benny McCoy, attracted frenzied interest in the free-agent market. Cullenbine received a twenty-five-thousand-dollar bonus and a five-thousand-dollar salary from MacPhail and the Dodgers. Connie Mack landed McCoy for the Athletics with a record free agent bonus of forty-five thousand dollars and a two-year contract at ten thousand dollars per year. With the Yankees' trust cash-poor as it struggled with estate-tax issues, Barrow found himself little more than a bystander. He chafed at being forced to sit on the sidelines while two of Detroit's top young players went on the auction block.

After Landis's vote against the new regulations and the Detroit decision, some of the owners began to turn up the heat on him regarding the farm system. They occasionally asked him, "If you don't like the farm system, give us an alternative." Landis believed, with some justification, that he had not in any material sense curtailed the farm systems, and that if the owners wanted an alternative they ought to design a system themselves. Regardless of this sentiment, Secretary Leslie O'Connor had spent considerable time and effort designing an alternative. In late January Landis decided to release the plan as a "proposal" by the commissioner's office.

O'Connor's brainchild essentially returned the relationship between the Majors and the Minors to its first years after the 1903 peace accord. Major League control of Minor League players would be prohibited, and option agreements would be abolished. Major League teams could acquire Minor Leaguers either through the draft or by outright purchase. Players could be sent to a lower classification only by outright assignment after a player passed through waivers at the higher level. Without a direct order, O'Connor's proposal had little hope of acceptance or implementation. A politician as wily as Landis certainly recognized this. Most likely he simply wanted to quiet the owners by showing he did, in fact, have an alternative, one they might not like, at that. Most owners recognized this for what it was, simply a suggestion to placate them. Most also understood Landis had little appetite for the fierce battle that would erupt if he tried to force this program on them. Therefore, few felt the need to criticize it directly. There was no need to antagonize Landis. Barrow, who had known the commissioner for many years, simply declined comment—a rarity for him—when questioned on the new plan. Without further advocacy and pressure from Landis, both he and the owners quickly forgot about it. Only O'Connor felt embittered.

Barrow loved the Yankees' presidency. He reveled in the prestige and controversies. He eagerly immersed himself in the radio and night baseball squabbles and was overly complacent with Griffith's crusade to "break up the Yankees." The team had just won a record fourth straight World Series in 1939, and Barrow basked in the many accolades for his brilliant team building. He maintained a sense of proportion, however, and rightly recognized that his presidency could only be temporary, and that the current Yankees ownership entity was only an interim solution. Fortunately for Barrow, the trusteeship would drag on for several more years.

Barrow had few interests outside baseball beyond hunting and fishing with his baseball cronies and boxing. His love of boxing had not diminished over the years; if anything, now that he had money, he may have enjoyed it even more. For example, in September 1941, Barrow anted up $1,440 to buy forty-eight ringside tickets to the Joe Louis–Lou Nova championship fight.

With Ruppert gone, Barrow no longer traveled to French Lick. In 1939 he spent his well-deserved November vacation with Boston owner Tom Yawkey at the latter's lodge in South Carolina. Accompanied by Krichell, Barrow enjoyed his usual postseason getaway. Upon his return, Barrow typically prepared for the league meetings in early December by reviewing the team's talent with Weiss, Krichell, and McCarthy. Prior to the meetings, Barrow needed to open preliminary consultations with other teams for the trades and other moves that he hoped to consummate. He also needed to lobby the other owners regarding league business that concerned him. As has been shown, in 1939 he was spectacularly unsuccessful on the political side.

In addition to the more-significant defeats, Barrow reintroduced his recommendation to eliminate the four-pitch intentional base on balls. He urged that the pitcher simply be allowed to tell the umpire he wished to issue a walk, and the umpire would award the batter first base. Barrow lost this one again when it was turned down at a rules meeting in February. Because of his longtime service to the American League, and perhaps because they voted against him on the major issues, his fellow magnates elected Barrow a league director, a largely ceremonial position. The other directors were Boston's Tom Yawkey, Cleveland's Alva Bradley, and Chicago's Harry Grabiner. Clark Griffith was the league's vice president, another mostly ceremonial position.

In February 1940 Barrow received a much more meaningful tribute when the Baseball Writers' Association of America presented him with an award for longtime meritorious service to the game. At the presentation dinner, Barrow, who, for all his bluster, disliked public speaking, said a few words before turning the microphone over to "a young fellow I signed forty-five years ago." Honus Wagner then ascended to the microphone and entertained the audience with the story of his signing by Barrow and other reminiscences.

Earlier in the evening the writers had performed humorous skits mocking baseball players and executives. In one with Tom Meany and Arthur Mann, Meany opened a letter: "Now, we have a letter from a Mr. E. G. Barrow of 55 West Forty-second Street. He sent it over by Paul Krichell and saved the price of a two-cent stamp. Mr. Barrow wants to know why the Giants suddenly developed a yen for night baseball."

Mann raised his hand.

Meany said, "Only one answer, and that from you, Mr. Mann. All right, Arthur, let's have 50 percent of your wit."

Mann responded, "Mr. Stoneham [the Giants owner with a reputation for late-night drinking] learned that afternoon games interfered with his sleep, so the night schedule fits baseball into his hours."

Barrow also involved himself in high-level Minor League operations. At the annual meeting of the Piedmont League, George Weiss stated that Bain Field in Norfolk was no longer an acceptable venue and the team planned to move its affiliate. According to one Yankees official, once this announcement became public, Barrow received more than twenty telegrams from other cities. He remarked, "[They offered] to build us a park, according to our specifications and rent free." (Some Minor League stadium matters have changed little over the past sixty years.)

Barrow approached the upcoming 1940 season confidently. The trade ban kept him from replacing Babe Dahlgren with George McQuinn, but other than that the team looked solid, and Barrow was satisfied standing pat. He acknowledged, though, that the Yankees still needed to "get the breaks," given that three stars, Red Ruffing, Lefty Gomez, and Bill Dickey, were getting up in age. While occasionally fretting over the ability of the farm system to provide long-term replacements, especially pitchers, he was optimistic. For the rotation he expected Marius Russo, Spud Chandler, and Atley Donald to step up. Regarding Dickey, Barrow reminded the Yankees' fans, "We've won pennants with and without great catchers. About the only trouble we expect from Dickey is signing him." He also spoke glowingly of the Kansas City keystone combo of shortstop Phil Rizzuto and second baseman Jerry Priddy.

Scout Bill Essick had discovered Priddy when the player was still in high school. Meanwhile, Paul Krichell had set up a youth tryout camp and baseball school in 1936. He brought in fifty-six top New York–area baseball amateurs for several days of schooling and tryouts. He invited Rizzuto because he had received four letters of recommendation. Despite Rizzuto's small stature, Krichell recognized his potential. After the camp Krichell signed him, and Rizzuto's play validated his assessment. The Yankees promoted him quickly through the Minors.

In the spring of 1940, Barrow's daughter, Audrey, decided to try marriage a second time. Now thirty-three years old, she wed the significantly older Mortimer Landsberg. Unfortunately, her marriage again ended badly. Two and a half years later she received a Reno divorce from Landsberg, one-time treasurer of the New York Stock Exchange, on the grounds of cruelty. At that time, many who could afford it traveled to Reno to file for divorce. Nevada had more liberal divorce laws than many other states and in 1942 required only a six-week stay to gain the necessary resident status.

Soon after her divorce from Landsberg, on October 31, 1942, Audrey married Ruppert's nephew H. Garrison Silleck III (son of Ruppert's sister Amanda), whom she had known for many years. The newlyweds had little time to enjoy matrimony, however. Almost immediately following the ceremony, Silleck was shipped overseas to head the Thirteenth Bombing Squadron. Fannie helped Audrey move into their new house in Rye, not far from the Barrows' residence in Larchmont. Audrey's luck in marriage, however, remained dismal, and this one did not long survive the end of the war.

The 1940 Yankees won only eighty-eight games and finished third in a close race behind the Tigers and the Indians. The Tigers' farm system may have been decimated by Landis's edict, but at the Major League level they still boasted MVP Hank Greenberg and several other excellent players. Barrow's anxiety over Dickey and Gomez proved prescient. A back injury suffered several years earlier while hunting in Canada hampered Gomez, and Dickey struggled though his worst season in New York. Furthermore, Red Rolfe had an off year, and Crosetti hit only .194. Russo pitched well, but Chandler, despite starting twenty-four games, was only adequate. Once it became clear that the Yankees' pennant hopes had dimmed, MacPhail challenged the Yankees to a postseason City Series with the Dodgers. Barrow deferred giving an answer by asserting that the Yankees were not yet eliminated from the pennant. When the season ended and MacPhail persisted, Barrow rejected the offer. If the Yankees did not qualify for the World Series, he had little interest in an exhibition series.

World War II had broken out in September 1939 with the German invasion of Poland. In the fall of 1940 Congress reinstituted the military draft and set October 13 as the deadline for registration. Baseball executives remained mostly unconcerned. America's entry into the war did not appear imminent. Also, because many players were married or had dependents, one estimate suggested that no more than six players per team would be subject to immediate call. Regardless, the owners had little choice but to carry on business as usual.

Barrow and McCarthy were determined to retool the team for 1941. Since Ruppert's death, however, they had little money to spend for Major League–ready players. Any influx or rearrangement of talent would have to come from the highly acclaimed farm system or trades of Major Leaguers. The two targeted Crosetti and Dahlgren for replacement after their disappointing seasons. Barrow offered both Selkirk, now the Yankees' fourth outfielder, and Dahlgren to Cleveland for first baseman Hal Trosky but was turned down. Barrow also planned to move out some of their more fragile pitchers. In December Barrow sold the effective but oft-injured Monte Pearson to Cincinnati for $20,000. He released Bump Hadley to the Giants for the $7,500 waiver price. Barrow also considered trading Gomez, whose career now appeared nearly over. Later that winter Barrow sold Dahlgren to the National League's Boston Braves.

To clear players for trading or selling to the National League, the Yankees needed to first clear waivers in the American League. Teams often asked waivers on players in preparation for trade or sale discussions with clubs in the other league. Usually the clubs in one's league passed on the waivers, freeing the players for trade to the other league. Under the rules in place at the time, if another American League team claimed a player, Barrow could withdraw the waiver request, but he was then prohibited from trading the player to the National League. Teams often allowed waivers to go through on a player they would otherwise like to have because they knew if they claimed him the waiving team would simply withdraw waivers and keep the player. And they themselves did not want to create a potential antagonist who might retaliate by claiming one of their players, effectively blocking a prospective trade. A team might also claim a player in order to negotiate a trade for the player itself.

Putting players though waivers was kept secret from the press to prevent unwarranted trade rumors. Plus public acknowledgment might lead the subject player, the press, and fans to feel the team no longer wanted him—a situation potentially detrimental to team morale. Reminiscent of the fiasco with the Cleveland owners in 1928, over the winter of 1940–41 word leaked to the press that Barrow had requested waivers on Dahlgren, Pearson, Hadley, and Gomez. When confronted, Barrow angrily acknowledged making requests for the hurlers but denied doing so for Dahlgren. After further insistence from a reporter that he was sure of his source, Barrow fumed and admitted that Dahlgren had in fact been run through waivers too. Outraged at the leaks, Barrow sent angry letters to Harridge and Landis insisting they be stopped.

Clark Griffith later grumbled about the sale of Dahlgren. He protested that Barrow was making a mockery of the rules. Barrow fired back: "Washington waives on Dahlgren November 18. It waives on Dahlgren January 27. All clubs in the National and American leagues waive on Dahlgren before he is sold to the Bees [the Boston National League team was briefly known as the Bees], and Washington had no right to be making any nasty cracks at the N.Y. Yankees."

Griffith expanded on the reason for his grievance: "Yes, we do waive on Dahlgren. But how does Barrow get the waiver? He sends us a list of players to waive on, and who is on the list with Dahlgren? Twenty guys and one of them is DiMaggio. What kind of stuff is that? They gotta change them rules. They gotta stop making a travesty out of the waiver lists."

Barrow, who was simply taking advantage of the existing system, retorted: "If Griffith is the smart guy which all the baseball history writers keep telling the world he is, why don't he claim DiMaggio? The Yankees is as pure as the driven snow."

To which Griffith rejoined: "Pure as the slag pile at Scranton."

While not feuding with Griffith, Barrow also spent part of the winter in a new spat with MacPhail. He hoped to trade or sell Gomez and Pearson to MacPhail, who was in the process of fine-tuning his team. Both men spent considerable time negotiating a deal in the press. MacPhail complained that Barrow wanted too much for the players—$25,000 each—and that he was using "high-pressure sales methods." MacPhail wanted to take both players to spring training on essentially a tryout basis; if they were not healthy, he could return them to New York. MacPhail's request was actually not as unreasonable as it sounds today. Barrow's sale of Hadley to the Giants had been on a returnable basis. When the Giants sent him back in late April for a refund—several weeks into the season—Barrow resold him for $2,500 to the Athletics. Barrow, though, had little interest in such an arrangement for Gomez. He bellowed in response to MacPhail's rant, "I am sending no one to the Brooklyn camp unless he is paid for in advance." Not surprisingly, these two antagonists, bickering in public, could not consummate a trade.

Barrow also expressed his displeasure at a new Landis Minor League–player decree. The commissioner had ruled that baseball-draft-eligible Minor League players purchased by a Major League team could not be optioned back to the Minors without first clearing waivers. The Major League teams complained bitterly. "We paid $25,000 to Hollywood for pitcher [Rugger] Ardizoia [one of the Yankees very few large money purchases in these years]," Barrow grumbled, "and we did so in the belief that we could educate him and option him out three times. It looks as if he will have to go out again. Are we going to take $7,500 for a $25,000 investment? I cannot believe the judge means it that way."

For spring training in 1941 the Yankees once again returned to St. Petersburg. The previous year, Cardinals owner Sam Breadon had approached Barrow to play an exhibition series in Havana that spring. Breadon told Barrow, "The guarantee is tremendous. How about it?"

Barrow's long memory dredged up the fiasco in Miami many years previously, and he declined the invitation: "Not a chance. I am not going to subject our ball club to the delights of Havana in March. Some of the bachelors might like the senoritas so well they might forget to return to St. Petersburg."

Breadon, not wanting to surrender the potentially large payday in Cuba, persisted: "You've got the whole thing wrong, Ed. Havana is no tougher on discipline than Tampa or Miami."

Barrow held his ground: "But we don't train in Tampa or Miami. I know all about Havana. It is very gay in March. I don't like to send ballplayers where it is gay."

"What do you call Broadway, a morgue?" Breadon continued.

To which Barrow replied, "New York is the best behaved city in the country."

Barrow may have been looking for additional sources of revenue, but he had little interest in letting his players loose in the Havana night life.

Unable to trade for acceptable replacements, Barrow and McCarthy settled on rebuilding their infield through the farm system. During spring training McCarthy promoted Kansas City's celebrated keystone combination of Phil Rizzuto and Jerry Priddy. To make room for Priddy at second base and replace Dahlgren, McCarthy shifted second baseman Joe Gordon over to first. Implementation was delayed for several games when Priddy twisted his ankle at the end of spring training, but once healthy, he joined Rizzuto to form an all-rookie middle infield. A month into the season, McCarthy abandoned his plan: Priddy was not hitting, and Rizzuto seemed to be struggling in the field. McCarthy moved Gordon back to second, re-inserted Crosetti at short, and handed first base over to Johnny Sturm, another Yankees farm product. When Hal Trosky spiked Crosetti in June sliding into second base, McCarthy put Rizzuto back at shortstop—a position he would hold (but for the war years) until 1954.

Rizzuto later recalled his first meeting with Barrow before the season. To appeal for a higher salary, he went to the Yankees' offices to see Barrow. When he arrived, he found a man in a frayed sweater being shaved by a barber known as "Goulash." Rizzuto waited silently as Goulash finished his shave. When the man in the chair sat up, he demanded: "Young man, what is your trouble?" Rizzuto now realized he was talking to Barrow and responded he wanted more money. Barrow barked back: "I give you this and no more. If okay, sign. If not, get the hell out of here." Rizzuto signed.

In the middle of the 1941 season, the baseball world was shocked by Lou Gehrig's death so soon after his diagnosis. Throughout 1940 and 1941 Gehrig's health had continued to decline, but he had maintained his job with the parole board. Barrow was one of the few who knew how sick Gehrig really was, but he was still surprised when he learned of Gehrig's death. Barrow, who had become as close to Gehrig as to any Yankees player, sadly reminisced that he "felt like he lost a son when Gehrig died."

Many of the Yankees rebounded from their subpar 1940 seasons, and the team recaptured the pennant. Sturm struggled at the plate, but the outfield of Charlie Keller, Tommy Henrich, and Joe DiMaggio finished second, third, and fourth in home runs. DiMaggio recorded his legendary fifty-six-game hitting streak and won the league's Most Valuable Player Award. Gordon hit twenty-four home runs, and rookie Rizzuto finished the season with a batting average of .307. The pitching held up as well. Only Russo pitched over 200 innings, but Gomez, Ruffing, Chandler, and Donald all pitched capably in over 150 innings each. Johnny Murphy turned in perhaps his best relief season with an ERA of 1.98 in thirty-five games.

In the World Series the Yankees faced Larry MacPhail's Brooklyn Dodgers, managed by Leo Durocher. Barrow felt especially gratified as the Yankees dispatched his occasional antagonist four games to one. The key play came in Game 4 with the Yankees batting, trailing 4–3 in the top of the ninth with two out. Brooklyn catcher Mickey Owen mishandled Hugh Casey's third strike on Tommy Henrich, who scrambled safely to first. The Yankees went on to score four runs in the inning to take the game 7–4 and a three-games-to-one lead in the Series. In recognition of the Yankees' rebound from their disappointing 1940 season, the *Sporting News* named Barrow executive of the year, the first executive to win the honor twice.

Once again, after the season Barrow traveled to Yawkey's retreat in South Carolina, this time for a three-week vacation. Both before leaving and upon his return Barrow, Krichell, Weiss, and McCarthy discussed the approaching 1942 season at length. Barrow hoped to integrate two Minor League pitchers, Johnny Lindell and Hank Borowy, into the Major League staff, but had no plans to restructure the position players. The brain trust still felt that Sturm would develop into a quality Major Leaguer. Nevertheless, when MacPhail approached him regarding star Dodgers first baseman Dolph Camilli, Barrow naturally expressed interest. MacPhail needed the cash so he could buy a first baseman from the Cardinals, either Johnny Mize or out-fielder/first baseman Johnny Hopp. Barrow offered twenty-five thousand dollars and two Minor Leaguers for the thirty-four-year-old Camilli, but MacPhail demanded sixty thousand dollars, an absurd amount for an aging slugger. In the meantime, the Cardinals sold Mize to the New York Giants and pulled Hopp off the market, removing MacPhail's incentive to sell Camilli. In one seemingly insignificant deal, the Yankees sent Minor League outfielder Tommy Holmes to the Boston Braves for cash and first baseman Buddy Hassett and outfielder Gene Moore. Holmes would go on to a solid Major League career in Boston, while Hassett would prove an important Yankees addition for 1942.

On December 7, 1941, with the Japanese attack on Pearl Harbor, baseball, along with the rest of American life, radically changed. Until the war ended nearly four years later, player personnel decisions mutated to include the player's military draft status as a central focus. Barrow, who had already led two baseball leagues and one team during two wars—the Spanish-American War and World War I—knew firsthand the difficulties that lay ahead. He had learned that the best approach was simply to struggle on as best possible and not worry too much about the war-imposed limitations beyond Organized Baseball's control. Baseball had to walk a fine line in advocating for itself yet not appearing either unpatriotic or as seeking preferential treatment. Over the winter Barrow announced that servicemen would be allowed free admission to Yankees' games. In becoming one of the first teams to enact such a policy, the Yankees made arrangements for five thousand such passes per game.

Because the armed services could induct and train only so many prospective servicemen at a time, many baseball executives failed at first to recognize the scope of the war's impending manpower needs. At first the loss of players to the war effort was mostly a trickle. As of the start of the 1942 season, the Yankees had lost only one significant player, first baseman Johnny Sturm. To compensate, McCarthy plugged recently acquired National League veteran Hassett into the role.

Contract negotiations during the war took on additional challenges. Coming off a World Championship season, the players naturally believed they were due a raise. Barrow, mindful of the impending revenue reduction caused by the war effort, was reluctant to overcommit to his players. "We don't want any of that [cutting salaries]," Barrow confirmed. "But I will say this—there will be few, very few, increases, and they will not be very big ones either." He had one of his most frustrating negotiations with Marius Russo. The two negotiated by phone and agreed to a contract. Barrow closed by saying he would courier the contract to Russo in St. Petersburg with traveling secretary Mark Roth. Not long after hanging up, Russo called back to demand another five hundred dollars. An annoyed Barrow stood firm, and Russo held out for the start of spring training.

In the early and uncertain days of America's entry into the war, many citizens and their leaders feared still worse could come. In addition to the usual spring preparation, baseball teams, particularly those on the coasts, girded for the possibility of an air raid. Barrow had signs painted on each Yankee Stadium seat with instructions for what to do in case of an air raid. He reassured the public that fifteen thousand fans could be protected beneath the bleachers and forty thousand under the grandstand. He also placed fire extinguishers, sand, and barrels of water throughout the stadium.

To support the war effort, each Major League team agreed to donate the proceeds of one 1942 game to the army-navy relief fund. The Yankees' charity date was scheduled for an August 23 doubleheader against Washington. Unfortunately, a Giants-Dodgers twin bill was also scheduled for that same date at Brooklyn's Ebbets Field. Barrow proposed that the Dodgers and the Giants instead play just a single game that day, while MacPhail argued that the Yankees should shift the date of the benefit game. The controversy gave Barrow and MacPhail another chance to feud publicly. The flamboyant MacPhail suggested letting the mayor arbitrate; Barrow had little interest in this suggestion.

Perhaps partially in response to the brouhaha, Barrow staged an extravaganza. He brought back Babe Ruth for a fungo hitting contest. He lined up all-time pitching great Walter Johnson to pitch a couple of balls to Ruth. He scheduled a track and field competition, which included a throwing contest, a sixty-yard dash, and a relay race. Barrow's program paid off. Despite competing with the Dodgers-Giants doubleheader, the Yankees drew a huge crowd and raised over seventy-five thousand dollars for the relief fund, the most of any team's relief day.

In one unexpected summer headache, the Yankees lost reserve catcher Buddy Rosar for a spell when he jumped the team on July 18 to travel home to Buffalo. He had hoped to join the Buffalo police department, which necessitated that he take the civil service exam. With Dickey out due to a shoulder injury, Barrow could ill afford to lose Rosar. He was forced to scramble to quickly find another backstop. Luckily, Cincinnati had recently released aging catcher Rollie Hemsley, and Barrow snatched him up. Rosar returned to New York three days later, whereupon McCarthy fined him $250. Desperate for a catcher, Barrow kept Rosar on the roster, but he remained in McCarthy's doghouse throughout the season. In August when the Buffalo Civil Service Commission released the test results, Rosar did not make the cut.

The Yankees suffered another meaningful loss to military service when Tommy Henrich joined the Coast Guard in August 1942. To restock his outfield, at the end of August Barrow claimed Roy Cullenbine off waivers from Washington. Cullenbine had been one of the main beneficiaries of Landis's freeing of numerous Detroit Tigers farmhands and had received a hefty signing bonus from Brooklyn. Cullenbine initially fell short of expectations but seemed to be reaching his potential in 1941 when he hit .317 for the Browns. He started slowly in 1942, however, and the Browns sent him to the Senators. When the Senators placed him on waivers in late August, Barrow wisely recognized he would be a relatively inexpensive, capable fill-in for Henrich. In twenty-one games down the stretch, Cullenbine exceeded Barrow's expectations, hitting .364 with a couple of home runs.

Griffith initially held out for more than just the $7,500 waiver price. He knew the Yankees desperately needed outfield help and hoped to squeeze Barrow. But Barrow could play hardball, too. He realized that Griffith was negotiating to sell pitcher Bobo Newsom to the Dodgers for around $30,000. As has been discussed, to transfer a player to the other league, he had to first clear waivers in his own. Barrow threatened to claim Newsom, thus effectively blocking Griffith's sale if he persisted in his demand for more than the waiver price. Barrow won this round against his old sparring partner, and Griffith released Cullenbine for $7,500; Barrow just beat the World Series eligibility deadline by landing Cullenbine on August 31.

Injuries were a bigger concern in 1942. Red Rolfe suffered from colitis and missed much of the season. McCarthy replaced him with ex-shortstop

Frank Crosetti, who could no longer hit. Two key pitchers from the previous year also missed significant time: Russo with a sore arm and Donald with an eye problem. Gomez, too, succumbed to a sore arm and started only thirteen games. Because the Yankees organization was well stocked with pitchers, Barrow could fill in with qualified replacements. Furthermore, Ruffing was still valuable, and Tiny Bonham, Spud Chandler, and the rookie Hank Borowy each finished in the top five in ERA in the American League.

Barrow and McCarthy's performance in 1942 was particularly impressive. Barrow's moves astutely addressed the team's fresh difficulties, while McCarthy intelligently juggled the new players into the lineup. In sum, the brain trust successfully overcame several personnel complications to win 103 games. The team once again excelled on both offense and defense, leading the league in both runs scored and runs allowed. In the World Series the Yankees faced the St. Louis Cardinals, a great team for the era (they won at least 105 games and three straight pennants from 1942 to 1944). The Yankees, who had won five of the past six world championships and had not lost a World Series since 1926, finally came up short, losing four games to one.

Joe DiMaggio was one of the last high-priced Minor Leaguers the Yankees splurged on. Barrow's collection of scouts—Paul Krichell, Gene McCann, Bill Essick, Joe Devine, and Johnny Nee for much of the 1930s—had delivered a consistent stream of high-quality amateurs to Weiss's Minor League system. When a bidding frenzy ensued for Seattle pitcher Fred Hutchinson after the 1938 season, Barrow surprised his rivals by sitting on the sidelines. Reportedly his scouts discounted Hutchinson's fastball, but in previous years Ruppert would have considered losing a bidding war a personal affront. When the dust cleared, Detroit had landed Hutchinson for fifty thousand dollars and five players.

While laying off the high-priced players, the Yankees' farm system still developed a surplus of talent, and in the late 1930s the Yankees began to sell some of their surplus Minor League players. After the death of Ruppert in January 1939 and the ensuing muddy financial situation, Barrow had directed George Weiss to step up his Minor League player sales. Weiss proved a brilliant salesman, peddling a number of players in the $20,000–$40,000 range. In transacting these sales, Weiss often garnered a throw-in

Minor Leaguer in return. The high quality of the Yankees' scouting organization meant that these afterthoughts occasionally developed into valuable ballplayers.

After the 1942 season, Barrow lost, for the time being anyway, his New York sparring partner when Larry MacPhail resigned to join the war effort. A disagreement within the Dodgers ownership probably hastened his departure. Rumors persisted that some board members were unhappy with the amount of money MacPhail had spent on players, the farm system, and ballpark improvements. At his departing news conference, MacPhail tearfully defended his record, emphasizing that by creating a winning team he had actually increased revenue and reduced the team's debt. It is a credit to the Dodgers' board that after McPhail's departure, they targeted some of baseball's best minds as his successor. The board considered Bill Terry, New York Giants manager and de facto general manager during the 1930s; Branch Rickey, legendary builder of the St. Louis Cardinals' farm system, who had recently been released by owner Sam Breadon; and George Weiss. MacPhail later recalled that when Barrow learned the Dodgers were considering Weiss (most likely through MacPhail's checking on his qualifications), Barrow ordered Weiss to either affirm his interest in the Yankees or quit to pursue the Dodgers job. MacPhail also gibed Rickey for his back-alley maneuvering to land the job. Fortunately for the Yankees, Weiss elected to remain. He recognized Barrow was likely nearing the end of his active role and hoped to succeed him. With Weiss no longer a candidate, the Dodgers opted for Rickey. As he had in St. Louis, Rickey created a consistently competitive team in Brooklyn.

By the end of 1942 the effect of the war on American society was becoming more pronounced. Harkening back to his World War I days, Barrow proposed shortening the 1943 season to 140 games. The other owners saw little reason to cut fourteen days of revenue from the schedule and rejected the suggestion. The need for men and material created shortages of each and led to rationing of many basic necessities. Because of the war effort's demand for rubber, the owners introduced a new baseball in 1943. For the new ball, Reach and Spalding substituted balata, a substance refined from the milky juice of tropical trees. Wartime travel restrictions made travel south for spring training unfeasible; Barrow and McCarthy settled on Asbury Park, New Jersey, for a training site. Because of northern weather conditions, the opening of camp was delayed until mid-March and the start of the season to April 20.

Of course, the loss of players to the war effort presented a more vexing and frustrating complication. A player's military draft classification and likelihood of entering the service became as important as his ability. Trading at the winter meetings fell off amid uncertainty regarding the players' military status. From experience Barrow grasped that players would soon be conscripted for the military or lost to war-related industry. At the winter meetings he proposed raising the player limit from twenty-five to thirty to help manage the uncertain exodus of players during the season. Initially he received little support from his fellow magnates, mainly because they had little interest in paying five additional players, but also because of their less-extensive farm systems. (A couple of years later, however, as the war drew to its conclusion, the limit was raised by five to accommodate returning veterans.)

In December 1942 the Yankees traded Cullenbine and Rosar to Cleveland for center fielder Roy Weatherly and utility infielder Oscar Grimes. While not a hitter of Cullenbine's caliber, Weatherly was a better fielder and could capably play center. Notably, all four were draft classified 3-A, generally meaning they were married with one or more children. The war's insatiable demand for manpower would eventually get around to the 3-As, but at this point they still seemed a relatively secure pool of talent.

The Yankees next lost first baseman Hassett to the service, and Barrow hoped to replace him with a Major League regular. He consulted with McCarthy regarding several options. Acting on McCarthy's recommendation, he sent a couple of second-rate ballplayers, pitcher Al Gettel and first baseman Ed Levy, and ten thousand dollars to the Phillies for starting first baseman Nick Etten, another 3-A player who would a prove a solid wartime performer. But Gettel refused to report and retired to his farm, and Levy was reclassified 1-A, first on the list to be inducted. With these changed circumstances, Philadelphia owner William Cox threatened to void the trade. In response Barrow, Cox, and Landis met to resolve the dispute. The three agreed Barrow could keep the rights to Gettel and Levy and substitute two other marginal ballplayers. The Yankees also had an opportunity to purchase outfielder Danny Litwhiler from Cox for thirty-five thousand dollars and three players. The Yankees no longer had an open checkbook to purchase players, but Barrow consulted with McCarthy anyway. McCarthy concurred that thirty-five thousand dollars was too much for Litwhiler, and Barrow declined the offer.

A year earlier when Levy had signed his contract for the 1942 season, he surprised Barrow by signing his name Ed Whitner. The New York teams were constantly on the lookout for Jewish ballplayers as an additional gate attraction for New York's Jewish fans. Barrow was never as fervent on this matter as the Giants, but as long as he had a player named Levy, he hoped to take advantage of his religion. Levy, it turned out, was Irish, not Jewish, but had assumed his stepfather's name. After meeting his natural father in the summer of 1941, he decided to go by his name, Whitner. When Barrow saw the signature and learned the story he told Levy/Whitner: "If you're going to play ball with the Yankees, your name's got to be Levy, understand? Man, that name will be worth a fortune to you in New York, if you ever become a good ballplayer." Unfortunately, he never became a good ballplayer.

Jerry Priddy thought he had won the starting second base job in the spring of 1941. His benching that season frustrated him, but he generally accepted his reserve status. In 1942, however, Priddy became increasingly disenchanted with McCarthy and his reserve role. He sulked when McCarthy mostly used the weak-hitting Crosetti to fill in for Rolfe at third and also felt he deserved a shot playing first base. A highly touted star in the Minors, Priddy could not understand McCarthy's refusal to give him another chance as a regular. McCarthy typically handled young players with intelligence and sensitivity. He was not afraid to play rookies and adeptly broke in a number of skilled youngsters. With Priddy, however, McCarthy never gave him another real opportunity after his short stint in early 1941. Notwithstanding his own culpability for Priddy's frustration, McCarthy had little tolerance for complainers. In January 1943 he and Barrow sent Priddy and a throw-in pitcher to Griffith for $7,500 and right-handed hurler Bill Zuber. In return for a favor, Barrow had once promised Griffith first dibs on Priddy should the Yankees decide to move him, and McCarthy liked Zuber. When Barrow first called Griffith, the Senators owner refused to include Zuber but demurred after Barrow threatened to shop Priddy elsewhere. The demand

for Zuber, a mediocre thirty-year-old pitcher, was driven by his military classification—he would play in the Majors throughout the war.

As the 1943 season opener neared, Barrow remained highly confident despite losing several more players to the war. For the first time in many years,
the team would be without its two future Hall of Fame pitchers, Ruffing
and Gomez. Barrow sold Gomez to the Boston Braves for the waiver price
after he had taken a job at a defense plant in Massachusetts. Ruffing was a
victim of the inevitable mistakes caused by the uneven application of the
draft rules. He was thirty-eight years old, supported a wife, children, and
mother-in-law, and was missing four toes on his left foot. After receiving
his draft notice, he reported to the induction center. On the verge of being
exempted, the last doctor whom Ruffing saw pronounced him fit. By 1943
both pitchers, however, had lost much of their effectiveness, and neither
would have been counted upon as a rotation anchor. The top of the 1942
rotation—Bonham, Chandler, and Borowy—were all returning, as were
Donald, Russo, and bullpen ace Johnny Murphy.

The regular lineup was slightly more problematic and uncertain. Of the
1942 regulars, DiMaggio, Rizzuto, Henrich, and Hassett were lost to the
military, and Rolfe retired to coach in college. Barrow anticipated many
of his losses, but DiMaggio caught him unaware. The star surprised both
Barrow and himself with a tepid announcement during the winter that he
might not have to worry about spring training. DiMaggio may have meant
this as a negotiating ploy, but many took it as a hint he would be enlist-
ing. The player and Barrow often butted heads on contract negotiations;
DiMaggio believed Barrow handled his contract last so he could "shame"
him into signing. At that time DiMaggio's draft board had actually temporarily closed enlistments, but DiMaggio was in the midst of marital troubles, and his wife was demanding he join the service. With the press now
seeking clarification of his comments and his wife pressing him, he reluctantly (at least in private) enlisted in the army.

DiMaggio and the former Dorothy Arnold had endured a rocky marriage for several years. The previous year, with DiMaggio slumping early in
the season, Dorothy left him for a short time and contemplated divorce. A
one-time actress, she chafed under DiMaggio's demand that she retire and
at his lack of attention at home. Barrow had acted as a marriage counselor
for his star; he met with Dorothy and convinced her to return home. He

selfishly hoped that resolving any marital troubles would improve DiMaggio's performance. At least as importantly, Barrow also realized that a married DiMaggio had a better chance of avoiding military service. This was not the first time Barrow had played marriage therapist. Several years earlier, Gomez, married to Broadway showgirl June O'Dea, had experienced difficulties of his own. Barrow had successfully intervened, and the two had reconciled. DiMaggio looked up to the older, New York–savvy Gomez, and this may have accounted for his tolerance of Barrow's intervention in his own marital troubles.

Barrow's optimism for 1943 stemmed from the fact that the Yankees still trotted out three of the American League's best players: Dickey, Gordon, and Keller. The Yankees' fortunes may also have benefited from a lucky turtle that Barrow's old pal Harry Wright Jr. sent him that winter. (In return Barrow sent Wright six opening-day passes.) On a more practical level, Nick Etten gave the Yankees their best first baseman since Gehrig, and Weatherly could buttress center in the absence of DiMaggio. To further man the outfield, McCarthy converted pitcher Johnny Lindell into an outfielder, and the club promoted Bob Metheny from Newark. Meanwhile, the club returned Crosetti to short and promoted third baseman Billy Johnson. Both Johnson and Lindell would remain key contributors after the war. The Yankees also promoted infielder Snuffy Stirnweiss from Newark. Stirnweiss was classified 3-A because he was recently married and supported his mother. He also remained a candidate to receive a 4-F designation, limited to those who could not serve in the armed forces due to medical conditions. Stirnweiss had undergone surgery in 1941 for a ruptured ulcer and suffered recurring stomach troubles. By one report the Yankees had only one unmarried player on their roster, Atley Donald, and he was classified 4-F because of an eye injury and a bad back.

The 1943 home opener drew barely seven thousand fans, a dismal start to the season. Barrow publicly remained unconcerned. He pointed out that the postponement of the original opening date due to weather cost the team some fans who could not get another day off work. Also, the cold weather discouraged advance sales and kept some fans away. For the season ahead, Barrow had little expectation of making a profit and merely hoped to break even. He fell short of this goal; for the year the Yankees lost $35,397. If one adds in another $53,224 loss attributable to the wholly owned farm teams, the total jumps to $88,521. Compared with 1939, the Yankees' revenues dropped from $1,355,183 to $925,514 in 1943 (a 31 percent decline), while salaries dropped from $361,471 to $301,229 (17 percent). In terms of overall player salaries, the baseball magnates proved surprisingly generous during the war. Despite a significant drop in revenues, player salaries fell only 12 percent between 1939 and 1943. Considering the exodus of star players to the war effort, this fact becomes even more remarkable.

By taking strict economy measures, the other American League teams (except the Red Sox) actually turned a profit. As table 17 illustrates, the Yankees still led the league in revenue, but Barrow struggled with high expenses. As reflected in table 13, the Yankees maintained a payroll of over $300,000, while no other team in the league exceeded $215,000. The trustees, struggling with the estate-tax obligation, could ill afford to sustain losses on the baseball team.

In July 1943 Barrow became peripherally involved in dispute with St. Louis Browns manager Luke Sewell. In the first game of a doubleheader in St. Louis, the Yankees led 2–1 heading into the bottom of the ninth. With Don Gutteridge on first, Milt Byrnes singled and Gutteridge reached third. When Lindell's wild throw from the outfield ended up in the Browns' dugout, Gutteridge trotted home. Byrnes had kept running as well, ending up on third. The umpire then awarded Byrnes home plate and the winning run. McCarthy correctly protested that a player is allowed only two bases from the last base he occupied at the time of the overthrow. Therefore, Byrnes, who had hit a single, should have remained at third. The other umpires agreed and recalled the Browns from the locker room to resume the game. When the Yankees held the Browns and went on to win in the eleventh inning, Sewell could not contain his irritation: "It's been my observation after twenty-one years in this league that the Yankees never have anything to fear from the umpires. They never have to worry about hitting at bad balls because they know the umpire won't call them."

Barrow immediately took umbrage at Sewell's comments. At an American League meeting shortly thereafter, St. Louis Browns owner Donald Barnes reportedly seconded Sewell's charge. Never one to back down from a confrontation, Barrow angrily denounced the allegation against the umpires and complained formally to American League president William Harridge. Harridge naturally supported his umpires, and Barnes soon smoothed things over with Barrow. A contrite Sewell ended the matter when he repudiated his accusation against the umpires and apologized to Barrow.

Once more the Yankees breezed to the pennant—their seventh in eight years—finishing thirteen and a half games ahead of the second-place Senators. The team again led the league in both runs scored and runs allowed. Spud Chandler won twenty against only four losses and recorded an ERA of 1.64. (It should be noted, however, that offense was down throughout baseball because the balata ball did not spring off the bat like a regular baseball.) For his performance the baseball writers named Chandler the league's Most Valuable Player. On offense Keller, Etten, and Gordon all turned in fine seasons. The thirty-six-year-old Dickey hit .351 while appearing in eighty-five games. In the World Series the Yankees gained a measure of revenge for 1942 as they dispatched the Cardinals four games to one.

After the first game of the World Series, Barrow suffered a heart attack. His physician did not immediately recognize the seriousness of his condition and merely restricted the seventy-five-year-old Barrow to rest at home. A couple of days later, with Barrow still seriously ailing, the doctor admitted him into the hospital in New Rochelle. Barrow spent over a month in the hospital and was forced to skip his annual sojourn in South Carolina with Yawkey. He finally returned home on November 24, just in time for Thanksgiving. After Barrow's discharge from the hospital, his doctors confined him to his home for another four weeks, and Barrow missed the winter meetings as well.

Barrow did not have to suffer alone, however; many baseball notables stopped by to visit and wish him well. He also received a number of gifts, some with strings attached. St. Petersburg's Al Lang sent him a basket of grapefruit with a note asking Barrow to lobby his fellow owners on the possibility of returning to Florida for spring training. Barrow did not return to his office until the second half of December and even then could not resume his full schedule for some time. His health problems also cost him a spot on a committee established that winter to discuss postwar planning.

As Barrow aged, he liked to maintain his ties to the "good old days." He had several old players, such as catcher Jack Warner and third baseman Arlie Latham, both retired before 1910, working at Yankee Stadium. Over the winter Barrow lost another of his longtime Yankees associates when traveling secretary Mark Roth passed away.

Two of Barrow's top priorities upon resuming his duties were re-signing McCarthy to a new three-year contract (at $37,500 per season) and selecting a new spring training location. Despite Lang's urging, Landis and the owners had little interest in challenging the government bureaucracy on travel. Asbury Park, however, had not worked out as well as hoped in 1943, so the Yankees shifted their spring training site to Atlantic City for 1944.

During the off-season the talent pool was further decimated when the government began removing the draft exemption from the 3-A classification. Now eligible for the draft, many either enlisted or sought war-related work. The changing manpower constraints made planning for the upcoming season futile. Projected lineups and pitching staffs changed weekly as players entered the armed forces. Purchasing or trading for a player made little sense when he could be gone at any time. Baseball executives, for the most part, had to passively watch as their fortunes for the upcoming season were determined by forces beyond their control.

That winter Barrow's old friend Boston Braves president Bob Quinn approached him regarding the possibility of Dickey assuming a player-manager role in Boston. Quinn offered little in exchange but hoped Barrow would allow Dickey to leave for the promotion to manager. Barrow refused on the entirely reasonable grounds that with the war-depleted player pool, Dickey was an extremely valuable asset, even at his advanced age. Before finalizing his decision, however, he was at least willing to consult with Dickey on the situation. "If I had insisted, I could have got my release," Dickey recalled.

Losses to the armed forces struck the Yankees particularly hard. During the off-season the team lost its three mainstays from the 1943 lineup: Dickey, Keller, and Gordon; not one of the 1942 regulars remained with the team. Of the 1943 regulars only Etten, Metheny, and Lindell returned in 1944. The pitching staff lost Chandler, Russo, and Murphy. Barrow and McCarthy could do little more than hope that their 4-F players, the best of whom were Donald and Stirnweiss, were better than those on the other clubs, and that they would get lucky with those with a riskier classification.

To ease the player shortage, St. Louis Browns general manager Bill De-Witt proposed allowing players classified 2-B, war-plant workers, to play on weekends. Rickey supported the plan, but Barrow ridiculed the suggestion:

"A man is either a Major League player or a war worker or a bricklayer. I think that using part-timers would demean big league ball. It would give us a semipro tone. The New York club wants none of it in any circumstances." Barrow further complained that the use of such players would require special permission from Landis. But Landis saw no need to rule on this proposal, and a couple of teams, most notably Washington and St. Louis, used otherwise-employed players.

With the complete turnover of rosters, no one really knew what to expect in 1944. For much of the season it was a four-team race between the Yankees, the Browns, the Tigers, and the Red Sox. In June with the club around .500, Barrow recognized that the Yankees might be a factor in the race but could use greater production from their left fielder. Barrow first targeted Hal Epps of the Browns. He believed he and Barnes had an understanding that the Yankees would have first shot at him in a trade. The Browns, however, perennial cellar dwellers, were in a pennant race for the first time in many years. Manager Luke Sewell resisted any move that might strengthen the Yankees, and he prevailed on Barnes to cut off trade discussions. As a second option, scout Bill Essick recommended thirty-four-year-old Hersh Martin, toiling in Milwaukee. Barrow purchased Martin, who debuted in late June and hit .302 over the remainder of the season.

As late as September 4 the Yankees gained a sliver of first place. Stirnweiss, now ensconced at second, Etten, and Lindell led the offense, and Borowy anchored the pitching staff. But the team fell off the pace in mid-September and finished six games behind the pennant-winning Browns. Both Barrow and McCarthy lauded the effort of what they considered an outmanned club. "Now, getting that lead back was one of the finest feats any Yankee club has accomplished," Barrow remarked in late September, "and I want to say right now that I take my hat off to this 1944 team, win or lose." He later went so far as to write a letter to the players praising them for their effort, an uncommon recognition from a man who typically would not settle for anything less than first place.

In mid-September a Yankees' night game in Philadelphia had to be postponed because the field was unplayable; an earlier professional football exhibition game in the rain had ripped it up. Barrow, in a foul mood as he watched his team slip out of the pennant race, angrily complained about the field conditions. Barrow's irritation did not subside after the season. At the winter meetings he sponsored a resolution prohibiting football games in baseball stadiums until the end of the baseball season, adding that for teams eligible for the World Series football games would be barred until the conclusion of the Series. The magnates adopted Barrow's recommendation along with a further expansion of night baseball.

After missing the previous fall hunting season because of his heart attack, in October Barrow returned to South Carolina to hunt and fish with Yawkey. On this excursion, however, Barrow became infested with chiggers. To remove them he tried a number of home remedies, including applying nail polish to various body parts.

In late November 1944 Commissioner Landis died, leaving baseball leaderless at a time of increasing uncertainty. Although the war was progressing favorably, the Western Allies were stalled at the German border. In the Pacific the invasions of well-fortified Pacific Islands, the Philippines, and the Japanese home islands still loomed. Some lawmakers and bureaucrats were pushing to reevaluate the service exemption of many 4-FS. Others discussed the possibility of using 4-FS, unfit for military service, in labor battalions. Furthermore, the Selective Service ruled that all men between the ages of twenty-six and thirty-seven, if not working in an essential industry, were subject to reclassification. Baseball magnates were uncertain what type of season they could expect in 1945. Barrow generally kept a low profile when questioned about all the lofty-sounding, ambiguous government edicts from various departments and bureaucrats. He felt it made little sense to complain publicly and, in effect, denigrate the very product they were putting on the field.

The opportunities to bolster one's team in the 1944–45 off-season were even more confounded by the uncertainties created by the war than in the previous two. Nevertheless, Barrow continued to maneuver wherever possible. Herb Pennock, now general manager of the Phillies, recounted Barrow's pursuit of once-feared slugger Jimmie Foxx. Well past his prime, Foxx had seen only minimal action in 1944 but offered at least the possibility of usefulness for 1945. Barrow approached his old pitcher and nonchalantly asked for Foxx's address on the pretense that he had some old business with him. When Pennock told Barrow that he had already signed him for 1945, Barrow "suddenly lost interest in Foxx."

24. "Over His Dead Body"

Not long after Jacob Ruppert's death, it became clear to the trustees of his estate that they had an estate-tax problem on their hands. Magnifying their predicament, the taxing authorities placed a much higher value on the estate than did the trustees. For example, the government valued the baseball franchise and all its holdings at roughly $5 million as opposed to around $2.4 million by the estate. The estate chose to litigate the issue, which also had the advantage of postponing any tax payment until a resolution had been achieved. Regardless of the outcome, it was now clear that either the team or the brewery would have to be sold to pay the estate tax. Because the team was more liquid than the brewery and theoretically a less-stable income generator, the Yankees organization seemed the more likely disposition.

As the dispute dragged on, the three trustees of Ruppert's estate, George Ruppert, Byron Clark Jr., and H. Garrison Sillick Jr., grew weary of the wrangling in which they had no financial stake. Furthermore, they had little desire to oversee all the complicated negotiations inherent in the sale of the team. On July 29, 1941, as permitted in the trust documents, they turned the administration of the estate over to the Manufacturers Trust Company. Barrow stayed on as president of the Yankees, but from now on he effectively had an unwanted and unanticipated partner: a financial institution looking to sell.

After the attack on Pearl Harbor, non-war-related economic activity quickly came to a standstill. Barrow and Manufacturers Trust both received several inquiries, but none at a price they felt reasonable. In 1943 Larry MacPhail, now unemployed in baseball and serving in the War Department, put together a ten-person syndicate to try to purchase the team. His lineup of investors included Del Webb and Dan Topping.

A playboy in his youth, Topping had been an excellent amateur athlete. He came from considerable family wealth, and after a couple of years working for a living, he "retired" to a life befitting a wealthy sportsman. He first moved into professional sports ownership in 1934, when he purchased an interest in the Brooklyn Tigers of the fledgling National Football League.

Because the team played in Ebbets Field, Topping was effectively a tenant of MacPhail's once MacPhail took over the Dodgers in early 1938. The two became friendly. When they ran into each other in California during the war—MacPhail was there on War Department business, Topping with the Marine Corps—MacPhail invited him to join his syndicate. Topping was also a logical investor because of his ownership in the Brooklyn football team. At the time he was having difficulty negotiating a lease renewal with Dodgers president Branch Rickey. Assuming he could get permission from the NFL to move to the Bronx (the New York football Giants played in Manhattan and controlled the rights to the area), owning Yankee Stadium would give him a playing venue he could control.

MacPhail first met Webb, a Phoenix-based self-made millionaire in the construction business, in Washington during the war. MacPhail worked as an assistant to Under Secretary of War Robert Patterson, while Webb frequently traveled to Washington to negotiate war-related construction work. At the time Webb was considering the purchase of the Pacific Coast League's Oakland Oaks team for seventy-five thousand dollars. When MacPhail contacted him regarding the Yankees opportunity, he quickly changed his focus. Other investors included Chicago taxi-cab magnate John Hertz, New York sanitation commissioner Bill Carey, and Ed Wetzel.

Barrow hated the idea of the boisterous, aggressive, and spotlight-seeking MacPhail taking control of "his" team. He went so far as to state that MacPhail would gain control of the Yankees only "over his [Barrow's] dead body."

MacPhail offered $2.8 million for 96.88 percent of the stock, $2.5 million for the 86.88 percent owned by the three Ruppert beneficiaries, and $300,000 for the 10 percent controlled by Barrow. The remaining 3.12 percent was owned by George Ruppert and two others. In February 1944, despite Barrow's distaste for MacPhail, acceptance of the offer by the trust company appeared imminent. Barrow managed to delay the sale, most likely because the estate had received another extension on its tax bill. Commissioner Landis helped slow MacPhail when he ruled that Hertz, who was involved in horse racing, was persona non grata in baseball ownership. Landis's edict forced MacPhail to restructure his ownership group.

The potential sale to MacPhail depressed Barrow. He knew the franchise and its Minor League operations were worth much more than $2.8 million. In 1923, when Ruppert had bought out Huston, the team had been valued at $2.5 million. Since then almost all profits had been reinvested in the club, revenues had increased dramatically, many championships had been won, and a valuable Minor League system had been developed. Plus Barrow had returned the team to profitability in 1944 as the Yankees earned over $150,000. After all his sweat and stress turning the franchise into one of the most dominant in American sports, how could its value have grown by only $300,000? And, personally, to receive nothing more than his original investment after nearly twenty-five years of building the premier organization in baseball disheartened him.

His delay in hand, Barrow sought to drive up the price or find another buyer. Unfortunately, finding a willing buyer with available cash under wartime circumstances was highly problematic. In one scheme he hoped to steer the franchise to his friend Tom Yawkey. This plan suffered from several shortcomings, most notably that Yawkey would first have to find a buyer for his Red Sox. Also, Yawkey's finances were potentially in limbo due to a recent divorce. Barrow also held out hope that James Farley could reformulate his syndicate, but that idea, too, came to nothing.

With little hope of either an alternate buyer or a delay until the end of the war and a reinvigoration of the civilian economy—which still seemed a long way off—the trust company was becoming impatient. Furthermore, Webb and Topping, both now awakened to the availability of the team and their own interest in acquiring it, continued to pursue the club. The trust company attempted to reinstate MacPhail's original terms by contacting Webb. They let him know that the estate might now be willing to sell on the original terms. The estate was also actively selling off some of its real-estate holdings, but the war had depressed prices in real estate as well. Only a fraction of the tax burden could be raised through the liquidation of real-estate assets.

Independent of Webb, Topping learned through his societal connections that the trust company was growing impatient. In late 1944, when Topping again encountered MacPhail in New York, he proposed that they try to revive the deal. MacPhail needed little prompting, and the two decided that they would simplify their proposed ownership by narrowing the syndicate to include only Webb in their re-formed venture. Topping, through his numerous connections, took the lead in contacting Barrow. Topping's fa-

ther and Harry Silleck had been friends, and through Garrison he became
friendly with Barrow's daughter, Audrey. She acted as an intermediary and
set up a meeting between Barrow and Topping. Once Barrow realized the
speed with which Manufacturers Trust planned to dispose of the franchise,
he merely hoped to preserve as much of his legacy as possible. He eagerly
met one-on-one with both Topping and Webb. With both he stressed the
importance of maintaining the status quo and running a first-class, well-
respected, championship organization. Both men gave him enough assurance that he could sell without too much trepidation—although he had little choice, in any case.

In late January 1945, MacPhail, Webb, and Topping finally purchased
the team. They put $250,000 down with the remainder to follow in March.
Prior to their final payment, the trio also agreed to purchase the remaining 3.12 percent interest from George Ruppert and associates, giving them
complete ownership of the team. Webb and Topping supplied the majority
of the capital, and MacPhail became president under a ten-year contract.
Barrow did not collect the windfall he once must have dreamed of for his
twenty-year investment in the Yankees. Based on the price of $305,000 re-
established three years earlier, he netted little if anything for his interest.

The final transfer of control occurred in late February. Barrow, who had
been working under a three-year contract, was given a so-called advisory role
and a new, fancy-sounding title, chairman of the board of directors. For his
new position, the Yankees' ownership awarded Barrow a five-year contract,
cancelable after two for a termination payment of one year's salary.

At the time of the purchase, both MacPhail and Barrow publicly proclaimed their ongoing interest in having Barrow be a part of the decision-
making team. But both men understood that this was now MacPhail's club,
and Barrow was little more than a seventy-six-year-old figurehead from the
past. The Yankees staged a newsreel film with Barrow and MacPhail to
commemorate the team's ownership transfer. Barrow, in his first speaking
appearance in a movie, acted with his usual bluntness. He did not particularly care for his prompted lines wishing MacPhail good luck and added:
"That's well enough but premature. I ought to tell Larry I wish him luck
in digging up a team [due to wartime depletion] before I wish him a flag."
MacPhail, in a generous mood after his acquisition responded, "Thanks,
Ed, for the congratulations and wishing the team wins the flag, but first we

must win the war, and then I hope to get as many pennants in the next fifteen years as you did in the last fifteen."

Baseball's Major League Agreement, concluded in January 1921, had created the office of commissioner and was due to expire in January 1946. Most observers expected the owners to wait until implementation of a new Major League agreement before selecting a new commissioner. At the 1944–45 winter meetings on the heels of Landis's death, the owners decided to temporarily reintroduce the three-man commission. In its reincarnation, the commission consisted of the league presidents and Leslie O'Connor, secretary to the commissioner's office and Landis's right-hand man. Termed the Advisory Council, the new commission would oversee baseball until a new commissioner could be picked. To begin that process, the magnates appointed a ten-man committee to vet the candidates.

Essentially leaderless just as the manpower crisis was reaching its zenith, many owners felt they needed a stronger voice in Washington. With the potential loss of 4-Fs and other rumors of further government inroads into baseball's limited personnel, the owners discussed submitting to a "sports coordinator," a quasi-governmental administrator who could represent baseball more formally within the government. Barrow blasted this idea, which would mean yielding some authority to Washington: "Baseball has proved that it can regulate itself and requires no outside political assistance."

The owners soon abandoned the idea of a coordinator and instead opted to renew the Major League agreement and select a new commissioner much more quickly; they moved the date for resolution up to early February 1945. Of course, getting twelve of sixteen men to agree on anything is never a simple task (a new commissioner required the consent of 75 percent of the owners). The selection process was further complicated by the split between those who wanted a baseball man and those who preferred an outsider, such as a prominent politician or judge. Barrow fell in the former camp; he recommended four candidates he could support: National League president Ford Frick, American League president William Harridge, Cincinnati Red general manager Warren Giles, and American League director of broadcasting Louis McAvoy. Behind the scenes another insider, Leslie O'Connor, campaigned for the position. Of the five, most observers felt Frick had the best chance. When Barrow remarked that an outsider would be nothing more than "a man for mere window dressing," it was the first public utterance on the commissioner controversy from a baseball executive.

Although MacPhail's group put the team under contract at the end of January, Barrow remained in control for several weeks thereafter, pending final payment and turnover of the organization. Thus Barrow represented the team at the early February meetings at which the magnates hoped to select a commissioner and ratify the new agreement. As the decisive meeting drew near, Barrow himself generated some interest as a possible candidate. But Barrow, now seventy-six, professed little interest in the job: "It's ten years too late. I am not a candidate."

The magnates ratified the new Major League Agreement, but agreeing on a commissioner was much more difficult. The debate centered on Frick, who had become the consensus choice for those wishing to promote an insider. After a spirited debate, Frick could garner no more than ten or eleven of the required twelve votes. His opponents believed that an outsider, free of the many entrenched relationships within baseball's boardrooms and with some clout in Washington, offered a better solution. But at the meeting they had no compromise candidate to put forward.

The failure to elect a new commissioner irked both Barrow and MacPhail. To move the process along, Barrow removed his objection to an outsider and even began to acknowledge its merits: "I now confess that I followed Judge Landis too blindly and was persuaded by him to adopt the wrong angle—that in no circumstances were we to approach the government in Washington. I have been won over to the belief that we have been too retiring. We must pick a commissioner and send him to the capital to holler now." To restart the selection process, a more streamlined four-man committee of two National League and two American League owners was established to cull the huge list of potential candidates.

To break the stalemate, the owners scheduled a meeting in Cleveland on April 24, 1945. As a fallback, the magnates considered appointing a temporary commissioner to serve until the war ended—most now believed it was in its final phase—at which time additional nominees would free up. Shortly before the Cleveland meeting, American League president William Harridge offered Barrow the temporary commissionership should the owners be unable to agree on a candidate.

Barrow declined due to his age and health; he complained of arthritis and rheumatism. As evidence of his restlessness and discontent in "retirement," Barrow irresponsibly announced Harridge's proposition to the press. Furthermore, in its characterization he did not qualify his remarks with the caveats that the offer was both temporary and conditional. To correct the record, Harridge was forced to publicly acknowledge the offer to Barrow and correct Barrow's characterization of the offer by adding the necessary qualifications.

At the Cleveland meeting the owners, in an upset, elected U.S. senator Albert "Happy" Chandler from Kentucky. Philadelphia's Connie Mack was so sure no decision would be made that he did not bother to attend and sent his son instead. St. Louis Browns president Donald Barnes, one of the four nominating committee members, intended to recommend selecting a temporary, six-month stopgap. MacPhail cornered Barnes and berated him for his indecision and the committee's lack of good alternatives. After further discussion among the full assemblage, the owners decided to try to elect a commissioner despite the apparent lack of agreement. The committee offered its six candidates, consisting of five outsiders and Frick. MacPhail demanded to know why Chandler was not on the list, and the owners agreed to add him.

To short-circuit a potentially fruitless discussion and gauge general interest, the owners began by each ranking his top five choices. Chandler finished no lower than third on any ballot. In the discussion that followed, the other hopefuls were eliminated for various reasons until only Chandler and Robert Hannegan, head of the Democratic National Committee, remained. In the first runoff, Chandler led 11–5, one shy of the twelve votes needed. After the count New York Giants owner Horace Stoneham announced he was willing to switch his vote. Thus, in the penultimate ballot, Chandler received the twelve votes necessary for election. With his election assured, the owners called for one final vote so that they could announce Chandler's unanimous election as the new commissioner.

Retirement started out painfully for Barrow. In June 1945 he had a tonsillectomy and his last three teeth pulled. He was also forced to watch as the Yankees' owners approved spending half a million dollars to light Yankee Stadium for the 1946 season. In spite of his lofty title, Barrow could be little more than a spectator as manager Joe McCarthy melted down and was replaced by Bill Dickey. Frustrated and tired of a job with no responsibility, Barrow officially resigned on December 31, 1946, two years into his contract as chairman. As called for in his contract, Barrow received one year's salary as severance. After more than twenty-five years in the organization, he was no longer a Yankee.

Barrow, now seventy-eight years old, and Fannie remained in decent health. Barrow had no hobbies outside of hunting and fishing, and these activities were becoming increasingly difficult. He quickly grew restless in retirement. In 1948 the *Sporting News* offered him a commission-based job selling advertising. They naturally hoped Barrow's celebrity and baseball stories would appeal to the ad buyers of various corporations. Not surprisingly, given his lack of tact and political savvy in dealing with his peers, a sales job neither appealed to nor suited Barrow.

One evening a couple of years later in New York, Barrow ran into his one-time amateur applicant Hank Greenberg, now a Cleveland Indians executive. Both were leaving Toots Shor's, one of New York's most fashionable restaurants, particularly for athletes. The nightspot had just previewed a film of the 1948 World Series, which Cleveland had won. As they left the restaurant, the two began talking, and Barrow complained of his restlessness in retirement. When Greenberg suggested a position might be available with the Indians, Barrow jumped at the opportunity. Greenberg must have been surprised at Barrow's eagerness; he replied he would consult with majority owner Bill Veeck Jr. That the conservative Barrow would gladly accept a position under the maverick Veeck testifies to Barrow's discontentment in retirement. Typical of many casual conversations after a night out on the town, in the end no position ever materialized.

As one outlet for his baseball fix, Barrow could still occasionally enjoy the limelight at various Yankees affairs. After the war, the Yankees organization began to appreciate and celebrate its storied history. Because Barrow had been one of the key contributors to its past successes, the Yankees often invited him to their commemorative functions. In April 1947 he attended Babe Ruth Day in Yankee Stadium. At the 1948 old-timers game, Barrow was introduced to an ovation and received a commemorative watch from Dan Topping. The Yankees' recognition of Barrow culminated at the old-timers game on May 13, 1950. As befitted the guest of honor, the game celebrated Barrow's enormous contributions to the Yankees organization. During the festivities many old players were invited back and given tokens of thanks. In one of the concluding ceremonies, Topping presented Barrow with a plaque in recognition of his service to the organization. At the dinner honoring him, Barrow received further salutes along with a television set, an expensive, exotic gift in 1950.

After three years running the Yankees, MacPhail began to crumple beneath the pressure and constant limelight. Near the end of the 1947 season, he arranged an initial public stock offering of shares in the New York Yankees franchise through a New York investment bank. MacPhail and the bankers worked out an offering that would make just under 50 percent of the club available to the public. The bankers estimated that they would raise about $3 million, implying a franchise value of roughly $6 million. MacPhail contrived the transaction to cash out part of his investment. Topping and Webb, however, had no desire to come under the scrutiny and reporting requirements of the public market. The two quickly resolved to buy out their partner. Just before the start of the World Series, Topping and Webb reached an agreement to acquire MacPhail's one-third interest for around $2 million, yielding him a nice profit over his initial investment, most of which he had borrowed. Despite selling his ownership interest, MacPhail would remain as president and de facto general manager. Barrow could not help but notice MacPhail's quick profit of over $1 million in stark contrast to his own lack of return after twenty years.

The agreement to sell did not calm MacPhail. Just the opposite, the decision to surrender his interest in the Yankees made him even more agitated and erratic. Rumors persisted that MacPhail feuded with other members of the Yankees' executive team, most of whom had been in place for many years and were protégés of Barrow and Ruppert. MacPhail's maniacal behavior culminated with his breakdown at the celebration dinner in the Biltmore Hotel after winning the 1947 World Series. He stumbled drunk around the dining room, alternating between bouts of sentimental crying and irrational raging. He saved his vilest epithets to denigrate Brooklyn's Branch Rickey, whose club the Yankees had just defeated. When John MacDonald, MacPhail's former traveling secretary in Brooklyn (against whom

MacPhail still harbored a grudge for a magazine story), defended Rickey, MacPhail punched him in the eye.

MacPhail next lurched over to Barrow's table, where Barrow was enjoying the celebration dinner with Fannie, Audrey, relative L. John Himes, restaurant entrepreneur Bob Cobb, and George Weiss and his wife. MacPhail started cursing Weiss and criticizing his work. Barrow's party watched in horror as MacPhail worked himself into a frenzy; he demanded a decision from Weiss regarding his future with the club within forty-eight hours: "Make up your mind what you are going to do." Weiss remained as calm as possible and suggested, "Larry, I don't want to make a decision here tonight. We have all been drinking. I would like to wait until tomorrow and discuss this with you." MacPhail, in no condition to be mollified, responded by firing Weiss on the spot. As MacPhail walked away, Weiss's wife chased after him to appeal for her husband's job, but he just ignored her. A shaken Weiss went outside to cool down and commiserate with Krichell. Weiss's wife returned to the table in tears.

Topping finally seized control of the situation. He tried to calm MacPhail only to be told that he had "been born with a silver spoon in [his] mouth." Topping then guided the still-crazed MacPhail into the kitchen, where the two huddled alone. After calming him somewhat, Topping ushered MacPhail out a side door so he could gather himself. Topping and Webb next accompanied Weiss to his hotel room to reassure him of his position with the Yankees. MacPhail actually returned later, still combative but no longer unglued. Webb and Topping, naturally, had no intention of leaving their $6 million operation in MacPhail's hands and quickly worked to quietly terminate his contract with the Yankees. To run the club the duo promoted Weiss to general manager, and Topping assumed the presidency.

The National Baseball Hall of Fame elected its first five immortals in 1936, and fans have been debating the merits of their favorites ever since. For the next twenty-five or so years, the selection process fluctuated among several schemes before finally settling down to a more stable system. During the first half of this trial-and-error period, Barrow actively shaped the process, first as an elector and later as a candidate. For many years Barrow belonged to the small committee empowered to grant Hall membership. Unfortunately, Barrow's committee did little to distinguish itself. In fact, it spawned much of the muddle over admittance standards that plague the Hall to this day.

From the beginning the Hall of Fame delegated the election of players to a select group of sportswriters to be overseen by the Baseball Writers' Association of America. The Hall initially restricted the writers' scope to those players active after 1900. Over the first few years writers intelligently elected a dozen of the twentieth century's best players. To accommodate the early pioneers, a committee led by Landis and the two league presidents, Ford Frick and William Harridge, added seven "builders of baseball," only one of whom, Morgan Bulkeley, was a poor choice. Many older fans agitated for the cohort still unrepresented: star players of the nineteenth century. To rectify this oversight, in 1939 Landis, Frick, and Harridge, in consultation with select writers and baseball executives, appointed six nineteenth-century stars. Overall they named an eclectic half-dozen, with one material but understandable miscalculation (Candy Cummings, reputed originator of the curve ball). To filter and appoint the remaining deserving players from the nineteenth century, Landis appointed a small committee that included Barrow, Connie Mack, Clark Griffith, and Bob Quinn.

Unfortunately, he created a flawed committee. Landis's choices consisted of the oldest active executives in the hope that they could accurately remember and assess players from the nineteenth century. All the executives were fully employed in baseball, however, and had little time or energy left for the difficult task of conscientiously sifting through the many deserving candidates. In retrospect the committee clearly needed a younger, energetic writer or executive to provide research and direct discussion.

In fact, the old-timers' committee never even managed to meet. Barrow and his fellow elderly members had little interest in traveling to a meeting and then sequestering themselves to decide on new members for the Hall of Fame. The apathy of the committee can be further seen in its response to a lobbying effort on behalf of Clark Griffith's Hall induction. Barrow, Mack, and Quinn—probably to avoid taking a stand on the merits of Griffith's qualifications—simply pled ignorance regarding their membership on the committee. Furthermore, the exact makeup of the old-timers' committee beyond the four executives remained ambiguous. In 1941 the retiring president of the Baseball Writers Association noted that Landis had told him that the committee also included ex-National League president John Heydler and retired umpire Bob Emslie. An authoritative source also placed veteran New York sportswriter Sid Mercer on the committee. In any case, the old-timers barely acknowledged the committee's existence, let alone actually selected anyone.

This lack of action would not have been such a problem if the writers had been electing anyone. In December 1939 they added Lou Gehrig by acclimation and then limited the voting to every third year. In 1942 the writers voted in just a single player, Rogers Hornsby, despite a long list of Hall of Fame–worthy players. Thus, as of mid-1944, the Hall of Fame had inducted only one new player during the 1940s. This lack of new blood exasperated the Hall's trustees by retarding the enthusiasm and excitement the directors were hoping to achieve.

In August, Landis tried to reenergize the old-timers' committee to its task. He appointed a new Permanent Hall of Fame Committee to name deserving players from the nineteenth century; he further verbally instructed the new committee that he wanted them to select ten old-time players. He also gave this new committee control over the rules and procedures for the Hall; in other words, it would be in charge of fine-tuning the voting rules to create the right balance between being too restrictive—as had been the case with the writers to date—and too liberal. In addition to Barrow, Mack, Quinn, and Mercer, Landis added Boston sportswriter Mel Webb. More importantly, he named National Baseball Museum (the technical owner of the Hall) president and financial backer Stephen Clark as chairman, and museum treasurer Paul Kerr as secretary.

The death of Landis in November finally provided the impetus for the committee to convene. In December they came together to elect Landis to the Hall and publicly announced their mission to name deserving old-timers. In Clark and Kerr the reconstituted committee now possessed the driving force to encourage meetings and elect players. Unfortunately, it still lacked an energetic, research-minded writer or junior executive, such as Ernest Lanigan, to provide the necessary factual correctives to the members' memories of players over forty years earlier.

In April 1945 Barrow hosted the committee in the Yankee Stadium offices, after the writers again failed to elect anyone. The 1945 list of nominees from the writer's ballots contained fifty-four players who would eventually become Hall of Famers, yet the writers did not elect a single one. This created the perception that the writers were being unnecessarily restrictive, although in fact the lack of new inductees resulted from a flawed voting system.

To be elected a player needed to be named on 75 percent of the ballots. Each writer was supposed to vote for ten candidates, and for the most part they did. The 247 eligible writers in 1945 cast 2,496 votes, almost exactly 10 per voter (it appears a couple managed to get in an extra vote). The problem, as Bill James has highlighted, is that with so many candidates, it is almost impossible for a player to be named on 75 percent of the ballots, even when each included ten players. To rectify the situation the committee addressed both issues: it inducted ten players and modified the voting rules. Unfortunately, it addressed neither particularly well.

The committee inducted seven players who had finished their careers after 1900 and were therefore also eligible through the writers. The seven had finished sixth, eighth, ninth, twelfth, fourteenth, fifteenth, and sixteenth in the 1945 writer voting. Although the selected players may not all have been great choices by today's more-sophisticated standards, all fit the nebulous definition of a Hall of Famer as it evolved over the next forty years: the top thirty-three candidates in the 1945 writers' election are all now in the Hall of Fame. The problem with the committee's selections was not so much who they were but rather the impression that the committee was usurping the authority of the writers by arbitrarily inducting several players the writers had just rejected.

The committee also named three exclusively nineteenth-century players: Dan Brouthers (who actually returned to play in two games in 1904), Mike (King) Kelly, and Jim O'Rourke. Brouthers was a great player; Kelly was the 1880s version of Joe Namath: a huge celebrity living the high life with a short but lofty peak. O'Rourke was a more whimsical choice: an excellent player, but certainly no better than a host of other nineteenth-century stars. In sum, many deserving players were available to the committee; they selected players who would have eventually made the Hall, but not the best ones available. The committee erred by neither objectively researching the players themselves nor appointing a qualified research assistant to review the data.

The committee also tinkered with the writers' voting process. To limit the number of eligible players, they instituted a preelection nominating procedure in which each writer would submit ten players. The top twenty players would be placed on the final ballot; the writers would be required to vote for five. To be elected, a player would still have to receive 75 percent of the vote on this final ballot. The committee also scheduled elections for every year instead of every third year. Unfortunately, this scheme failed as well. All twenty-one players on the 1946 slate (two tied for the twentieth spot) would eventually be inducted into the Hall of Fame. In the January election, however, no single player could command 75 percent of the vote.

At their meeting in April 1946, Barrow and the committee named eleven new Hall of Famers, including seven of the twenty-one on the writers' ballot. From that slate they essentially named the seven players with the highest vote totals who had played before 1910 (with the exception of Three Finger Brown, who finished sixth). Again, all were reasonable selections given the rough standard that existed over the next forty years. But the fact that none was admitted by the writers amplified the overall confusion and the writers' dissatisfaction with the process. The committee also added Eddie Plank, intelligently picking up a good player overlooked by the writers, and Jesse Burkett, a reasonable selection who had hit over .400 a couple of times in the 1890s. The committee seriously erred, however, with its other two choices. Tommy McCarthy was little more than an average nineteenth-century outfielder and may be the worst player in the Hall of Fame. The other, Jack Chesbro, who had played nearly his entire career after 1900, received only one vote from the nominating poll. In other words, only 1 of the 202 writers who sent in ten nominations felt Chesbro should even be on the final ballot. The committee fell short on two counts: first, it selected only one true nineteenth-century player and therefore appeared to be in competition with the writers' vote; and second, with two highly questionable selections, the committee essentially set the bar so low that one could now argue for almost any long-career, above-average player.

Kerr advocated within the committee that the Hall be reserved exclusively for players. This seems a peculiar position given that the Hall already included a number of executives and managers. Nevertheless, in 1946 the committee, convinced that nonplayers should and would be restricted in the future, named an Honor Roll of twelve writers, eleven executives, five managers, and eleven umpires. Ignored or unknown today, the Honor Roll created no significant lasting negative consequences, but at the time it sowed additional confusion. What was the relative status of the members of the Honor Roll? Were new names to be added on an ongoing basis? The committee further compromised itself by naming three of its own to the Honor Roll: Barrow and Quinn to the executives' list and Harry Cross (who took Mercer's spot when he died) to the writers' section. Little ever became of the Honor Roll, and the committee soon pretended it had never existed.

For 1947 the committee again changed the voting rules. Many members felt that the early twentieth-century players were not receiving a fair shot in the writers' vote. Therefore, it made two more changes to the writers' procedures: (1) it limited voting eligibility to only those writers who had been in the writers' association for at least ten years, and (2) selections were restricted to players whose careers had ended after 1920; the committee would be responsible for those prior to 1920. In fact, the writers had treated the old-time players surprisingly well in the voting. In 1946 early twentieth-century stars finished first, second, and fourth, ahead of more-recent and better players such as Mickey Cochrane, Lefty Grove, and Carl Hubbell. Despite their unfounded rationale, the new rules helped by limiting the pool of players eligible through the writers. This made it more likely they would name the same players on their ballots. The nominating process was also now made a part of the actual voting. If any players were named on at least 75 percent of the initial poll, they were granted Hall membership and no follow-up election was held. If no one was elected, the top twenty would be resubmitted to the writers, and they could vote for five of the twenty. With this reduction in the number of eligible players, the writers finally elected four players to the Hall in 1947.

Barrow and his fellow aging baseball executives had little energy or inclination to carry on as overseers for the Hall of Fame. After 1946 the group rarely, if ever, met and conducted its business by mail. The committee made no Hall of Fame selections in 1947 or 1948. When they finally admitted Three Finger Brown and Kid Nichols in 1949—two deserving choices—they carried out the entire voting process by mail. The committee then disintegrated.

Clark and Kerr, as the Hall's representatives, recognized that the committee needed to be reenergized. Accordingly, in the summer of 1953, on behalf of the Hall of Fame's board of directors, Kerr announced the formation of a new eleven-man "committee on veterans" to be chaired by *Sporting News* publisher J. G. Taylor Spink. Clark and Kerr, who stayed on as secretary to the new committee, limited the committee to the selection of old-time inductees only; the Hall's board of directors reclaimed the rule-making and voting-policy functions. A new directive also extended the period of time a player must be retired before becoming eligible from one to five years.

The board tasked the new Veterans Committee with promptly electing two players, two umpires, and two managers from a list of seventy nominees. To narrow the list for the meeting, Kerr directed each committee member to rank his top ten for each of the three categories. For the manager classification, Barrow clearly led the field: he received seven first-place votes and three seconds. When the committee met on September 28, it quickly named Barrow to the Hall of Fame. After deciding on Barrow, the committee struggled before finally settling on a second manager. Barrow's credentials as a Hall of Fame manager are marginal at best. But the committee principally wanted to honor him for his role as architect of the Yankees' thirteen pennants and ten World Series championships. Barrow's ego and self-worth were completely wrapped up in his baseball success. It is impossible to overstate what his election meant to the eighty-five-year-old Barrow. Fannie observed that being chosen for the Hall "kept him alive longer than he would have lived otherwise."

Meanwhile, as the Second World War drew to a close, Barrow moved to 367 Locust Avenue in Rye, New York. He had earned an upper-middle-class income for the past twenty-five years and had accumulated some savings, but he also continued to have bad luck on several of his investments. In the early 1940s, after making nine years of payments on an annuity contract to the Fidelity Assurance Association, he learned the company was insolvent. Fidelity had been based in Barrow's old stomping grounds of Wheeling, West Virginia, and the contract had undoubtedly been sold to him by a one-time associate. The West Virginia insurance commissioner's office placed the company into receivership, and in 1942 it sent Barrow a letter letting him know that he had a claim for the $7,447 cash value of his annuity. After writing off the entire amount, two years later Barrow was relieved to receive sixty cents on the dollar of his annuity.

Table 18 lays out Barrow's earnings after joining the Yankees. By the late 1920s Barrow was making twenty-seven thousand dollars a year, a healthy salary for the era. Ruppert soon raised his salary to thirty thousand dollars but cut it back to twenty-five thousand during the Depression. While Ruppert was alive, Barrow earned slightly less than McCarthy, which surely grated on his pride, although he never showed it publicly. After he became president, the board bumped his pay to thirty-five thousand dollars, where it stayed until he retired several years later. Although he obviously no longer earned a salary after retirement, Barrow still received a significant income. He received his termination payment, spread over the first couple of years after he left the Yankees; he also had enough savings and investments to provide for a comfortable retirement.

Often a person who has a gruff exterior is assumed to have a generous heart—the "tough on the outside, but soft on the inside" cliché. If Barrow had a generous side, he showed it through his treatment of friends and old ballplayers; he did not donate much money to charitable causes. As indicated by his tax returns, he declared surprisingly few charitable deductions. For example, in 1942 when Barrow earned over $35,000, his charitable deductions totaled $166. And that year was not unique; in 1938 he listed only $105 in charitable deductions.

Aside from the occasional Yankees' tribute and press interview comparing the modern game to the good old days, after retirement Barrow missed the day-to-day association with baseball that had consumed his life for so long. Barrow and Fannie also worried about Audrey, whose life remained troubled. She and Silleck divorced after the war. Shortly thereafter Audrey tried marriage for a fourth time with F. Culver Shafer, manager of the Rye office of a Westchester-based real-estate firm. Tragically, in August 1950 Shafer died in their home of a heart ailment, widowing Audrey for a second time.

The following July, still despondent from the death of her husband, Audrey died after falling or jumping from her eleventh-floor apartment.

A copy of Barrow's recent autobiography, inscribed: "To my daughter Audrey Barrow Shafer, May 25, 1951"—not a particularly warm dedication—was found in her apartment. Furthermore—as far as I can tell—Barrow never referred to her in his autobiography, which could only have exacerbated her anguish.

In late 1951 Barrow's health began to fail. On January 1, 1952, he was admitted to United Hospital in Port Chester, New York, with "hemorrhages and other complications." Two weeks later he underwent a prostatic operation. Barrow convalesced at home for the remainder of 1952 and the start of 1953. On July 7, 1953, he was rehospitalized for emergency cancer surgery, which was only nominally successful. Barrow remained hospitalized until November, when he lapsed into a coma. He briefly regained consciousness, but at 8:35 in the evening on December 15, with his wife at his side, Barrow passed away in the Port Chester hospital.

Barrow's funeral took place on December 19 at the St. Thomas Protestant Episcopal Church in New York. Numerous baseball executives, players, ex-players, umpires, baseball writers, and local dignitaries came to pay their final respects. Baseball commissioner Ford Frick and American League president William Harridge led the honorary pallbearers, which included a long list of former players and associates. The funeral was followed with the burial at the Kensico Cemetery in Westchester, New York.

Several years after Barrow's death, Fannie was forced out of her apartment because of financial problems. Barrow had not left a large estate, but it should have been sufficient to support his widow. One story reported that some of the securities in her portfolio collapsed in value. In any case, Dan Topping and Tom Yawkey agreed to provide her with an allowance of $1,000 per month for the remainder of her life. They expected to make the payment anonymously, but when the press learned of it, Fannie's stipend became public.

On April 15, 1954, before the home opener, the Yankees honored Barrow in a tribute like one previously accorded Jacob Ruppert. The team dedicated a plaque to Barrow on the center field wall of Yankee Stadium, adjacent to Ruppert's and right behind the monuments to Gehrig and Ruth.

Several years after he retired, Barrow and long-time rival Branch Rickey were sitting at the same table at a dinner of Major League executives and writers. When one of the writers mentioned a compliment Rickey had recently received on his own legendary baseball acumen, Rickey graciously accepted the tribute and then pointed across the table at Barrow:

> *That fellow sitting across the table is the smartest man who ever was in baseball. I will take this glass to prove my point. [Rickey held up an empty champagne glass as a prop.] I adjudge this glass to be perfect in appearance, of excellent material and sound and exquisite construction. Now if I am a connoisseur of glassware, you accept my opinion of it. I am an expert. I have spoken. Now mark the distinction between Mr. Barrow and myself. I have said this is a fine glass. It is Mr. Barrow, however, who could tell you far better than I whether this table, with its silverware, its glasses, its china, and its floral decorations, is properly laid out. He knows whether it is balanced or not. That is the difference between Mr. Barrow and myself. That is why I say there has never been a smarter baseball man than Mr. Barrow. He knows what a club needs to achieve balance, what a club needs to become a pennant winner. I, perhaps, can judge the part, but Mr. Barrow can judge the whole.*

Appendix

Table 1. Estimated Salaries, 1897

	Youngsters	*Veterans*
National League	$1,050–1,500	up to $3,000
Eastern League	$600–1,080	$1,200–1,500 for stars
Western League	$450–900	$1,200 (nominal limit); $1,800 (real limit)
Atlantic League	$450–725	$1,200–1,500 for stars
Western Association	$390–690 overall for all players	
Southern Association	$420–600 overall for all players	
New England League	$450–725 overall for all players	

Source: *The Sporting News*, December 11, 1897.

Table 2. Toronto Financial Statements, 1901

Balance sheet

Assets

Cash on hand	$1.70	
Cash in Union Bank	$360.18	
Franchise value	$6,000.00	
Grandstand, fences, etc.	$8,250.77	
Ballgrounds improvements	$671.13	
Due from Philadelphia for Brown	$450.00	
League guarantee	$250.00	
Balance due from stockholder	$25.00	
F. J. Leonard Loan	$310.50	
Balls, uniforms, etc.	$390.30	
Total assets		$16,709.58

Liabilities

Bills payable	$1,400.00	
Accrued interest on debenture	$157.50	
Debenture	$4,500.00	
Capital stock	$9,700.00	
Net income	$952.08	
Total liabilities and equity		$16,709.58

(continued)

Toronto Financial Statement *(continued)*

Income statement		
Revenue		$36,128.27
Expenses		
League assessments	$1,205.00	
Manager salary	$1,800.00	
Player salaries	$12,135.98	
Share to visiting clubs	$9,885.55	
General expenses[a]	$8,440.88	
Assistant secretary salary	$500.00	
Rent and taxes	$861.78	
Accrued interest	$157.50	
Total Expenses[b]		$35,176.19
Net income		$952.08

Source: *The Sporting News*, November 9, 1901.

Note: In 1901 the Canadian dollar was at par with the U.S. dollar.

[a] Includes travel, wages of help, interest on loan, advertising, etc.

[b] The total does not exactly equal the sum of the shown expenses.

Table 3. Payments by Majors to Minors, 1909–14

	1909	1910	1911	1912	1913	1914
Draft	$100,550	$84,500	$83,850	$103,000	$117,550	$56,500
Purchases	$145,000	$152,000	$158,000	$196,350	$188,250	$167,870
Total	$245,550	$236,500	$241,850	$299,350	$305,800	$224,370

Source: *The Sporting News*, November 26, 1914.

Table 4. 1914 Profit Summary

City	National League	American League	Federal League	International League
New York	$120,000	-$20,000		
Chicago	$50,000	$70,000	$20,000	
Brooklyn	-$25,000		-$60,000	
Philadelphia	-$20,000	$18,000		
St. Louis	$30,000	-$10,000	-$50,000	
Boston	$90,000	$75,000		
Cleveland		-$80,000		
Baltimore			$10,000	-$43,000
Pittsburgh	-$30,000		-$38,000	
Montreal				-$40,000
Detroit		$30,000		
Buffalo			-$30,000	NA
Toronto				-$30,000
Cincinnati	-$5,000			
Newark				-$30,000
Washington		-$15,000		
Jersey City				NA
Kansas City			-$40,000	
Indianapolis			$12,000	
Providence				-$12,000
Rochester				NA
Total[a]	$210,000	$68,000	-$176,000	-$200,000

Source: *New York Times*, January 31, 1915; *Atlanta Constitution*, February 7, 1915; *The Sporting News*, various dates.

[a] It is likely that, in the aggregate, the American, and in particular the National and Federal League all performed worse than suggested by this table. International League losses were variously estimated at $150,000 and $200,000. Based on information uncovered that spotlights individual team losses, the aggregate loss for the league most likely approaches the high end of the estimates.

Table 5. 1914 Population and Attendance Comparison

City	City population[a]	Metropolitan population[a]	National League	American League	Federal League[e]	International League	American Association[g]
New York[b]	2,615,483	6,474,568	364,313	359,477			
Chicago	2,185,283	2,446,921	202,516	469,290	200,729		
Brooklyn[c]	2,065,331	6,474,568	122,671		77,101		
Philadelphia	1,549,008	1,972,342	138,474	346,641			
St. Louis	687,029	828,733	256,099	244,714	47,586		
Boston	670,585	1,520,470	382,913	481,359			
Cleveland/Toledo[f]	560,663	613,270		185,997			99,732
Baltimore	558,485	658,715			124,072	NA	
Pittsburgh	533,905	1,042,855	139,620		63,482		
Montreal	471,000	NA				NA	
Detroit	465,766	500,982		416,225			
Buffalo	426,715	488,661			71,225	NA	
Toronto	377,000	NA				NA	
Milwaukee	373,857	427,175					177,875
Cincinnati	363,591	563,804	100,791				
Newark	347,469	6,474,568				NA	
Washington	331,069	367,869		243,888			
Minneapolis	301,408	526,256					104,975
Jersey City	267,779	6,474,568				NA	
Kansas City	248,381	340,446			65,846		99,438
Indianapolis	233,650	237,783			136,186		98,189
Providence	224,326	395,972				NA	
Louisville	223,928	286,158					190,438

Rochester	218,149	248,512			75,621
St. Paul	214,744	526,256		NA	1,290,320
Columbus	181,511	221,567			156,861
Total attendance	1,707,397	2,747,591	786,227		1,003,129
1913 total	2,891,531	3,526,805			1,290,320
Effective population[d]	4,005,519	4,732,473	2,990,671	2,398,323	1,816,795

Source: In addition to the sources in notes a–g, the attendance columns for the American League and the National League are from Thorn, *Total Baseball.*

[a] 1910 census (1911 census for Canadian cities).

[b] Manhattan and Bronx; entire NY area for metropolitan population.

[c] Brooklyn and Queens; entire NY area for metropolitan population.

[d] For cities with more than one team, city population divided by the number of teams (except Cleveland in the case of the American League).

[e] *Washington Post,* November 24, 1914. Based on estimates from Organized Baseball; thus, the figures may be understated. Chicago owner Charles Weeghman, for example, claimed 312,000 in paid attendance.

[f] Charles Somers owned both the Cleveland Indians and the Toledo franchise in the American Association. He moved the Toledo team to Cleveland in 1914 to provide continuous baseball throughout the summer to discourage the Federal League from invading his city. Toledo had a population of 168,497 in 1910.

[g] Hearings, Subcommittee on the Study of Monopoly Power.

Table 6. International League Treasurer's Report, 1917

Receipts and disbursements

Opening cash balance		$1,880.01
1914 sinking fund		$2,000.00
Receipts		
League assessments		
Toronto	$2,500.00	
Montreal	$2,500.00	
Rochester	$2,500.00	
Richmond	$2,500.00	
Newark	$2,500.00	
Providence	$2,500.00	
Baltimore	$2,125.00	
Buffalo	$1,875.00	
Player's fines	$670.00	
Western Union Telegraph, on account	$525.00	
Sale of umpire Bransfield	$500.00	
Bank interest	$23.43	
Balance from sale of Newark, 1916	$1,252.87	
Balance from Harrisburg, 1915	$14.64	
Subtotal		$21,985.94
Disbursements		
Umpire salaries	($8,777.50)	
Umpire traveling expenses	($2,231.06)	
Barrow salary	($7,500.00)	
Barrow traveling expenses	($658.82)	
Office help wages (W. J. Manley)	($1,150.00)	
Office rent	($840.00)	
Telegraph tolls	($456.09)	
Telephone costs	($184.93)	
Advertising (*Sporting Life and News*)	($180.00)	
Printing and stationary	($154.50)	
Miscellaneous expenses	($111.76)	
Postage stamps	($108.22)	
Umpire McBride's release from NY State League	($100.00)	
Compiling player averages	($100.00)	
Hotel expenses—league meetings	($89.05)	
Office supplies	($87.68)	
Manley vacation allowance	($50.00)	
Auditing expense	($25.00)	
Exchange on checks and protest fees	($14.06)	
Subtotal		($22,818.67)
Balance on hand at year end, 1917		$3,047.28

(continued)

Loan accounts		
Advanced from American League in 1914	$5,000.00	
Advanced from National League in 1914	$5,000.00	
Total loans		$10,000.00
Repaid to American League in 1915	$2,500.00	
Repaid to National League in 1915	$2,500.00	
Repaid to American League in 1916[a]	$1,000.00	
Repaid to National League in 1916[a]	$1,000.00	
Total repaid		$7,000.00
Net loans outstanding		$3,000.00

Source: Barrow's file at the National Baseball Hall of Fame, Cooperstown, New York.

Note: There were also two unpaid notes from Thomas Fogarty and William Devery totaling $3,650. These were given in return for money advanced to the Jersey City Club in 1914 out of a National Commission loan. The International League attorney had been unable to enforce payment on these notes by Forgarty and Devery.

[a] One thousand dollars of the money repaid in 1916 came from the sale of the Newark franchise; this amount was charged against Charles Ebbets.

Table 7. Team Profits, 1920–24 (Five-Year Totals)

American League	Profit	Dividends	Retained earnings
Boston	-$53,125	$0	-$53,125
Chicago	$553,643	$0	$553,643
Cleveland	$858,822	$469,615	$389,207
Detroit	$983,620	$300,000	$683,620
New York	$1,634,218	$0	$1,634,218
Philadelphia	$235,293	$200,000	$35,293
St. Louis	$692,394	$320,000	$372,394
Washington	$626,356	$130,000	$496,356
National League	Profit	Dividends	Retained earnings
Brooklyn	$844,923	$120,000	$724,923
Boston	$46,244	$0	$46,244
Chicago	$388,159	$141,929	$246,230
Cincinnati	$424,439	$0	$424,439
New York	$988,743	$175,000	$813,743
Philadelphia	$115,280	$60,000	$55,280
Pittsburgh	$976,079	$143,200	$832,879
St. Louis	$311,710	$28,317	$283,393

Source: Hearings, Subcommittee on the Study of Monopoly Power.

Table 8. Select New York Yankees Purchases from the Minor Leagues, 1920s

Player(s)	Minor League team	Price	Comments	Date
Earle Combs	Louisville	$50,000	+ Elmer Smith	January 4, 1924
Walter Beall	Rochester	$30,000		June 24, 1924
Pat Collins	St. Paul	$20,000	+ 2 Players	September 3, 1924
Mark Koenig	St. Paul	$50,000	+ 5 Players	May 29, 1925
Tony Lazzeri	Salt Lake City	$50,000	+ 5 Players	August 3, 1925
Julian Wera	St. Paul	$40,000	+ 2 Players	December 21, 1926
Eugene Robertson	St. Paul	$25,000	+ 1 Player	August 8, 1927
Lyn Lary and Jimmy Reese	Oakland	$125,000		August 12, 1927
Fred Heimach	St. Paul	$20,000	+ 1 Player	August 6, 1928
Fay Thomas	Oklahoma City	$25,000		September 4, 1928
Ivy Andrews	Mobile	$20,000		July 24, 1929
Lefty Gomez	San Francisco	$45,000		August 17, 1929

Source: New York Yankees business and financial records, on file at the National Baseball Hall of Fame, Cooperstown, New York.

Table 9. Select Philadelphia Athletics Purchases from the Minor Leagues, 1920s

Player(s)	Minor League team	Price	When[a]
Sammy Hale	Portland	$40,000	1923
Paul Strand	Salt Lake City	$40,000	1924
Al Simmons	Milwaukee	$30,000	1924
Max Bishop	Baltimore	$25,000	1924
Mickey Cochrane	Portland[b]	$50,000	1925
Lefty Grove	Baltimore	$100,600	1925
Dud Branom	Kansas City	$50,000	1927
Joe Boley	Baltimore	$25,000	1927
George Earnshaw	Baltimore	$50,000	1928

Source: Purchase prices are from various printed sources. In the event of conflicting amounts, preference was given to contemporary newspaper accounts.

Note: Players purchased late in the season are shown in the following year.

[a] The purchase occurred prior to or during the season shown.

[b] Previously, Philadelphia owner Connie Mack had purchased a controlling interest in the Portland franchise.

Table 10. Select Top Purchases from the Minor Leagues, 1920s (American League)[a]

Major League team	Player(s)	Minor League team	Price	When[b]
Boston	Dudley Lee	Tulsa	$30,000	1924
Chicago	Willie Kamm	San Francisco	$100,000	1922
	Stubb Mack	Seattle	$25,000	1923
	Maurice Archdeacon	Rochester	$50,000	1924
	Leo Mangum and Johnny Grabowski	Minneapolis	$40,000	1925
	Bert Cole	San Francisco	$30,000	1927
	Bill Cissell	Portland	$75,000	1928
	Clarence Hoffman	Sacramento	$25,000	1929
	Smead Jolley	San Francisco	$40,000	1930
Detroit	Herman Pillette and Syl Johnson	Portland	$40,000	1924
	Red Wingo	Toronto	$50,000	1924
	Mervyn Shea	Sacramento	$40,000	1927
	Roy Johnson	San Francisco	$75,000	1929
	Dale Alexander and Johnny Prudhomme	Toronto	$100,000	1929
St. Louis	Fred Schulte	Milwaukee	$100,000	1927

Source: Purchase prices are from various printed sources. In the event of conflicting amounts, preference was given to contemporary newspaper accounts.

Note: Players purchased late in the season are shown in the following year.

[a] This excludes the Yankees and the Athletics.

[b] The purchase occurred prior to or during the season shown.

Table 11. Select Top Purchases from the Minor Leagues, 1920s (National League)

Major League team	Player(s)	Minor League team	Price	When[a]
Brooklyn	John Jones and Rube Byron	Portland	$50,000	1924
Chicago	Woody English	Toledo	$50,000	1927
Cincinnati	Jakie May	Vernon	$35,000	1924
	Walter Christensen	St. Paul	$24,000	1926
	Ray Kolp	St. Paul	$25,000	1927
New York	Jimmy O'Connell	San Francisco	$75,000	1922
	Jack Bentley	Baltimore	$65,000	1923
	Wayland Dean	Louisville	$50,000	1924
	Carl Hubbell	Beaumont	$40,000	1928
Pittsburgh	Paul Waner and Hal Rhyne	San Francisco	$100,000	1926

Source: Purchase prices are from various printed sources. In the event of conflicting amounts, preference was given to contemporary newspaper accounts.

Note: Players purchased late in the season are shown in the following year.

[a] The purchase occurred prior to or during the season shown.

Table 12. Team Profits, 1925–29 (Five-Year Totals)

American League	Profit	Dividends	Retained earnings
Boston	-$189,044	$0	-$189,044
Chicago	$471,669	$0	$471,669
Cleveland	-$65,929	$149,100	-$215,029
Detroit	$587,503	$450,000	$137,503
New York	$1,637,996	$0	$1,637,996
Philadelphia	$809,299	$150,000	$659,299
St. Louis	$120,405	$42,000	$78,405
Washington	$583,712	$452,750	$130,962

National League	Profit	Dividends	Retained earnings
Brooklyn	$474,195	$684,000	-$209,805
Boston	-$41,737	$0	$41,737
Chicago	$1,073,385	$300,000	$773,385
Cincinnati	-$98,636	$0	-$98,636
New York	$843,178	$1,100,000	-$256,822
Philadelphia	$16,489	$40,000	-$23,511
Pittsburgh	$1,332,869	$565,500	$767,369
St. Louis	$1,169,371	$79,117	$1,090,254

Source: Hearings, Subcommittee on the Study of Monopoly Power.

Table 13. Team Payroll

League	1929	1933	1939	1943	1946
AL					
Boston	$171,260	$145,896	$227,237	$212,982	$511,625
Chicago	$220,000	$150,000	$243,041	$213,129	$386,377
Cleveland	$215,523	$178,598	$272,359	$204,864	$378,773
Detroit	$185,771	$138,758	$297,152	$172,733	$504,794
New York	$365,741	$294,982	$361,471	$301,229	$442,854
Philadelphia	$255,231	$166,533	$165,268	$135,405	$271,925
St. Louis	$200,312	$140,789	$159,925	$186,441	$221,789
Washington	$231,618	$187,059	$165,849	$192,190	$356,631
NL					
Boston	$238,260	$218,776	$171,159	$138,000	$322,000
Brooklyn	$245,309	$179,702	$204,047	$271,424	$313,369
Chicago	$310,299	$266,431	$292,178	$251,026	$348,546
Cincinnati	$224,655	$160,788	$231,389	$196,329	$316,137
New York	$291,368	$210,645	$291,448	$201,661	$344,635
Philadelphia	$140,422	$171,322	$144,255	$158,008	$302,471
Pittsburgh	$250,000	$197,503	$234,141	$185,624	$312,312
St. Louis	$219,815	$197,267	$192,085	$195,597	$313,530

Source: Hearings, Subcommittee on the Study of Monoply Power.

Note: Payroll figures include players, managers, and coaches.

Table 14. Team Profits, 1930–34 (Five-Year Totals)

American League	Profit	Dividends	Retained earnings
Boston	-$798,611	$0	-$798,611
Chicago	-$593,432	$0	-$593,432
Cleveland	-$229,733	$4,000	-$233,733
Detroit	$265,563	$50,000	$215,563
New York	$176,988	$0	$176,988
Philadelphia	$114,467	$250,050	-$135,583
St. Louis	-$388,604	$0	-$388,604
Washington	-$28,288	$39,300	-$67,588

National League	Profit	Dividends	Retained earnings
Brooklyn	$74,448	$300,000	-$225,552
Boston	-$143,323	$0	-$143,323
Chicago	$342,244	$470,000	-$127,756
Cincinnati	-$433,589	$1,952	-$445,541
New York	$77,957	$512,500	-$434,543
Philadelphia	$107,111	$0	$107,111
Pittsburgh	-$55,363	$100,000	-$155,363
St. Louis	$530,597	$253,920	$276,677

Source: Hearings, Subcommittee on the Study of Monoply Power.

Table 15. Where the Yankees Acquired Players

Position	1923		1927		1939	
	Name	Where acquired	Name	Where acquired	Name	Where acquired
Catcher	Wally Schang	Boston Red Sox	Pat Collins	High Minors	Bill Dickey	High Minors
1st base	Wally Pipp	Detroit Tigers	Lou Gehrig	College	Babe Dahlgren	Boston Red Sox
2nd base	Aaron Ward	Low Minors	Tony Lazzeri	High Minors	Joe Gordon	College
3rd base	Joe Dugan	Boston Red Sox	Joe Dugan	Boston Red Sox	Red Rolfe	College
Shortstop	Everett Scott	Boston Red Sox	Mark Koenig	High Minors	Frankie Crosetti	High Minors
Outfield	Babe Ruth	Boston Red Sox	Earle Combs	High Minors	George Selkirk	High Minors
Outfield	Whitey Witt	Philadelphia Athletics	Babe Ruth	Boston Red Sox	Joe DiMaggio	High Minors
Outfield	Bob Meusel	High Minors	Bob Meusel	High Minors	Charlie Keller	College
Outfield					Tommy Henrich	Minor League Free Agent
Starting pitcher	Bob Shawkey	Philadelphia Athletics	Waite Hoyt	Boston Red Sox	Red Ruffing	Boston Red Sox
Starting pitcher	Joe Bush	Boston Red Sox	Urban Shocker	St. Louis Browns	Lefty Gomez	High Minors
Starting pitcher	Waite Hoyt	Boston Red Sox	Herb Pennock	Boston Red Sox	Atley Donald	College
Starting pitcher	Sam Jones	Boston Red Sox	Dutch Ruether	Washington	Monte Pearson	Cleveland
Starting pitcher	Herb Pennock	Boston Red Sox	George Pipgras	Boston Red Sox	Bump Hadley	Washington
Relief pitcher			Wilcy Moore	Low Minors	Johnny Murphy	High Minors

Source: New York Yankees business and financial records, on file at the National Baseball Hall of Fame, Cooperstown, New York; contemporary newspaper accounts, www.retrosheet.org, and www.baseball-reference.com.

Table 16. Team Profits, 1935–39 (Five-Year Totals)

American League	Profit	Dividends	Retained earnings
Boston	-$958,586	$0	-$958,586
Chicago	-$60,042	$0	-$60,042
Cleveland	$482,601	$167,844	$314,757
Detroit	$1,079,968	$400,000	$679,968
New York	$1,257,691	$520,000	$737,691
Philadelphia	-$141,211	$0	-$141,211
St. Louis	-$511,132	$0	-$511,132
Washington	$55,797	$58,550	-$2,753

National League	Profit	Dividends	Retained earnings
Brooklyn	-$180,399	$0	-$180,399
Boston	-$74,283	$0	-$74,283
Chicago	$307,328	$100,000	$207,328
Cincinnati	$675,153	$108,620	$566,533
New York	$955,754	$794,474	$161,280
Philadelphia	-$107,869	$0	-$107,869
Pittsburgh	$267,874	$235,900	$31,974
St. Louis	$257,460	$406,080	-$148,620

Source: Hearings, Subcommittee on the Study of Monopoly Power.

Table 17. American League Team Income, 1943

	Boston	Chicago	Cleveland	Detroit	New York	Philadelphia	St. Louis	Washington
Games at home	$245,566	$372,569	$378,748	$506,131	$463,568	$254,845	$154,473	$902,622
Games away	$128,188	$109,033	$119,093	$118,987	$208,794	$119,426	$117,601	$131,500
Exhibition games	$11,116	$8,032	$4,318	$5,572	$82,242	$4,682	$12,219	$41,216
Radio	$40,000	$41,000	$87,500	$60,000	$0	$40,000	$39,200	$22,500
Concessions (net)	$47,376	$71,205	$29,066	$76,808	$131,022	$5,600	$38,892	$41,856
Gross operating income	$489,196	$651,880	$603,173	$810,857	$925,514	$537,227	$369,850	$729,391
Gross operating expenses	$608,748	$546,701	$505,700	$543,567	$882,511	$434,737	$341,872	$481,492
Net operating income	($119,552)	$105,179	$97,473	$267,290	$43,003	$102,790	$27,978	$247,898
Cost of player contracts	$85,500	$61,850	$51,800	$47,800	$78,300	$92,150	$29,800	$144,008
Net income before taxes	($205,052)	$43,329	$45,673	$219,490	($35,297)	$10,640	($1,822)	$103,891
Farm losses	$107,365	$0	$0	$0	$53,234	($9,245)	($47,197)	$26,174
Consolidated net income before taxes	($312,417)	$43,329	$45,673	$219,490	($86,521)	$19,885	$45,375	$77,717
Income taxes income	$0	$18,906	$17,800	$87,444	$0	$0	$0	$31,086
Consolidated net	($312,417)	$24,423	$27,873	$132,046	($88,521)	$19,885	$45,375	$46,631
Dividends	$0	$0	$20,250	$0	$0	$0	$0	$19,400
Retained earnings	($312,417)	$24,423	$7,623	$132,046	($88,521)	$19,885	$45,375	$27,231

Source: Hearings, Subcommittee on the Study of Monopoly Power.

Table 18. Barrow's Income after Joining the Yankees

Year	Salary	Other[a]
1928	$27,000	$0
1931	$30,000	$0
1934	$25,000	$0
1935	$25,000	$0
1937	$25,000	$0
1938	$25,000	$0
1940	$35,000	$0
1941	$35,060	$18,200
1942	$35,240	$0
1943	$35,220	$0
1944	$35,240	$0
1948	$0	$17,370[b]
1949	$0	$17,302[c]
1950	$0	$31,370
1951	$0	$15,120
1952	$0	$15,620

Source: The data for 1934, 1935, and 1937 is based on published information. All other years are based on Barrow's income tax returns.

[a] Dividend, interest, and other income.

[b] $5,250 in interest income; $12,120 in other income.

[c] $5,182 in interest income; $12,120 in other income.

Bibliography

Note on Sources

Chronicling and interpreting Barrow's life in baseball required reviewing the events of his time through contemporary sources. The digitization of several newspapers made this task much less tedious. A number of papers, including the *New York Times* and the *Boston Globe* (at least through Barrow's time in Boston) are available through ProQuest. The historical *Toronto Star* is available and searchable at that newspaper's Web site. The weekly sporting newspaper, the *Sporting News*, is available through Paper of Record. Unfortunately, the search function for the *Sporting News* works only haphazardly through the early 1920s, necessitating a detailed review of the microfilm for Barrow's early years in baseball. The following papers were also combed extensively: *Atlanta Constitution, Chicago Defender, Chicago Tribune, Des Moines Daily News, Des Moines Leader, Los Angeles Times, Montreal Gazette* (1910), *Paterson Daily Guardian*, and *Washington Post.* Several annual publications also offer valuable insights into the seasons they review. Those consulted include the *Reach Official American League Base Ball Guide*, published by the A. J. Reach Company, for the years 1895 to 1939; *Spalding's Official Base Ball Guide*, published by the American Sports Publishing Company, for the years 1895 to 1939; the *Spalding-Reach Official Base Ball Guide* for 1940 and 1941; the *Sporting News Baseball Register*, published by the Sporting News Publishing Company, for the years 1940 to 1945; and the *Sporting News Official Baseball Guide*, published by the Sporting News Publishing Company, for the years 1940 to 1947.

Six large albums containing documents relating to Barrow were auctioned by Sotheby's several years ago. The National Baseball Hall of Fame and Museum possesses four, which include personal correspondence, several years of tax returns, saved newspaper articles, and financial documents. An examination of the four albums on file at the Hall offered a number of insights and previously unreported experiences. More recently Sotheby's auctioned two collections of papers pertaining to Yankees and American League business from roughly 1915 through 1930. These collections also contained a number of personal letters to and from Barrow that reveal previously unknown incidents. Barrow's relatively short autobiography, written late in life, glosses over or only tangentially mentions several critical events.

The Hall of Fame has created a "file" for many baseball individuals and topics. These files contain an extensive collection of newspaper, magazine, and other articles on the subject. Scrutiny of these files for many of the most important people in Barrow's life, such as Frank Navin, Jacob Ruppert, Tillinghast L'Hommedieu Huston, Miller Huggins, Joe McCarthy, and George Weiss, provided further coverage of the people and events affecting Barrow. The *Sporting News* also maintains clipping files on baseball players and executives that contain articles from other papers as well; the Barrow file provided several valuable pieces. The task of tracking down the many references to Barrow and others in the baseball literature was eased tremendously by The Baseball Index. Other critical information came via the extensive government records available at Ancestry.com. The most important information came from U.S. Census records and Canadian birth and death records. Barrow's reticence in writing about family matters made these records invaluable.

Regarding the business operation, three excellent relatively untapped sources exist. The Hall of Fame possesses a huge collection of New York Yankees business and financial records for 1913 to 1950. These records include player salaries, player sale price information, trial balance financial statements, and general ledgers. From these documents one can establish the cost of capital items such as Yankee Stadium and its later expansion along with the revenue and expenses from various business matters. The U.S. House of Representatives Judiciary Committee hearings in 1951 on baseball's monopoly, chaired by Emanuel Celler, led to two indispensable publications, a 232-page report and a 1,643-page transcript and appendix. The latter contained important testimony on the business of baseball and generally undisclosed financial materials and transcripts of league meetings.

Part 1: Every Job in Baseball, 1868–1920

For general American and business history there are many excellent sources. In the bibliography I have listed some that were particularly helpful for this biography. These include Nevins and Commager, and Gordon on some of the broader history; Drucker, Sloan, and Chandler on American business management; and Dubofsky, McCraw, Porter, and Reiss on American economic history. Also, the four-volume *Encyclopedia of the United States in the Twentieth Century* offers outstanding background on all areas of American society.

Several researchers have captured the reminiscences of players who played under Barrow. Ritter interviewed Sam Crawford, Stan Coveleski, Harry Hooper, and Sam Jones. Murdock visited with Waite Hoyt, Stan Coveleski, and Bob Shawkey. McGarigle tracked down Carl Mays. Honig interviewed George Pipgras, Spud Chandler, Tommy Henrich, Bill Werber, Tommy Holmes, Joe Sewell, Joe McCarthy, and Bob Shawkey. Langford also tracked down Joe Sewell, and Westcott talked with Holmes and Werber. These (and other) researchers also interviewed numerous other players who interacted extensively with Barrow's teams.

The Dave Bancroft waiver story came from the newspapers and Kieran's 1930 *Saturday Evening Post* article. A principal source for information on Bob Quinn was an article by Fred Lieb in the *Sporting News* of March 24, 1954. The general manager background came from a number of sources; the *Baseball Magazine* articles by Drebinger and Crusinberry were especially helpful. Quotes were also taken from sources not listed in the bibliography, including the *New York World Telegram* and the *New York Sun*.

The principal sources for Barrow's years in Des Moines include Christian's paper, the *Des Moines Daily News* and the *Des Moines Leader*, Taylor's article, and Barrow's many autobiographical and biographical pieces. Betts offers a nice summary of the effect of technology on sports in the second half of the nineteenth century. Much of the information on Barrow's interaction with Fred Clarke comes from two *Sporting News* essays: one by Lieb on August 24, 1960, and a three-part article by Joe King carried from March 14, 1951, thorough March 28, 1951. The story of Barrow declining an opportunity to box Jim Corbett in Pittsburgh comes from his autobiography. Two main sources of biographical information on Harry Stevens are Reynolds's article and one by J. G. Taylor Spink in the *Sporting News* of February 13, 1940.

Reiss provides an excellent discussion of the socioeconomic makeup of early baseball owners. Details on Lizzie Arlington come primarily from the 1983 *Baseball Research Journal*; a story in the *Philadelphia Inquirer* on July 8, 1898; Bryson's story; and Barrow's recollections. The story of Honus Wagner's signing has many slightly different permutations. I relied heavily on a piece by Barrow in the *Sporting News* on March 26, 1908, written after he had left baseball. Because he was then in the hotel business, Barrow had little reason to shade the story to create any particular favor within the game (but for his own self-importance). Furthermore, the incident was still recent enough that others who knew the specifics would be around to see the article. The DeValerias' book was also helpful regarding Wagner's time with Barrow.

In addition to the materials in Frank Navin's Hall of Fame file, his entry by Anthony J. Papalas in Porter's book and Lieb's Tigers history proved especially useful. Spink wrote a short biography of William Yawkey in the November 26, 1947, issue of the *Sporting News*. Fred Buelow's story of getting caught by Barrow after a might on the town with Frank McManus was recounted in the *Sporting News*, February 2, 1906. The main source for the Lichtenhein hockey story was www.jewsinsports.org. A long article in the *Sporting News* of May 21, 1936, provided helpful insights into the history and organization of the Minor Leagues.

A number of excellent sources on the Federal League exist but no definitive history. The bitterness of the battle and the high level of interest in its outcome ensured that many of the controversies would be covered in the press. *Sporting Life* and the *Sporting News* were both closely examined, as were many newspapers. The extensive history of the league in Seymour's book has held up surprisingly well. Pietrusza provides valuable detail and along with Okkonen also offers helpful background information. The two publications coming out of the Celler committee contain a wealth of information on the struggle between the Federal League and Organized Baseball. The story of the Players' Fraternity during and after the Federal League was also well followed in the press. It has been synthesized and considered in several more-recent publications as well. See, for example, Longert, Burk, Lowenfish, and Seymour.

Barrow's time in Boston is well covered in newspapers and the *Sporting News*. Because the Red Sox had Babe Ruth and attained their last World Series championship prior to 2004 during Barrow's tenure, numerous books focus on these years. Wood's book addresses the 1918 season in detail and is particularly comprehensive on the World Series. Zingg's and Creamer's biographies both add important insights to Barrow's term in Boston. Creamer also includes excerpts of correspondence between Frazee, Ruppert, and Huston regarding Frazee's need for cash. Lieb, as well as Stout and Johnson, provide good background on both the personalities and specific incidents. McGarigle's book is useful but uneven. The Harry Frazee papers archived at the University of Texas contain a wealth of information about Frazee's life, including many documents from his years owning the Red Sox. A review of his tax returns, team financial statements, and numerous letters testify to his precarious financial situation and haphazard recordkeeping. Several articles tell of Johnny Cooney's tryout with the Red Sox. The main source for my account is the *Sporting News*, August 31, 1949.

Part 2: The Yankees Years, 1920–1953

Many books have been written on the New York Yankees and their stars. Graham, Meany, and Stout and Johnson all offer insightful histories that include large sections on Barrow's time with the Yankees. Fetter recognizes the importance of a general manager in the rise of the Yankees. Spatz provides an excellent background and overview of the Yankees' trades. The many player biographies and autobiographies also offer valuable perspective on significant events. Creamer's volume remains the definitive biography of Ruth; Montville's more recent treatment is also extremely useful; Eig and Robinson both provide valuable material on Lou Gehrig; Cramer's shrewd biography of Joe DiMaggio furnishes additional original information.

Meany and Graham provide revealing material on the key Yankees executives and managers. A number of articles published in various periodicals (in addition to the *Sporting News*) and newspapers over many years, however, furnish the bulk of the material on Barrow's main confidants. The extensive newspaper clippings in the Hall of Fame files proved especially helpful. As to the specific front-office and on-field staff, a biographical sketch of Paul Krichell and several scouting stories are related by Heinz and Camerer. Of the many articles on Jacob Ruppert, his autobiographical series in the *World-Telegram* was especially useful. George Weiss's long history in baseball is well recounted in the many magazine articles listed in the bibliography. Also, a short newspaper series by Dan Daniel discussed his many player sales from the Yankees' Minor Leagues. Regarding Miller Huggins, Trachtenberg, Steinberg, and a short biography by Arthur Mann in the *Sporting News* on November 2, 1939, effectively supplement the newspaper articles. Extensive magazine articles by Williams and Fitzgerald provide good summaries of Joe McCarthy's tenure with the Yankees. Levy's lengthy biography is comprehensive and authoritative.

The battle between American League president Ban Johnson and the renegade owners around 1920 was well chronicled in the press at the time. Huggins's quote on the importance of character comes from the *Philadelphia Public Ledger*. Lieb related the details of Huston's meltdown after the 1922 World Series in the *Sporting News* in 1963. Regarding the site-selection process for Yankee Stadium, in addition to the itemized sources, a column by J. G. Taylor Spink in the *Sporting News* in which he quotes an interview with stadium superintendent Charley McManus provides an insider's perspective. Barrow's 1925 phone conversation with Huggins is recounted in the *Sporting News* of November 2, 1939. Krichell's recollection of the Lazzeri and Cooke signings are from Camerer. Much of the unsanitized version of the Wilcy Moore signing and its aftermath comes from letters in the Barrow albums and an article in the *Wilkes-Barre Evening News* of August 23, 1930. The story of the fatal Yankee Stadium panic in 1929 was taken mainly from the *New York Times* with background provided by Weeks's article. Barrow's confrontation with Leo Durocher leading up to his trade was recounted in Durocher's autobiography. Insight into the Shawkey hiring and firing comes from a *Sporting News* article by Frank Graham in 1947 and Shawkey's comments in Murdock and Honig. As to the hiring of McCarthy, Brown revealed his conversations with George Perry in his history of the Chicago Cubs.

The transcripts for the 1929 and 1931 Joint Meeting of the Major Leagues can be found in the appendix to the Celler subcommittee hearings. Both the hearings and the subcommittee report were extremely valuable for both background and specific rules related to Major League roster restrictions and Major League–Minor League relations and regulations. Cliff Blau's excellent website also offers extensive information on Major League operating rules. The text of Judge Lindley's decision in the Bennett case (in which St. Louis owner Phil Ball challenged Commissioner Landis's ruling regarding the Minor Leaguer's disposition) is reprinted in the *Sporting News*, April 30, 1931. Lindley's discussion of the case illuminates the rules and a number of the issues and controversies surrounding them. The Barrow-Combs correspondence comes from the Earle Combs papers that were generously donated to the Society for American Baseball Research by his grandson.

The terms of the operating agreement with Oakland for 1936 are from the Yankees' financial records. The Jake Powell embarrassment is well researched by Lamb. In addition to the mainstream press, helpful articles were found in the *Chicago Defender*, the *Afro-American* (Maryland), and the *Norfolk Journal and Guide*. Halberstam's book presents an excellent background to the early days of radio in New York and provides the context for interpreting the contemporary newspaper stories. The radio-rights revenue information is from the Celler subcommittee hearings appendix. Mead and Goldstein provide good background for the war years. The account of Barrow's public feud with Clark Griffith over the sale of Babe Dahlgren comes principally from the *Sporting News*, March 13, 1941. Barrow's conversation with Sam Breadon on scheduling a spring training trip to Cuba was recounted in the *Sporting News*, May 2, 1940.

The *Sporting News* and the *New York Times* carried revealing articles, both at the time and several years later, on various features of the Yankees transfer to the Ruppert estate and the later sale to Del Webb, Dan Topping, and Larry MacPhail. J. G. Taylor Spink writes the inside scoop of Happy Chandler's election as commissioner in the *Sporting News* of March 3, 1945. Dan Daniel relates the story of MacPhail's rampage at the Biltmore Hotel in the *Sporting News* of October 15, 1947.

Published Works

Adair, Robert K. *The Physics of Baseball*. 3rd. ed., revised, updated, and expanded. Perennial, 2002.

Allen, Lee. *The Cincinnati Reds*. G. P. Putnam's Sons, 1948.

———. *Cooperstown Corner: Columns from the Sporting News, 1962–1969*. Society for American Baseball Research, n. d.

Allen, Mel, and Ed Fitzgerald. *You Can't Beat the Hours: A Long, Loving Look at Big-League Baseball—Including Some Yankees I Have Known*. Harper & Row, 1964.

Alexander, Charles C. *Breaking the Slump: Baseball in the Depression Era*. Columbia University Press, 2002.

————. *John McGraw*. Penguin Books, 1989.

————. *Our Game: An American Baseball History*. Henry Holt, 1995.

————. *Rogers Hornsby: A Biography*. Henry Holt, 1991.

Angus, Jeff. *Management by Baseball: The Official Rules for Winning Management in Any Field*. Collins, 2006.

Armour, Mark A., and Daniel R. Levitt. *Paths to Glory: How Great Baseball Teams Got That Way*. Brassey's, 2003.

Associated Press. "Sox Didn't Sell Ruth to Finance Play, Book Says." http://www.msnbc.com/id/11545612.

Auker, Elden, with Tom Keegan. *Sleeper Cars and Flannel Uniforms: A Lifetime of Memories from Striking Out the Babe to Teeing It Up with the President*. Triumph Books, 2001.

Barber, Frederick Courtenay. "The Star Ball-Players and Their Earnings." *Munsey's Magazine*, 1913.

Barrow, Edward Grant, as told to John Drebinger. "Why the Yankees Won't Break Up." *Liberty*, March 16, 1940.

Barrow, Edward Grant, with James M. Kahn. "My Baseball Story." Parts 1–6, *Colliers*, May 10, 1950; May 27, 1950; June 3, 1950; June 10, 1950; June 17, 1950; June 24, 1950.

————. *My Fifty Years in Baseball*. Coward-McCann, 1951.

Barrow, Edward Grant, as told to Arthur Mann. "Baseball Cavalcade." *The Saturday Evening Post*, April 24, 1937.

"Baseball Businessman." *Forbes*, August 1, 1951.

Berger, Lance A., with Dorothy R. Berger. *Management Wisdom from the New York Yankees' Dynasty: What Every Manager Can Learn from a Legendary Team's 80-Year Winning Streak*. John Wiley & Sons, 2005.

Betts, John Rickards. "The Technological Revolution and the Rise of Sport, 1850–1900." *The Mississippi Valley Historical Review*, September 1953.

"Big League Baseball." *Fortune*, August 1937.

Bjarkman, Peter C., ed. *Encyclopedia of Major League Baseball—American League*. Carroll & Graf, 1993.

————, ed. *Encyclopedia of Major League Baseball—National League*. Carroll & Graf, 1993.

Blau, Clifford. "Original Baseball Research." http://mysite.verizon .net/brak2.o/

Bloodgood, Clifford. "Spring Training at Toronto." *Baseball Magazine*, March 1938.

———. "Yankee Stadium." *Baseball Magazine*, April 1946.

Bradley, Hugh. "The Ed Barrow Story." Parts 1–4. *New York Journal American*, December 1953.

Brown, Warren. *The Chicago White Sox.* G. P. Putnam's Sons, 1946, 1952.

Bryson, Bill. "Lizzie Started It." *Baseball Digest*, September 1949.

Bucek, Jeanine, et al. *The Baseball Encyclopedia.* 10th ed. Macmillan, 1996.

Bulger, Bozeman. "The Baseball Business from the Inside." *Collier's*, March 25, 1922.

———. "A Big League Club Owner Tells the Truth." *Liberty*, September 27, 1924. (An interview with Colonel Huston.)

Burk, Robert F. *Much More Than a Game: Players, Owners, & American Baseball Since 1921.* University of North Carolina Press, 2001.

———. *Never Just a Game: Players, Owners, & American Baseball to 1920.* University of North Carolina Press, 1994.

Chamberlin, Jo. "Safe At Home!" *Review of Reviews*, May 1935.

Chandler, Alfred D., Jr. *Strategy and Structure: Chapters in the History of Industrial America.* MIT Press, 1962, 1990.

Christian, Ralph. "Edward Grant Barrow: The Des Moines Years." Paper presented at the Society for American Baseball Research convention, Scottsdale AZ, 1999.

Chusid, Irwin. "The Short, Happy Life of the Newark Peppers." *Baseball Research Journal.* Society for American Baseball Research, 1991.

Cohen, Richard M., and David S. Neft, with text by Jordan A. Deutsch. *The World Series.* Dial, 1979.

Combs, Earle. Papers on file with the Society for American Baseball Research.

Connery, Thomas J. "An Analysis of the Chain System." *Baseball Magazine*, February 1946.

Cooke, Bob, ed. *Wake Up the Echoes: From the Sports Pages of the New York Tribune.* Hanover House, 1956.

Craig, Peter S. *Organized Baseball: An Industry Study of a $100 Million Spectator Sport.* Bachelor's thesis, Oberlin College, 1950.

Camerer, Dave. "Secret Weapon of the N.Y. Yankees." *Esquire*, May 1957.

Cramer, Richard Ben. *Joe DiMaggio: The Hero's Life*. Simon & Schuster, 2000.

Creamer, Robert W. *Babe: The Legend Comes to Life*. Fireside, 1992.

———. *Baseball in '41: A Celebration of the Best Baseball Season Ever—in the Year America Went to War*. Penguin Books, 1992.

———. *Stengel: His Life and Times*. Fireside, 1990.

Crichton, Kyle. "Vinegar Bill, the Ivory Scout." *Collier's*, March 12, 1938.

Crusinberry, James. "General Managers." *Baseball Magazine*, June 1950.

Daniel, Daniel M. "DiMaggio, Lazzeri, Moore Deals Stand Out in Barrow's Recollection." *Baseball Magazine*, May 1950.

———. "Draft System, Legalistic Necessity, Rises to New Dignity With 26 Choices." *Baseball Magazine*, January 1948.

———. "From Peanuts to Pennants: The Story of Ed Barrow." Parts 1–11. *New York World Telegram*, January–February, 1938.

———. "Major Leagues Set Up New Defenses against Plottings of Baseball Fixers." *Baseball Magazine*, April 1947.

———. "Those Yankees Carry On." *Baseball Magazine*, March 1939.

———. "Weiss Brought Varied Talents into General Managership of Yankees." *Baseball Magazine*, February 1948.

———. "Yankees Spark Fresh Flair as Ebullient MacPhail Moves In." *Baseball Magazine*, April 1945.

Danzig, Alison, and Joe Reichler. *The History of Baseball: Its Great Players, Teams and Managers*. Prentice Hall, 1959.

DeValeria, Dennis, and Jeanne Burke DeValeria. *Honus Wagner: A Biography*. Henry Holt, 1995.

Dewey, Donald, and Nicholas Acocella. *The Ball Clubs*. Harper Perennial, 1996.

———. *The Biographical History of Baseball*. Triumph Books, 2002.

Dorward, Jane Finnan. "Ed Barrow's Toronto Years." In *Dominionball: Baseball above the 49th*. Society for American Baseball Research, 2005.

Drebinger, John. "Baseball's Millionaires." *Baseball Magazine*, July 1939.

———. "The Changing Trend." *Baseball Magazine*, February, 1940.

———. "Were They Worth the Money?" *Baseball Magazine*, March 1946.

Drucker, Peter F. *The Essential Drucker: The Best of Sixty Years of Peter Drucker's Essential Writings on Management*. HarperCollins, 2001.

Dubofsky, Melvyn. *Industrialism and the American Worker: 1865–1920*. 3rd ed. Harlan Davidson, 1975, 1985, 1996.

Dunn, Don. *The Making of No, No, Nanette*. Citadel, 1972.

Durocher, Leo, with Ed Linn. *Nice Guys Finish Last*. Simon & Schuster, 1975.

Durso, Joseph. *Yankee Stadium: Fifty Years of Drama*. Houghton Mifflin, 1972.

Eig, Jonathan. *The Luckiest Man: The Life and Death of Lou Gehrig*. Simon & Schuster, 2005.

Eisenhammer, Fred, and Jim Binkley. *Baseball's Most Memorable Trades: Superstars Swapped, All-Stars Copped and Megadeals That Flopped*. McFarland, 1997.

Enright, Jim, ed. *Trade Him: 100 Years of Baseball's Greatest Deals*. Follett, 1976.

Eskenazi, Gerald. *The Lip: A Biography of Leo Durocher*. William Morrow, 1993.

Fetter, Henry D. *Taking on the Yankees: Winning and Losing in the Business of Baseball, 1903–2003*. W. W. Norton, 2003.

Fitzgerald, Ed. "Nobody's Neutral about McCarthy." *Sport*, August 1950.

Forman, Sean. Baseball Reference Website. www.baseball-reference.com.

Foster, John B., ed. *A History of the National Association of Professional Baseball Leagues, 1902–1926*. National Association of Professional Baseball Leagues, n.d.

Frank, Stanley. "Boss of the Yankees." *Saturday Evening Post*, April 16, 1960.

———. "Yankee Farmer." *Elks Magazine*, August 1944.

———. "Yankee Kingmaker." *Saturday Evening Post*, July 24, 1948.

Frick, Ford C. *Games, Asterisks, and People: Memoirs of a Lucky Fan*. Crown, 1973.

Frommer, Harvey. *The New York Yankee Encyclopedia*. Macmillan, 1997.

Fullerton, Hugh S. "Baseball—The Business and the Sport." *American Review of Reviews*, April 1920.

———. "Earnings in Baseball." *North American Review*, June 1930.

Gallico, Paul. *Lou Gehrig: Pride of the Yankees*. Grosset & Dunlap, 1942.

Gehrig, Eleanor, and Joseph Durso. *My Luke and I*. Signet, 1977.

Ginsberg, Daniel E. *The Fix Is In: A History of Baseball Gambling and Game Fixing Scandals*. McFarland, 1995.

Goldstein, Richard. *Spartan Seasons: How Baseball Survived the Second World War*. Macmillan, 1980.

Gordon, John Steele. *An Empire of Wealth: The Epic History of American Economic Power*. Harper-Collins, 2004.

Graham, Frank. *The Brooklyn Dodgers*. G. P. Putnam's Sons, 1945.

———. "The Man behind the Yankees." *Esquire*, April 1942.

———. *McGraw of the Giants: An Informal Biography*. G. P. Putnam's Sons, 1944.

———. *The New York Giants*. Southern Illinois University Press, 2002.

———. *The New York Yankees*. Southern Illinois University Press, 2002.

Greenberg, Hank. *Hank Greenberg: The Story of My Life*. Edited by Ira Berkow. Times Books, 1989.

Hageman, William. *Honus: The Life and Times of a Baseball Hero*. Sagamore, 1996.

Hailey, Gary. "Anatomy of a Murder: The Federal League and the Courts." *The National Pastime*. Society for American Baseball Research, Spring 1985.

Halberstam, David J. *Sports on New York Radio: A Play-by-Play History*. Masters, 1999.

Harper, William A. *How You Played the Game: The Life of Grantland Rice*. University of Missouri Press, 1999.

Haupert, Michael. "Purchasing Pennants: The New York Yankees Then and Now, Part 1: Yankee Revenues and Expenses." *Outside the Lines*, publication of the Society of American Baseball Research Business of Baseball Committee, Summer 2005.

Haupert, Michael J., with Ken Winter. "Pay Ball: Estimating the Profitability of the New York Yankees, 1915–1937." *Essays in Economic and Business History* 21, Spring 2003.

———. "Yankee Profits and Promise: The Purchase of Babe Ruth and the Building of Yankee Stadium." In *The Cooperstown Symposium on Baseball and American Culture*, edited by William Simons. McFarland, 2003.

Hayes, Neil. "Debunking the Curse of the Bambino." http://www.msnbc .msn.com/id/6236116.

Heinz, W. C. "I Scout for the Yankees." *Collier's*, July 11, 1953.

Henrich, Tommy, with Bill Gilbert. *Five O'clock Lightning: Ruth, Gehrig, DiMaggio, Mantle and the Glory Years of the NY Yankees*. Birch Lane, 1992.

Holtzman, Jerome, ed. *No Cheering in the Press Box*. Holt, Rinehart, & Winston, 1973, 1974.

Honig, Donald. *Baseball America: The Heroes of the Game and the Times of Their Glory*. Macmillan, 1985.

———. *Baseball between the Lines*. Coward, McCann & Geoghegan, 1976.

———. *Baseball When the Grass Was Real*. Coward, McCann & Geoghegan, 1975.

———. *A Donald Honig Reader*. Fireside, 1988.

———. *The Man in the Dugout*. University of Nebraska Press, 1995.

———. *The New York Yankees*. Crown, 1987.

Hornsby, Rogers, and Bill Surface. *My War with Baseball*. Coward-McCann, 1962.

Hoyt, Waite, and Frank Graham. "The Private Life of the New York Yankees." Parts 1 and 2. *Liberty*, February 28, 1941; March 7, 1942.

Huggins, Miller. "The Difficulty of Doping Out a Pennant Race." *Baseball Magazine*, July 1925.

Huggins, Myrtle, as told to John B. Kennedy. "Mighty Midget." *Collier's*, May 24, 1930.

Information Concepts, Inc. *The Baseball Encyclopedia*. Macmillan, 1969.

James, Bill. *The Bill James Guide to Baseball Managers*. Scribners, 1997.

———. *The Bill James Historical Baseball Abstract*. Villard, 1986.

———. *The New Bill James Historical Baseball Abstract*. Free Press, 2001.

———. *The Politics of Glory*. Macmillan, 1994.

James, Bill, and others, eds. *Bill James Presents . . . STATS All-Time Major League Handbook*. STATS, 1998.

———. *Bill James Presents . . . STATS All-Time Baseball Sourcebook*. STATS, 1998.

"Jim Corbett Playing First Base." *Baseball Research Journal* 12 (1983): 183–87.

Johnson, Lloyd, and Miles Wolff, eds. *The Encyclopedia of Minor League Baseball*. 2nd ed. Baseball America, 1997.

Johnston, Alva. "Beer and Baseball." *New Yorker*, September 24, 1932.

Kaese, Harold. *The Boston Braves*. G. P. Putnam's Sons, 1948.

Karst, Gene, and Martin J. Jones Jr. *Who's Who in Professional Baseball*. Arlington House, 1973.

Keener, Sid C. "Baseball's Rags-to-Riches Story." Parts 1–6. *St. Louis Star Times*, January 1946.

Kerrane, Kevin. *Dollar Sign on the Muscle: The World of Baseball Scouting*. Avon, 1984, 1985.

Kieran, John. "Big-League Business." *Saturday Evening Post*, May 31, 1930.

Koppett, Leonard. *Koppett's Concise History of Major League Baseball*. Temple, 1998.

——. *The Man in the Dugout*. Crown, 1993.

——. *The Thinking Man's Guide to Baseball*. Dutton, 1967.

Kutler, Stanley I., ed. *Encyclopedia of the United States in the Twentieth Century*. 4 vols. Charles Scribner's Sons, 1996.

Lahman, Sean. *Baseball Player Database*. www.baseball1.com.

Lamb, Chris. "L'Affaire Jake Powell: The Minority Press Goes to Bat against Segregated Baseball." *J & MC Quarterly*, Spring 1999.

Lane, F. C. "Baseball's Master Builder." *Baseball Magazine*, October 1936. (An interview with Colonel Ruppert.)

——. "The Big Man of the Minor Leagues." *Baseball Magazine*, February 1918.

——. "The Enormous Financial Hazards of Running a Major League Baseball Club." *Baseball Magazine*, January 1923.

Langford, Walter M. *Legends of Baseball: An Oral History of the Game's Golden Age*. Diamond Communications, 1987.

Levesque, John. "For Harry Frazee III, 'the Curse' Has Different Meaning." *Seattle Post-Intelligencer*, September 26, 2003.

Levy, Alan H. *Joe McCarthy: Architect of the Yankee Dynasty*. McFarland, 2005.

Lewis, Franklin. *The Cleveland Indians*. G. P. Putnam's Sons, 1949.

Lieb, Fred. *The Baltimore Orioles*. Southern Illinois University Press, 2005.

——. *Baseball as I Have Known It*. Coward, McCann & Geoghegan, 1976.

———. *The Boston Red Sox*. G. P. Putnam's Sons, 1947.

———. *Connie Mack*. G. P. Putnam's Sons, 1945.

———. *The Detroit Tigers*. G. P. Putnam's Sons, 1946.

———. *The Pittsburgh Pirates*. Southern Illinois University Press, 2003.

———. *The St. Louis Cardinals*. Southern Illinois University Press, 2001.

Linn, Ed. *The Great Rivalry: The Yankees and the Red Sox, 1901–1990*. Ticknor & Fields, 1991.

Longert, Scott. "The Players' Fraternity." *Baseball Research Journal*. Society for American Baseball Research, 2001.

Lowenfish, Lee. *The Imperfect Diamond: A History of Baseball's Labor Wars*. Da Capo, 1991.

Luisi, Vincent. *Images of Sports, the New York Yankees: The First 25 Years*. Arcadia, 2002.

MacFarlane, Paul, ed., in collaboration with Leonard Gettelson. *Daguerreotypes of Great Stars of Baseball*. Sporting News, 1971.

Madden, Bill. *Pride of October: What It Was Like to Be Young and a Yankee*. Warner Books, 2003.

Mann, Arthur. *Branch Rickey: American in Action*. Riverside, 1957.

———. "Pillars of Progress." *Baseball Magazine*, March 1944.

McCraw, Thomas K. *American Business, 1920–2000: How It Worked*. Harlan Davidson, 2000.

McCuster, John J. *How Much Is That in Real Money? A Historical Commodity Price Index for Use as a Deflator of Money Values in the Economy of the United States*. American Antiquarian Society, 2001.

McGarigle, Bob. *Baseball's Great Tragedy: The Story of Carl Mays—Submarine Pitcher*. Exposition, 1972.

McGeehan, W. O. "The Ivory Industry." *Saturday Evening Post*, February 11, 1928.

Mead, William B. *Baseball Goes to War*. Broadcast Interview Source, 1998.

Meany, Tom. *Baseball's Greatest Teams*. Barnes, 1949.

———. *The Yankee Story*. E. P. Dutton, 1960.

Mercer, Sid. "The Colonel." Parts 1 and 3–6. *New York Journal and American*, January 14–January 20, 1939.

"Monopsony in Manpower." *Yale Law Journal*, March 1953.

Montville, Leigh. *The Big Bam: The Life and Times of Babe Ruth*. Doubleday, 2006.

Murdock, Eugene. *Ban Johnson: Czar of Baseball.* Greenwood, 1982.

———. *Baseball between the Wars: Memories of the Game by the Men Who Played It.* Meckler, 1992.

———. *Baseball Players and Their Times: Oral Histories of the Game, 1920–1940.* Meckler, 1991.

Neft, David S., Richard M. Cohen, and Michael L. Neft. *The Sports Encyclopedia: Baseball 2001.* St. Martins Griffin, 2001.

Nevins, Alan, and Henry Steele Commager with Jeffrey Morris. *A Pocket History of the United States.* 8th rev. ed. Washington Square Press, 1986.

Neyer, Rob, and Eddie Epstein. *Baseball Dynasties.* Norton, 2000.

Obojski, Robert. *Bush League: A History of Minor League Baseball.* Macmillan, 1975.

Okkonen, Marc. *The Federal League of 1914–1915: Baseball's Third Major League.* Society for American Baseball Research, 1989.

Okrent, Daniel, and Harris Lewine, eds. *The Ultimate Baseball Book.* Houghton Mifflin, 1988.

Palmer, Pete, and Gary Gillette, eds. *The 2006 ESPN Baseball Encyclopedia.* Sterling, 2006.

Parker, Dan. "Cousin Egbert, the Star Maker." *Elks Magazine,* May 1948.

Peterson, Robert. *Only the Ball Was White: A History of Legendary Black Players and All-Black Professional Teams.* Gramercy Books, 1999.

———. *Pigskin: The Early Years of Pro Football.* Oxford University Press, 1997.

Pietrusza, David. *Judge and Jury: The Life and Times of Judge Kenesaw Mountain Landis.* Diamond Communications, 1998.

———. *Major Leagues: The Formation, Sometimes Absorption and Mostly Inevitable Demise of 18 Professional Baseball Organizations, 1871 to Present.* McFarland, 1991.

Pietrusza, David, Matthew Silverman, and Michael Gershman, eds. *Baseball: The Biographical Encyclopedia.* Sports Media, 2000, 2003.

Porter, David L., ed. *Biographical Dictionary of American Sports: Baseball.* Greenwood, 1987.

Porter, Glenn. *The Rise of Big Business: 1860–1920.* 2nd ed. Harlan Davidson, 1977, 1992.

Powers, Jimmy. *Baseball Personalities.* Rudolph Field, 1949.

Quirk, James, and Rodney D. Fort. *Pay Dirt: The Business of Professional Sports Teams*. Princeton University Press, 1997.

Reidenbaugh, Lowell. *100 Years of National League Baseball*. Sporting News, 1976.

Reiss, Steven A. "The Baseball Magnates and Urban Politics in the Progressive Era: 1895–1920." *Journal of Sports History*, Spring 1974.

———. *Sport in Industrial America*. Harlan Davidson, 1995

Rennie, Rud. "Free Agent." *Collier's*, July 17, 1937.

Reynolds, Quentin. "Ivory Hunter." *Collier's*, July 15, 1939.

———. "Peanut Vendor." In *More Than a Game*, compiled by Lawrance Holmes, introduction by Paul Gallico, 182–89. Macmillan, 1967.

Ribowsky, Mark. *A Complete History of the Negro Leagues, 1884–1955*. Citadel, 2002.

Ritter, Lawrence S. *The Glory of Their Times: The Story of the Early Days of Baseball Told by the Men Who Played It*. Vintage Books, 1966, 1984, 1995.

Robinson, Ray. *Iron Horse: Lou Gehrig in His Time*. HarperPerennial, 1991.

———. *Matty: An American Hero*. Oxford University Press, 1993.

———. Telephone interview with the author. July 26, 2006.

Robinson, Ray, and Christopher Jennison. *Yankee Stadium: 75 Years of Drama, Glamor, and Glory*. Viking Studio, 1998.

Rogosin, Donn. *Invisible Men: Life in Baseball's Negro Leagues*. Kodansha America, 1995.

Rothe, Emil H. "Was the Federal League a Major League?" *Baseball Research Journal*. Society for American Baseball Research, 1981.

Ruppert, Jacob, as told to [Dan] Daniel. "Behind the Scenes of the Yankees." Parts 1–6. *New York World-Telegram*, February 14–February 21, 1938.

———. "The Ten-Million-Dollar Toy." *Saturday Evening Post*, March 28, 1931.

Ruth, Mrs. Babe, with Bill Slocum. *The Babe and I*. Prentice-Hall, 1959.

Seymour, Harold. *Baseball: The Early Years*. Oxford University Press, 1960.

———. *Baseball: The Golden Age*. Oxford University Press, 1971.

Shaplen, Robert. "The Yankees' Real Boss." *Sports Illustrated*, September 20, 1954.

Shatzkin, Mike, and Jim Charlton, creators and developers. *The Ballplayers: Baseball's Ultimate Biographical Reference.* Arbor House, 1990.

Sheridan, J. B. "Base Ball Cannot Be Cheaply Conducted." *Sporting Life,* February 26, 1916.

Sloan, Alfred P., Jr. *My Years with General Motors.* Macfadden Books, 1965.

Slocum, Bill. "Miller Huggins as I Knew Him." Parts 3–6. *New York American,* October 1929.

Smelser, Marshall. *The Life That Ruth Built: A Biography.* Quadrangle, 1975.

Smith, David, et al. Retrosheet Web site. www.retrosheet.org.

Smith, Ken. *Baseball's Hall of Fame.* Tempo Books, 1977.

Snelling, Dennis. *The Pacific Coast League: A Statistical History, 1903–1957.* McFarland, 1995.

Solomon, Burt. *The Baseball Timeline: The Day-by-Day History of Baseball, from Valley Forge to the Present Day.* Avon Books, 1997.

Sowell, Mike. *July 2, 1903: The Mysterious Death of Hall-of-Famer Big Ed Delahanty.* Macmillan, 1992.

———. *The Pitch That Killed.* Macmillan, 1989.

Spatz, Lyle. *Yankees Coming, Yankees Going: New York Yankee Player Transactions, 1903 through 1999.* McFarland, 2000.

Spink, Alfred H. *The National Game.* Southern University Library Press, 1910, 2000.

Spink, J. G. Taylor. *Judge Landis and 25 Years of Baseball.* Sporting News, 1974.

Steinberg, Steve. "Heralding Hug." *Yankees Magazine,* July 2005.

Stout, Glenn, and Richard Johnson. *Red Sox Century: One Hundred Years of Red Sox Baseball.* Houghton Mifflin, 2000.

———. *Yankees Century: 100 Years of New York Yankees Baseball.* Houghton Mifflin, 2002.

Sullivan, Neil J. *The Minors: The Struggles and the Triumph of Baseball's Poor Relation from 1876 to the Present.* St. Martin's, 1990.

"Taps for Huggins: A Great Little Bear-Tamer." *Literary Digest,* October 12, 1929.

Tarvin, A. H. "Another Wagner Tale." *Baseball Magazine,* February 1948.

Taylor, Sec. "Ed Barrow." Parts 1 and 2. *Des Moines Register,* January 27, 1939; January 28, 1939.

Thomas, Henry W. *Walter Johnson: Baseball's Big Train*. Phenom, 1995.

Thorn, John et al., eds. *Total Baseball: The Ultimate Baseball Encyclopedia*. Sport Media, 2004.

Thorn, John, and John Holway. *The Pitcher*. Prentice Hall, 1987, 1988.

Thorn, John, and Pete Palmer. *The Hidden Game of Baseball: A Revolutionary Approach to Baseball and its Statistics*. Doubleday, 1984.

Thornley, Stew. *Land of the Giants: New York's Polo Grounds*. Temple University Press, 2000.

Tofel, Richard J. *A Legend in the Making: The New York Yankees in 1939*. Ivan R. Dee, 2002.

Trachtenberg, Leo. "Ed Barrow: Founder of the Yankees Dynasty." *Yankees Magazine*, April 12, 1984.

———. "Jake Ruppert Built Dynasties." *Yankees Magazine*, June 20, 1985.

———. "Mighty Mite Miller Huggins: An American Sports Legend." *Yankees Magazine*, June 20, 1985.

———. "The Travails of Miller Huggins." *Baseball History*, Summer 1987.

U.S. Bureau of the Census. *Historical Statistics of the United States: Colonial Times to 1970*. Bicentennial ed. 1975.

U.S. House of Representatives. Hearings before the Subcommittee on the Study of Monopoly Power of the Committee of the Judiciary: Organized Baseball. 82nd Cong., 1st sess., 1952.

———. *Report of the Subcommittee on the Study of Monopoly Power of the Committee of the Judiciary: Organized Baseball*. 82nd Cong., 2nd sess., 1952.

Vecchione, Joseph J., ed. *The New York Times Book of Sports Legends*. Fireside, 1991.

Veeck, Bill, with Ed Linn. *The Hustler's Handbook*. Fireside, 1989.

———. *Veeck . . . As in Wreck*. Fireside, 1989.

Voigt, David Q. *American Baseball*. Vol. 1: *From Gentleman's Sport to the Commissioner System*. Pennsylvania State University Press, 1983.

———. *American Baseball*. Vol. 2: *From the Commissioners to Continental Expansion*. Pennsylvania State University Press, 1983.

———. *American Baseball*. Vol. 3: *From Postwar Expansion to the Electronic Age*. Pennsylvania State University Press, 1983.

Wallace, Frances. "College Men in the Big Leagues." *Scribner's*, October 1927.

Warfield, Don. *The Roaring Redhead: Larry MacPhail—Baseball's Great Innovator*. Diamond Communications, 1987.

Weeks, David. "Foul Play: Fan Fatalities in Twentieth-Century Organized Baseball." *NINE*, Fall 2003.

Weiss, George, with Robert Shaplen. "The Best Decision I Ever Made." *Sports Illustrated*, March 13, 1961.

———. "The Man of Silence Speaks." *Sports Illustrated*, March 6, 1961.

Werber, Bill. Telephone interview with the author. November 16, 2005.

Werber, Bill, and C. Paul Rogers III. *Memories of a Ballplayer: Bill Werber and Baseball in the 1930s*. Society for American Baseball Research, 2001.

Westcott, Rich. *Masters of the Diamond: Interviews with Players Who Began Their Careers More than 50 Years Ago*. McFarland, 1994

Williams, Joe. "Busher Joe McCarthy." *Saturday Evening Post*, April 15, 1939.

———. *The Joe Williams Reader*. Edited by Peter Williams. Algonquin Books of Chapel Hill, 1989.

Williams, Peter. *When the Giants Were Giants: Bill Terry and the Golden Age of New York Baseball*. Algonquin Books of Chapel Hill, 1994.

"Women Players in Organized Baseball." *Baseball Research Journal* 12 (1983): 157–61.

Woolley, Edward Mott. "The Business of Baseball." *McClure's Magazine*, July 1912.

Wood, Allan. *Babe Ruth and the 1918 Red Sox*. Writers Club, 2000.

Wright, Marshall D. *The American Association*. McFarland, 1997.

———. *The International League: Year-by-Year Statistics, 1884–1953*. McFarland, 1998.

Wrigley, William, Jr. "Owning a Big-League Ball Team." *Saturday Evening Post*, September 13, 1930.

"The Yankees." *Fortune*, July 1946.

Zingg, Paul J. *Harry Hooper: An American Baseball Life*. University of Illinois Press, 1993.

Zingg, Paul J., and Mark D. Medeiros. *Runs, Hits, and an Era: The Pacific Coast League, 1903–58*. University of Illinois Press, 1994.

Index